PARABLES FOR THE VIRTUAL

POST-CONTEMPORARY INTERVENTIONS

Series Editors: Stanley Fish and Fredric Jameson

Brian Massumi

PARABLES FOR THE VIRTUAL

Movement,

Affect,

Sensation

Duke University Press   Durham & London   2002

Designed by C. H. Westmoreland

Typeset in Plantin Light with Frutiger display

by Keystone Typesetting, Inc.

Library of Congress Cataloging-

in-Publication Data

Massumi, Brian

Parables for the virtual: movement, affect,

sensation / Brian Massumi.

p. cm.–(Post-contemporary interventions)

Includes bibliographical references and index.

ISBN 0-8223-2882-8 (cloth : alk. paper)–

ISBN 0-8223-2897-6 (pbk. : alk. paper)

1. Movement (Philosophy) 2. Senses and

sensation. 3. Affect (Psychology)

I. Title. II. Series.

B105.M65 M37 2002

128/.6 21   2001058211

CONTENTS

ACKNOWLEDGMENTS

I would like to thank the Australian Research Council (ARC) for its most generous support. The research and writing of this book was largely carried out under a fellowship from the ARC that provided me the most precious commodity a writer can have: time to think. My gratitude also goes to the Humanities Research Centre of the Australian National University (HRC) which as my host institution provided something just as rare: a conducive environment in which to think. To find an institutional home truly fostering of scholarship is a privilege too few academics experience. I would like to thank Julie Gorrell, Ian McCalman, Caroline Turner, Leena Messina, Judy Buchanan, and the rest of the directorship and staff of the HRC for making the Centre such a place, and also for all their help and hard work. I would also like to thank the English Department of the University of Queensland, in particular Graeme Turner, John Frow, and David Marshall, for their hospitality and generous assistance in providing me my first institutional home in Australia. Additional support, also much appreciated, was provided by the Center for Cultural Studies of the University of California-Santa Cruz, the Canadian Centre for Architecture in Montreal, and the Social Sciences and Humanities Research Council of Canada.

Those who contributed to this project through their personal and intellectual generosity and the stimulation of their ideas, reactions, and interactions are too numerous to cite. A partial list would include Gordon Bull, Chris Connery, William Connolly, Dipesh Chakrabarty, Kuan-Hsing Chen, Kevin Dahl, Penelope Deutscher, Lorne Falk, Heidi Gilpin, Lawrence Grossberg, Freda Guttman, Gail Hershatter, Alice Jardine, Michael Jasper, Michael Hardt, Thomas Lamarre, Greg Lynn, Tim Murphy, Toni Negri, Paul Patton, Naoki Sakai, Sue Sargent, Steven Shaviro, Shane Wilcox, and my past and now far-flung students from McGill University. Special thanks to Ken Dean, Toni Dove, Meaghan Morris, and Isabelle Stengers for their friendship, patience, and inspiration. Most special thanks for these same things and much, much more to Sandra Buckley, unwavering. And to Jesse Aravaipa for a ten-year (and counting) crash course (literally) in qualitative transformation. Spinach and Protector have contributed many seasons of fur to the cracks in my keyboard in a testament to their companionship and their undying love of CRTs. I won't mention Spike. But I will mention Glenn Hendler.

Portions of this book have appeared, partially and/or in earlier drafts, in the journals *Cultural Critique* (chapter 1); *Architectural Design* (chapter 8); *Cultural Studies* (chapter 9); the Wexner Center catalog *Body Méca-nique: Artistic Explorations of Digital Realms,* ed. Sarah Rodgers (chapter 7); and in the following edited volumes: *Anybody,* ed. Cynthia Davidson (MIT Press) (chapter 3); *Rethinking Borders,* ed. John Welchman (University of Minnesota Press) (chapter 2); *Deleuze: A Critical Reader,* ed. Paul Patton (Blackwell) (reprint of chapter 1); and *Observing Complexity: Systems Theory and Postmodernism,* ed. William Rasch and Cary Wolfe (University of Minnesota Press) (reprint of chapter 1). Finally, my gratitude goes to Ken Wissoker, my editor at Duke University Press, for his faith in this project.

INTRODUCTION

Concrete Is as Concrete Doesn't

When I think of my body and ask what it does to earn that name, two things stand out. It *moves*. It *feels*. In fact, it does both at the same time. It moves as it feels, and it feels itself moving. Can we think a body without this: an intrinsic connection between movement and sensation whereby each immediately summons the other?

If you start from an intrinsic connection between movement and sensation, the slightest, most literal displacement convokes a qualitative difference, because as directly as it conducts itself it beckons a feeling, and feelings have a way of folding into each other, resonating together, interfering with each other, mutually intensifying, all in unquantifiable ways apt to unfold again in action, often unpredictably. Qualitative difference: immediately the issue is change. Felt and unforeseen.

The project of this book is to explore the implications for cultural theory of this simple conceptual displacement: body—(movement/sensation)—change. Cultural theory of the past two decades has tended to bracket the middle terms and their unmediated connection. It can be argued that in doing so it has significantly missed the two outside terms, even though they have been of consistent concern—perhaps *the* central concerns in the humanities. Attention to the literality of movement was deflected by fears of falling into a "naive realism," a reductive empiricism that would dissolve the specificity of the cultural domain in the plain, seemingly unproblematic, "presence" of dumb matter. The slightness of ongoing qualitative change paled in comparison to the grandness of periodic "rupture." Against that possibility, the everyday was the place where nothing ever happens. Culture occupied the gap between matter and systemic change, in the operation of mechanisms of "mediation." These were ideological apparatuses that structured the dumb material interactions of things and rendered them legible according to a dominant signifying scheme into which human subjects in the making were "interpellated." Mediation, although inseparable from power, restored a kind of movement to the everyday. If the everyday was no longer a place of rupture or revolt, as it had been in glimpses at certain privileged historical junctures, it might still be a site of modest acts of "resistance" or "subversion" keeping alive the possibility of systemic change. These were practices of "reading" or "decoding" counter to the dominant ideological scheme of things. The body was seen to be centrally involved in these everyday practices of resistance. But this thoroughly mediated body could only be a "discursive" body: one with its signifying gestures. Signifying gestures make sense. If properly "performed," they may also unmake sense by scrambling significations already in place. Make and unmake sense as they might, they don't *sense*. Sensation is utterly redundant to their description. Or worse, it is destructive to it, because it appeals to an unmediated experience. Unmediated experience signals a danger that is worse, if anything can be, than naive realism: its polar opposite, naive subjectivism. Earlier phenomenological investigations into the sensing body were largely left behind because they were difficult to reconcile with the new understandings of the structuring capacities of culture and their inseparability both from the exercise of power and the glimmers of counterpower incumbent in mediate living. It was all about a subject without subjectivism: a subject "constructed" by external mechanisms. "The Subject."

"The Body." What is it to The Subject? Not the qualities of its moving experience. But rather, in keeping with the extrinsic approach, its *positioning*. Ideological accounts of subject formation emphasize systemic structurings. The focus on the systemic had to be brought back down to earth in order to be able to integrate into the account the local cultural differences and the practices of resistance they may harbor. The concept of "positionality" was widely developed for this purpose. Signifying subject formation according to the dominant structure was often thought of in terms of "coding." Coding in turn came to be thought of in terms of positioning on a grid. The grid was conceived as an oppositional framework of culturally constructed significations: male versus female, black versus white, gay versus straight, and so on. A body corresponded to a "site" on the grid defined by an overlapping of one term from each pair. The body came to be defined by its pinning to the grid. Proponents of this model often cited its ability to link body-sites into a "geography" of culture that tempered the universalizing tendencies of ideology.

The sites, it is true, are multiple. But aren't they still combinatorial permutations on an overarching definitional framework? Aren't the possibilities for the entire gamut of cultural emplacements, including the "subversive" ones, precoded into the ideological master structure? Is the body as linked to a particular subject position anything more than a local embodiment *of* ideology? Where has the potential for change gone? How does a body perform its way out of a definitional framework that is not only responsible for its very "construction," but seems to prescript every possible signifying and countersignifying move as a selection from a repertoire of possible permutations on a limited set of predetermined terms? How can the grid itself change? How can what the system has pinpointedly determined flip over into a determining role capable of acting on the systemic level? The aim of the positionality model was to open a window on local resistance in the name of change. But the problem of change returned with a vengeance. Because every body-subject was so determinately local, it was boxed into its site on the culture map. Gridlock.

The idea of positionality begins by subtracting movement from the picture. This catches the body in cultural freeze-frame. The point of explanatory departure is a pinpointing, a zero-point of stasis. When positioning of any kind comes a determining first, movement comes a problematic second. After all is signified and sited, there is the nagging problem of how to add movement back into the picture. But adding movement to stasis is about as easy as multiplying a number by zero and getting a positive product. Of course, a body occupying one position on the grid might succeed in making a move to occupy another position. In fact, certain normative progressions, such as that from child to adult, are coded in. But this doesn't change the fact that what defines the body is not the movement itself, only its beginning and endpoints. Movement is entirely subordinated to the positions it connects. These are predefined. Adding movement like this adds nothing at all. You just get two successive states: multiples of zero.

The very notion of movement as qualitative transformation is lacking. There is "displacement," but no transformation; it is as if the body simply leaps from one definition to the next. Since the positional model's definitional framework is punctual, it simply can't attribute a reality to the interval, whose crossing is a continuity (or nothing). The space of the crossing, the gaps between positions on the grid, falls into a theoretical no-body's land. Also lacking is the notion that if there is qualitative movement of the body, it as directly concerns sensings as significations. Add to this the fact that matter, bodily or otherwise, never figures into the account *as such*. Even though many of the approaches in question characterize themselves as materialisms, matter can only enter in indirectly: as mediated. Matter, movement, body, sensation. Multiple mediated miss.

The present project began almost ten years ago in response to these problems. It was based on the hope that movement, sensation, and qualities of experience couched in matter in its most literal sense (and sensing) might be culturally-theoretically thinkable, without falling into either the Scylla of naive realism or the Charybdis of subjectivism and without contradicting the very real insights of poststructuralist cultural theory concerning the coextensiveness of culture with the field of experience and of power with culture. The aim was to put matter unmediatedly back into cultural materialism, along with what seemed most directly corporeal back into the body. Theoretically, the point of departure would have to be to part company with the linguistic model at the basis of the most widespread concepts of coding (almost always Saussurian in inspiration, often with Lacanian inflections) and find a semiotics willing to engage with continuity (in fact, a major preoccupation of the founder of the discipline, C. S. Peirce). This was undertaken not in a spirit of opposition to "Theory" or "cultural studies," but in the hope of building on their accomplishments, perhaps refreshing their vocabulary with conceptual infusions from neglected sources or underappreciated aspects of known sources.

If at any point I thought of this refreshing in terms of regaining a "concreteness" of experience, I was quickly disabused of the notion. Take movement. When a body is in motion, it does not coincide with itself. It coincides with its own transition: its own variation. The range of variations it can be implicated in is not present in any given movement, much less in any position it passes through. In motion, a body is in an immediate, unfolding relation to its own nonpresent potential to vary. That relation, to borrow a phrase from Gilles Deleuze, is real but abstract. The positional grid was abstract, despite the fact that it was meant to bring cultural theory back down to the local level, since it involved an overarching definitional grid whose determinations preexisted the bodies they constructed or to which they were applied. The abstract of Deleuze's real-but-abstract is very different from this. It doesn't preexist and has nothing fundamentally to do with mediation. If ideology must be understood as mediating, then this real-abstract is not ideological. (Chapters 2, 3, and 9 tackle the description of nonideological mechanisms of power.) Here, abstract means: never present in position, only ever in passing. This is an abstractness pertaining to the transitional immediacy of a real relation—that of a body to its own *indeterminacy* (its openness to an elsewhere and otherwise than it is, in any here and now).

The charge of indeterminacy carried by a body is inseparable from it. It strictly coincides with it, to the extent that the body is in passage or in process (to the extent that it is dynamic and alive). But the charge is not itself corporeal. Far from regaining a concreteness, to think the body in movement thus means accepting the paradox that there is an incorporeal dimension *of the body*. Of it, but not it. Real, material, but incorporeal. Inseparable, coincident, but disjunct. If this is "concrete," the project originally set out on will take some severe twists.

One way of starting to get a grasp on the real-material-but-incorporeal is to say it is to the body, as a positioned thing, as energy is to matter. Energy and matter are mutually convertible modes of the same reality. This would make the incorporeal something like a phase-shift of the body in the usual sense, but not one that comes after it in time. It would be a conversion or unfolding of the body *contemporary* to its every move. Always accompanying. Fellow-traveling dimension of the same reality.

This self-disjunctive coinciding sinks an ontological difference into the heart of the body. The body's potential to vary belongs to the same reality as the body as variety (positioned thing) but partakes of it in a different mode. Integrating movement slips us directly into what Michel Foucault called *incorporeal materialism*.[1] This movement-slip gives new urgency to questions of ontology, of ontological difference, inextricably linked to concepts of potential and process and, by extension, event—in a way that bumps "being" straight into becoming. Paraphrasing Deleuze again, the problem with the dominant models in cultural and literary theory is not that they are too abstract to grasp the concreteness of the real. The problem is that they are not *abstract enough* to grasp the real incorporeality of the concrete.

When it comes to grappling productively with paradoxes of passage and position, the philosophical precursor is Henri Bergson. The slip into an incorporeal materialism follows the logic of Bergson's famous analysis of Zeno's paradoxes of movement.[2] When Zeno shoots his philosophical arrow, he thinks of its flight path in the commonsense way, as a linear trajectory made up of a sequence of points or positions that the arrow occupies one after the other. The problem is that between one point on a line and the next, there is an infinity of intervening points. If the arrow occupies a first point along its path, it will never reach the next—unless it occupies each of the infinity of points between. Of course, it is the nature of infinity that you can never get to the end of it. The arrow gets swallowed up in the transitional infinity. Its flight path implodes. The arrow is immobilized.

Or, if the arrow moved it is because it was never *in* any point. It was in *passage* across them all. The transition from bow to target is not decomposable into constituent points. A path is not composed of positions. It is nondecomposable: a dynamic unity. That *continuity* of movement is of an order of reality other than the measurable, divisible space it can be confirmed as having crossed. It doesn't stop until it stops: when it hits the target. Then, and only then, is the arrow in position. It is only after the arrow hits it mark that its real trajectory may be plotted. The points or positions really appear *retrospectively,* working backward from the movement's end. It is as if, in our thinking, we put targets all along the path. The in-between positions are logical targets: *possible* endpoints. The flight of the arrow is not immobilized as Zeno would have it. We stop it in thought when we construe its movement to be divisible into positions. Bergson's idea is that space itself is a retrospective construct of this kind. When we think of space as "extensive," as being measurable, divisible, and composed of points plotting possible positions that objects may occupy, we are stopping the world in thought. We are thinking away its dynamic unity, the continuity of its movements. We are looking at only one dimension of reality.

A thing is when it isn't doing. A thing is concretely where and what it is—for example a successfully shot arrow sticking in a target—when it is in a state of arrest. *Concrete is as concrete doesn't.*

Solidify?[3]

Fluidifying with Bergson has a number of far-reaching consequences:

(1) It suggests that a distinction between extensive and intensive is more useful than any opposition between the "literal" and the "figural" if what we are interested in is change. Extensive space, and the arrested ob-

jects occupying the positions into which it is divisible, is a back-formation from cessation. The dynamic enabling the back-formation is "intensive" in the sense that movement, in process, cannot be determinately indexed to anything outside of itself. It has withdrawn into an all-encompassing relation with what it will be. It is in becoming, absorbed in occupying its field of potential. For when it comes to a stop in the target, it will have undergone a qualitative change. It will not just be an arrow. It will have been a successfully shot arrow. It is still the same thing by definition, but in a different way, qualitatively changed by the passing event. But if it is qualitatively changed, isn't it only nominally the "same"? Shouldn't we assert, with Leibniz, that all the predicates that can be stated of a thing— all the "accidents" that might befall it (even those remaining in potential)—are of its nature?[4] If so, "nature" changes at the slightest move. The concept of nature concerns modification not essence (chapter 9).

(2) The emphasis is on process before signification or coding. The latter are not false or unreal. They are truly, really stop-operations. Or, if they have movement, it is derivative, a second-order movement between back-formed possibilities (a kind of zero-point movement that can be added back, against all odds). The models criticized earlier do not need to be trashed. They are not just plain wrong. It's just that their sphere of applicability must be recognized as limited to a particular mode of existence, or a particular dimension of the real (the degree to which things coincide with their own arrest). Einstein's theories of relativity did not prove Newton's laws wrong. It showed them to be of limited applicability: accurate, but only at a certain scale of things (where the law of entropy holds). The same goes for the Bergsonian revolution. Cultural laws of positioning and ideology are accurate in a certain sphere (where the tendency to arrest dominates). Right or wrong is not the issue. The issue is to demarcate their sphere of applicability—when the "ground" upon which they operate is continuously moving. This "limitation" does not belittle the approaches in question. In fact, it brings wonder back into them. From this point of view, the operations they describe are little short of miraculous. Like multiplying by zero and yielding a positive quantity. "Miraculation" should figure prominently in the semiotic vocabulary.[5]

(3) The Bergsonian revolution turns the world on its head. Position no longer comes first, with movement a problematic second. It is secondary to movement and derived from it. It is retro movement, movement residue. The problem is no longer to explain how there can be change given

positioning. The problem is to explain the wonder that there can be stasis given the primacy of process. This is akin to late-twentieth-century problematics of "order out of chaos."

(4) Another way of putting it is that positionality is an emergent quality of movement. The distinction between stasis and motion that replaces the opposition between literal and figurative from this perspective is not a logical binarism. It follows the modes by which realities pass into each other. "Passing into" is not a binarism. "Emerging" is not a binarism. They are dynamic unities. The kinds of distinction suggested here pertain to continuities under qualitative transformation. They are directly processual (and derivatively signifying and codifying). They can only be approached by a logic that is abstract enough to grasp the self-disjunctive coincidence of a thing's immediacy to its own variation: to follow how concepts of dynamic unity and unmediated heterogeneity reciprocally presuppose each other. The concept of field, to mention but one, is a useful logical tool for expressing continuity of self-relation and heterogeneity in the same breath (chapters 3 and 6). Embarrassingly for the humanities, the handiest concepts in this connection are almost without exception products of mathematics or the sciences.

(5) It is not enough for process concepts of this kind to be ontological. They must be *ontogenetic*: they must be equal to emergence.

(6) If passage is primary in relation to position, processual indeterminacy is primary in relation to social determination (chapters 2, 4, 9). Social and cultural determinations on the model of positionality are also secondary and derived. Gender, race, and sexual orientation also emerge and back-form their reality. Passage precedes construction. But construction does effectively back-form its reality. Grids happen. So social and cultural determinations feed back into the process from which they arose. Indeterminacy and determination, change and freeze-framing, go together. They are inseparable and always actually coincide while remaining disjunctive in their modes of reality. To say that passage and indeterminacy "come first" or "are primary" is more a statement of ontological priority than the assertion of a time sequence. They have ontological privilege in the sense that they constitute the field of the emergence, while positionings are what emerge. The trick is to express that priority in a way that respects the inseparability and contemporaneousness of the disjunct dimensions: their ontogenetic difference. The work of Gilbert Simondon is exemplary in this regard.

8

(7) As Simondon reminds us, it is important to keep in mind that there is a contemporaneous difference between social *determination* and sociality.[6] The approach suggested here does not accept any categorical separation between the social and the presocial, between culture and some kind of "raw" nature or experience (chapters 1, 8, 9). The idea is that there is an ontogenesis or becoming of culture and the social (bracketing for present purposes the difference between them), of which determinate forms of culture and sociability are the result. The challenge is to think that process of *formation,* and for that you need the notion of a taking-form, an inform on the way to being determinately this or that. The field of emergence is not presocial. It is *open-endedly social.* It is social in a manner "prior to" the separating out of individuals and the identifiable groupings that they end up boxing themselves into (positions in gridlock). A sociality without determinate borders: "pure" sociality. One of the things that the dimension of emergence is ontogenetically "prior to" is thus the very distinction between the individual and the collective, as well as any given model of their interaction. That interaction is precisely what takes form. That is what is socially determined—and renegotiated by each and every cultural act. Assume it, and you beg the whole question (chapter 3). Not assuming it, however, entails finding a concept for interaction-in-the-making. The term adopted here is *relation* (chapters 1, 3, 9).

(8) That there is a difference between the possible and the potential needs to be attended to (chapters 4, 5, 9). Possibility is back-formed from potential's unfolding. But once it is formed, it also effectively feeds in. Fedback, it prescripts: implicit in the determination of a thing's or body's positionality is a certain set of transformations that can be expected of it by definition and that it can therefore undergo without qualitatively changing enough to warrant a new name. These possibilities delineate a region of nominally defining—that is, normative—variation. Potential is unprescribed. It only feeds forward, unfolding toward the registering of an event: bull's-eye. Possibility is a variation *implicit in* what a thing can be said to be when it is on target. Potential is the *immanence* of a thing to its still indeterminate variation, under way (chapters 3, 4, 5, 8, 9). Implication is a code word. Immanence is process.[7]

(9) If the positional grid feeds back, then the success of that operation changes the field conditions from which the determinate positions emerged. The distinction between potential and possibility is a distinction

between conditions of emergence and re-conditionings of the emerged. Conditions of emergence are one with becoming. Re-conditionings of the emerged define normative or regulatory operations that set the parameters of history (the possible interactions of determinate individuals and groups). History is inseparably, ontogenetically different from becoming. But if feedback from the dimension of the emerged re-conditions the conditions of emergence, then it also has to be recognized that conditions of emergence change. Emergence emerges. Changing changes. If history has a becoming from which it is inseparably, ontogenetically different, then conversely becoming has a history (chapter 9).

(10) The difference between the actual stopping that occurs when a continuity exhausts itself and reaches a terminus and the logical stopping that goes back over what then appears as its path, in order to cut it into segments separated by plottable points, is not as great as it might seem at first. The retrospective ordering enables precise operations to be inserted along the way, in anticipation of a repetition of the movement—the possibility that it will come again. If the movement does reoccur, it can be captured (chapters 1, 2, 3, 9). It comes to a different end. At that terminus, its momentum may be diverted into a new movement. The backformation of a path is not only a "retrospection." It is a "retroduction": a production, by feedback, of new movements. A dynamic unity has been retrospectively captured and qualitatively converted. Space itself is a retroduction, by means of the standardization of measurement (chapters 7, 8). Before measurement, there was air and ground, but not space as we know it. Ground is not a static support any more than air is an empty container. The ground is full of movement, as full as the air is with weather, just at different rhythm from most perceptible movements occurring with it (flight of the arrow). Any geologist will tell you that the ground is anything but stable. It is a dynamic unity of continual folding, uplift, and subsidence. Measurement stops the movement in thought, as it empties the air of weather, yielding space understood as a grid of determinate positions. The practices enabled by the spatialization of ground convert it into a foundation for technological change. This is not simply a "cultural construction." It is a becoming cultural of nature. The very ground of life changes. But it remains as natural as it becomes-cultural. This becoming-cultural of nature is predicated on the capture of processes already in operation. Putting up a new target to stop an arrow connects with forces of mass and inertia. The arrest of the arrow prolongs

a tendency toward stoppage belonging to the ground, converting it into a cultural function—the foundation, say, for an archery competition. The anticipation of a next arrow prolongs powers of repetition also incumbent in nature, converting them into a basis for scoring. The point is that the "natural" and the "cultural" feed forward and back into each other. They relay each other to such an extent that the distinction cannot be maintained in any strict sense. It is necessary to theorize a *nature-culture continuum* (chapters 1, 9). Logical operations prolong and convert forces already in nature, and forces of nature divert into cultural operations normatively regulated (rulered) by the logical conversion. Nature and culture are in mutual movement into and through each other. Their continuum is a dynamic unity of reciprocal variation. Things we are accustomed to placing on one side or another of the nature-culture divide must be redistributed along the whole length of the continuum, under varying modes of operation, in various phases of separation and regrouping, and to different degrees of "purity." (As was suggested for sociality, note that "pure" sociality is found at the "nature" end of the continuum, in culture's just-becoming, "prior to" its separations; chapter 9.) On the list of distinctions it becomes difficult to sustain in any categorical way are those between artifact and thing, body and object—and even thought and matter. Not only do these relay in reciprocal becomings; together they ally in process. They are tinged with event.

(11) The status of "natural law" (the normative self-regulation of nature; nature's self-rule) becomes a major theoretical stake, as does the naturalizing of cultural laws with which cultural theory has more traditionally been concerned. The problem has been that the concern for "naturalization" was one-sided, only attending to half the becoming. Of tremendous help in looking at both sides is the concept of *habit*. Habit is an acquired automatic self-regulation. It resides in the flesh. Some say in matter. As acquired, it can be said to be "cultural." As automatic and material, it can pass for "natural." Sorting out the identity or difference between law and habit (chapter 9), and distributing the result along the nature-culture continuum, becomes a promising direction for inquiry. Of course, a preoccupation with precisely this question accompanied the birth of *empiricism* (with Hume). "Incorporeal materialism" has a date with empiricism (chapter 9).[8]

(12) The kinds of codings, griddings, and positionings with which cultural theory has been preoccupied are no exception to the dynamic

unity of feedback and feed-forward, or double becoming. Gender, race, and orientation are what Ian Hacking calls "interactive kinds": logical categories that feed back into and transform the reality they describe (and are themselves modified by in return).[9] Ideas about cultural or social construction have dead-ended because they have insisted on bracketing the *nature* of the process.[10] If you elide nature, you miss the becoming of culture, its emergence (not to mention the history of matter). You miss the continuum of interlinkage, feed-forward and feedback, by which movements capture and convert each other to many ends, old, new, and innumerable. The world is in a condition of constant qualitative growth. Some kind of constructivism is required to account for the processual continuity across categorical divides and for the reality of that qualitative growth, or ontogenesis: the fact that with every move, with every change, there is something new to the world, an added reality. The world is self-augmenting. Reality "snowballs," as William James was fond of saying. Perhaps "productivism" would be better than constructivism because it connotes emergence. "Inventionism" wouldn't be going too far, for even if you take nature in the narrowest sense, it has to be admitted that it is inventive in its own right. There is a word for this: evolution. There is no reason not to use the same word for the prolongation of "natural" processes of change in the emergent domain of "culture." Is a constructivist evolutionism conceivable? An evolutionary constructivism (chapters 4, 9)?

(13) If you want to adopt a productivist approach, the techniques of critical thinking prized by the humanities are of limited value. To think productivism, you have to allow that even your own logical efforts feedback and add to reality, in some small, probably microscopic way. But still. Once you have allowed that, you have accepted that activities dedicated to thought and writing are inventive. Critical thinking disavows its own inventiveness as much as possible. Because it sees itself as uncovering something it claims was hidden or as debunking something it desires to subtract from the world, it clings to a basically descriptive and justificatory modus operandi. However strenuously it might debunk concepts like "representation," it carries on as if it mirrored something outside itself with which it had no complicity, no unmediated processual involvement, and thus could justifiably oppose. Prolonging the thought-path of movement, as suggested here, requires that techniques of negative critique be used sparingly. The balance has to shift to *affirmative* methods: tech-

niques which embrace their own inventiveness and are not afraid to own up to the fact that they add (if so meagerly) to reality. There is a certain hubris to the notion that a mere academic writer is actually inventing. But the hubris is more than tempered by the self-evident modesty of the returns. So why not hang up the academic hat of critical self-seriousness, set aside the intemperate arrogance of debunking—and enjoy? If you don't enjoy concepts and writing and don't feel that when you write you are adding something to the world, if only the enjoyment itself, and that by adding that ounce of positive experience to the world you are affirming it, celebrating its potential, tending its growth, in however small a way, however really abstractly—well, just hang it up. It is not that critique is wrong. As usual, it is not a question of right and wrong—nothing important ever is. Rather, it is a question of dosage. It is simply that when you are busy critiquing you are less busy augmenting. You are that much less fostering. There are times when debunking is necessary. But, if applied in a blanket manner, adopted as a general operating principle, it is counterproductive. Foster or debunk. It's a strategic question. Like all strategic questions, it is basically a question of timing and proportion. Nothing to do with morals or moralizing. Just pragmatic.

(14) The logical resources equal to emergence must be limber enough to juggle the ontogenetic indeterminacy that precedes and accompanies a thing's coming to be what it doesn't. *Vague* concepts, and concepts of vagueness, have a crucial, and often enjoyable, role to play.

(15) Generating a paradox and then using it as if it were a well-formed logical operator is a good way to put vagueness in play. Strangely, if this procedure is followed with a good dose of conviction and just enough technique, presto!, the paradox actually becomes a well-formed logical operator. Thought and language bend to it like light in the vicinity of a superdense heavenly body. This may be an example of miraculation. (As if lucidity itself could be invented.)

These are just some of the directions that the simple aim of integrating movement into the account gets going: a lot of leverage for a small amount of applied conceptual pressure. A lot of new problems.

This is without even mentioning the associated problem of sensation. Briefly: sensation also presents a directly disjunctive self-coinciding (how's that for vague?). It's simply this: sensation is never simple. It is always doubled by the feeling of having a feeling. It is self-referential. This is not necessarily the same as "self-reflexive." The doubling of sensation does not assume a subjective splitting and does not of itself constitute a distancing. It is an immediate self-complication. It is best to think of it as a resonation, or interference pattern (chapters 1, 9). An echo, for example, cannot occur without a distance between surfaces for the sounds to bounce from. But the resonation is not on the walls. It is in the emptiness between them. It fills the emptiness with its complex patterning. That patterning is not at a distance from itself. It is immediately its own event. Although it is complex, it is not composed of parts. It is composed of the event that it is, which is unitary. It is a complex dynamic unity. The interference pattern arises where the sound wave intersects with itself. The bouncing back and forth multiplies the sound's movement without cutting it. The movement remains continuous. It remains in continuity with itself across its multiplication. This complex self-continuity is a putting into relation of the movement to itself: self-relation. The self-relation is immediate—in and of itself, only its own event—even though it requires distance to occur. The best word for a complicating immediacy of self-relation is "intensity" (chapters 1, 2, 3, 4). Resonation can be seen as converting distance, or extension, into intensity. It is a qualitative transformation of distance into an immediacy of self-relation.

With the body, the "walls" are the sensory surfaces. The intensity is experience. The emptiness or in-betweenness filled by experience is the incorporeal dimension of the body referred to earlier. The conversion of surface distance into intensity is also the conversion of the materiality of the body into an *event* (chapters 2, 3, 6, 8). It is a relay between its corporeal and incorporeal dimensions. This is not yet a subject. But it may well be the conditions of emergence of a subject: an incipient subjectivity. Call it a "self-." The hyphen is retained as a reminder that "self" is not a substantive but rather a relation. Sorting out "self-reflexivity," "self-referentiality," and "self-relation" and, in the process, distributing subjectivity and its incipiency along the nature-culture continuum, becomes another major theoretical stake.

The feeling of having a feeling is what Leibniz called the "perception of perception." That raises another thorny issue: the identity or difference between the terms "sensation" and "perception" (chapters 2, 4, 5).[11] It gets thornier. Leibniz notes that the perception of perception "occurs without characters and therefore that memory does also."[12] Add memory to issues of sensation and perception. Then pause. Memory, sensation, perception occurring without "characters"? In other words, without properties? Without determinate form or content? What is a memory without content? One answer might be that it is just pastness, a pure pastness that would be the condition of emergence for determinate memory. But that would make the past contemporary to the present of sensation and perception. Leibniz goes on to say that although the perception of perception is without characters, it does carry a "distinguishing sense of bodily direction." Distinguishing bodily direction without a determinate form? (chapter 8). In other words, without distance? That could only be *tendency*, pure tendency (chapter 4).[13] Tendency is futureness: pure futurity. So there is a futurity that is contemporary with the past's contemporaneousness with the present.

All of this is to say that feedback and feed-forward, or recursivity, in addition to converting distance into intensity, folds the dimensions of time into each other. The field of emergence of experience has to be thought of as a space-time continuum, as an ontogenetic dimension prior to the separating-out of space and time (adopting the same approach as with nature-culture; chapters 2, 8).[14] Linear time, like position-gridded space, would be emergent qualities of the event of the world's self-relating.

Leibniz's allusion to tendency brings up one more issue and also points to a way of making the link between movement and sensation developed in the work of Spinoza. Spinoza defined the body in terms of "relations of movement and rest."[15] He wasn't referring to actual, extensive movements or stases. He was referring to a body's *capacity* to enter into relations of movement and rest. This capacity he spoke of as a *power* (or potential) to affect or be affected. The issue, after sensation, perception, and memory, is *affect*. "Relation between movement and rest" is another way of saying "transition." For Spinoza, the body was one with its transitions. Each transition is accompanied by a variation in capacity: a change in which powers to affect and be affected are addressable by a next event and how readily addressable they are—or to what degree they are present as futurities. That "degree" is a bodily intensity, and its present futurity a tendency. The Spinozist problematic of affect offers a way of weaving together concepts of movement, tendency, and intensity in a way that takes us right back to the beginning: in what sense the body coincides with its own transitions and its transitioning with its potential.

The link to sensation comes in with the added remark that the variation in intensity is *felt*. This brings us back to where we just were, at self-relation: the feeling of transition by nature stretches between phases of a continuing movement. The sensed aspect of intensity doubles the affect understood as pure capacity: we are back at self-multiplication. And we are back at emergence, because the sensation is the first glimmer of a determinate experience, in the act of registering itself as itself across its own event. A first glimmer of definable self-experience: back at incipient subjectivity. We have looped, taking an affective shortcut across many of the salient problems raised by the question of the body's passing powers of "concreteness."

Where we might loop into shortly is empiricism, at the other end of its history. William James made transition and the feeling of self-relation a central preoccupation of his latter-day "radical" empiricism. "The relations that connect experiences," he wrote, "must themselves be experienced relations, and any kind of relation must be accounted as 'real' as anything else in the system."[16] If incorporeal materialism is an empiricism it is a radical one, summed up by the formula: *the felt reality of relation*. A complication for radical empiricism is that the feeling of the relation may very well not be "large" enough to register consciously. It may be what Leibniz termed a "small perception," or microperception (chapter 8). The vast majority of the world's sensations are certainly nonconscious. Nonconscious is a very different concept from the Freudian unconscious (although it is doubtless not unrelated to it). The differences are that repression does not apply to nonconscious perception and that nonconscious perception may, with a certain amount of ingenuity, be argued to apply to nonorganic matter (chapters 1, 8, 9). Whereas the feeling of the relation may be "too small" to enter perception (it is *infraempirical*), the relation it registers, for its part, is "too large" to fit into a perception since it envelops a multiplicity of potential variations (it is *superempirical*). A radical empiricism, if it is to be a thorough thinking of relation, must find ways of directly, affectively joining the infraempirical to the superempirical (chapters 2, 6). "Actualization" does this.

Affect, sensation, perception, movement, intensity, tendency, habit, law, chaos, recursion, relation, immanence, the "feedback of higher forms." Emergence, becoming, history, space, time, space-time, space and time as emergences. Nature-culture, matter, feeling, matter feeling. Event, capture, possible, potential, power. Not all the concepts in this crowd figure in each essay, of course. And when they do come up, it is often to different emphasis, in different constellations. Other concepts slip in like uninvited guests (image, effect, force, new, openness, singularity, situation, belonging). The concepts appear and reappear like a revolving cast of characters, joining forces or interfering with each other in a tumble of abstract intrigues—at times (I admit) barely controlled. (Or is it: with miraculous lucidity? I might as well also admit that my prose has been compared to a black hole.) The first chapter, "The Autonomy of Affect," sets the stage. It begins by following a long-standing engagement with the work of Deleuze, Guattari, and Deleuze/Guattari back to some of their inspirations, in particular Bergson, Spinoza, and Simondon. It is in the concluding essay, "Too-Blue: Color-Patch for an Expanded Empiricism," that incorporeal materialism meets up with radical empiricism. Bergson, Spinoza, and Simondon make way for James, who tumbles onto A. N. Whitehead and Isabelle Stengers. The intervening chapters bring together the usual conceptual suspects in varying combinations. At times, under the pressure of the uncouth company they find themselves keeping, they undergo a bit of a personality change or may even assume a pseudonym.

The reason for the constant reconstellation of concepts, and the differences in their casting when they make repeat appearances, is that I have tried to take seriously the idea that writing in the humanities can be affirmative or inventive. Invention requires experimentation. The wager is that there are methods of writing from an institutional base in the humanities disciplines that can be considered experimental practices. What they would invent (or reinvent) would be concepts and connections between concepts. The first rule of thumb if you want to invent or reinvent concepts is simple: don't apply them. If you apply a concept or system of connection between concepts, it is the material you apply it to that undergoes change, much more markedly than do the concepts. The change is imposed upon the material by the concepts' systematicity and constitutes a becoming homologous of the material to the system. This is all very grim. It has less to do with "more to the world" than "more of the same." It has less to do with invention than mastery and control.

One device for avoiding application is to adopt an "exemplary" method. Logically, the example is an odd beast. "It holds for all cases of the same type," Giorgio Agamben writes, "and, at the same time, is included in these. It is one singularity among others, which, however, stands for each of them and serves for all."[17] An example is neither general (as is a system of concepts) nor particular (as is the material to which a system is applied). It is "singular." It is defined by a disjunctive self-inclusion: a belonging to itself that is simultaneously an extendibility to everything else with which it might be connected (one for all, and all in itself). In short, exemplification is the logical category corresponding to self-relation.

As a writing practice, exemplification activates detail. The success of the example hinges on the details. Every little one matters. At each new detail, the example runs the risk of falling apart, of its unity of self-relation becoming a jumble. Every detail is essential to the case. This means that the details making up the example partake of its singularity. Each detail is like another example embedded in it. A microexample. An incipient example. A moment's inattention and that germ of a one-for-all and all-in-itself might start to grow. It might take over. It might shift the course of the writing. Every example harbors terrible powers of deviation and digression.

The essays in this volume work through examples. The writing tries not only to accept the risk of sprouting deviant, but also to invite it. Take joy in your digressions. Because that is where the unexpected arises. That is the experimental aspect. If you know where you will end up when you begin, nothing has happened in the meantime. You have to be willing to surprise yourself writing things you didn't think you thought. Letting examples burgeon requires using inattention as a writing tool. You have to let yourself get so caught up in the flow of your writing that it ceases at moments to be recognizable to you as your own. This means you have to be prepared for failure. For with inattention comes risk: of silliness or even outbreaks of stupidity. But perhaps in order to write experimentally, you have to be willing to "affirm" even your own stupidity. Embracing one's own stupidity is not the prevailing academic posture (at least not in the way I mean it here).

The result is not so much the negation of system as a setting of systems into motion. The desired result is a systematic openness: an open system. For the writing to continue to belong in the humanities, it must take into account and put into use already established concepts drawn for one or another humanities discipline, or better, from many all at once (philosophy, psychology, semiotics, communications, literary theory, political economy, anthropology, cultural studies, and so on). The important thing, once again, is that these found concepts not simply be applied. This can be done by extracting them from their usual connections to other concepts in their home system and confronting them with the example or a detail from it. The activity of the example will transmit to the concept, more or less violently. The concept will start to deviate under the force. Let it. Then reconnect it to other concepts, drawn from other systems, until a whole new system of connection starts to form. Then, take another example. See what happens. Follow the new growth. You end up with many buds. Incipient systems. Leave them that way. You have made a systemlike composition prolonging the active power of the example. You have left your readers with a very special gift: a headache. By which I mean a problem: what in the world to do with it all. That's their problem. That's where their experimentation begins. Then the openness of the system will spread. *If* they have found what they have read compelling. Creative contagion.

As mentioned earlier, in this project scientific and mathematical models are often foregrounded. The concept of field was mentioned. Concepts from chaos theory come in time and again (chapters 1, 3, 4, 6, 9). And, given all the doublings back and foldings over on itself that characterize the body's dynamic unity, models from topology take on increasing emphasis (chapters 5, 8). Given the touchiness surrounding the issue of thefts from science for the humanities, it is probably wise to say a word about it. Defenders of the disciplinary purity of the sciences consider it shameless poaching. I wholeheartedly agree. It's not science anymore, they say, once those silly humanities people get their hands on it. It's all "wrong."

As well it should be. Getting it "right" could only mean one thing: applying the results of science to the humanities. If carried out systematically, this simply annexes the target area to the sciences, in what amounts to a form of imperialist disciplinary aggression. The success of this approach would erase whatever specificity or singularity a humanities discipline might have. Sociobiology and its younger cousin evolutionary psychology are prime examples. This kind of wholesale application is usually practiced by scientists without training in the humanities (and often with a great deal of animus toward trends in the humanities of the last few centuries). People in the humanities, for their part, tend to take a piecemeal approach to application. They will isolate an attractive scientific or mathematical concept and add it to the repertoire of their own disciplinary system, like an exotic pet. Scientists might rightly object that the concept has ceased to have anything remotely scientific about it and is just functioning as a metaphor. Statements like "James Joyce's *Finnegan's*

Wake is a chaotic system" too often and too easily translate as: "the rhetorical form of the text is 'like' a chaotic system." A more deliberate "chaos" you could not find. Is it really chaos, a scientist might be forgiven for asking. An even worse case scenario, however, is when "chaos" is treated as a theme. This boils down to the banal observation that the novel might be illustrating a scientific concept, representing it on the level of its content.

The optimal situation would be to take a scientific concept and use it in such a way that it ceases to be systematically scientific but doesn't end up tamed, a metaphorical exhibit in someone else's menagerie. This might be done by treating the scientific concept the way any other concept is treated in the approach advocated here. It was said that a concept could be severed from the system of connections from which it is drawn and plopped into a new and open environment where it suffers an exemplary kind of creative violence. This is only half the story. A concept is by nature connectible to other concepts. A concept is defined less by its semantic content than by the regularities of connection that have been established between it and other concepts: its rhythm of arrival and departure in the flow of thought and language; when and how it tends to relay into another concept. When you uproot a concept from its network of systemic connections with other concepts, you still have its *connectibility.* You have a systemic connectibility without the system. In other words, the concept carries a certain residue of activity from its former role. You can think of it as the rhythm without the regularity, or a readiness to arrive and relay in certain ways. Rhythm, relay, arrival and departure. These are relations of motion and rest: *affect.* When you poach a scientific concept, it carries with it scientific affects. Thus the transmission is two-way. The activity of the example is transmitted to the scientific concept, and affects of science are transmitted to the example. A kind of conceptual struggle ensues, producing a creative tension that may play itself out in any number of ways (depending in part on how much the importer of the concept actually understands of the system left behind—or cares). However it plays out, it is certain that the humanities project into which the concept has been imported will be changed by the encounter. This is the kind of shameless poaching from science I advocate and endeavor to practice: one that betrays the system of science while respecting its affect, in a way designed to force a change in the humanities.

The point, once again, is not to make the humanities scientific. The point is to borrow from science in order to make a difference in the humanities. But not only that. The point is not just to make the humanities differ, but also to make them differ from the sciences in ways they are unaccustomed to. In other words, part of the idea is to put the humanities in a position of having continually to renegotiate their relations with the sciences—and, in the process, to rearticulate what is unique to their own capacities (what manner of affects *they* can transmit). This imperative to renegotiate adds an element of diplomacy to the piracy. Although it is unlikely that the sciences for their part will feel much inclination to negotiate. Having an immeasurably more secure institutional and economic base gives them the luxury of isolationism. The fact of the matter is that the humanities need the sciences—entirely aside from questions of institutional power but rather for their own conceptual health—a lot more than the sciences need the humanities. It is in this connection that the issue of empiricism takes on added importance. Reopening the question of what constitutes empiricism is perhaps one way to get the attention of the sciences (chapter 9).

Scientists shouldn't feel threatened by these respectful betrayals. If it is any consolation, concepts from humanities disciplines undergo similarly "diplomatic" treatment. Aside from that, poaching a scientific concept in no way prevents it from continuing to function in its home environment. It's not a zero-sum game. It's additive. The concept still belongs to the culture of science but has also been naturalized into the humanities. If I were a concept, I could emigrate *and* stay behind in my home country. (I have tried this, but it didn't work.)

Which just leaves the title. The genre of writing most closely allied with the logical form of the example is the *parable*. A word for the "real but abstract" incorporeality of the body is the *virtual*. The extent to which the virtual is exhausted by "potential," or how far into the virtual an energeticism can go, is a last problem worth mentioning. For only "an insensible body is a truly continuous body": there's the rub.[18] There's the ultimate paradox of the dynamic unity of movement and sensation: the unity is purely virtual. For the virtual to fully achieve itself, it must recede from being apace with its becoming. This problem (of the void) is not entirely absent from the "parables for the virtual" that follow (chapters 4, 6). But a thorough grappling with it will have to wait for a next project, whose own problems are perhaps already just beginning to be felt in these essays.

1

THE AUTONOMY OF AFFECT

I

A man builds a snowman on his roof garden. It starts to melt in the afternoon sun. He watches. After a time, he takes the snowman to the cool of the mountains where it stops melting. He bids it good-bye and leaves.

Just images, no words, very simple. This was a story depicted in a short film shown on German television as filler between programs. The film drew complaints from parents reporting that their children had been frightened. That drew the attention of a team of researchers. Their subsequent study was notable for failing to find very much of what it was studying: cognition.[1]

Researchers, headed by Hertha Sturm, used three versions of the film: the original wordless version and two versions with voice-overs added. The first voice-over version was dubbed "factual." It added a simple step-by-step account of the action as it happened. A second version was called "emotional." It was largely the same as the factual version but included, at crucial turning points, words expressing the emotional tenor of the scene under way.

Groups of nine-year-old children were tested for recall and asked to rate the version they saw on a scale of "pleasantness." The factual version was consistently rated the least pleasant and was also the least remembered. The most pleasant was the original wordless version, which was rated just slightly above the emotional. And it was the emotional version that was most remembered.

This is already a bit muddling. Something stranger happened when the subjects of the study were asked to rate the individual scenes in the film both on a "happy-sad" scale and a "pleasant-unpleasant" scale. The "sad" scenes were rated the *most pleasant;* the sadder the better.

The hypothesis that immediately suggests itself is that in some kind of precocious anti-Freudian protest, the children were equating arousal with pleasure. This being an empirical study, the children were wired. Their physiological reactions were monitored. The factual version elicited the highest level of arousal, even though it was the most unpleasant (that is, "happy") and made the least long-lasting impression. The children, it turns out, were physiologically split: factuality made their heart beat faster and deepened their breathing, the original nonverbal version elicited the greatest response from their skin. The arousal effect faded with repetition as measured by heart beat and breathing, but remained high as registered by the skin. Galvanic skin response measures *autonomic* reaction.

From the tone of their report, it seems that the researchers were a bit taken aback by their results. They observed that the difference between sadness and happiness is not all that it's cracked up to be and worried that the difference between children and adults was also not all that it was cracked up to be (judging by studies of adult retention of news broadcasts). Their only positive conclusion emphasized *the primacy of the affective* in image reception.

Accepting and expanding upon that, it may be noted that the primacy of the affective is marked by a gap between *content* and *effect*: it would appear that the strength or duration of an image's effect is not logically connected to the content in any straightforward way. This is not to say that there is no connection and no logic. What is meant here by the content of the image is its indexing to conventional meanings in an intersubjective context, its sociolinguistic qualification. This indexing fixes the determinate *qualities* of the image; the strength or duration of the image's effect could be called its *intensity*. What comes out here is that there is no dependable correspondence or conformity between qualities and intensity. If there is a relation, it is of another nature.

To translate this negative observation into a positive one: the event of image reception is multilevel, or at least bi-level. There is a bifurcation in response into two systems. The level of intensity is characterized by a crossing of semantic wires: on it, sadness is pleasant. The level of intensity is organized according to a logic that does not admit the excluded middle. This is to say that it is not semantically or semiotically ordered. It does not fix distinctions. Instead, it vaguely but insistently connects what is normally indexed as separate. When asked to signify itself, it can only do so in a paradox. There is disconnection of signifying order from intensity—which constitutes a different order of connection operating in parallel. The gap noted earlier is not only between content and effect. It is also between the form of content—signification as a conventional system of distinctive difference—and intensity. The disconnection between form/content and intensity/effect is not just negative: it enables a different connectivity, a different difference, in parallel.

Both levels, intensity and qualification, are immediately embodied. Intensity is embodied in purely autonomic reactions most directly manifested in the skin—at the surface of the body, at its interface with things. Depth reactions belong more to the form/content (qualification) level, even though they also involve autonomic functions such as heartbeat and breathing. The reason may be that they are associated with expectation, which depends on consciously positioning oneself in a line of narrative continuity. Modulations of heartbeat and breathing mark a reflux of consciousness into the autonomic depths, coterminous with a rise of the autonomic into consciousness. They are a conscious-autonomic mix, a measure of their participation in one another. Intensity is beside that loop, a nonconscious, never-to-be-conscious autonomic remainder. It is outside expectation and adaptation, as disconnected from meaningful sequencing, from narration, as it is from vital function. It is narratively delocalized, spreading over the generalized body surface like a lateral backwash from the function-meaning interloops that travel the vertical path between head and heart.

Language, though headstrong, is not simply in opposition to intensity. It would seem to function differentially in relation to it. The factual version of the snowman story was dampening. Matter-of-factness dampens intensity. In this case, matter-of-factness was a doubling of the sequence of images with narration expressing in as objective a manner as possible the commonsense function and consensual meaning of the movements perceived on screen. This interfered with the images' effect. The emotional version added a few phrases that punctuated the narrative line with qualifications of the emotional content, as opposed to the objective-narrative content. The qualifications of emotional content enhanced the images' effect, as if they resonated with the level of intensity rather than interfering with it. An emotional qualification breaks narrative continuity for a moment to register a state—actually to re-register an already felt state, for the skin is faster than the word.

The relationship between the levels of intensity and qualification is not one of conformity or correspondence but rather of resonation or interference, amplification or dampening. Linguistic expression can resonate with and amplify intensity at the price of making itself functionally redundant. When on the other hand it doubles a sequence of movements in order to add something to it in the way of meaningful progression—in this case a more or less definite expectation, an intimation of what comes next in a conventional progression—then it runs counter to and dampens the intensity. Intensity would seem to be associated with nonlinear processes: resonation and feedback that momentarily suspend the linear progress of the narrative present from past to future. Intensity is qualifiable as an emotional state, and that state is static—temporal and narrative noise. It is a state of suspense, potentially of disruption. It is like a temporal sink, a hole in time, as we conceive of it and narrativize it. It is not exactly passivity, because it is filled with motion, vibratory motion, resonation. And it is not yet activity, because the motion is not of the kind that can be directed (if only symbolically) toward practical ends in a world of constituted objects and aims (if only on screen). Of course, the qualification of an emotion is quite often, in other contexts, itself a narrative element that moves the action ahead, taking its place in socially recognized lines of action and reaction. But to the extent that it is, it is not in resonance with intensity. It resonates to the exact degree to which it is in excess of any narrative or functional line.

In any case, language doubles the flow of images on another level, on a different track. There is a redundancy of resonation that plays up or amplifies (feeds back disconnection, enabling a different connectivity) and a redundancy of signification that plays out or linearizes (jumps the feedback loop between vital function and meaning into lines of socially valorized action and reaction). Language belongs to entirely different orders depending on which redundancy it enacts. Or, it always enacts both more or less completely: two languages, two dimensions of every expression, one superlinear, the other linear. Every event takes place on both levels—and between both levels, as they resonate together to form a larger system composed of two interacting subsystems following entirely different rules of formation. For clarity, it might be best to give different names to the two halves of the event. In this case, *suspense* could be distinguished from and interlinked with *expectation* as superlinear and linear dimensions of the same image-event, which is at the same time an expression-event.

Approaches to the image in its relation to language are incomplete if they operate only on the semantic or semiotic level, however that level is defined (linguistically, logically, narratologically, ideologically, or all of these in combination, as a Symbolic). What they lose, precisely, is the expression *event*—in favor of structure. Much could be gained by integrating the dimension of intensity into cultural theory. The stakes are the new. For structure is the place where nothing ever happens, that explanatory heaven in which all eventual permutations are prefigured in a self-consistent set of invariant generative rules. Nothing is prefigured in the event. It is the collapse of structured distinction into intensity, of rules into paradox. It is the suspension of the invariance that makes happy happy, sad sad, function function, and meaning mean. Could it be that it is through the expectant suspension of that suspense that the new emerges? As if an echo of irreducible excess, of gratuitous amplification, piggybacked on the reconnection to progression, bringing a tinge of the unexpected, the lateral, the unmotivated, to lines of action and reaction. A change in the rules. The expression-event is the system of the inexplicable: emergence, into and against regeneration (the reproduction of a structure). In the case of the snowman, the unexpected and inexplicable that emerged along with the generated responses had to do with the differences between happiness and sadness, children and adults, not being all they're cracked up to be, much to our scientific chagrin: a change in the rules. Intensity is the unassimilable.

For present purposes, intensity will be equated with affect. There seems to be a growing feeling within media, literary, and art theory that affect is central to an understanding of our information- and image-based late capitalist culture, in which so-called master narratives are perceived to have foundered. Fredric Jameson notwithstanding, belief has waned for many, but not affect. If anything, our condition is characterized by a surfeit of it. The problem is that there is no cultural-theoretical vocabulary specific to affect.[2] Our entire vocabulary has derived from theories of signification that are still wedded to structure even across irreconcilable differences (the divorce proceedings of poststructuralism: terminable or interminable?). In the absence of an asignifying philosophy of affect, it is all too easy for received psychological categories to slip back in, undoing the considerable deconstructive work that has been effectively carried out by poststructuralism. Affect is most often used loosely as a synonym for emotion.[3] But one of the clearest lessons of this first story is that emotion and affect—if affect is intensity—follow different logics and pertain to different orders.

An emotion is a subjective content, the sociolinguistic fixing of the quality of an experience which is from that point onward defined as personal. Emotion is qualified intensity, the conventional, consensual point of insertion of intensity into semantically and semiotically formed progressions, into narrativizable action-reaction circuits, into function and meaning. It is intensity owned and recognized. It is crucial to theorize the difference between affect and emotion. If some have the impression that affect has waned, it is because affect is unqualified. As such, it is not ownable or recognizable and is thus resistant to critique.

It is not that there are no philosophical antecedents to draw on. It is just that they are not the usual ones for literary and cultural studies. On many of these points there is a formidable philosophical precursor: on the difference in nature between affect and emotion; on the irreducibly bodily and autonomic nature of affect; on affect as a suspension of action-reaction circuits and linear temporality in a sink of what might be called "passion," to distinguish it both from passivity and activity; on the equation between affect and effect; and on the form/content of conventional discourse as constituting a separate stratum running counter to the full registering of affect and its affirmation, its positive development, its expression as and for itself. On all of these points, it is the name of Baruch Spinoza that stands out. The title of his central work suggests a designation for the project of thinking affect: *Ethics*.[4]

II

Another story, this time about the brain: the mystery of the missing half second.

Experiments were performed on patients who had been implanted with cortical electrodes for medical purposes. Mild electrical pulses were administered to the electrode and also to points on the skin. In either case, the stimulation was felt only if it lasted more than half a second: half a second, the minimum perceivable lapse. If the cortical electrode was fired a half second before the skin was stimulated, patients reported feeling the skin pulse first. The researcher speculated that sensation involves a "backward referral in time"—in other words, that sensation is organized recursively before being linearized, before it is redirected outwardly to take its part in a conscious chain of actions and reactions. Brain and skin form a resonating vessel. Stimulation turns inward, is folded into the body, except that there is no inside for it to be in, because the body is radically open, absorbing impulses quicker than they can be perceived, and because the entire vibratory event is unconscious, out of mind. Its anomaly is smoothed over retrospectively to fit conscious requirements of continuity and linear causality.[5]

What happens during the missing half second? A second experiment gave some hints.

Brain waves of healthy volunteers were monitored by an electroencephalograph (EEG) machine. The subjects were asked to flex a finger at a moment of their choosing and to recall the time of their decision by noting the spatial clock position of a revolving dot. The flexes came 0.2 seconds after they clocked the decision, but the EEG machine registered significant brain activity 0.3 seconds *before* the decision. Again, a half-second lapse between the beginning of a bodily event and its completion in an outwardly directed, active expression.

Asked to speculate on what implications all this might have for a doctrine of free will, the researcher, Benjamin Libet, proposes that "we may exert free will not by initiating intentions but by vetoing, acceding or otherwise responding to them after they arise."[6]

In other words, the half second is missed not because it is empty, but because it is overfull, in excess of the actually-performed action and of its ascribed meaning. Will and consciousness are *subtractive*. They are *limitative, derived functions* that reduce a complexity too rich to be functionally expressed. It should be noted in particular that during the mysterious half second, what we think of as "free," "higher" functions, such as volition, are apparently being performed by autonomic, bodily reactions occurring in the brain but outside consciousness, and between brain and finger but prior to action and expression. The formation of a volition is necessarily accompanied and aided by cognitive functions. Perhaps the snowman researchers of our first story couldn't find cognition because they were looking for it in the wrong place—in the "mind," rather than in *the body* they were monitoring. Talk of intensity inevitably raises the objection that such a notion involves an appeal to a prereflexive, romantically raw domain of primitive experiential richness—the nature in our culture. It is not that. First, because something happening out of mind in a body directly absorbing its outside cannot exactly said to be experienced. Second, because volition, cognition, and presumably other "higher" functions usually presumed to be in the mind, figured as a mysterious container of mental entities that is somehow s eparate from body and brain, are present and active in that now not-so-"raw" domain. Resonation assumes feedback. "Higher functions" belonging to the realm of qualified form/content in which identified, self-expressive persons interact in conventionalized action-reaction circuits, following a linear time line, are fed back into the realm of intensity and recursive causality. The body doesn't just absorb pulses or discrete stimulations; it infolds *contexts,* it infolds volitions and cognitions that are nothing if not situated. Intensity is asocial, but not presocial—it *includes* social elements but mixes them with elements belonging to other levels of functioning and combines them according to different logic. How could this be so? Only if the *trace* of past actions, *including a trace of their contexts,* were conserved in the brain and in the flesh, but out of mind and out of body understood as qualifiable interiorities, active and passive respectively, directive spirit and dumb matter. Only if past actions and contexts were conserved and repeated, autonomically reactivated but not accomplished; begun but not completed. Intensity is *incipience,* incipient action and expression. Intensity is not only incipience. It is also the beginning of a selection: the incipience of mutually exclusive pathways of action and expression, all but one of which will be inhibited, prevented from actualizing themselves completely. The crowd of pretenders to actualization tend toward completion in a new selective context. Its newness means that their incipience cannot *just* be a conservation and reactivation of a past. They are *tendencies*—in other words, pastnesses opening directly onto a future, but with no present to speak of. For the present is lost with the missing half second, passing too quickly to be perceived, too quickly, actually, to have happened.

This requires a reworking of how we think about the body. Something that happens too quickly to have happened, actually, is *virtual.* The body is as immediately virtual as it is actual. The virtual, the pressing crowd of incipiencies and tendencies, is a realm of *potential.* In potential is where futurity combines, unmediated, with pastness, where outsides are infolded and sadness is happy (happy because the press to action and expression is life). The virtual is a lived paradox where what are normally opposites coexist, coalesce, and connect; where what cannot be experienced cannot but be felt—albeit reduced and contained. For out of the pressing crowd an individual action or expression *will* emerge and be registered consciously. One "wills" it to emerge, to be qualified, to take on sociolinguistic meaning, to enter linear action-reaction circuits, to become a content of one's life—by dint of inhibition.

Since the virtual is unlivable even as it happens, it can be thought of as a form of superlinear abstraction that does not obey the law of the excluded middle, that is organized differently but is inseparable from the concrete activity and expressivity of the body. The body is as immediately abstract as it is concrete; its activity and expressivity extend, as on their underside, into an incorporeal, yet perfectly real, dimension of pressing potential.

It is Henri Bergson who stands as a philosophical precursor on many of these points: the brain as a center of indetermination; consciousness as subtractive and inhibitive; perception as working to infold extended actions and expressions, *and* their situatedness, into a dimension of intensity or *in*tension as opposed to extension; the continual doubling of the actual body by this dimension of intensity, understood as a superlinear, superabstract realm of potential; that realm of the virtual as having a different temporal structure, in which past and future brush shoulders with no mediating present, and as having a different, recursive causality; the virtual as cresting in a liminal realm of emergence, where half-actualized actions and expressions arise like waves on a sea to which most no sooner return.[7]

Bergson could profitably be read together with Spinoza. One of Spinoza's basic definitions of affect is an "affection [in other words an impingement upon] the body, *and at the same time the idea of the affection*" (emphasis added). This starts sounding suspiciously Bergsonian if it is noted that the body, when impinged upon, is described by Spinoza as being in state of passional suspension in which it exists more outside of itself, more in the abstracted action of the impinging thing and the abstracted context of that action, than within itself, and if it is noted that the idea in question is not only not conscious but is not in the first instance in the "mind."

In Spinoza, it is only when the idea of the affection is doubled by an *idea of the idea of the affection* that it attains the level of conscious reflection. Conscious reflection is a doubling over of the idea on itself, a self-recursion of the idea that enwraps the affection or impingement at two removes. For it has already been removed once by the body itself. The body infolds the *effect* of the impingement—it conserves the impingement minus the impinging thing, the impingement abstracted from the actual action that caused it and actual context of that action. This is a first-order idea produced spontaneously by the body: the affection is immediately, spontaneously doubled by the repeatable trace of an encounter, the "form" of an encounter, in Spinoza's terminology (an infolding, or contraction, of context in the vocabulary of this essay). The trace determines a tendency, the potential, if not yet the appetite, for the autonomic repetition and variation of the impingement. Conscious reflection is the doubling over of this dynamic abstraction on itself. The order of connection of such dynamic abstractions among themselves, on a level specific to them, is called mind. The autonomic tendency received secondhand from the body is raised to a higher power to become an activity of the mind. Mind and body are seen as two levels recapitulating the same image/expression event in different but parallel ways, ascending by degrees from the concrete to the incorporeal, holding to the same absent center of a now spectral—and potentialized—encounter. Spinoza's ethics is the philosophy of the becoming-active, in parallel, of mind and body, from an origin in passion, in impingement, in so pure and productive a receptivity that it can only be conceived as a third state, an excluded middle, prior to the distinction between activity and passivity: affect. This "origin" is never left behind, but doubles one like a shadow that is always almost perceived, and cannot but be perceived, in effect.

In a different but complementary direction, when Spinoza defines mind and body as different orders of connection, or different regimes of motion and rest, his thinking converges in suggestive ways with Bergson's theories of virtuality and movement.

It is Gilles Deleuze who reopened the path to these authors, although nowhere does he patch them directly into each other. His work and theirs could profitably be read together with recent theories of complexity and chaos.[8] It is all a question of *emergence,* which is precisely the focus of the various science-derived theories that converge around the notion of self-organization (the spontaneous production of a level of reality having its own rules of formation and order of connection). Affect or intensity in the present account is akin to what is called a critical point, or a bifurcation point, or singular point, in chaos theory and the theory of dissipative structures. This is the turning point at which a physical system paradoxically embodies multiple and normally mutually exclusive potentials, only one of which is "selected." "Phase space" could be seen as a diagrammatic rendering of the dimension of the virtual. The organization of multiple levels that have different logics and temporal organizations, but are locked in resonance with each other and recapitulate the same event in divergent ways, recalls the fractal ontology and nonlinear causality underlying theories of complexity.

The levels at play could be multiplied to infinity: already mentioned are mind and body, but also volition and cognition, at least two orders of language, expectation and suspense, body depth and epidermis, past and future, action and reaction, happiness and sadness, quiescence and arousal, passivity and activity, and so on. These could be seen not as binary oppositions or contradictions, but as resonating levels. Affect is their point of emergence, in their actual specificity, and it is their vanishing point, in singularity, in their virtual coexistence and interconnection—that critical point shadowing every image/expression-event. Although the realm of intensity that Deleuze's philosophy strives to conceptualize is transcendental in the sense that it is not directly accessible to experience, it is not transcendent, it is not exactly outside experience either. It is immanent to it—always in it but not of it. Intensity and experience accompany one another like two mutually presupposing dimensions or like two sides of a coin. Intensity is immanent to matter and to events, to mind and to body and to every level of bifurcation composing them and which they compose. Thus it also cannot but be experienced, in effect—in the proliferations of levels of organization it ceaselessly gives rise to, generates and regenerates, at every suspended moment.[9] Deleuze's philosophy is the point at which transcendental philosophy flips over into a radical immanentism, and empiricism into ethical experimentation. The Kantian imperative to understand the conditions of possible experience as if from outside and above transposes into an invitation to recapitulate, to repeat and complexify, at ground level, the real conditions of emergence, not of the categorical, but of the unclassifiable, the unassimilable, the never-yet felt, the felt for less than half a second, again for the first time—the new. Kant meets Spinoza, where idealism and empiricism turn pragmatic, becoming a midwifery of invention—with no loss in abstractive or inductive power. Quite the contrary—both are heightened. But now abstraction is synonymous with an unleashing of potential, rather than its subtraction. And the sense of induction has changed, to a triggering of a process of complexifying self-organization. The implied ethics of the project is the value attached—without foundation, with desire only—to the multiplication of powers of existence, to ever-divergent regimes of action and expression.

Feedback (Digression)

A key to the rethinking of affect is the feedback of atoms of "higher" modes of organization into a level of emergence.[10] The philosopher of science Gilbert Simondon sees this functioning even on the physical level, where "germs" of forms are present in an emergent dimension along with unformed elements such as tropisms (attractors), distributions of potential energy (gradients defining metastabilities), and nonlocalized relations (resonation). According to Simondon, the dimension of the emergent— which he terms the "preindividual"—cannot be understood in terms of form, even if it infolds forms in a germinal state. It can only be analyzed as a continuous but highly differentiated *field* that is "out of phase" with formed entities (that is, has a different topology and causal order from the "individuals" which arise from it and whose forms return to it).[11] A germinal or "implicit" form cannot be understood as a shape or structure. It is more a bundle of potential functions localized, as a differentiated region, within a larger field of potential. In each region a shape or structure begins to form, but no sooner dissolves as its region shifts in relation to the others with which it is in tension. There is a kind of bubbling of structuration in a turbulent soup of regions of swirling potential. The regions are separated from each other by dynamic thresholds rather than by boundaries. Simondon calls these regions of potential "quanta," even as they appear on the macrophysical level and on the human level—hence the atomic allusion.[12] The "regions" are as abstract as they are actual, in the sense that they do not define boundaried spaces but are rather mobile differentiations within an open field characterized by action at a distance between elements (attractors, gradients, resonation). The limits of the region and of the entire field (the universe) are defined by the reach of its elements' collective actions at a distance. The limit will not be a sharp demarcation but more like a multidimensional fading to infinity. The field is open in the sense it has no interiority or exteriority: it is limited *and* infinite.

"Implicit" form is a bundling of potential functions, an infolding or

34

contraction of potential interactions (intension). The playing out of those potentials requires an *unfolding* in three-dimensional space and linear time—extension as actualization; actualization as *expression*. It is in expression that the fade-out occurs. *The limits of the field of emergence are in its actual expression.* Implicit form may be thought of as the effective presence of the sum total of a thing's interactions minus the thing. It is a thing's relationality autonomized as a dimension of the real. This *autonomization of relation* is the condition under which "higher" functions feed back. Emergence, once again, is a two-sided coin: one side in the virtual (the autonomy of relation), the other in the actual (functional limitation). What is being termed affect in this essay is precisely this two-sidedness, the simultaneous participation of the virtual in the actual and the actual in the virtual, as one arises from and returns to the other. Affect is this two-sideness *as seen from the side of the actual thing,* as couched in its perceptions and cognitions. Affect is *the virtual as point of view,* provided the visual metaphor is used guardedly. For affect is synesthetic, implying a participation of the senses in each other: the measure of a living thing's potential interactions is its ability to transform the effects of one sensory mode into those of another. (Tactility and vision being the most obvious but by no means the only examples; interoceptive senses, especially proprioception, are crucial.)[13] Affects are *virtual synesthetic perspectives* anchored in (functionally limited by) the actually existing, particular things that embody them. The autonomy of affect is its participation in the virtual. *Its autonomy is its openness.* Affect is autonomous to the degree to which it escapes confinement in the particular body whose vitality, or potential for interaction, it is. Formed, qualified, situated perceptions and cognitions fulfilling functions of actual connection or blockage are the capture and closure of affect. Emotion is the most intense (most contracted) expression of that *capture*—and of the fact that something has always and again escaped. Something remains unactualized, inseparable from but unassimilable to any *particular,* functionally anchored perspective. That is why all emotion is more or less disorienting, and why it is classically described as being outside of oneself, at the very point at which one is most intimately and unshareably in contact with oneself and one's vitality. If there were no escape, no excess or remainder, no fade-out to infinity, the universe would be without potential, pure entropy, death. Actually existing, structured things live in and through that which escapes them. Their autonomy is the autonomy of affect.

The escape of affect *cannot but be perceived,* alongside the perceptions that are its capture. This side-perception may be punctual, localized in an event (such as the sudden realization that happiness and sadness are something besides what they are). When it is punctual, it is usually described in negative terms, typically as a form of *shock* (the sudden interruption of functions of actual connection).[14] But it is also continuous, like a background perception that accompanies every event, however quotidian. When the continuity of affective escape is put into words, it tends to take on positive connotations. For it is nothing less than the *perception of one's own vitality,* one's sense of aliveness, of changeability (often signified as "freedom"). One's "sense of aliveness" is a continuous, nonconscious self-perception (unconscious self-reflection or lived self-referentiality). It is the perception of this *self-perception,* its naming and making conscious, that allows affect to be effectively analyzed—as long as a vocabulary can be found for that which is imperceptible but whose escape from perception cannot but be perceived, as long as one is alive.[15]

Simondon notes the connection between self-reflection and affect. He even extends the capacity for self-reflection to all living things—although it is hard to see why his own analysis does not force him to extend it to all things, living or not.[16] (Is not resonation a kind of self-reflection?) Spinoza could be read as doing this in his definition of the idea of the affection as a trace—one that is not without reverberations. More radically, he sees ideas as attaining their most adequate (most self-organized) expression not in us but in the "mind" of God. But then he defines God as Nature (understood as encompassing the human, the artificial, and the invented). Deleuze is willing to take the step of dispensing with God. One of the things that distinguishes his philosophy most sharply from that of his contemporaries is the notion that ideality is a dimension of matter (also understood as encompassing the human, the artificial, and the invented).[17]

The distinction between the living and the nonliving, the biological and the physical, is not the presence or absence of reflection, but its directness. Our brains and nervous systems effect the autonomization of relation, in an interval smaller than the smallest perceivable, even though the operation arises from perception and returns to it. In the more primitive organisms, this autonomization is accomplished by organism-wide networks of interoceptive and exteroceptive sense-receptors whose impulses are not centralized in a brain. One could say that a jellyfish is its brain. In all living things, the autonomization of relation is effected by a center of indetermination (a localized or organism-wide function of resonation that delinearizes causality in order to relinearize it with a change of direction: from reception to reaction). At the fundamental physical level, there is no such mediation.[18] The place of physical nonmediation between the virtual and the actual is explored by quantum mechanics. Just as "higher" functions are fed back—all the way to the subatomic (that is, position and momentum)—quantum indeterminacy is fed forward. It rises through the fractal bifurcations leading to and between each of the superposed levels of reality. On each level, it appears in a unique mode adequate to that level. On the level of the physical macrosystems analyzed by Simondon, its mode is potential energy and the margin of "play" it introduces into deterministic systems (epitomized by the "three-body problem" so dear to chaos theory). On the biological level, it is the margin of undecidability accompanying every perception, which is one with a perception's transmissibility from one sense to another. On the human level, it is that same undecidability fed forward into thought, as evidenced in the deconstructability of every structure of ideas (as expressed, for example, in Gödel's incompleteness theorem and in Derrida's *différance*). Each individual and collective human level has its own peculiar "quantum" mode; various forms of undecidability in logical and signifying systems are joined by emotion on the psychological level, resistance on the political level, the specter of crisis haunting capitalist economies, and so forth. These modes are fed back and fed forward into one another, echoes of each other one and all.

The use of the concept of the quantum outside quantum mechanics, even as applied to human psychology, is not a metaphor. For each level, it is necessary to find an operative concept for the objective indeterminacy that echoes what on the subatomic level goes by the name of quantum. This involves analyzing every formation as participating in what David Bohm calls an *implicate order* cutting across all levels and doubled on each.[19] Affect is as good a general term as any for the interface between implicate and explicate order.[20] Returning to the difference between the physical and the biological, it is clear that there can be no firm dividing line between them, nor between them and the human. Affect, like thought or reflection, could be extended to any or every level, providing that the uniqueness of its functioning on that level is taken into account. The difference between the dead, the living, and the human is not a question of form or structure, nor of the properties possessed by the embodiments of forms or structures, nor of the qualified functions performed by those embodiments (that is, their utility or ability to do work). The distinction between kinds of things and levels of reality is a question of degree: of the way in which modes of organization (such as reflection) are differentially present on every level, barring the extremes. The extremes are the quantum physical and the human, inasmuch as it aspires to or confuses itself with the divine (which occurs wherever notions of eternity, identity, and essence are operative). Neither extreme can be said to exist, although each could be said to be real in entirely different ways: the quantum is productive of effective reality, and the divine is effectively produced as a fiction. In between lies a continuum of existence differentiated into levels, or regions of potential, between which there are no boundaries, only dynamic thresholds.

As Simondon notes, all of this makes it difficult to speak of either transcendence or immanence.[21] No matter what one does, they tend to flip over into each other, in a kind of spontaneous Deleuzian combustion. It makes little difference if the field of existence (being plus potential; the actual in its relation with the virtual) is thought of as an infinite interiority or a parallelism of mutual exteriorities. You get burned either way. Spinoza had it both ways: an indivisible substance divided into parallel attributes. To the extent that the terms transcendence and immanence connote spatial relations—and they inevitably do—they are inadequate to the task. A philosophical sleight of hand like Spinoza's is always necessary. The trick is to get comfortable with productive paradox.[22]

All of this—the absence of a clear line of demarcation between the physical, the vital, the human, and the superhuman; the undecidability of immanence and transcendence—also has implications for ethical thought. A common thread running through the varieties of social constructivism currently dominant in cultural theory holds that everything, including nature, is constructed in discourse. The classical definition of the human as the rational animal returns in new permutation: the human as the chattering animal. Only the animal is bracketed: the human as the chattering of culture. This reinstates a rigid divide between the human and the nonhuman, since it has become a commonplace, after Lacan, to make language the special preserve of the human (chattering chimps notwithstanding). Now saying that the quantum level is transformed by our perception is not the same as saying that it is only *in* our perception; saying that nature is discursively constructed is not necessarily the same as saying that nature is *in* discourse. Social constructivism easily leads to a cultural solipsism analogous to subjectivist interpretations of quantum mechanics. In this worst-case solipsist scenario, nature appears as immanent to culture (as its construct). At best, when the status of nature is deemed unworthy of attention, it is simply shunted aside. In that case it appears, by default, as transcendent to culture (as its inert and meaningless remainder). Perhaps the difference between best and worst is not all that it is cracked up to be. For in either case, nature as naturing, nature as having its own dynamism, is erased. Theoretical moves aimed at ending Man end up making human culture the measure and meaning of all things in a kind of unfettered anthropomorphism precluding—to take one example—articulations of cultural theory and ecology. It is meaningless to interrogate the relation of the human to the nonhuman if the nonhuman is only a construct of human culture, or inertness. The concepts of nature and culture need serious reworking, in a way that expresses the irreducible *alterity* of the nonhuman in and through its active *connection* to the human and vice versa. Let matter be matter, brains be brains, jellyfish be jellyfish, and culture be nature, in irreducible alterity and infinite connection.

A final note: the feedback of "higher" functions can take such forms as the deployment of narrative in essays about the breakdown of narrative.

III

Next story.

The last story was of the brain. This one is of the brainless. His name is Ronald Reagan. The story comes from a well-known book of pop-neurophysiology by Oliver Sacks.[23]

Sacks describes watching a televised speech by the "Great Communicator" in a hospital ward of patients suffering from two kinds of cognitive dysfunction. Some were suffering from global aphasia, which rendered them incapable of understanding words as such. They could nonetheless understand most of what was said, because they compensated by developing extraordinary abilities to read extraverbal cues: inflection, facial expression, and other gesture—body language. Others on the ward were suffering from what is called tonal agnosia, which is the inverse of aphasia. The ability to hear the expressiveness of the voice is lost, and with it goes attention to other extraverbal cues. Language is reduced to its grammatical form and semantic or logical content. Neither group appeared to be Reagan voters. In fact, the speech was universally greeted by howls of laughter and expressions of outrage. The "Great Communicator" was failing to persuade. To the aphasics, he was functionally illiterate in extraverbal cuing; his body language struck them as hilariously inept. He was, after all, a recycled bad actor, and an aging one at that. The agnosiacs were outraged that the man couldn't put together a grammatical sentence or follow a logical line to its conclusion. He came across to them as intellectually impaired. (It must be recalled that this is long before the onset of Reagan's Alzheimer's disease—what does that say about the difference between normality and degeneration?)

Now all of this might come as news to those who think of Reagan and other postmodern political stars on the model of charismatic leadership, in which the fluency of a public figure's gestural and tonal repertoire mesmerize the masses, lulling them into bleary-eyed belief in the content of the mellifluous words. On the contrary, what is astonishing is that Reagan wasn't laughed and jeered off the campaign podium, and was swept into office not once but twice. It wasn't that people didn't hear his verbal fumbling or recognize the incoherence of his thoughts. They were the butt of constant jokes and news stories. And it wasn't that what he lacked on the level of verbal coherence was glossed over by the seductive fluency of his body image. Reagan was more famous for his polyps than his poise, and there was a collective fascination with his faltering health and regular shedding of bits and pieces of himself. The only conclusion is that Reagan was an effective leader not in spite of but because of his double dysfunction. He was able to produce ideological effects by nonideological means, a global shift in the political direction of the United States by falling apart. His means were affective. Once again: affective, as opposed to emotional. This is not about empathy or emotive identification, or any form of identification for that matter.[24]

Reagan politicized the power of mime. That power is in interruption. A mime decomposes movement, cuts its continuity into a potentially infinite series of submovements punctuated by jerks. At each jerk, at each cut into the movement, the potential is there for the movement to veer off in another direction, to become a different movement. Each jerk suspends the continuity of the movement, for just a flash, too quick really to perceive but decisively enough to suggest a veer. This compresses into the

40

movement under way potential movements that are in some way made present without being actualized. In other words, each jerk is a critical point, a singular point, a bifurcation point. At that point, the mime almost imperceptibly intercalates a flash of virtuality into the actual movement under way. The genius of the mime is also the good fortune of the bad actor. Reagan's gestural idiocy had a mime effect. As did his verbal incoherence in the register of meaning. He was a communicative jerk. The two levels of interruption, those of linear movement and conventional progressions of meaning, were held together by the one Reagan feature that did, I think, hold positive appeal: the timbre of his voice, that beautifully vibratory voice. Two parallel lines of abstractive suspense resonated together. His voice embodied the resonation. It embodied the abstraction. It was the embodiment of an asignifying intensity doubling his every actual move and phrase, following him like the shadow of a mime. It was the continuity of his discontinuities.[25]

Reagan operationalized the virtual in postmodern politics. Alone, he was nothing approaching an ideologue. He was nothing, an idiocy musically coupled with an incoherence. But, that's a bit unfair. He was an incipience. He was unqualified and without content. But, his incipience was prolonged by technologies of image transmission and then relayed by apparatuses such as the family or the church or the school or the chamber of commerce, which in conjunction with the media acted as part of the nervous system of a new and frighteningly reactive body politic. It was on the receiving end that the Reagan incipience was qualified, given content. Receiving apparatuses fulfilled the inhibitory, limitative function. They selected one line of movement, one progression of meaning, to actualize and implant locally. That is why Reagan could be so many things to so many people; that is why the majority of the electorate could disagree with him on major issues but still vote for him. Because he was actualized, in their neighborhood, as a movement and a meaning of their selection—or at least selected for them with their acquiescence. He was a man for all inhibitions. It was commonly said that he ruled primarily by projecting an air of confidence. That was the emotional tenor of his political manner, dysfunction notwithstanding. Confidence is the emotional translation of affect as *capturable* life potential; it is a particular emotional expression and becoming-conscious of one's side-perceived sense of vitality. Reagan transmitted vitality, virtuality, tendency, in sickness and interruption. ("I am in control here," cried the general, when Reagan was shot. He wasn't, actually.) The actualizations relaying the Reagan incipience varied. But, with the exception of the cynical, the aphasic, and the agnosiac, they consistently included an overweening feeling of confidence—that of the supposedly sovereign individual within a supposedly great nation at whose helm idiocy and incoherence reigned. In other words, Reagan was many things to many people, but always within a general framework of affective jingoism. Confidence is the apotheosis of affective capture. Functionalized and nationalized, it feeds directly into prison construction and neocolonial adventure.

What is of dire interest now, post-Reagan, is the extent to which he contracted into his person operations that might be argued to be endemic to late-capitalist, image- and information-based economies. Think of the image/expression-events in which we bathe. Think interruption. Think of the fast cuts of the video clip or the too-cool TV commercial. Think of the cuts from TV programming to commercials. Think of the cuts across programming and commercials achievable through zapping. Think of the distractedness of television viewing, the constant cuts from the screen to its immediate surroundings, to the viewing context where other actions are performed in fits and starts as attention flits. Think of the joyously incongruent juxtapositions of surfing the Internet. Think of our bombardment by commercial images off the screen, at every step in our daily rounds. Think of the imagistic operation of the consumer object as turnover times decrease as fast as styles can be recycled. Everywhere the cut, the suspense—incipience. Virtuality, perhaps?

Affect holds a key to rethinking postmodern power after ideology. For although ideology is still very much with us, often in the most virulent of forms, it is no longer encompassing. It no longer defines the global mode of functioning of power. It is now one mode of power in a larger field that is not defined, overall, by ideology.[26] This makes it all the more pressing to connect ideology to its real conditions of emergence. For these are now manifest, mimed by men of power. One way of conceptualizing the non-ideological means by which ideology is produced might deploy the notions of *induction* and *transduction*—induction being the triggering of a qualification, of a containment, an actualization, and transduction being the transmission of an impulse of virtuality from one actualization to another and across them all (what Guattari calls transversality). Transduction is the transmission of a force of potential that cannot but be felt, simultaneously doubling, enabling, and ultimately counteracting the limitative selections of apparatuses of actualization and implantation.[27] This amounts to proposing an *analog* theory of image-based power: images as the conveyors of forces of emergence, as vehicles for existential potentialization and transfer. In this, too, there are notable precursors. In particular, Walter Benjamin, whose concept of shock and image bombardment, whose analyses of the unmediated before-after temporality of what he called the "dialectical image," whose fascination with mime and mimicry, whose connecting of tactility to vision, all have much to offer an affective theory of late-capitalist power.[28]

At this point, the impression may have grown such that affect is being touted here as if the whole world could be packed into it. In a way, it can and is. The affective "atoms" that overfill the jerk of the power-mime are monads, inductive/transductive virtual perspectives fading out in all directions to infinity, separated from one another by dynamic thresholds.[29] They are autonomous not through closure but through a singular openness. As unbounded "regions" in an equally unbounded affective field, they are in contact with the whole universe of affective potential, as by action at a distance. Thus they have no outside even though they are differentiated according to which potentials are most apt to be expressed (effectively induced) as their "region" passes into actuality. Their passing into actuality is the key. Affect *is* the whole world: from the precise angle of its differential emergence. How the element of virtuality is construed— whether past or future, inside or outside, transcendent or immanent, sublime or abject, atomized or continuous—is in a way a matter of indifference. It is all of these things, differently in every actual case. Concepts of the virtual in itself are important only to the extent to which they contribute to a pragmatic understanding of emergence, to the extent to which they enable triggerings of change (induce the new). It is the edge of virtual, where it leaks into actual, that counts. For that seeping edge is where potential, actually, is found.

Resistance is manifestly not automatically a part of image reception in late capitalist cultures. But neither can the effect of the mass media and other image- and information-based media simply be explained in terms of a lack: a waning of affect, a decline in belief, or alienation. The mass media are massively potentializing, but the potential is inhibited, and both the emergence of the potential and its limitation are part and parcel of the cultural-political functioning of the media, as connected to other apparatuses. Media transmissions are breaches of indetermination. For them to have any *specific* effect, they must be determined to have that effect by apparatuses of actualization and implantation that plug into them and transformatively relay what they give rise to (family, church, school, and chamber of commerce, to name but a few). The need to actively actualize media transmission is as true for reactive politics as it is for a politics of resistance and requires a new understanding of the body in its relation to signification and the ideal or incorporeal. In North America at least, the far right is far more attuned to the imagistic potential of the postmodern body than the established left and has exploited that advantage for at least the last two decades. Philosophies of affect, potential, and actualization may aid in finding countertactics.

IV

Last story:

> A man writes a health-care reform bill in his White House. It starts to melt in the media glare. He takes it to the Hill, where it continues to melt. He does not say good-bye.

And, although economic indicators show unmistakable signs of economic recovery, the stock market dips. By way of explanation, TV commentators cite a secondhand feeling. The man's "waffling" on other issues has undermined the public's confidence in him and is now affecting the health care initiative. The worry is that President Clinton is losing his "presidential" feel. What does that have to do with the health of the economy? The prevailing wisdom among the same commentators is that *passage* of the health care reform would harm the economy. It is hard to see why the market didn't go *up* on the news of the "unpresidential" falter of what many "opinion-makers" considered a costly social program inconsistent with basically sound economic policy inherited from the previous administration that was credited with starting a recovery. However, the question does not even arise, because the commentators are operating under the assumption that the stock market registers affective fluctuations in adjoining spheres more directly than properly economic indicators. Are they confused? Not according to certain economic theorists who, when called upon to explain to a nonspecialist audience the ultimate foundation of the capitalist monetary system, answer "faith."[30] And what, in the late capitalist economy, is the base cause of inflation according to the same experts? A "mindset," they say, in which feelings about the future become self-fulfilling prophesies capable of reversing "real" conditions.[31]

The ability of affect to produce an economic effect more swiftly and surely than economics itself means that affect is a real condition, an intrinsic variable of the late capitalist system, as infrastructural as a factory. Actually, it is beyond infrastructural, it is everywhere, in effect. Its ability to come secondhand, to switch domains and produce effects across them all, gives it a metafactorial ubiquity. It is beyond infrastructural. It is transversal.

This fact about affect—its matter-of-factness needs to be taken into account in cultural and political theory. Don't forget.

2

THE BLEED

Where Body Meets Image

Scenario

PASSAGE PRECEDES POSITION.

The Bleed

It is 1937. The future president of the United States is beginning his first acting job. "There I was—," confesses Ronald Reagan, "faced with my nemesis, reading. It isn't that I flubbed the words, or stumbled and mispronounced; I even placed the emphasis on the right syllable. I just lack personality when I read. . . . The second day I was introduced to the rushes. This is the custom of going at the end of each day's work and seeing on the screen what you shot the previous day. What a shock it was!"[1]

Fast-forward, mid-paragraph, to 1965, the writing present of the now experienced actor on the cusp of a spectacularly improbable political career. Poised for the campaign for the governorship of California that was to set him on the road to the White House and apparently no more comfortable with writing than reading, he is coauthoring his first autobiography. One of its primary functions is to explain how half a lifetime as a bad actor actually qualified him for high office, contrary to the then-public perception that the roles of entertainer and governor were fundamentally incompatible. He couches his explanation in terms of a shocking deficiency in movie acting that can only be overcome in the public arena.

> It has taken me many years to get used to seeing myself as others see me, and also seeing myself instead of my mental picture of the character I'm playing. First of all, very few of us ever see ourselves except as we look directly at ourselves in a mirror. Thus we don't know how we look from

behind, from the side, walking, standing, moving normally through a room. It's quite a jolt. Second is the fact that when you read a story you create a mental picture of each character. For the first few years this is true even in reading a script. You don't see yourself because you haven't had much experience in seeing yourself. Thus as you act the part, in your mind you envision your mental picture of the author's character. You go to the rushes and somebody has stolen that heroic figure, and there you are—just plain old everyday you—up on the screen. It's one hell of a letdown.[2]

This deceptively complex statement does not condemn acting wholesale, for example, on the grounds that it traffics in fakery, substituting appearance for reality. In fact, it implies that there is power in acting, which is faulted not for the kind of process it sets in motion but rather for its inability to take that process far enough to realize the power inherent in it. The process in question is seeing. A seeing of *oneself*. Specifically, a seeing of oneself *as others see one*. The problem with acting isn't that it carries the actor out of himself, out of his character into another, out of his real self into a false double; it is that it doesn't take the actor *far enough* outside of himself. The movie actor's success hinges on his ability to see himself as others see him, but this is circumvented by what Reagan calls "mental pictures." These are private images the actor forms of the character he is portraying, developed from the script. The actor makes words into images, visualizes text, then renders that visualization public by embodying it before the camera. Watching the rushes is a jolt for Reagan *precisely because he recognizes himself* on the screen. "There you are—just plain old everyday you."

That Reagan should be jolted by this is jolting. As he sits in the screening room watching the day's shoot, he is seeing himself exactly as the director and his fellow actors simultaneously see him and as the public will later see him. He is indeed seeing himself as others see him. So what's the problem? And who did he expect to see on the screen, if not himself? And if seeing a film of himself embodying a visualized text is seeing his plain old everyday self, does that mean that in everyday life he is an actor following a script?

What is clear is that Reagan is not concerned with the difference between reality and appearance. He seems to be speaking of two orders of reality—both of which are composed of appearance, understood more in a performative than epistemological sense. The relevant distinction is not between reality and appearance, true and false, acting and not acting, seeing and not seeing oneself as others see one. The pertinent criterion of evaluation is ontological and cuts across those registers. It bears on the completeness of an appearance, which it locates on a scale of intensity, as a higher- or lower-degree reality.

The plain, old, everyday self is an actor playing an ordinary role in the ordinary way. Reagan defines that as mirrorlike. *Mirror-vision* is by definition partial. There is a single axis of sight. You see yourself from one angle at a time and never effectively in movement. If you keep your head motionless and your eyes level, you can see parts of yourself move, for example your arms, from one perspective. You can change perspective by immobilizing your body and moving your head. But if you try to move your body and your head together in an attempt to catch yourself in motion, you only succeed in jumping from one frozen pose to another. The movement between is a blur, barely glimpsed. You can never see yourself "moving normally" as another sees you. Either you see movement, but the movement is partial, riveted to a stationary visual axis, stiffened by the effort of maintaining that line of vision, made wooden, deadened, turned into a caricature of itself, or you make a live movement at the price of losing sight of yourself for the duration. Every time you really see yourself, well, there you are. The single axis of vision stretches you between two surfaces recapitulating the same. On that axis, you resemble yourself perfectly. Stilted, static, a perfect picture. Change is excluded. Change is movement. It is rendered invisible.

This specular structure of doubled identity can be transposed into an intersubjective structure with only slight adjustment. In the everyday intersubjective world there are of course multiple axes of vision, but they are still strung out along a single line that subordinates them to resemblance and self-sameness. This line is itself nonvisual, it is a narrative line. In the family or at work, you perform your assigned social role. You interpret the script, you visualize or form a "mental picture" of what it means for you to be what you are, parent or child, mother or father, boss or employee, cop or criminal, and embody that visualization for the benefit of others occupying the contrasting but complementary character roles. For each role there is a privileged other in whose recognition of you, you recognize yourself. You mirror yourself in your supporting actor's eyes, and they in yours. A reciprocal difference stretches between paired retinal surfaces. Between them runs a narrative line carrying both social players across a series of regulated thresholds. You resemble each other more fundamentally than you differ, by virtue of your shared participation in the same narrative. The difference between you and your specular complement is the minimal difference allowing movement. The axes of vision are at slightly skewed angles, so that the mutually self-defining recognition always imperceptibly misses. This perspectival disjunction creates just enough of an imbalance to prevent fusion. Saved from stasis, life goes on. There is change but only minimal change, a skew-induced dynamic distortion generally consistent with sameness. You grow up, grow old, even reverse certain roles, perhaps becoming a parent, in any case turning into an adult after spending your entire life as a child. But you never outgrow yourself, however distorted your aging body and increasingly unfocused mind become. Privileged moments stand out clearly, perfect as pictures in a family album: birthday, graduation, marriage, anniversary, celebrating the raise, retirement. Plain, old, everyday you progresses through a sequence of life passages photographically preserved as stilted poses. Your life passes before you in succeeding tableaux, continuity shots punctuating a banal script just bad enough to systematically but modestly miss the mark. There is progression but no real transformation, the movement barely glimpsed. Wherever you go, there you are again. Unavoidably you. Then you die. This is utopia, 1950s-style.

Reagan is not content with that. He wants to transcend, to be someone else. He wants to be extraordinary, a hero. It jolts him that when he strikes the pose he sees himself. Acting keeps him him, in spite of the fame, because it only allows him to cross a minimal distance, between himself and his complement, in this case the moviegoer. Sitting in the screening room, he anticipates his fans crossing that same distance in the opposite direction. He sees them seeing themselves in their recognition of him. He sees himself seen, as privileged other. He wants out of that mirror-vision, but the film stock fixes him in it by objectifying the partial mental picture he embodied. As long as he is in the movies, he is condemned to be what he is, a second-rate actor in a bad fifties film, complementing, compensating small lives, on a larger-than-life screen. He is destined for greater things.

Complementarity is not completeness. The completeness Reagan yearns for is to be found in a way of appearing that goes beyond text and visualization, script and picture, beyond the dual structuring of specular identity in which one compensates for a lack in the other. He invokes a kind of vision that grasps exactly and exclusively what mirror-vision misses: the movement, only the movement ("walking, standing, moving normally through a room"). Reagan wants to see the lack in specular identity and, in the process, transform it into a peculiar kind of fullness. The *movement-vision* he looks to is also perspectival ("from behind, from the side"). But its perspectives lie on the far side of a maximum distance, one that can be crossed but not bridged. Occupying one of these perspectives would render Reagan instantly unrecognizable to himself. In that instant, he would have *become* other, in a way unassimilable to reflective identity. Mirror-vision and movement-vision are discontinuous; between them there is no mediation. The first is relative (ongoing reciprocal determination of I-me/I-you), the second is absolute (self-distancing).

Movement-vision is not only discontinuous with mirror-vision. It is discontinuous with itself. To see oneself standing as others see one is not the same as seeing oneself walking as others see one. Maintaining a simple continuity across standing and walking entails positing a commonality between moving and not moving, a generality in which their difference is resolved. It would miss, again, precisely what is being sought: movement as such, in its difference from stasis. The same goes for seeing oneself walking from behind and seeing oneself walking from the side. Movement is relational. Its specificity is compromised if any aspects of the relation are lost to generality—even if it is the generality *of* the terms in the relation, their self-sameness across time or in different coordinates in space.

Only as a generality can there be said to be a continuity between states (a body standing then walking) guaranteed by a unity of the observer (a subject that remains the same across changes of state in the object). The elementary unit of the space of movement-vision is not a generalizing subject coupled with an object in general, a self-identical observer who recognizes the object as the same, as what is common to different movements and to movement and stasis. Its elementary unit is the singularity of a movement that includes a perspective which occludes the actual functioning of both the subject and the object. The objectness of the object is attenuated as the subject, seeing itself as others see it, comes to occupy the object's place as well as its own. Simultaneously occupying its place and the object's, the subject departs from itself. The subject-object symmetry of mirror-vision is broken. The subject overlays itself on the object in a super position of reciprocal functions. The gap left by the subject's self-departure is filled not by a new subject or object but by a process encompassing their disjunction in a tide of change. This disjunctive encompassing is a kind of continuity but is in no way a simple one like that of mirror-vision (one whose implications may be exhausted following a single narrative line). It complicates things. The continuity of movement-vision is an *included disjunction*. It is a continuous displacement of the subject, the object, and their general relation: the empirical perspective uniting them in an act of recognition. It is an opening onto a space of transformation in which a de-objectified movement fuses with a de-subjectified observer. This larger processuality, this *real movement,* includes the perspective from which it is seen. But the perspective is that of a *virtual observer* that is one only with the movement (of the subject's self-departure). Not: I see you standing then walking. But: I (other than) sees me (now you) standing (from-the-side), standing (from-behind), walking (from-the-side), walking (from-behind), and so on. The elementary unit of the space of movement-vision is a *multiply* partial other-perspective included in a fractured movement-in-itself: change. Change: that which includes rupture but is nevertheless continuous (but only with itself, without complement).[3]

When Reagan enters the space of movement-vision, he is leaving behind the empirical world as he knew it. He is coinciding with a perspective that is neither that of his plain old self vis-à-vis the others and objects populating his everyday world, nor that of the others in that world vis-à-vis him as an object in their sight. He leaves the intersubjective world of the other-in-the-self, self and other identity-bound in mutual missed-recognition, for a space of dislocation, the space of movement-as-such, sheer transformation. There, movement is continuously fractured, unhinged from subject and object, and they from each as other. The eye is out of its socket, hovering on an exorbital axis of vision, seeing elsewhere as a kind of other without other, actually *seeing distance,* the in-itself of distance, the as-such of difference-from. Seeing oneself as others see one in fact means occupying an axis of vision on a tangent to self and other, both as actual entities and as conditions of identity. It is to enter a space that opens an outside perspective on the self-other, subject-object axis. The tangent point at which movement-vision meets mirror-vision and diverges from it is the space between the subject-object poles, superposed, fractured, multiplied. It is relationality in itself, freed from its terms.[4]

How can this be construed as completeness? Clues can be found in

Reagan's recounting of the only time that he achieved this vision as an actor. It happened when he was called upon "to portray a scene of total shock."[5] It was in *King's Row,* and he had to play a young, handsome "blade" who has an accident and wakes up to find that the bottom half of his body has been amputated. "Coming from unconsciousness to full realization of what had happened in a few seconds, it presented me with the most challenging acting problem in my career." Reagan continues:

> A whole actor would find such a scene difficult; giving it the necessary dramatic impact as half an actor was murderous. I felt I had neither the experience nor the talent to fake it. I had to find out how it really felt, short of actual amputation. I rehearsed the scene before mirrors, in corners of the studio, while driving home, in the men's room of restaurants, before selected friends. At night I would wake up staring at the ceiling and automatically mutter the line before I went back to sleep. I consulted physicians and psychologists; I even talked to people who were so disabled, trying to brew in myself the cauldron of emotions a man must feel who wakes up one sunny morning to find half of himself gone. I got a lot of answers. I supplied some more for myself. None of mine agreed with any of theirs. Theirs did not agree with each other. I was stumped.[6]

"Wan and worn" from a sleepless night, a despairing Reagan stumbles into the studio for the shoot.

> I found the prop men had arranged a neat deception. Under the gay patchwork quilt, they had cut a hole in the mattress and put a supporting box beneath. I stared at it for a minute. Then, obeying an overpowering impulse, I climbed into the rig. I spent almost that whole hour in stiff confinement, contemplating my torso and the smooth undisturbed flat of the covers where my legs should have been. Gradually, the affair began to terrify me. In some weird way, I felt something horrible had happened to my body. Then gradually I became aware that the crew had quietly assembled, the camera was in position, and the set all lighted. . . . There were cries of "Lights!" and "Quiet, please!" I lay back and closed my eyes, as tense as a fiddlestring. I heard [the director's] low voice call, "Action!" There was a sharp *clack* which signaled the beginning of the scene. I opened my eyes dazedly, looked around, slowly let my gaze travel downward. I can't describe even now my feeling as I tried to reach for where my legs should be. . . . I asked the question—the words that had been haunting

me for so many weeks—"Where's the rest of me?" There was no retake. It was a good scene and it came out that way in the picture. Perhaps I never did quite as well again in a single shot. The reason was that I had put myself, as best I could, in the body of another fellow. . . . No single line in my career has been as effective in explaining to me what an actor's life must be. . . . Seeing the rushes, I could barely believe the colored shadow on the screen was myself.[7]

Reagan was so touched by his truncated self that he organized not just the opening chapter but his entire autobiography around this bed scene and took that fateful line for the book's title: *Where's the Rest of Me?* The passage is so rich that a close reading, especially in connection with Reagan's later presidential performances, would prove inexhaustible.[8] The discussion here will be limited to retracing and retranslating the process he relives in it.

Reagan begins by saying that he was called upon to "portray" not a character but a "scene." What he has to embody as an actor is more fundamentally an *event* than a personality. It is something that can't be faked. He needs to know "how it really felt, short of actual amputation": his challenge is to produce and coincide with a reality "short of" the actual. The event at issue is the culmination, in a verbalized coming to consciousness, of a transformation from one bodily state (characterized by mobility, the ability to walk) to a radically different one (characterized by stasis, being bedridden). Reagan must embody the scene of a man *recognizing himself as irretrievably changed,* as having been transported in total darkness and, unbeknown to himself, from one perspective on life to another that is irreconcilably different. The actor's labor is not one of the intellect; the act of recognition is the end result, not the means by which the scene's reality is produced. Acting is a labor of feeling, but not only that. The feeling is inseparable from motility. Reagan becomes a traveling rehearsal. He moves from one place to another and from one kind of observer to another, repeating the culminating phrase, "Where's the rest of me?" He starts from a difference between two unbridgeable perspectives which, in their disjunction, encompass an entire life, as telescoped into the absolute distance between being able to walk and being crippled. Then he tries to learn how to cross from one of these perspectives to the other by multiplying relative perspectives on the event that they delimit but do not contain: the accident, by which the self becomes other than it was. The phrase marking the culmination of the event in an act of instantaneous recognition of self-as-other is dragged by his body through his everyday world. It functions through repetition as a trace of the transformation, a spectre of an ungraspable, unthinkable event that haunts the flesh. He recites the phrase to different people from different angles: to himself in mirrors, alone in the car, in front of friends, physicians, psychologists, and amputees. He repeats it so often that it becomes automatic. The event, still a trace, begins to circulate freely through all of the interlocking visual fields composing Reagan's empirical world. Finally, Reagan's realm, that of the ordinary, and the realm of the extraordinary, the realm of the ungraspable event, begin to contaminate one another in a gradual contagion. Reagan's entire world becomes colored by amputation. He is stumped, repeatedly referring to himself as a cripple. But he isn't, actually, and he hasn't yet produced the short-of-actual reality of amputation. He only embodies its anticipation. The problem is that the perspectives he has connected to the event remain relative. They do not "agree." They now communicate across their difference but cannot be superposed. It takes an artifice to jolt them into a synthesis—one that Reagan is incapable of constructing. His compulsive rehearsing has only exhausted him and driven him into a panic. He can no longer act in any sense of the word. His manic activity has only succeeded in working him into a state of heightened excitability that is at the same time the pitch of passivity: he has become a peripatetic panic autonomically repeating a line.

This marks the end of the first phase of the process. The second begins with a "deception" prepared without Reagan's knowledge and to which he is passively subjected. He loads himself into a "rig," a bed with a hole in it to conceal his legs. His activity in the real world is now suspended by artifice; his anticipation of the event is turned into dramatic suspense as he sinks, quilted, into the scene. Will it happen? For a painful hour, he contemplates his torso. A feeling slowly wells within him. The time of contemplation is like an infolding of his previous activity. As if all of the relative perspectives he placed into communication were overlaying themselves on one another and on the disjunct but encompassing perspectives of the before and after between which he now lies suspended. In this state of suspended animation, he is more than himself but less than whole. His eyes close. "Action!" His eyes reopen.

Phase three. The suspension of the suspense by the director's signal transports him across a blackout of vision into the space of transformation. The feeling that was welling inside his body bursts forth in a gesture and a phrase. He bolts up, crying his line. At that moment, he enters the body of another fellow. It's for real (short of actual). This time he cannot recognize himself in the rushes.

In a way, it is both real and actual. Reagan has been changed by the experience. An actual event really did occur. He feels afterward that as an actor he is "only half a man." He is cut to the quick by his moment of triumph. The event he recreated has bled into his everyday life, coloring it forever. Reagan laments that he has "become a semi-automaton," and will remain one as long as he is just an actor. The autonomic repetition into which he collapses during the preparatory phase leading up to the event has carried over into his everyday life. He can't go on that way. He resolves to find the rest of him. He will look for it in conservative politics.

If the event was in a sense real and if it made him a semiautomaton, does that mean that finding the rest of him entails becoming a *complete* automaton? The question is answered by his subsequent career.

The reason Reagan gives for his determination to complete his transformation is that he felt like "a shut-in invalid, nursed by publicity. I have always liked space," he writes, "the feeling of freedom, a broad range of friends, and variety (not excluding the publication [of the same name])." Again, it is not the fakeness of acting, nor the media hype, that he is objecting to. Hollywood is simply not big enough for him. He needs more space, more friends and observers, a greater variety of relative perspectives through which to circulate as he repeats his lines. Politics will allow him to multiply incalculably the contexts through which he drags his founding event of reality-producing, acted amputation, extending the trajectory of its trace, widening the space it colors. If accompanied by adequate artifice, this will allow Reagan to enter innumerable bodies of other "fellows." These bodies, in their eagerness (or at least willingness) to play their social roles, will have worked themselves into a state of heightened receptivity, a kind of panicked passivity marked by autonomic repetition of assigned lines and a susceptibility to becoming-other, on cue. All the world will be a stage, with Reagan in the leading role as carrier of a dehumanizing contagion.

To recapitulate: Reagan invents a technology of the event that is also a technology of the self and a technologizing of the self. He starts from the need to portray a scene culminating in an event that can be taken as exemplary. The accident, in the suddenness of its inclusively disjunctive transformation not only of the shape of a body but of an entire life, can be seen as a figure of the event in general. The generic or exemplary event is short of actual. It need only be acted. But its acting yields a reality of its own. Through his performance of the exemplary event, Reagan effects an actual change in his life. That change is expressed as a blend between the exemplary event and his ordinary world, a bleed between the two. The bleed occurs in a moment of prolonged suspense. Reagan's activity both as screen actor and as actor in the everyday world is artificially suspended. Reagan's line of sight is trained on his own body. It moves down his torso toward his waist, his center of gravity, and then disappears as if moving through his body's center into another space, experienced as one of affect. A feeling wells. Reagan's vision and body collapse into an intensity that increases in pitch the longer it lasts. The way for the welling of that intensity was prepared by extensive means.

Reagan had spent his time leading up to the bleed moving between empirical contexts, each of which was characterized by a certain kind of relative perspective in the sense defined above: an object (always Reagan) appeared before the eyes of various observers (sometimes Reagan) and was recognized as itself. In each context, Reagan repeated the same words. The words were treated as a kind of incantation, as if they enveloped something of the desired event, contained its trace. Their repetition deposited a trace of the event in each of the contexts, gradually coloring the everyday world. Conversely, each context left its own trace in the words. It is as if the words were absorbing the relative perspectives, absorbing traces of the movements accomplished within them, as well as the movement from one to the other, blending the motion of acting the exemplary event with ordinary circulation through the world. The accumulation immobilizes Reagan under its weight. He enters a state of passivity marked by heightened excitability.

When he places himself in the rig, he continues to move, but only in place. He is reeling, overtaken by vertigo, as if his previous movements were repeating themselves in intensity. Unmoving, he circulates between empirical contexts and incantations of the exemplary event. He relives them sequentially and simultaneously, as if he can pass into each of those contexts and perform all of his rehearsals at the same time without moving his body or parting his lips. He is all eyes and emotion. When his eyes descend to the blankness at his waist, he is only emotion. He is no one, nowhere, in darkness. He is in an in-between space composed of accumulated movements bled into one another and folding in upon the body. And he is in an in-between time after before but before after, in a gap of suspended animation following the preparation of the event but preceding its culmination. He is in the space of the duration of an ungraspable event.[9] The feeling of the event washes through him (or that in-between of space and time), a wave or vibration that crests in the spoken lines. This time, the repetition of the lines effectively produces the event. But the event, as produced, is different. It has the reality of an acted event, a performance: short of actual. The "short of actual" is expressed as a prolonging of the intensive in-betweenness of the event in the empirical world. It is a subsidence of the emotion, a flattening of the wave as it spreads out to fill a wider area. Reagan will now be extensively what he just was intensively. He will be an ambulant blend of the ordinary everyday and of the exemplary event: he will be a walking amputee. His flesh will carry the mark of the artifice that jolted him into the event, endowing it with a kind of half-life: he will be a semiautomaton. He will find a method that will take this new self, semitechnologized through acting, through a similar transformation, after which he will feel it to be complete.

Fleshing Out: Definitions

Call the closing of Reagan's eyes as he sees himself at the pitch of panic and exhaustion *movement-vision*. It is a vision that passes into the body and through it to another space. Call that infra-empirical space, what the blind-sight of movement-vision sees, *the body without an image*. The body without an image is an accumulation of relative perspectives and the passages between them, an additive space of utter receptivity retaining and combining past movements, in intensity, extracted from their actual terms. It is less a space in the empirical sense than a gap in space that is also a suspension of the normal unfolding of time. Still, it can be understood as having a spatiotemporal order of its own.

   In its spatial aspect, the body without an image is the involution of subject-object relations into the body of the observer and of that body into itself. Call the spatiality proper to the body without an image *quasi corporeality*.[10] The quasi corporeal can be thought of as the superposition of the sum total of the relative perspectives in which the body has been implicated, as object or subject, plus the passages between them: in other words, as an interlocking of overlaid perspectives that nevertheless remain distinct. The involution of space renders these relative perspectives absolute: it registers movement as included disjunction. Subject, object, and their successive emplacements in empirical space are subtracted, leaving the pure relationality of process. Quasi corporeality is an abstract *map* of transformation. Its additive subtraction simultaneously constitutes the spatiality of the body without an image and translates it into another kind of time. For pure relationality extracted from its terms can be understood, at the extreme, as a time out of space, a measureless gap in and between bodies and things, an incorporeal interval of change.

Call that substanceless and durationless moment the pure *event*. The time of the event does not belong per se to the body in movement-vision or even to the body without an image. They incur it. It occurs to them. As time-form it belongs to the *virtual*, defined as that which is maximally abstract yet real, whose reality is that of potential—pure relationality, the interval of change, the in-itself of transformation. It is a time that does not pass, that only comes to pass. It cannot be suspended because, unlike empirical time, it does not flow. The event is superempirical: it is the crystallization, out the far side of quasi corporeality, of already actualized spatial perspectives and emplacements into a time-form from which the passing present is excluded and which, for that very reason, is as future as it is past, looping directly from one to the other. It is the immediate proximity of before and after. It is nonlinear, moving in two directions at once: out from the actual (as past) into the actual (as future). The actuality it leaves as past is the same actuality to which it no sooner comes as future: from being to becoming.

Thus far the body without an image has been discussed exclusively as an optical effect. But there are other modes of perception involved. The spatiality of the body without an image can be understood even more immediately as an effect of *proprioception*, defined as the sensibility proper to the muscles and ligaments as opposed to tactile sensibility (which is "exteroceptive") and visceral sensibility (which is "interoceptive").[11] Tactility is the sensibility of the skin as surface of contact between the perceiving subject and the perceived object. Proprioception folds tactility into the body, enveloping the skin's contact with the external world in a dimension of medium depth: between epidermis and viscera. The muscles and ligaments register as conditions of movement what the skin internalizes as qualities: the hardness of the floor underfoot as one looks into a mirror becomes a resistance enabling station and movement; the softness of a cat's fur becomes a lubricant for the motion of the hand. Proprioception translates the exertions and ease of the body's encounters with objects into a muscular memory of relationality. This is the cumulative memory of skill, habit, posture. At the same time as proprioception folds tactility in, it draws out the subject's reactions to the qualities of the objects it perceives through all five senses, bringing them into the motor realm of externalizable response.

Proprioception effects a double translation of the subject and the object into the body, at a medium depth where the body is only body, having nothing of the putative profundity of the self nor of the superficiality of external encounter. This asubjective and nonobjective medium depth is one of the strata proper to the corporeal; it is a dimension of the *flesh*. The memory it constitutes could be diagrammed as a superposition of vectorial fields composed of multiple points in varying relations of movement and rest, pressure and resistance, each field corresponding to an action. Since it is composed of interactions subtracted from their actual terms, it is abstract in the same sense as is the included disjunction of movement-vision. Proprioceptive memory is where the infolded limits of the body meet the mind's externalized responses and where both rejoin the quasi corporeal and the event. As infolding, the faculty of proprioception operates as a corporeal transformer of tactility into quasi corporeality. It is to the skin what movement-vision is to the eyes. Its vectors are perspectives of the flesh. Although movement-vision opens onto the same space as proprioception, the latter can be said to be the mode of perception proper to the spatiality of the body without an image because it opens exclusively onto that space and registers qualities directly and continuously as movement. The eyes also see in the intersubjective space of mirror-vision, but they do not register movement without also registering its arrest, in other words form (the visual image insofar as it is susceptible to geometric expression; movement as captured in a still, snapshot, or tableau giving it measure and proportion). It is because vision interrupts movement with formed images that it must interrupt itself to see movement as such. Movement-vision is sight turned proprioceptive, the eyes reabsorbed into the flesh through a black hole in the geometry of empirical space and a gash in bodily form (the hole in Reagan's stage bed; amputation). Vision is a mixed mode of perception, registering both form and movement. For it to gain entry into the quasi corporeal, the realm of pure relationality, pure movement, it must throw aside form in favor of unmediated participation in the flesh. Movement-vision is retinal muscle, a visual strength flexed in the extremities of exhaustion.[12]

The temporality of the body without an image coincides with the eclipse of the subject in emotion. It is a time of interruption, the moment vision plunges into the body's suspended animation. It is a gap, like the event, but one that is still attached to empirical time as a punctuation of its linear unfolding. It can be understood as the double, in the actual, of the event, whose reality as pure interval of transformation is virtual, on the order of potential, more energetic than bodily, incorporeal. Or, its attachment to empirical time can be understood as the durational equivalent of the edge of the hole in empirical space into which the eyes of movement-vision disappear, in which case it would be the rim of the virtual at the crossroads of the actual. Reserve the term *suspense* for the temporality proper to the body without an image.

Just as the spatiality of the body without an image opens out onto another time-form, its temporality opens out onto another space. This opening occurs in a second dimension of the flesh: one that is deeper than the stratum of proprioception, in the sense that it is farther removed from the surface of the skin, but it is still at a medium depth in that it also intervenes between the subject and the object. It, too, involves a cellular memory and has a mode of perception proper to it: *viscerality* (interoception). Visceral sensibility immediately registers excitations gathered by the five "exteroceptive" senses even before they are fully processed by the brain.[13] Walking down a dark street at night in a dangerous part of town, your lungs throw a spasm before you consciously see and can recognize as human the shadow thrown across your path. As you cross a busy noonday street, your stomach turns somersaults before you consciously hear and identify the sound of screeching brakes that careens toward you. Having survived the danger, you enter your building. Your heart stops before you consciously feel the tap on your shoulder and identify it as the greeting of a friend. The immediacy of visceral perception is so radical that it can be said without exaggeration to precede the exteroceptive sense perception. It anticipates the translation of the sight or sound or touch perception into something recognizable associated with an identifiable object. Call that "something recognizable" a quality (or property). Movement-vision as proprioception subtracts qualified form from movement; viscerality subtracts quality as such from excitation. It registers *intensity*.

The dimension of viscerality is adjacent to that of proprioception, but they do not overlap. The dimension of proprioception lies midway between stimulus and response, in a region where infolded tactile encounter meets externalizing response to the qualities gathered by all five senses. It performs a synthesis of those intersecting pathways in the medium of the flesh, thus opened to its own quasi corporeality. Viscerality, though no less of the flesh, is a rupture in the stimulus-response paths, a leap in place into a space outside action-reaction circuits. Viscerality is the perception of suspense. The space into which it jolts the flesh is one of an inability to act or reflect, a spasmodic passivity, so taut a receptivity that the body is paralyzed until it is jolted back into action-reaction by recognition. Call it the space of *passion*.[14] Its elementary units are neither the absolute perspectives of movement-vision nor the vectorial fields of proprioception proper, but rather *degrees* of intensity. The space of passion constitutes a quasi-qualitative realm adjacent to the quasi corporeal.[15] Say that every absolute perspective/vectorial field composing the quasi corporeal is associated with a certain intensity, a higher or lower degree of spasmodic passivity. The intensity can be thought of as filling the interval of quasi-corporeal space with a time-derivative, as bathing its relationality with spatialized suspense. If quasi corporeality is a maximally abstract spatial matrix, intensity is the nonqualified substance occupying it. Passion, then, is best understood less as an abstract space than as the time-stuff of spatial abstraction. Call the coupling of a unit of quasi corporeality with a unit of passion an *affect*: an ability to affect and a susceptibility to be affected. An *emotion* or *feeling* is a recognized affect, an identified intensity as reinjected into stimulus-response paths, into action-reaction circuits of infolding and externalization—in short, into subject-object relations. Emotion is a contamination of empirical space by affect, which belongs to the body without an image.

(The need to keep deriving time from space and space from time testifies to the inadequacy of the terms. The body without an image is a seamless spatiotemporal mix [as is empirical space as understood by physics]. Still, time and space concepts are necessary heuristic devices for thinking the specificity of the interlocking processes contributing to the construction of the body without an image. See chapter 8 below for more on spatiotemporality.)

Call proprioception and viscerality taken together—as two complementary dimensions of the "medium"-depth perception most directly implicated in the body's registration of the in-betweenness of the incorporeal event—*mesoperception*. Mesoperception is the synesthetic sensibility: it is the medium where inputs from all five senses meet, across subsensate excitation, and become flesh together, tense and quivering. Mesoperceptive flesh functions as a corporeal transformer where one sense shades into another over the failure of each, their input translated into movement and affect.[16] Mesoperception can be called *sensation* for short.

Action!

Affect contaminates empirical space through language. Entranced in his trick bed, Reagan moves through quasi-corporeal space, accumulating perspectives and passages and, with them, affects. As regions of his quasi corporeality are superimposed upon one another, their associated intensities mount. It is as if the body's abstract matrix and its nonqualified filling form a resonating vessel rising to an unbearable pitch, reaching the point where it can no longer contain itself. The virtual resonation overflows as actual sound. A voice, perhaps his own, speaking words charged with feeling but whose meaning Reagan will not fully understand until many years later. "Where's the rest of me?"

Bedded in passivity, Reagan cannot jolt himself out of his condition. He is freed from the body without an image and returned to the everyday world, albeit a changed man, by the words of another called out as a cue: "Action!" Call the cue-call an *order-word*. Call the question-response an *expression*—keeping in mind that the expression is preconceptual and even presubjective, more an existential *cry* than a communication. The expression is the unmediated and unmediated speaking of the event by the flesh. It culminates Reagan's transformation into half a man. It gives him a demi-self. What it expresses is less an idea or an emotion formed by a signifying subject than an ontological *problem* posing as an open question the very possibility of constructing such a subject. Feelings and ideas will follow from the expression and, before solving the problem it poses, will develop its problematic nature even further. The line Reagan speaks makes him feel like a cripple and gives rise to the idea that he has become a semiautomaton. He has found half of himself, but he happens to have found it in the "body of another fellow." He is on the road to completing himself, to identifying his body, but he got there by mouthing a pre-scripted line that made him into a foreshortened other. Many secondary questions arise. All of them can be condensed into one: how can exalted difference be derived from banal repetition? Repeat: how can a difference born of becoming-other be self-identity? Again: how can higher being arise from abject becoming?

The cue-call or order-word that jolted Reagan into the body of another fellow had the force of a magic incantation. It induced a phenomenon of *possession* verbally manifested in the automaton mouthing of pre-scripted words, that is to say as *ventriloquism*. Susceptibility to possession and ventriloquism are the requisite skills of the true actor Reagan now embodies. Together they define the actor's talent: *self-affectation*. That term should be understood in the double sense of the artificial construction of a self and of the suffusing of that self with affect.

Again, nothing would have happened without artifice. Reagan is extracted from the body without an image and delivered to the actuality of his becoming-actor by the good graces of a "rig." The order-word simply tripped the rig into operation. Call the rigging of becoming *induction*. The activation of the rig by the order-word culminated his passion by inducing his possession of his body. Although he may think of himself as having been possessed by the other fellow of the script, it is ultimately the body without an image that takes his body, endowing it with a measure of potential. Reagan is now in becoming; his being is "short of actual." That is to say, his actual perceptions are colored by the virtual. Unable to recognize the virtual-in-the-actual, Reagan develops it into feelings and ideas whose combined effect is to transpose it into a future possibility: an ultimate actuality in which the potential that has seeped into his body has been fully realized as the complete man that he desperately wants to become but which, as an ideal of being, prefigures the end of becoming. Reagan's body reenters linear time, although it still carries with it traces of the body without an image, transposed into a phantom amputation. Call the phantom amputation that comes to stand for the body without an image in Reagan's mind and emotions the *exemplary event* (or central phantasm) of his life. Call each threshold he passes on the road to his ideal of being, each movement culminated in an everyday context or between contexts, an *ordinary event* (also a *phantasm*). (As used here, the word phantasm does not connote irreality; quite the contrary, it connotes the mode of reality proper to events, however exalted or ordinary: insistent ontological ungraspability).[17]

The exemplary event is a deferred completion. But the fact that it takes over his life indicates that Reagan has already attained a completion of sorts. For the ideal implied by the exemplary event to have been produced, Reagan had to have rejoined the body without an image for a spasmodic moment. His empirical body was completed by its virtual double. The word "completion" is misleading. In the case of the exemplary event, it is misleading because it is not attainable: it denotes an ideal being and, as such, lies beyond the reach of becoming. Call the ideal of being-complete *unity*. The ideas, emotions, and mirror-vision images attached to unity keep the ideal alive as the object of a compulsion or tendency. Call them *whole attractors*. In the case of the body without an image, "completion" is misleading because it is always-already attained at every turn. Call that perpetual future-past doubling ordinary events *supplementarity*. The exemplary event is the transposition of supplementarity into the lure of unity. Transposed supplementarity is the mode of being of the pure event. Call the event, to the extent that it continues to call from across its transposition, defining a compulsion or tendency to fracture the integrity attributed to the body in everyday action-reaction circuits and to shatter the symmetry attributed to subject and object in their mirrored mutuality, a *fractal attractor*.

Call the seeing of the body without an image by the blind-sight of movement-vision *blank mimicry*. The activity of the actor is less to imitate a character in a script than to mimic in the flesh the incorporeality of the event. Blank mimicry is supplemented seeming (acting injected with real passion and yielding real change) and seeming supplemental (the attainment of real passion and real change through the staging of the body in suspended animation). The rig, the order-word, the question-response, induction, possession, ventriloquism, the development of an emotionally charged ideal of unity and the quest to reach that ideal—all of these are technologies for *making seeming being*,[18] for making a life of acting, for making something unified of supplementarity, something central of liminality, for filling the fractal rim to make a (w)hole.

Reagan could not recognize himself in the rushes of *King's Row*. In the screening room, he misrecognized himself as his new ideal. He looked back into the mirror, even as he was marked forever by movement-vision. He saw himself as other without other that is the body without an image, then blinked and saw himself again as self-in-other, in a mirror image of his own future. His subsequent career would be characterized by a continual flicker between these two visions.

Reagan was a bad actor. This was not an accident. It was *the* accident, the accident of his career, his fate, his professional crippledom. If he had been a good actor, he would not have had to turn to politics in a quest to complete himself. He would have found passion in each new movie. Repetition of that rush would have been enough. He was a real actor only once. He became a politician for life. It is not that there is anything to prevent a good actor from going into politics, but it would be experienced as a career choice, not a compulsion. And the kind of political success a good actor could have would be very different, and undoubtedly lesser, than the success Reagan had. As a politician, Reagan did not stop acting, despite his tendency in his first autobiography to portray the two roles as mutually exclusive. He went about completing himself as a political actor.

"He once described to me how he got into politics by accident," says a former senior Administration official. "He told me he told someone, 'By God, what am I doing in politics? The kinds of things I've done so far are far away from this. But then I thought that a substantial part of the political thing is acting and role playing and I know how to do that. So I used to worry, but I don't anymore.'"[19]

There he goes again. Repeating lines: "He told me he told someone." Ventriloquizing himself. Still at it after all those years. Reagan not only did not let go of the technologies of making seeming being, he did nothing to hide them. His spectacular political success in fact hinged on making seeming being visible. Reaganism is the regime of the visibility of seeming being. Reagan's professional crippledom, his entry into public life, was the exemplary event allowing the population of an entire nation to develop emotions and ideas along those same lines. As political actor, he catalyzed processes already at work in society. He was the Great Inducer, the national actor-cum-stage director who called a country to action in pursuit of the lofty lure of postwar unity. The amputation written into this script was the "wound" of Vietnam. The all-too-visible rig was TV.[20]

Scenario

Find a cultural-theoretical vocabulary specific to the body. Use it to express the unmediated participation of the flesh in the image (whether "natural" or mass-mediated). Find a logic for the corporeal (body *and* image) that does not oppose it to the virtual, even as it distinguishes them, as dimensions of each other. Find a logic for the virtual (imagelessness *and* potential) that does not remove it from the real; for example by equating it with the imaginary. Dis-sever, instead, the imageless from the Ideal.

For an incorporeal materialism.[21]

See the body get rigged. See the flesh suffuse with artifice, making it as palpably political as it is physical. For the artifice is always cued, and the cuing is collective.

Consider that there is no "raw" perception. That all perception is rehearsed. Even, especially, our most intense, most abject and inspiring, self-perceptions.

REPETITION PRECEDES RESEMBLANCE (even to oneself).[22]

Consider that although change is compatible with repetition, it is nonetheless ontologically prior to sameness. See stasis, see station, as a special case of movement (a special case of reiterative movement: that allowing recognition).

PASSAGE PRECEDES POSITION.[23]

Rethink body, subjectivity, and social change in terms of movement, affect, force, and violence—before code, text, and signification. These latter reiterate arrest (the Law: where bodies cease, only to mean, and where meaning carries a sentence).

Even an arch-conservative politician can see and reach beyond the law long enough to catalyze a movement. A special case of reiterative movement (one that allows misrecognition of the fractured time of the virtual as a future Unity). This is becoming—against itself, because subsumed under that Ideal. Against itself—because its self-assigned meaning ("our Unity!") contradicts its own senseless, eminently effective, rallying cry ("the rest of me?"). Remember the becoming-Reaganoid of America through the 1980s. And well beyond.[24] Remember how one bad actor shed his self-likeness to steer a nation sameward. This is becoming—at once highly virulent and self-arresting.

What is left of *us*, after "our" unity has completed "his" amputation?

Do we, cultural theorists, recognize ourselves in the rushes?

Rig writing, unarresting.

DISSEVER THE IMAGELESS FROM THE IDEAL.

THE POLITICAL ECONOMY OF BELONGING

and the Logic of Relation

Which came first? The individual or society?

Which is the chicken and which is the egg?

Too much cultural and social theorizing has proceeded as if this were a reasonable place to begin. On one side are those who look first to the individual and see feathers. When notions such as function, exchange, contract, or reason are used to explain the constitution of society, the individual is the chicken. The inaugural gesture is to conjure away society with the fiction of an atomistic flock of individuals who forge a relation with one another on the basis of a normative recognition of shared needs and common goods. These "foundationalist" approaches have been roundly criticized, in particular since deconstruction, for appealing more or less explicitly to a myth of origins. But what has not been re-marked often enough is that approaches defining themselves against the individual-chicken wing are, in their own way, just as foundationalist. Approaches privileging such notions as structure, the symbolic, semiotic system, or textuality look first to what the other wing puts second: an intersubjective frame. Society now figures as an a priori, a principle of intersubjectivity hatching individual subject-eggs. The "foundation" in this case is not a mythic origin, but a foundation it is nevertheless. It effects an inversion of the first foundationalism. The inaugural gesture in this case is to conjure away the individual in order for it to return as determined by society rather than determining of it. The individual is defined by its "positioning" within the intersubjective frame. The foun-dation is transposed from a time axis to a spatial one, becoming topo-graphical, the lay of the social land: we are no longer in the once-upon-a-time, but in the always-already. For in this approach, the individual is in a sense prehatched, since the topography determining it is itself predetermined by a mapped-out logic of baseline positions and combinations or permutations of them.

Along came a third, mutant wing that saw this quarrel as little better than the Swiftian controversy over whether it is better to spoon the egg out of the narrow end or the wide end. Why can't they see that it's best to break it in the middle? More recent theories privileging notions of hybridity, bordering and border culture, and queering attempt to defuse the chicken-and-the-egg scenario by valorizing the in-between. The ultimate aim is to find a place for change again, for social innovation, which had been squeezed out of the nest by the pincer movement of the needful or reasonable determination of a legislative norm on one side and topographical determination by a constitutive positionality on the other. But to the extent that the in-between is conceived as a space of interaction of already-constituted individuals and societies, middle-feeders end up back on the positional map. The tendency is to describe the in-between as a blending or parody of the always-already positioned. Social change is spatially relegated to precarious geographical margins, where unauthorized positional permutations bubble up from the fermenting mixture. Even more precariously, in the case of theories of subjectivity as performance, change is confined to sites whose "marginality" is defined less by location than the evanescence of a momentary parodic rupture or "subversion." How the subversion could react back on the positionalities of departure in a way that might enduringly change *them* becomes an insoluble problem. Concepts of mixture, margin, and parody retain a necessary reference to the pure, the central, and the strait-laced and straight-faced, without which they vaporize into logical indeterminacy. Erase the progenitors and the hybrid vanishes: no terms have been provided with which to understand it in its own right. The middle wing ends upon the same plate as the others: determination. When everything is served up in founding terms of determination—"of" or "by"—by design or by default—change can only be understood as a negation of the determination: as the simply indeterminate. This dilemma haunts all three wings in different ways, and its valorization is characteristic of postmodern celebrations of aporia.

Similar conundrums haunt other oppositional pairings that contemporary theorists try to think with or around: body and culture, community and state, East and West.

There may be another approach, close in many ways to the mutant third wing of the hybrid, but mutated again, with a different philosophical twist—away from determination. From one point of view, the weakness pointed to in theories of performance is a strength. Articulating change in a way that retains a necessary reference to the already-constituted preserves a crucial role for formations of power and marks a refusal of spontaneism or voluntarism. The problem arises when no way is provided to conceptualize the in-between as having a logical consistency, and even ontological status, of its own. The necessary connection to the already-constituted then becomes a filiative dependence to which the "subversion" must continually return in order to re-engender itself. The foundation eternally returns.

What would it mean to give a logical consistency to the in-between? It would mean realigning with a logic of relation. For the in-between, as such, is not a middling being but rather the being *of* the middle—the being of a relation. A positioned being, central, middling, or marginal, is a *term* of a relation. It may seem odd to insist that a relation has an ontological status separate from the terms of the relation. But, as the work of Gilles Deleuze repeatedly emphasizes, it is in fact an indispensable step toward conceptualizing change as anything more or other than a negation, deviation, rupture, or subversion. The terms of a relation are normally assumed to precede their interrelating, to be already-constituted. This begs the question of change, because everything is given in advance. The interrelating simply realizes external configurations already implicit as possibilities in the form of the preexisting terms. You can rearrange the furniture, even move it to a new location, but you still have the same old furniture. Assuming the precedence of terms in the relation is common to approaches characterized as empirical. Taking pregiven terms, extracting a permutational system of implicit positionings from their form, projecting that system to metaphysical point before the givenness of the terms, and developing the projection as a generative a priori mapping—these moves are common, in varying ways, to phenomenological, structuralist, and many poststructuralist approaches. They back-project a stencil of the already-constituted to explain its constitution, thus setting up a logical time-slip, a vicious hermeneutic circle. What is given the slip, once again, is change.

It is only by asserting the exteriority of the relation to its terms that chicken and egg absurdities can be avoided and the discussion diverted from an addiction to foundation and its negation to an engagement with change as such, with the unfounded and unmediated in-between of becoming. The need for this diversion is nowhere more evident than in terms like "body" and "culture" or "individual" and "society." Is it possible even to conceive of an individual outside of a society? Of a society without individuals? Individuals and societies are not only empirically inseparable, they are strictly simultaneous and consubstantial. It is an absurdity even to speak of them using notions of mediation, as if they were discrete entities that enter into extrinsic relation to one another, let alone to wonder which term takes precedence over the other in determining stasis and change. If they cannot be seen as terms in extrinsic relation, then perhaps they can be seen as products, effects, coderivatives of an immanent relation that would be change in itself. In other words, they might be seen as differential emergences from a shared realm of relationality that is one with becoming—and belonging. Seen from this point of view, the "terms" might look so different that it might be necessary to redefine them thoroughly, reconfigure them, or perhaps forego them entirely. What follows is just a beginning.

An example: Michel Serres's ball. A soccer ball. Bruno Latour is well known for taking up Serres's concept of the quasi object, introduced through the example of a ball in a sports game. Serres and Latour used it to rethink the relation between the subject and the object. More recently, Pierre Lévy has used the same example to redeploy the relation between the individual and the collectivity.[1] What follows flows from Lévy, moving toward a notion of collective individuation around a catalyzing point. Here, that point will be called not a quasi object but a part-subject.

To the question of what founds a formation like a sport, or what its conditions of existence are, an obvious answer would be "the rules of the game." But in the history of sport, as with virtually every collective formation, the codification of rules *follows* the emergence of an unformalized proto-sport exhibiting a wide range of variation. The formal rules of the game capture and contain the variation. They frame the game, retrospectively, describing its form as a set of constant relations between standardized terms. A codification is a framing derivative that arrogates to itself the role of foundation. It might be argued that all foundations are of this nature: ex post facto regulatory framings rather than effective foundings. Once they apply themselves, the rules do effectively frame and regulate the play, taking precedence. Their precedence is retrospective, or fictional, but effective. It has all the reality of a formation of power, of which usurpation might be argued to be the model—usurpation of variation.

If the rules are ex post facto captures that take precedence, what do they take it from?: from the process from which the game actually emerged, and continues to evolve, to the extent that circumstances arise that force modifications of the rules. The foundational rules follow and apply themselves to forces of variation that are endemic to the game and constitute the real conditions of the game's emergence. The rules formally determine the game but do not condition it. (They are its formal cause, not its efficient cause.)

So what is the condition? Quite simply, a field. No field, no play, and the rules lose their power. The field is what is common to the proto-game and the formalized game, as well as to informal versions of the game coexisting with the official game and any subsequent evolution of it. The field-condition that is common to every variation is unformalized but not unorganized. It is minimally organized as a polarization. The field is polarized by two attractors: the goals. All movement in the game will take place between the poles and will tend toward one or the other. They are physical limits. The play stops when the ball misses or hits the goal. The goals do not exist for the play except tendentially, as inducers of directional movement of which they mark the outside limits (winning or losing). The goals polarize the space between them. The field of play is an in-between of charged movement. It is more fundamentally a field of potential than a substantial thing, or object. As things, the goals are signs for the polar attraction that is the motor of the game. They function to *induce* the play. The literal field, the ground with grass stretching between the goals, is also an inductive limit-sign rather than a ground in any foundational sense. The play in itself is groundless and limitless, taking place above the ground-limit and between the goal-limits.

Put two teams on a grassy field with goals at either end and you have an immediate, palpable tension. The attraction of which the goals and ground are inductive signs is invisible and nonsubstantial: it is a tensile force-field activated by the presence of bodies within the signed limits. The polarity of the goals defines every point in the field and every movement on the field in terms of force—specifically, as the potential motion of the ball and of the teams toward the goal. When the ball nears a goal, the play reaches a pitch of intensity. Every gesture of the players is supercharged toward scoring a goal or toward repelling one. The ball is charged to the highest degree with potential movement toward the goal, by its position on the field, by the collective tending of the team homing in for a score. The slightest slip or miscalculation will depotentialize that movement. When that happens, a release of tension as palpable as its earlier build-up undulates across the field.

If the goalposts, ground, and presence of human bodies on the field induce the play, the ball catalyzes it. The ball is the focus of every player and the object of every gesture. Superficially, when a player kicks the ball, the player is the subject of the movement, and the ball is the object. But if by subject we mean the point of unfolding of a tendential movement, then it is clear that the player is not the subject of the play. The ball is. The tendential movements in play are collective, they are team movements, and their point of application is the ball. The ball arrays the teams around itself. Where and how it bounces differentially potentializes and depotentializes the entire field, intensifying and deintensifying the exertions of the players and the movements of the team. *The ball is the subject of the play.* To be more precise, the subject of the play is the displacements of the ball and the continual modifications of the field of potential those displacements effect. The ball, as a thing, is the object-marker of the subject: its sign. Like the goal and the ground, the ball as a substantial term doubles the subject of the play, which itself is invisible and nonsubstantial, the catalysis-point of a force-field, a charge-point of potential.

Since the ball is nothing without the continuum of potential it doubles, since its effect is dependent on the physical presence of a multiplicity of other bodies and objects of various kinds; since the parameters of its actions are regulated by the application of rules, for all these reasons the catalytic object-sign may be called a part-subject. The part-subject catalyzes the play as a whole but is not itself a whole. It attracts and arrays the players, defining their effective role in the game and defining the overall state of the game, at any given moment, by the potential movement of the players with respect to it. The ball moves the players. *The player is the object of the ball.* True, the player kicks the ball. But the ball must be considered in some way an autonomous actor because the global game-effects its displacements produce can be produced by no other game element. When the ball moves, the whole game moves with it. Its displacement is more than a local movement: it is a global event.

If the ball is a part-subject, each player is its part-object. The ball does not address the player as a whole. It addresses the player's eyes, ears, and touch through separate sensory channels. These separate sensory impressions are synthesized not into a subjective whole but into a state of intensive readiness for reflex response: they are synthesized into an actionability. The response is expressed through a particular body part—in the case of soccer, the foot. The ball addresses the player in a limited way, as a specific kind of actionability flowing through the player's body and following very particular channels. The kick is indeed an expression, but not of the player. It is an "ex-pression" of the ball, in the etymological sense, since the ball's attractive catalysis "draws out" the kick from the player's body and defines its expressive effect on the globality of the game. The player's body is a node of expression, not a subject of the play but a material channel for the catalysis of an event affecting the global state of the game. While the ball is a catalyzer and the goals are inducers, the node of expression is a transducer: a channel for the transformation of a local physical movement into another energetic mode, that of potential energy. Through the kick, human physicality transduces into the insubstantiality of an event, releasing a potential that reorganizes the entire field of potential movement.

The players, in the heat of the game, are drawn out of themselves. Any player who is conscious of himself as he kicks, misses. Self-consciousness is a negative condition of the play. The players' reflective sense of themselves as subjects is a source of interference that must be minimized for the play to channel smoothly. When a player readies a kick, she is not looking at the ball so much as *she is looking past it.* She is reflexively (rather than reflectively) assessing the potential movement of the ball. This involves an instantaneous calculation of the positions of all the players of the field *in relation to each other* and in relation to the ball and both goals. This is by nature a vague perception more than a conscious calculation, because there are too many terms to be reflectively processed, and each term is a variable rather than a constant. Since the players are in constant motion, their relation to each other, the ball, and the goals is also in flux, too complex to measure, only registerable as heightenings and releases of eddies of intensity in the midst of which appear openings for the potential movement of the ball. The player must let his trained body synthesize his separate perceptual impressions into a global sense of the intensity. The sensing of the intensity will be vague but goal-directed in such a way as to draw a maximally exact reflex expression from him. He looks past the ball—directly sensing the potential as such, as an immeasurable but actionable degree of intensity affecting the polar continuum of the field. The player must pare himself down to a channeling of the play. The player's subjectivity is disconnected as he enters the field of potential in and as its sensation. For the play, the player *is* that sensation. The sensation is a channeling of field-potential into local action, from which it is again transduced into a global reconfiguration of the field of potential. Sensation is the mode in which potential is present in the perceiving body. The player does not play on the ground. He looks past it and past the ball to the field of potential—which is insubstantial, real but abstract. He plays the field of potential directly.

It would be a mistake to equate the reflex with the purely physical. Perception is never only impression. It is already composite. Studding each impression are shards of intentions and conscious memories, most presently bearing on pregame strategy—shimmers of reflection and language. These do not frame the perception so much as they enter its field, partialized by the separation of the sensory channels in-gathering the impressions they ride. Sharded elements remix to shared effect. Toward that effect, in that sensation, a heterogeneity of levels contract into the body from which they reissue in *an* action—in a unity of movement through which their multiplicity is singularly expressed. The physicality of the reflex is the shared passage through the body of a disparateness of elements and levels. The "rather than" reflective of the reflexive does not mark an exclusion or opposition, so much as a conversion. The reflex action is the differentiation of human actuality, including elements of reflection and language, rechanneled through the body. The body figures not as an object, one substantial element among others, but as a part-object, a conversion channel, a transducer—of the substantial elements of mixture, along with the shards of already-abstracted elements they carry, into sensed potential.[2]

Potential sensed, the player plays her field directly. Potential is the space of play—or would be, were it a space. It is a *modification* of a space. The space is the literal field, the ground between the goals. Any and every movement of a player or the ball in that space modifies the distribution of potential movement over it. Each such modification is an event. The play is the event-dimension doubling the empirical event-space in which the substantial terms in play physically intermix. The dimension of the event is above the ground, between the goals, between the players, and around the ball on all sides. It is that through which the substantial elements interrelate and effect global transformations. It is nothing without them. They are inert and disconnected without it, a collection of mere things, no less isolated for the shards of reflection and language they ferry. It is the event-dimension of potential—not the system of language and the operations of reflection it enables—that is the effective dimension of the interrelating of elements, of their belonging to each other. That belonging is a dynamic corporeal "abstraction": the "drawing off" (transductive conversion) of the corporeal into its dynamism (yielding the event). Belonging is unmediated, and under way, never already-constituted. It is the openness of bodies to each other and to what they are not—the incorporeality of the event. In direct channeling. That is, in a directional channeling: ontological vector. The transductive conversion is an ontological vector that in-gathers a heterogeneity of substantial elements along with the already-constituted abstractions of language ("meaning") and delivers them together to change.

Although the event-dimension of potential is in-between, it is in no sense a hybrid or mixture. It is inseparable from and irreducible to the collection of substantial and already-abstracted elements through whose inductive, catalytic, and transductive mixing its potential is released and reconfigured. The field of potential is the *effect* of the contingent intermixing of elements, but it is logically and ontologically distinct from them. In itself, it is composed not of parts or terms in relation, but of *modulations*, local modifications of potential that globally reconfigure (affects). The field of potential is exterior to the elements or terms in play, but it is not inside something other than the potential it is. It is immanent. It is the immanence *of* the substantial elements of the mix to their own continual modulation. The field of immanence is not the elements in mixture. It is their becoming. In becoming is belonging.

Only apparently do the players relate to each other empirically as discrete terms, mediated by reflection and language. They relate to each other in their collective becoming, as a distinct ontological level doubling their substantial being. It is this collective becoming that is the condition of a formation like a sport, common to the proto-game, the official game, unofficial versions coexisting with it, and subsequent variations of them all. Although inseparable from the empirical elements of whose contingent mixing it is an effect, the field of immanence is superempirical—in excess over the substantiality of already-constituted terms. As a dimension of becoming, gathering proto-, present, and post-, it is also transhistorical—uncontainable in the closure of any particular historical moment. It is superempirical and transhistorical without being foundational. For it is *the contingent effect of that which it conditions.* This is a logical circularity, but not a vicious one, because it is also an ontological circuit around an opening: a phase shift between the substantial and the potential without which the movement would be simple repetition of pregiven terms entering preauthorized, pre-meant relations. The circuit is between the substantial—or, more broadly the actual (including the already-constituted abstractions of meaning)—and the potential. The phase-shift of the substantial to the potential is the opening through which empirical contingency—the intermixing of already-constituted bodies, things, and signs—expresses itself as coordinated becoming. This *expression* is the effective condition of collective change (open-ended belonging).

Change is emergent relation, the becoming sensible in empirical conditions of mixture, of a modulation of potential. Post-emergence, there is capture and containment. Rules are codified and applied. The intermixing of bodies, objects, and signs is standardized and regulated. Becoming becomes reviewable and writable: becoming becomes history.

It is only by leaving history to reenter the immanence of the field of potential that change can occur. Even in a codified and regulated sport, there is an opening for this. It is called style. Style is what makes the player. What makes a player a star is more than perfection of technique. Technical perfection merely makes a player most competent. To technical perfection the star adds something extra. Perhaps a way of catching the eye of players on the opposite team to make them self-conscious and throw them off their own game. Perhaps a feint added to every kick. Or an imperceptible spin. Little extras. Small but effective ways of skewing the potential movements composing the field. The star player is one who modifies expected mechanisms of channeling field-potential. The star plays against the rules but not by breaking them. He plays around them, adding minute, unregulated contingencies to the charged mix. She adds free variations: "free" in the sense that they are modulatory actions unregulated or unsubsumed by the rules of the game. A star's style is always a provocation to the referee, who must scrutinize and judge barely tangible extras that amount to very little separately but, as disproportionately effective channelings of potential, add up to an advantage. If the provocation goes too far, new rules need to be invented to subsume the modulation devices.

It is through stylistic, free variations that an already-constituted sport evolves. The "individuality" of the style is a collective individuation: it is "collective" in its absolute dependence on an intermixing of the multiple and heterogeneous elements of the sport, and it is an "individuation" in the sense that it is the mother of the sport's unique evolution. A style is a germinal individuation *of the sport*. The single body channeling the evolutionary potential is a node of expression of a collective becoming. A body has style only in and through its role as part-object. The star is the one who most effectively melds with the collectivity, toward its becoming. That becoming is inextricably aesthetic (stylistic) and ontological (emergent).[3]

The mention of the referee scrutinizing the star's little extras might be seen as a back-door admission that the rules of the game are indeed determining. Is not the referee on the field, applying rules and regulating movements? Doesn't it all come back to the rock-solid foundation of the rule of law?

Look at what a referee actually does. A referee *stops* the action. The referee stops and reflects. The intervention of the referee is an interruption that opens the way for an application of the rules. A different kind of opening, onto an inverse movement. The rules, it was argued above, are retrospective. They are a codifying follow-up to emergence that folds back on becoming. The operation of the application is to isolate a move in a way that pins responsibility for its sensible effects on a single playing body. What the move and the body are being isolated from is the immanence of the field of potential. The disciplinary stoppage momentarily depotentializes the field in a way that makes its intensive elements *appear* to the trained perceiver as separate terms in extrinsic relation to one another. Channelings of global modulations of the field whose conditions are thoroughly collective are reduced to local moves of individual origin and deviant effect. It is now the player, not the sport, that is individualized by the disciplinary, regulatory, group-authorized and group-recognized application of the rules. This individualization is a fiction—an effectively regulating fiction—predicated on a stoppage of the play. The rules of the game and their application are transcendent to the play. It is the intervention of a transcendent operation in the continual variation of the field of immanence that makes the nodes of expression appear as discrete, substantial terms in extrinsic relation to each other. From the point of view of the rules, the codifiable form of that extrinsic relating determines the intrinsic properties of the play: fair or foul. The field of immanence is interrupted by an operation of transcendence that institutes a regime of intrinsic-extrinsic relationality predicated on the interruption of immanent relationality. The authorized set of movements between already-constituted terms is reaffirmed. The dimension of the play is reduced to a repetitive space of disciplinary regulation. Change, variation, is captured and contained. Immanent modulation of the play cedes to an overaching model of the game.

The capture and containment is not simply negative. Its very transcendence becomes a productive element in the mix whose effect is the field of immanence. The rules become an integral part of the play without ceasing to be a transcendent intervention. Just as in reflex language becomes body, in play transcendence as such becomes-immanent. It circuits into immanence. The rules are a preservative organ of the field of play. They are the condition of the play's identity across its serial repetitions in disparate times and places. The positivity of the rules is in preservation. This is also, precisely, their negativity. Codifying capture cuts both ways. Negatively, it stops and contains variation. Positively, it preserves the game for repetition. If the game were not repeated, variation would never have a chance to restart. No occasion would arise for variation to reassert itself. From one point of view (the rulemakers' and referees') variation is a departure from identity. From another point of view, identity is a moment (a productive lapse) in the continuation of variation.

The second point of view is the creative, or aesthetic. Except that the creative is not a point of view. It is not a perspective on the game or on anything. It is amidst. A dynamic midst. The being of the collective middle: belonging in becoming. Perspective is the sign of a separation from change.[4] It is a mark of codifying capture: a demarcation of the space of interruption. *A perspective is an anti–event-space.* Just as transcendence becomes a productive element of the mix to immanence, the anti–event space of perspective becomes a productive element of the event-space. The ground includes the viewpoints on it. Officially speaking, what would a soccer field be without a referee? Unofficial. The inclusion of that anti–event-space in the event space not only allows particular moves in the game to be qualified as to type (attributed intrinsic properties of fairness or foulness common to any number of other moves). It typifies the game as a whole: as "official," as in conformity. The anti–event-space is the injection of *generality* into the *particularity* of the game, with which it channels into the *singularity* of the play (the game as *such*, *this* game, *an* event). The history of the game operates, through codification, between the level of the general and of the particular. The game's becoming is the transductive conversion of the general-particular (the historical) into what it is not (singular). In general, nothing happens. In particular, things are typically about to happen or have already happened (fair or foul, win or loss). *Happening* is singularly outside "such" as "this," model and type, above, around, between. In the making, in the midst, in the openness of outcome.

There are other perspectives on the game other than the referee's. The fans also individualize players and teams, attributing to them intrinsic properties and ordering the seriality of their extrinsic relatings into the linearity of a recognizable history (a model progression). The way in which the audience's perspective is included in the game is not through regulatory application but by affective means. The excitement or disappointment of the stadium audience adds auditory elements to the mix that directly contribute to modulating the intensity of the field of potential. The audience feedback is itself modulated by the spectators' accumulated individualizations of the game—their already-constituted knowledge of and attachment to the histories of the players and teams.

The point of view of the television audience is different. Its individuations do not fold directly back on the field of play. Quite to the contrary, through the TV audience the play folds out of its own event space and into another. The televised game enters the home as a domestic player. Take for example American football. Super Bowl Sunday, the peak event of the football season, is said to correspond to an increase in domestic violence.[5] The home entry of the game, at its crest of intensity, upsets the fragile equilibrium of the household. The pattern of relations between house-held bodies is reproblematized. The game event momentarily interrupts the pattern of extrinsic relations generally obtaining between domestic bodies, as typed by gender. A struggle ensues: a gender struggle over clashing codes of sociality, rights of access to portions of the home and its contents, and rituals of servitude. The sociohistorical home place converts into an event-space. The television suddenly stands out from the background of the furnishings, imposing itself as a catalytic part-subject, arraying domestic bodies around itself according to the differential potentials generally attaching to their gender type. For a moment, everything is up in the air—and around the TV set, and between the living room and the kitchen. In proximity to the TV, words and gestures take on unaccustomed intensity. The home space is repotentialized. Anything could happen. The male body, sensing the potential, transduces the heterogeneity of the elements of the situation into a reflex readiness to violence. The "game" is rigged by the male's already-constituted propensity to strike. The typical pattern of relations is reimposed in the unity of movement of hand against face. The strike expresses the empirical reality of the situation: recontainment by the male-dominated power formation of the domestic. The event short-circuits. The event is recapture. The home event-space is back to the place it was: a container of asymmetric relations between terms already constituted according to gender. Folding back onto domestication. Coded belonging, no becoming.

The transmission of media images has transductively converted sports potential-and-containment into gender potential-and-containment. The event has migrated, changing in nature as it went. Media transmission is the becoming *of the event*. All of the operations figuring on the playing field refigure in the striking field. Refigure, and reconfigure: induction, transduction, catalysis; signs, part-object, part-subject; expression application (folding back), coding; capture and containment. When the event-dimension migrates to a new space, its elements modulate. There is no general model for the catalysis of an event. Every time an event migrates, it is re-conditioned. In the home space, the television and the images it transmits are inductive signs. The images are also transducers. And they contribute to the catalysis of the domestic event. The television set combines sign, part-object, and part-subject functions, making it a key term in the home space. In spite of multiple operations attached to it, the television is a less powerful catalyzer than the soccer ball. Although domestic violence events are widespread, they do not occur with the same regularity as soccer play is triggered by the arrival of the ball in an event-primed stadium. In both cases, the overall field of potential within which the event transpires is composed of subfields. For example, in the stadium the application of the rules of the game and the audience reactions can be seen as having their own fields of potential, primed by inductive signs proper to them and having their own specialized transducers. Every field of potential occurs at the intersection of a plurality of subfields of potential, each composed of a heterogeneity of elements. The fields intersecting around the home event-space are just as complexly layered as those of the stadium, if not more so. However, its subfields (home architecture, dwelling habits, unconscious gender patterning, conscious gender ideology, and so on) are more loosely held together. The home space is not *codified;* there is no rule book governing the production of the event of domestic violence (or, on the other hand, of caring). Domesticity is *coded.* Coding is also modeling, but not through formal regulation. The modeling occurs through the accumulation of already-constituted relations, contracted into bodies as habit (which includes belief: habituated meaning). Of course, formal regulation is part of the mix (civil law covering marriage and cohabitation and criminal law covering assault). But overall the power formation of the domestic operates through the informal production of *regularities,* as opposed to the formal application of *regulations.*

There is a constant communication between and cofunctioning of power formations that operate predominantly through accumulation and regularization, and those that operate through application and regulation. Broadly, power formations of the regulatory kind are Static—State, proto-State, and State-like formations. The Static is defined by the separation of a dedicated institution of application, a specialized bureaucracy whose judgments fold back down upon the event-space from which it has emerged and diverged, and to which it belongs, in an operation of transcendence. The temptation is to call power formations having to do with regularization "social" or "cultural," since they have no dedicated bureaucracy other than the State in the narrow sense. But it is self-evident that the "social" or "cultural" do not coincide with the field of regulatory application of the State, even though they cannot be separated from it. That is precisely the point: this is precisely why they require separate appellation and analysis. The "social" and the "cultural" leak from State regulation on every side. There are transnational and prenational cultures, just as there are sub-State social fields, often officially recognized by the State as beyond its purview (the "personal" and "private"). Their official recognition amounts to a partial—indirect or negative—regulation. For example, negatively, domestic violence may occasion State intervention. Violence, or any interruption of smoothly patterned social functioning, provides the opening into which the State can insert itself into spaces formally defined as non-Static (Foucault's disciplinary power). Positively, the State can help induce the emergence of smoothly patterned social functioning in State-friendly forms, for example, through civil marriage, profamily policy, and health and welfare measures (Foucault's biopower). But caring cannot be legislated. Effective expressions of the positivity of belonging elude the State. This is why the State, like any regulatory apparatus, *follows* that which it regulates. Its applications are always retrospective, sniffing out and running after feral belongings it must attempt to recoup, to rechannel into State-friendly patterns. The Static is incapable of perceiving the distinction between an infraction of its rules and the emergence of a new belonging, a new field of potential. It only knows the negative. It can only construe change negatively, as a prospective transgression of the regulations it will, by right, impose. The Static is by nature reactive ("static" also in the sense of favoring stasis, changing only in response to an outside it can only perceive as an impingement on itself, or as a perturbation). Like sports style, social or cultural emergence is against the rules—without having broken them. Complicating things further, if the "social" and "cultural" elude the Static, the Static for its part is a component element of the "social" and "cultural." Its transcendence folds back down on them, becomes-immanent to them. A bureaucracy participates in catalyzing the social or cultural. Furthermore, every bureaucracy has a culture specific to it: its separation from that to which it becomes-immanent constitutes it as a minisociety.

There is another level of complication to calling event-spaces "social" or "cultural." As event-spaces bifurcate into the regularizing and the regulatory, the event-dimension undergoes a different but associated split. The event-dimension bifurcates into two subdimensions:

First, coding and codification are forms of event self-referentiality—the folding back of the event onto itself, toward its repetition. The folding back, the self-referencing, is what converts the event into an event-space. The regularization or regulation effecting this conversion must be conceived as having its own conditions and field of potential. The physicality of the event-space (house or stadium) is doubled by a dynamic abstraction proper to it, one governing its own repeatability, as distinct from the repeatability of the events it hosts. Every event-space proliferates. Houses come by the suburb and stadiums in leagues. As coded or codified, the event-space is reproducible. Its reproduction provides an inductive ground for the serial emergence of subsequent events. These are deemed to be the "same" by virtue of occurring in what has become a recognizable space. A type of space. This time in the usual sense. It is the typing of the physical event-space—the invariance (regularity or regulation) of the substantial elements entering the mix—that makes the incorporeal events that emerge from it recognizably the "same." (This is why

"isolation," "defamiliarization," "distancing," or "decontextualization"—
ways of freeing the event from its regular event-space—are so often cited
as conditions of "art," as a practice of transformation resisting containment by social or cultural power formations.) The recognizability of the
space lends itself to the event, like an afterimage of substantial invariance
on the incorporeality of variation. The typing of the space tinges the
multiple events doubling it with generality, giving already-constituted
meaning and reflection a tongue-hold on the unspeakably singular (only
sensible) self-expression of the events—each of which retains a residue
of uniqueness in excess over its recognition as belonging to a type. Recognition makes an event typical. That is to say, boring. Its residue of
uniqueness makes it "interesting" (an attractor, an inducting sensation)
for a body positioned outside its space (with a perspective on it). The
event dimension of self-referentiality is the inclusion in becoming (as a
multiple-singular, a proliferation of uniqueness) of the anti–event-space
of generality (recognizability, sameness) and its perceptual concomitant
(perspective). Self-referentiality, as a subdimension of the event, is the
field of potential of transcendence-become-immanent. "Interest" is the
sign of that inclusion.

Second, media transmission involves another subdimension of the
event, interlinking with and inseparable from event self-referentiality.
This is the dimension of event-transitivity. The transitivity of the event is
also proliferating. But this proliferation crosses a qualitative threshold.
When the event passes from the stadium to the home, piggybacked on
televisual images, it changes in nature. Whereas self-referentiality has to
do with reproduction, event-transitivity has to do with differentiation. In
transformational transit, the event returns to its becoming as pure immanence. The *interval* of transmission is thus very different from the interruption of regulation. In the media interval, the event is a material but
incorporeal immanence (an electron flow) moving through a dedicated
technological milieu. When it is analogically reexpressed in televisual
images, its conditions have drastically changed. Its substantial elements
have been homogenized and reduced to fit sound speaker and screen.
The event's ability to trigger a catalytic effect is no longer certain. It is no
longer necessarily a part-subject and must be assisted in that role. Its
catalysis must be catalyzed. "Nothing" is ever on TV. It is rarely "interesting." In the new event-space, distraction is more catalytically operational than interest. Television is not predominantly perspectival as the

old catchphrase "window on the world" would have it. What is analogically rendered on screen is only a fraction of the operative event-space, which includes the content of the home, as well as the screen and its content. The home, however, is less a container than a membrane: a filter of exteriorities continually entering and traversing it.

Television is more about delivery into a more-or-less open milieu than it is about the perspective of one closed space onto another, or of a closed space onto an open space. The collective expressions occurring in the porosity of the domestic space, including the television as one humble element in a complex and loosely integrated mix, are highly variable. However, the variability and porosity, the fact that the TV-hosting home is not a container should not be construed to mean that the events regularly triggered with televisual participation are not containment events and that the home is not a formation of power. Containment has more to do with the patterning of exits and entries across thresholds than with the impermeability of boundaries. This is as true for the regulation of codified event-spaces as for spaces characterized by coding. What is pertinent about an event-space is not its boundedness, but what elements it lets pass, according to what criteria, at what rate, and to what effect. These variables define a regime of passage. Self-reference through application or through regulation by a transcendent formation, can assure a stricter regime of passage (more selective openness). The around-the-clock access to the home by communication technologies (mail delivery, telephone and answering machine, fax, e-mail, radio, TV) opens wide its codings to high-volume and highly random passage, of signs if not of human bodies. In spite of the locks on the door, the event-space of the home must be seen as one characterized by a very loose regime of passage. As a regime of openness to sign circulation—to the delivery, absorption, and relay of sounds, words, and visions—the home is a node in a circulatory network of many dimensions (each corresponding to a technology of transmission). Awash in transitivity, the home is a node in an indefinitely extended field of immanence, to which the technologies of transmission give body (provide a dedicated event-space). That technologized field of immanence is punctuated by formations of transcendence (generalities, perspectives; State, proto-State, and State-like formations), but they do not effectively regulate it. Rather, the network distributes (effectively connects) the transcendences. Formations of transcendence are also nodes, encompassed by a technologically body-doubled field of immanence that by nature eludes their rule (however hard they might try at times to tame it—communication deregulation is still the governmental name of the game).

Technologically assisted channeling of event-transitivity constitutes a qualitatively different mode of power than either the regulating codifications of the Static or the regularizing codings of the "social" or "cultural," at whose self-referential thresholds it is continually knocking. The *transitive* (a less fraught term than "communicational") must be seen as the dominant mode of power in what some are apt to call the postmodern condition. Its network is what connects coding to coding, codification to codification, coding to codification, and each to its own repetitions in an ebb and flow of potentialization-and-containment. The network distributes. Interlinks. Relates. The network is the relationality of that which it distributes. It is the being of collective becoming. Communicational technologies *give body to relationality as such* and as set in motion—as the passing-on of the event. The passing of the event is distinct both from the technology of transmission that is its corporeal double and from its delivery on the other side of the threshold. The passing, event-transitivity in itself: in its becoming, is the interval that encompasses—occupying every threshold.

Every "enclosure" is encompassed by a pure immanence of transition. The medium of "communication" is not the technology. It is the interval itself: the moveability of the event, the displacement of change, relationality outside its terms, "communication" without content, communicability.[6] Encompassed by transitivity (understood in this way as a special kind of transduction), the Static and the regularized transpire in a rarefied atmosphere of modulation. As "communications" ever more insistently pipes itself in through a multidimensional delivery line, it increasingly thresholds spaces of potentialization-and-containment with indeterminate event-transitivity. Both the singular *and* the general-particular come to hinge on the indeterminate. Or swim in it, since the encompassing threshold is not a door but an inundatory medium of flow. "Communications" is the traffic in modulation. It is a special mode of power that lubricates event spaces in a bath of indeterminacy, smoothing the thresholds of containment. If local or individual style is resistance (understood more in the frictional sense than the oppositional one: a rub against the rules rather than a breaking of them), then resistance *and* containment are contained—in flow. They are wafted. Their wafting indexes them to the not-self-referentiality of their threshold, the interval: something that is not exactly outside but is still exorbital to the event-space of arrival. A pseudo exoreferentiality—to the indeterminate. Not the "simply" indeterminate. Not the simply logically indeterminate: the complexly, technologically, ontologically, indeterminate.

From the perspective of containment and regularized modes of opposition to it (countercontainment), this situation can only be experienced as a "crisis." Everything from architecture to "the family" to religion to "the Left and the Right" to government itself fell into a self-declared state of perpetual crisis, all around the same moment—when the thresholding approached the saturation point. Yet they are all still very much with us. The change is not a disappearance but an encompassing. What has changed is that none of them, no apparatus of coding or of codification, can claim to encompass, because they are all encompassed. They waft and bathe, and by virtue of that shared condition, connect. Not negated: networked. Delivered one and all to transitivity, to the indeterminate event (for which "crisis" is as good a name as any).

The networkability of event transmission must be seen as pertaining not only to mass-media images but to information in general, to commodities, and to money: to any sign whose basic operation is to flow, and whose inductive/transductive effect must be "realized" (whose catalytic role must be catalyzed; whose expression must be expressed). All of these event transmitters carry a high charge of indeterminacy, of unrealized (or, in the present vocabulary, "unactualized") potential. What they are, what their event will be, what will be expressed with or through them, is highly variable, since they are complexly cocatalyzed by the heterogeneous elements populating the proliferating spaces they enter. Event transmitters are inductive/transductive signs roving for catalysis, across many a proliferation.[7] Their readiness to catalyze—their aptitude for part-subjecthood—is also highly variable. The ready-most is money, a sign whose simple appearance in any context is sure to incorporeally transform it in one way or another. The least catalytic is information. Each event transmitter is sustained and delivered by a dedicated collective apparatus deploying at least one technology of channeling that gives it body in the interval, where it disappears into its own immanence (even low-tech transmitters return to immanence: letters are mailed in a sealed envelope, their meaning re-latent). The intervallic bodies are of many types, ranging from mailboxes and post offices to telephone lines to computers to the many and varied institutions and instruments of finance. These knot together in an expanding capillary network traversing every event-space with ever-increasing complexity (most recently converging on the Internet). It is in the complexity of their technological interlinkage that they form an encompassing threshold-space of transitivity that can no longer be ignored as a global power formation in its own right.

This new power formation has an old name: capitalism. For money, as means of payment or investment, is the only event transmitter that traverses every event-space and piggybacks every intervallic body without exception. Present-day capital is the capillary network of the capillary, the circulator of the circulation, the motor of transitivity—the immanence of immanence-embodied. The *inside limit of the relational.* The current capitalist mode of power could be called control: neither coding nor codification, neither regularization nor regulation, but the *immanently encompassing modulation of both.*[8] The power of control is predicated on decoding (the rendering immanent of signs as vectors of indeterminate potential) and deterritorialization (the drawing off of the event from its general-particular spaces of expression and, in this case, its consignment to a distributed, intervallic space of its own). The power of control is decoding and deterritorialization, *delivered* (ready for catalysis, into a potentialization-and-containment in a new space; ready for recoding/recodification and reterritorialization). Control is modulation made a power factor (its flow factor). It is the powering-up—or powering-away—of potential. The ultimate capture, not of the elements of expression, not even of expression, but of the movement of the event itself.

It is in no way underestimating capitalist control to call its worldwide trafficking in modulation the stylization of power. It was argued earlier that the model of power was usurpation. What is being usurped here? The very expression of potential. The movement of relationality. Becoming-together. Belonging. *Capitalism is the global usurpation of belonging.* This is not merely a lament: power, it must be recognized, is now massively potentializing, in a new planetary mode. But neither is it necessarily cause for celebration: the potentialization is just as massively delivered to proliferating spaces of containment. It is the inescapable observation that belonging per se has emerged as a problem of global proportions. Perhaps *the* planetary problem. Neither celebration nor lament: a challenge to rethink and reexperience the individual and the collective.

Which goes last?

THE EVOLUTIONARY ALCHEMY OF REASON
Stelarc

PROJECT: "extend intelligence beyond the earth."[1]
MEDIUM: the body.
Correction: the body is "obsolete."

Now there's a bind: a "body artist" who wants to operate upon intelligence. Wouldn't that make him a "conceptual" artist? Stelarc gives every sign of wanting to have it both ways, making his medium the body *and* ideas. But then he goes on to say that the first is "obsolete,"[2] all the while protesting that his work operates entirely outside of the "outmoded metaphysical distinctions of soul-body or mind-brain."[3] Talk about difficult to please.

One thing that is clear is that Stelarc is not a conceptual artist. He is not interested in communicating concepts *about* the body. What he is interested in is experiencing the body *as* concept. He thinks of his performances, which involve minutely prepared, "austere" probings of the functional limits of the body, as a direct "physical experience of ideas."[4] In performance, "expression and experience join," making the body an "actual manifestation of a concept."[5] The *manifestation* of a concept: the concepts Stelarc is interested in cannot be communicated about in the performance, because they only come into being through the performance. The ideas he takes as his medium, on a par with the body, do not preexist their physical expression. That is why his first performances were accompanied by no "notices, manifestos, or written explanations."[6] It was only after the manifestation of the ideas began in the body that they were able to be disengaged enough from it to enter speech and writing.

Stelarc's art starts from and continually returns to a point at which idea and body have not yet split or have rejoined. His medium is the body as a *sensible concept.*

PROBLEM: in what way is the body an idea, and the idea bodily? In what way can probing one extend the other? "*How is it that the body thinks itself?*"[7]

This is the problem Stelarc's work poses. And this is the problem that the art writer must re-pose if the concern is to approach the work on its own terms—or even meet it halfway—rather than imposing an outside frame of judgment upon it. The challenge is to write the rejoining of body and thought that Stelarc performs. This requires a willingness to revisit some of our basic notions of what a body is and does as an acting, perceiving, thinking, feeling thing.

The Matter of Intelligence

Imagine for a moment that you are an intelligent insect. Would things be different? This is the question Stelarc seems to be asking in some of his first performances, in which the artist and the audience donned helmets designed to scramble binocular vision by superimposing fragmented rear and side views onto the normal frontal view, thus producing a technologically assisted humanoid version of the compound eye of the insect.[8] If you had compound eyes would the properties of the things you perceived be the same? Couldn't be. If their properties were different, would they be the same things? More or less.

In other words, no. This is not an argument for the relativity of perception. Far from it—it is an argument for its necessity. What does the bee see and smell in the flower? Enough to extract pollen from it. A creature's perception is exactly proportioned to its action upon the thing. The properties of the perceived thing are properties of the action, more than of the thing itself. This does not mean, on the other hand, that the properties are subjective or in the perceiver. On the contrary, they are tokens of the perceiver's and the perceived's concrete inclusion in each other's world. The perception lies *between* the perceiver and the perceived. The sight of the flower is an actual bodily conjunction, a joint material connection of the perceiver and the perceived to different ends of the same reflected light wave, in different ways. That differential conjunction is the latency of a next conjunction. The contour and fragrance of the flower are the presence to both perceiver and perceived, in different ways, of a possible touch where once there was only sniff and see. It is an understatement to say that a creature's perceptions are exactly proportioned to its actions. Its perceptions *are* its actions—in their latent state. *Perceptions are possible actions.*[9] They belong to two orders simultaneously: an order of substitution (one conjunction relayed by another: action) and an order of superposition (the latent presence of the next conjunction in the actual one it will relay: anticipation). Both orders are real and express a material necessity (nourishment).

Orders of substitution and superposition are orders of thought defined as *the reality of an excess over the actual.* This is clearest in the case of anticipation, which in a real and palpable way extends the actual moment beyond itself, superposing one moment upon the next, in a way that is not just thought but also bodily felt as a yearning, tending, or tropism. But the definition also applies to substitution, which never come in ones. There are any number of possible next connections. The bee may be laden and skip the flower. Or, instead of collecting, it may return to the hive to signal the source of food. Or it may be duped by a blossoming mimic into trying to mate instead. Or it may mate and eat. Substitutions are cases in a combinatoric (a system of "either-ors" sometimes conjoined as an "and"). Not all possible actions are present as perception to the same degree. All of the permutations composing the combinatoric are not actionably present to the same degree in every perception. Each perception is surrounded by a fringe of unlikelihood, of impalpable possibility.[10] Perception shades off into a systematicity whose exact contours can *only* be thought.

Perception and thought are two poles of the same process. They lie along a continuum. At one pole, more than one substitution is actively superposed, enveloped in the feeling of anticipation of a next action, not yet determined. This is the perception pole. At the other pole, all possible substitutions are present, deactivated and without overlap, unenveloped in feeling. They are unfolded from action and feeling, arrayed in extrinsic (either-or) relation to one another, determined as alternatives to one another. This is the thought pole. The poles of perception and thought are at the limits of the same continuum. One limit is the mixture of experience as it passes on: action under way and on the way to the next; sensory plug-in; the recognition of having actively plugged-in before, memory or the already-thought; the feeling of tending to act-think again. The other is a purification of experience, thought-out (the only-thought). At any given conjunction, a creature's activity, or lack thereof, will place it in the perceptual in-mix and, simultaneously, at a certain degree along the continuum toward the out-thought, depending on the extent to which it can project into a future an array of action-substitutions to choose from. This forward projection of perception into latent action-choice is its *possibilization*. To possibilize is to stretch perception down the continuum in the direction of the only-thought. Each actual conjunction is a dynamic mixture of different orders materially combining the experience of the actually under way with possibilizing extensions beyond itself. The inextricability of the experiencing and the extension make perception an *analysis in action* and the perceived "thing" a sensible concept.

Every creature connecting with a flower will think-perceive it differently, extending the necessity of its perception into the only-thought of possibility to a varying degree. The lower the degree of possibilization, the vaguer the anticipation, and the more mixed are the alternatives it presents and the feeling of tending enveloped in the action under way: the less thought-out it is. The flower is each of the thought-perceptions in which it is implicated, to whatever degree of thought-perception. Which is not to say that there are as many flowers as there are florally conjoined creatures. The flower-thing is *all* of the thought-perceptions in which it is implicated. Latent in the flower are all of the differential conjunctions it may enter into. The flower, as a thing "in itself," is its connectability with other things outside itself. That connectability is not of the order of action or thought-out anticipation and is therefore not in the mode of possibility. It is of the order of *force*. Each connection is a shared plug-in to a force emitted or transmitted by the flower-thing. Like a light wave. The latency in this case is in the mode not of the possible but of energetic *potential*. There is more potentially emitted or transmitted by the flower than any necessary perception of it picks up on (more . . .). The bee's hungry or horny perception is not "relative" to the flower. It is selective of it (*and less*). Perception, even before its thinking out, is a limited selection, an actualization of potential plug-ins. There is *more* in the "thing" than in the perception of it. The feeling of anticipation as such—as enveloped in action under way in all its mixity, and as distinct from the alternatives it can think out into—is a registering of potential. This pending feeling of being selectively plugged-in to forces, this registering of a nextness betokening always more: this may be called *sensation*. Sensation is the registering of the multiplicity of potential connections in the singularity of *a* connection actually under way. It is the direct experience of a more to the less of every perception.[11] It may be considered a third pole or limit of experience, accompanying each degree of action-perception (that is to say: it is a limit of experience immanent to every step along the continuum).

The latency of the potentials in the flower constitutes an order that follows different rules of formation and is broader in bandwidth and more complexly woven than any possible combinatoric extracted from it. The thought-system of the possible is a necessary *loss of order* relative to potential.[12] The latency of the flower is inexhaustible. There are no doubt insectile ways of plugging into floral forces that no bug has yet experienced. More than that, the humblest flower enfolds forces that no creature, not even a human, will ever know how to connect to: colors outside the visible spectrum, forces too small, too large, too subtle, or simply too different to conjoin. To answer the question, the flower the bee sees is not the "same" flower a human sees. It is a particular, need-oriented selection from the experience of the singular multiplicity that is its inexhaustible complexity as a thing "in itself" (in its potential connections).

So what does a human see in a flower? More than the bee, but by no means the full range of its inexhaustible complexity. A human will see enough to extract not just pollen for immediate collection but also, for example, a pharmaceutical for profitable distribution. Human perception is unique in the degree to which it can extend itself into the only-thought and, thus, into the future in more and more varied ways. It can do this because it is capable of connecting with a thing as if it somehow existed outside of any particular perception of it. Saying that a thing might be considered to be *outside* any particular perception is very different from saying it is *not all in* any particular perception. Taking a thing as "not all in" the particular is to singularly sense the multiplicity of the potential for perceptions it connectively envelops. Taking it as "outside" the particular is to approach it *in general*, as if unconnected. Both are operations of abstraction. The mode of abstraction pertaining to the thing in general concerns the possible, purified of any unplanned interference from unselected-for potentials. The possible is not just an active selection of potential, but a systematic simplification of it. Taken in general, the flower-thing becomes the object of a set of regularized floral connections systematized in such a way as to ensure the maximum repeatability of the largest number of actions with the maximum uniformity of result. Predictability: anticipation perfected. The *object* is the systematic stock-piling for future use of the possible actions relating to a thing, systematically thought-out on the general level of abstraction. Existing only in general, the object is imperceptible. The thought-unseen flower-object doubles each given flower-thing in the order of the possible. It is the future-looking shadow of the actually repeatedly perceived, blooming scentless. Regularized, repeatable, uniform connection—the systematicity of a thing—constitutes a profitable disengagement of the thing's thinking from its perceiving in such a way as to maximize its extension into thought under a certain mode of abstraction.

Paradoxically, this perfecting of the order of substitution is an intensification of the order of superposition pertaining to potential at the same time as it is a disengagement from it. Objectivity makes more possibilities more anticipatable, and thus more accessible as next connections. Objectivity shadows the perception with an increased charge of possibility, which cycles back into perception to augment the potentiality of the thing it began by purifying, or thinking out. The forces enveloped in the thing have actually gained in the diversity of effects into which they feed. The connectability of the thing has been increased: it now has more potentials. They have been sur-charged, intensified. The thing's general selection returns to it as an augmentation of its singular multiplicity. Its simplification returns to it as a complexification, its loss as a gain in order. Possibilization and potentialization, simplification and complexification, fold into and out of each other. The loss of order is only a moment in an expansive process in which perception and thought form a positive feedback loop (as do things and thought, by way of perception). Things, perception, and thought are in a reciprocal movement into and out of each other and themselves. They are moments or dimensions of the same process of mutual reinforcement and co-conversion. Sensation is the point of co-conversion through which the variations of perception and thought play out. It is the singular point where what infolds is also unfolding.

The overall process of the actual extending into the possible and then looping through sensation into a mutual intensification of potential, perception, and thought: this is *intelligence*. The part of that process consisting in the systematization of intelligence in the general mode of possibility is what goes by the name of *instrumental reason*. Instrumental reason is by no means all of intelligence and is not even the only only-thought. It is a thought-variety (an analytic variety of the only-thought). Intelligence is

94

an outgrowth of need. Instrumental reason is the extension of need into utility: a greater co-presence of possibilities that enables a systematic construction of a combinatoric and, by virtue of that, a calculated choice between possible next connections. This may even include a methodical invention of new connections as previously inaccessible aspects of forces emerge in the course of probings of the thing designed to set its limits of possibility. A bee intelligently analyzes-in-action the flower, toward the fulfillment of a need. The instrumentally reasoning human extends the analysis-in-action in thought toward the invention of utilities. There is no clear and distinct dividing line between intelligence and instrumental reason. Every thought-perception is both, to a varying degree, in mixture and co-conversion.

What else does a human see in a flower? Besides pharmaceuticals? Poetry, for one thing. The extension from need to utility can extend again.

Stelarc's bug goggles fulfilled no need. They extended no-need into no-utility. And they extended no-utility into "art." They were an exercise in the perceptual poetry of instrumental reason.

We started out saying that Stelarc was a body artist, and we are now saying that his art is in some (poetic) way objective. This is not a contradiction. For the object is an extension of the perceived thing, and the perceived thing is a sensible concept, and the sensible concept is a materialized idea embodied not so much in the perceiving or the perceived considered separately as in their between, in their felt conjunction. But are the terms independent of the conjunction? What is a perceiving body apart from the sum of its perceivings, actual and possible? What is a perceived thing apart from the sum of its being-perceiveds, actual and potential? Separately, each is no action, no analysis, no anticipation, no thing, no body. The thing *is* its being-perceiveds. A body *is* its perceivings. "Body" and "thing" and, by extension, "body" and "object" exist only as implicated in each other. They are differential plug-ins into the same forces, two poles of the same connectability. The thing is a pole of the body and vice versa. Body and thing are extensions of each other. They are mutual implications: co-thoughts of two-headed perception. That two-headed perception is the world.[13]

Extensions. The thing, the object, can be considered *prostheses* of the body—provided that it is remembered that the body is equally a prosthesis of the thing.

Matter as it enters into the double analytic order of necessary substitution and superposition and then extends again into utility—matter as it enters into things and objects—*matter itself is prosthetic*. Things and objects are literally, materially, prosthetic organs of the body.[14] But if bodies and objects exist only as implicated in each other, in necessary and useful reciprocity, then isn't it just as accurate to say that the body is literally, materially, an organ of its things? In mutual implication, it is not clear who is used by whom.[15]

Having an instrumentally reasoning body for an organ can be most useful to a thing. A flower in which humans see a pharmaceutical will grow in abundance. Is the flower an aid to the perpetuation of the human, or is the human, like the mimic-duped bee, a reproductive organ of the flower? Both. You can have it either way. It's just a question of from which pole you approach the problem. Human and flower are in differential, polar cofunctioning. They meet in the reciprocity of perception. But the reciprocity is not a symmetry, since the two plug in differently to contrasting poles of shared forces and travel, through their forcible conjunction, in different directions: one toward individual health maintenance, the other toward species reproduction. Thought-perception is *asymmetrical prosthetic symbiosis*.

A flower in which humans see poetry rather than pharmaceuticals will also grow widely. And differentiate. The poetics of roses has led to a multiplication of strains, each bearing the name of its first human prosthesis. Need and utility lead to self-same reproduction. Uselessness, on the other hand, lends itself to invention.

This link between uselessness and invention even applies to instrumental reason: a true invention is an object that precedes its utility. An invention is something for which a use must be created. Once the utility is produced, it rapidly self-converts into a need. This is the direction of flow of the history of technology (of which bodies, things, and objects are the first artifacts): backward. With invention, the perceptual direction of travel between the poles of necessity and utility, between the intelligence and instrumentality, possibility and reason, is reversed. An invention is a sensible concept that *precedes and produces its own possibility* (its system of connection-cases, its combinatoric). An invention is an in situ plumbing of potential rather than an extrapolation of disengaged possibility. It is a trial-and-error process of connecting with new forces, or in new ways with old forces, to unanticipated effect. Invention is a plug-in to the

96

impossible. It is only by plumbing that connection that anything truly new can arise.

The goggles Stelarc invented effected an inventive reversion from human instrumental reason to humanoid-insect intelligence. Needlessly. The goggles are still waiting for a use to be created for them (and doubtless have a long wait ahead of them still). Stelarc's art, in its first carefully engineered gesture, sets for itself the project of applying instrumental reason in such a way as to *suspend need and utility.* His technically accomplished body-objects precede their possibility—but stop short of producing it. If he is a body artist whose medium is also ideas, then he is not content with his medium. He converts it. He began by approaching ideas as materialized thoughts and making them into *unthinkable objects*— artifacts that can *only be sensed*—pure sensation. Then he put the unthinkable objects on the body to see what might become of it. The body and thought converge toward a shared indeterminacy. They are together in the sensation. You can't begin to know what bug goggles can do until you don them. You have to experience them even to begin to imagine a use for them, and what your body is with them. "Imagine" is still too reasoned a term: any eventual use is impossibly enveloped in a definitely felt but still undefined experience, compoundly unpreviewed. Which is why the goggles were deployed in *performances* requiring audience participation.[16] The goggles were the trigger for a collective thought-body event ever so tentatively suggesting the just-beginnings of a symbiosis: a pending tending-together.

Stelarc's is an art of sensation. Sensation is the direct registering of potential. It is a kind of zero-degree of thought-perception, and of the possibility it disengages, at the point at which it all folds vaguely together, only sensed, pending action and a reconnect to need and utility (whose impending is also sensed, only just). Despite its constitutive vagueness, it is a pole of thought-perception, whose every conjunction is accompanied to a varying degree by sensation—by the real unthinkability of things, the as-yet unnecessary and stubbornly useless, registering as a tending, as a to-come to be in the world.

Sensation is an extremity of perception. It is the immanent limit at which perception is eclipsed by a sheerness of experience, as yet unextended into analytically ordered, predictably reproducible, possible action. Sensation is a state in which action, perception, and thought are so intensely, performatively mixed that their in-mixing falls out of itself. Sensation is fallout from perception. Endo-fallout: *pure mixture,* the in-mixing-out of the most-mixed. A receding into a latency that is not just the absence of action but, intensely, a poising for more: an augmentation.

However poised, sensation *as such* is inaccessible to active extension and systematic thinking-out. It is an always-accompanying, excessive dimension, of the purely infolded. Like the possibility that thoughtfully unfolds, it doubles present perception. Two modes of abstraction, doubly doubling perception: the only-thought and the only-felt, the possible and the impossibly potentialized. These modes can be understood as concurrent movements of abstraction running in opposite directions (before feeding back), one receding into felt-tending, the other laying out thinkable alternatives for the active unfolding of what had been only in tendency. The world concretely appears where the paths cross.

Both generality (thought possibility) and singularity (sensed potential) are in excess over any and every actual conjunction. The first because it projects itself outside into a systematic alternative to the actually given; the second because it folds into every given connection so intensely that it falls out of it into pure mixture (reciprocal immanence). Sensation and thought, at their respective limits as well as in their feedback into each other, are *in excess over experience:* over the actual. They extend into the nonactual. If the alternative mode of abstraction into which perception extends is the possible, the intense mode of abstraction into which sensation potentially infolds is, at the limit, the *virtual.* Intelligence stretches between the extremes of thought-perception, from the actual to the possible, dipping at every connection into the vortex of the virtual.

Although the distinction between the virtual and potential will not be crucial here, a quick indication is in order: yet another pair of poles. (As Deleuze was fond of saying, always multiply distinctions). This time the poles are of sensation itself. The potential and the virtual can be considered the constitutive limits of the endo-fallout that is sensation. The virtual would be the highest degree of infolding-out. Potential would be its least degree, as it just begins to recede from action-perception and thinking-out into nonpossible latency. In what follows, "pure potential" can be taken as a marker of the "virtual": sensation most latent. The continuum between potential and virtuality is of degrees of latency-by-infolding, or of intensity. The continuum of thought and perception with which this essay will be most concerned is composed of degrees of extension (development or unfolding). The distinction between the potential and the virtual, and their respective differences with possibility, will be a main focus of the following chapter.

If you were an intelligent insect, would you be reading this?

Suspended Animations

At a certain point, Stelarc realized that fourteen hooks weren't enough.[17] A doctor advised him that he should use eighteen, at minimum, so that the weight of his body would be more evenly distributed. That way his wounds would be smaller, and there would be less danger of his flesh tearing.

Stelarc's body suspensions were careful, calculated, literally antiseptic. They weren't about risk. They weren't about danger for danger's sake. They weren't shamanistic or mystical or ecstatic. And they most certainly weren't masochistic. The pain wasn't sought after or reveled in. It was a soberly accepted by-product of the project. Again, notions such as shamanism and masochism applied to his work are "irrelevant" and "utterly wrong."[18] The point was never to awe the audience with the artist's courage or hubris. Neither was it to treat the audience to a dramatic staging of symbolic suffering in order to shed light on or heal some supposedly founding agony of the human subject. For one thing, there wasn't an audience (and, if there were, it is not clear that they would have seen that symbolism through compound eyes).

So what's the project again? "*Extending intelligence beyond the earth.*"[19] Hold that thought.

"What is important is the body as an object, not a subject—not being a particular someone but rather becoming something else."[20] Stelarc applies instrumental reason—careful, calculated, medically-assisted procedure—to the body, taken as an object, in order to extend intelligence into space, by means of a suspension. Now how does suspending the body-object extend intelligence? And what is the something else the body becomes, beyond its objectivity and subjectivity?

To begin to answer these questions, it is necessary to clarify what precisely is suspended. It is not simply the actual body of the artist, because once again the body as an *object* is in excess over any given actual conjunction it enters into by virtue of the shadow of generality that is one with its objectivity (reproducibility, predictability, uniformity of anticipated result). By targeting the body as object, Stelarc is targeting the body in its generality; he is targeting the generality of the body. But how, without symbolizing, without communicating to an audience, can a particular performance target a generality? How can a single performance raise itself to the amplitude of the objective? It can't.

> I didn't honestly think I'd be doing more than one suspension event but there have been a series of ideas that I felt compelled to realize. In the first four suspension events the body was rotated through 360 degrees in space. The next series of suspensions were involved with all kinds of structural supports. . . . More recently there have been the environmental suspensions.[21]

On second thought, maybe it can: if suspensions, like substitutions, do not come in ones. Rolled up in the first suspension event was an indefinite series of others that were unanticipated. These were present in the first, somehow implicit in it, but not in a way available for conscious elaboration. The first accomplished suspension event set in motion a serial unfolding of variations that were implicit in it or immanent to it. That first event only explored what comes of suspending the body in one particular way. But what of other ways? Is it the same to be suspended upright as horizontal? Upside down as right-side up? Inside from a frame of poles and outside from the top of a building in Manhattan or over a rocky coastline? James Paffrath and Stelarc's book *Obsolete Bodies/Suspensions/Stelarc* (1984) follows the unfolding exploration of the field opened up by the implicitly serial ur-idea of suspension. Each developed event was a variation on that idea, approached from a different angle—permutations in an unfolding combinatoric.

The suspended body is a sensible concept: the implications of the event are *felt* first, before being thought-out. They are felt in the form of a "compulsion": an abstractness with all the immediacy of a physical force. What the apparatus of suspension did was to set up the body's unfolding relation to itself as a problem, a compulsion, and to construe that problem in terms of force. The compulsion was a problem-posing force that moved through the series. It was its momentum, immanent to the first event and each after, as well as bridging the intervals between them. The compulsive force of unfolding was thus responsible for the felt intensity of each event taken separately, as well as for their continuity.

This serializing force of compulsion operated in relation with other forces. The basic device employed throughout was an interruption of the body's necessary relation to the grounding force of human action: gravity. The hooks turned the skin into a countergravity machine.[22] The consequences of using the resident forces of the flesh—its elasticity and strength—to counteract gravity were not clearly anticipatable, as illustrated by the fact that the first suspension event was blocked at the last minute by the sponsoring institution, which feared it might be left with a shredded artist.[23] Stelarc's suspensions methodically unraveled the implications of hooking up the body as a countergravity machine. Only after a wide range of the possible countergravity connections were actualized—only after the combinatoric implicit in the first event was close to being exhausted—did the artist feel uncompelled to continue. This process took more than ten years.

The suspension variations should not be confused with answers to the problem posed. The problem posed by a force cannot be "solved," only *exhausted*. In a need- or utility-oriented context, the permutations comprising the combinatoric of possible action doubling the given conjunction can indeed be thought-out as cases of solution that inform and precede a choice, the selection of the "right" (most functional) solution. The combinatoric is based on an analysis of past conjunctions abstracted from the singularity of their occurrence and then generally projected into the future in the form of a set of functional alternatives to choose from. But here it is precisely need and utility that are suspended and with them the linear projection from past conjunctions to generally laid-out alternatives. The regularized, needful, useful actions of the human body all hinge in one way or another on its bipedal upright posture, the body's usual way of counteracting gravity. Interrupt that and you have profoundly disconnected the human body from its normal realm of activity, from its possible actions. The suspended body is in no position to extend its present situation into a logically expressible next step by choosing from a set of possible actions. It is not only in a needless and useless condition, it is in an utterly dysfunctional one. It is in no condition to choose. No analysis-in-action leading to selection here. Not even a presentiment of eventual use-value as with the bug goggles. The usual mode in which the body *functions* as a sensible concept—possibility—is radically suspended. The body is placed at the limit of its functionality.

The answer to the question of what is being suspended: embodied human *possibility*. Each suspension in the series was not a possible answer but a re-posing of a problem that stubbornly remains a problem from end to end of its serial unfolding, that refuses solution as long as the human body is the kind of sensible concept it normally is and functions the way it does. The repeated explorations resolved nothing. Each time, the body was left hanging. By the end of the series, the body was, well, exhaustively hung. Nothing more. No need or use, let alone an effectively conveyed symbolism or even a communicable meaning, was generated. A process, simply, had been set in motion and had run its course.

What is important to Stelarc is approaching the body as an object, in other words, as an objectivized sensible concept whose abstract mode is that of possibility. Stelarc starts at the end. He starts from the pole of possibility *as a limit*, the outside limit of the body's functionality, its already-extension into the only-thought of instrumental reason. He assumes the body as a known object of instrumental reason with known, regularized functions of need and utility. Then he applies that same instrumental reason—in the engineering of scaffolding, in the medical knowledge used to take health precautions—in a way carefully calculated to cause it to self-interrupt. That the suspensions were not initially operating in a mode of possibility is amply demonstrated by the fact that their seriality was unforeseen. It is only retrospectively that the series can be resolved into a combinatoric of possible alternatives or permutations. Only *retroactively* are the suspension events an operation on possibility, on the body at the limit of its generality.

Normally, possibility comes before, for a better after: it consists in a certain abstractive operation on the past that projects it usefully into a future, or extrapolates it. Each step toward that future is seen to be conditioned by the possible: what that future comes to be, in particular, is affected by the possible alternatives laid out before it. The possible moves in linear fashion from past particulars, through a generality doubling each present conjunction (the combinatoric of alternatives), and to a next and future particular (selected from the combinatoric). With Stelarc's suspension series, things are radically different. There is no extrapolation. Here, the possibility of the series *results from* the series rather than conditioning it.[24] The possible appears only at the end, after the movement it concerns has exhausted itself. The limit-state in which Stelarc's suspensions place the body has possibility only in its pastness. Since the momentum carrying the series forward into the future has already lost its momentum by the time its combinatoric is apparent, there is nowhere for its possibility to go. The possible belongs to the suspension series as a pure *past,* unprojected, only arrived at after everything is already over. The body's limit-state prior to its possibility, before it catches up with its past, in the course of its serial unfolding, is an onward momentum of "becoming something else." The body is in a state of invention, pure and not so simple. That inventive limit-state is a pre-past suspended present. The suspension of the present without a past fills each actual conjunction along the way with unpossibilized *futurity:* pure potential. Each present is entirely filled with *sensation:* felt tending, pending.

Stelarc's project is to use particular bodily conjunctions to counteract generality in order to pack the body's singularity into sensation. That singularity is experience falling out of the particular moment, but not into a generality. Rather: into the impending moreness of serial continuation immanent to each body event—save the last. Actually, including the last. There is still something immanent to the last: another first, no less. A whole new series, beyond suspension. The momentum will leap to the next series in a move that will be as unanticipated, as aberrant from the point of view of any normal logic of linear development, as was the transition from goggles to hooks. The end of possibility envelops *more,* and more varied, potential: multiplicity. The project is to invent an indeterminate bodily future, in an uncommon intensity of sensation packing more multiplicity into bodily singularity. Paul Virilio, so obstinately wrong about so many aspects of Stelarc's work, got this one right: Stelarcian suspensions approach the body-as-object in order to "negate" it (counteract it) "in favor of pure sensation."[25]

In the only suspension in which the body was actively doing something while suspended (hoisting itself on a pulley), what Stelarc registered was a "split between what the body was feeling and what it was doing."[26] The mix of activity and suspended animation only made perceptible the divergence between action and sensation: the way in which sensation falls out from action-perception into a futurity that precedes and doubles the body's past. The seriality of the performances was a multiplying of that infolded future-singular before it was the laying-out of a combinatoric.

Why explore sensation when the project is intelligence? The suspensions in themselves do not extend intelligence beyond the gravitational field of the earth. If they did, they would not be suspensions of the human body-object but, precisely, free-floating continuations of it. What they do is prepare the ground. The suspended body expresses nothing of need or use, nothing of symbolic or semantic value. As a sensible concept, it is an undetermined one from the point of view of function and meaning. It is a corporeal *opening*. Etymologically, the "extrapolation" of possibility is an "altering out." Here, the body, infolded, is "altered in." Stelarc's art is an *interpolation* of the body's openness.

Functions, as well as meanings, are expressions. Every action of a body is a physical expression of its analysis-in-action of the perceptual world, of the plug-in to forces of which the body and its things are complementary poles. The hung body is not actively expressive. But it is expressive nevertheless. Stelarc repeatedly evokes the pattern of ripples and hills that form on the hook-stretched skin, calling it a "gravitational landscape."[27] The body visibly expresses the force whose counteracting posed the problem. The "something else," the something other than an object that it becomes by being approached as an object in this way, is a *transducer:* a local organization of forces (epidermal elasticity and strength) responding to and transformatively prolonging another force (gravity).[28] A transducer transformatively "manifests rhythms and flows of energy."[29] The body-transducer transforms gravity from an invisible condition of station, locomotion, and action into a visibility.[30] Light waves are not the only sensible force into which gravity transduced. Many of Stelarc's suspension events also amplified the sounds of the body. The rush of blood through the artist's veins as his body rises in a state of heightened receptivity to the effects of gravity are transformed into amplified sound waves that fill the room. The transducing of the body is extended beyond the skin to propagate through the surrounding space.[31] The transductive physicality of the body extends to the limits of its spatial containment. The body-as-transducer literally, physically fills its space, becoming architectural as blood flows sonically to the walls, echoing its built limits.[32] The body, in becoming a transducer, has become two more things: a visibility of gravity and a sonic architecturality. A corporeal opening onto sound, image, architecture, and more. The future. Sensation is the key to accessing the more-than regularized action and perception that is the body-thing.

The suspended more-thans of sound and vision are already extensions, but not yet of intelligence. It is better to call them extendabilities than extensions, because there is no receiver, no audience: there is no one present to register and relay them. They expire with the event. They are beginnings of extensions, incipient extensions. Among the many directions in which a gravitational landscape and a sonic body-architecturality might be extended is into a mystical symbolism of nature-culture fusion with inevitable overtones of shamanism and exalted masochism. The absence of an audience works precisely to block that extension. The audience will be included again in Stelarc's art only when the conditions are right for an extension in an entirely different direction—a machinic direction, toward the cyborg, reached by extending the plug-in to gravity, across an interseries leap, to another fundamental force of human existence: electromagnetism.[33]

In retrospect, the suspension events composing the series can be considered to have been most exhaustively performed in their mutual implication, most intensely rolled into each other in indeterminate futurity, most problematically enveloped in a singular event—one that was not to be repeated. That event is the veritable "first," even though chronologically it came in the middle. It is the first in the sense of taking a logical precedence of sorts, embodying as it does the sensible concept of the suspended body in an unthinkably extreme form. It is the most intense embodiment of the ur-idea of suspension. It is of this event that all the others were multiples. It comes "first" in the sense that it is the *virtual* center of the suspension series.

> The body was contained between two planks and suspended from a quadrapod pole structure in a space littered with rocks. The eyes and mouth were sewn shut. Three stitches for the lips, one each for the eyelids. The body was daily inserted between the planks and in the evening was extracted to sleep amongst the rocks. Body participation was discontinued after seventy-five hours.[34]

All bodily expression was closed down. Barely glimpsed between the planks, the body generated no gravitational landscape by day. By night, it slipped into a surrounding landscape, reduced to one gravity-stranded object among others, a body-mineral among the rocks, in darkness, unseen even by itself. Not only did the body not transduce and externalize its sounds, it could not speak. It had ceased to speak, to see and make visible, even to eat. It was shut down. Unplugged. Disconnected from every form of meaningful, need-based, useful function. Delivered supine unto the force of gravity. Stranded abject object.

It was argued earlier that there was not a difference in nature between object and organ. The terms are just conventional designations for differential regions of the same polarized perceptual field. If the transductive suspensions in which the body began to extend into image and sound were counteractions of the body's *objectivity*, then the sewn suspension goes one step further, countering the *organicity* of the body. A body that can express nothing, not even incipient let alone possible action, is supremely dysfunctional. It is what a Deleuze and Guattari call a body without organs.[35] On hold. Sewn and suspended, the body folds in on itself to the point that it is not only no longer an object or an organism, it is even stretched to the limit of things. This is what Stelarc dubs the "Anaesthetized Body."[36]

Distraught and disconnected.[37]

The body was passified, but the mind was restless.[38]

The body is corporeally challenged, its active engagement with the world interrupted. But the forced passivity of the interruption is filled with ferment. The "restlessness" of the body is not "action," since it produces no outward effect and disengages no possibility. It is a kind of activity prior to action. It is like the unextended, incipient expression of the unsewn suspensions, only even more incipient, not even an unheard echo, only a gravitational vibration still swaddled in the matter of the body.

The body is no longer a transducer but rather a *resonation* chamber, a resonating vessel that compulsively, ineffectually registers the force of gravity—as what? In states of near-sensory deprivation and, more importantly, of deprivation of expression, the mind cannot stop but neither can it continue.[39] The dividing line between sleep and waking blurs. "Imploding the dichotomy."[40] At the dividing line, their mutual limit, there is a ferment of what might be action or might be thought, a hallucinatory (or hyper-lucid?) indistinction between mind-states and body-states, between actions and echoes, sights and dreams, thoughts and adventures. Since there is no follow-through, no perceivable effect of any kind, it is impossible to tell and all the more impossible to stop. The dividing line between passivity and activity blurs. The body, passified to the limit, separated from any possibility of being active, becomes uncontrollably *activated*, inwardly animated. That inwardness is badly served by the word "mind." Nothing is conclusively distinguished. Everything impinges. Everything is felt. Between the planks, it is the force of gravity, carried to its inertial extreme, that materially registers and resonates, its effect transformatively infolded in the sensitized flesh. The body turns into a hobbled receiver tuned to the frequency of gravity. The received force undergoes the beginning of a transduction. But instead of being unfolded again, continued, extended into a perceptible, actionable, or thinkable transmission, it bubbles into every mode at once, compulsively, with no letup and no outlet. "Everything in motion, connected and contained."[41] This is the zero-degree of sensation, sensation as the zero-degree of everything that a body can do. *Suspended animation.* "Between gravity and fantasy."[42] Thought and action return together to the body, and the body compulsively restarts them and their every mix, spontaneously regenerating all that goes into making a body and its complements. Sensation is body-substance, the indeterminate matter from which the body and its objects and organs unfold: felt futurity. Resonating, animated body-substance: corporeal unfolding infolded. Not transductive enough to be called a thing, it is the stuff of things, turned in on itself: restless matter, action wanting, waiting for perception. The sensible concept of the body turned ur-idea of potential.

"Everything in motion": compound eyes are adapted "for perceiving motion almost exclusively."[43] The bug goggles really were looking forward (or inward) to this moment. Without even knowing it, they focused the project of performing the body as sensible concept away from the peripheral problem of the form of things (their objectivity or organicity) and onto their modalities of motion. It is this problem that lies at the virtual center: what constitutes a transformative movement, extraplanetary or otherwise? The suspensions make clear that it is across intervals of intensive movements that the body becomes something else. This raises the further problem: how can extensive movements turn intensive and contribute to a transformation of the very nature of the body (as opposed simply to adding permutations on its actions as the object it already is, with the organs it already has)? What subsequent extensions might then unfold? These problems are re-performed, exhaustively, in a non suspension series of experimentations with prostheses (including the Third Hand, Extended Arm, Extra Ear, Exoskeleton) and then in a further series of cyborg experimentations where the body takes its place in a cybernetic network rewiring its motional limits in radically new ways (Split Body, Fractal Flesh, Stimbod, Ping Body, Virtual Arm, Virtual

Body, Parasite, Movatar).[44] All of Stelarc's performances can be seen as operations which, to use Deleuze and Guattari's most arthropod formula, "look only at the movements."[45] Eyes sewn shut (or goggled open).

At virtual center, with the sewn body, ur-idea of potential, instrumental reason has returned to activated matter, the transformative stuff of things, sweeping everything associated with intelligence back with it. The direction of perception has been reversed,[46] and the reversion pushed to the limit where the inverse movement, into extension, is suspended. But, if you unsew the still suspended body-substance, hook it up again, and amplify it, you get the beginnings of visible and sonic extension. The matter of the body starts to unfold again, to re-extend, to feed forward, still shy, however, of utility and need. Lower the ropes, stand it up, attach a robotic arm to it, and then you can perhaps just begin to imagine a use. The body starts to reorganize in response to the unaccustomed connection. Its matter just starts to resystematize. Its analysis-in-action just barely starts to possibilize. You can feel utility just over the horizon. But it won't arrive until the world can accommodate its budding usefulness in more than a presentiment. When a way is invented to attach the robotic arm to a computer and remotely control it—now then there are possibilities. It really could be used in hostile off-world environments, for equipment repair or mining. It could fulfill so many wondrous functions. Why, it would be a necessity in any extraterrestrial extension of the body's sphere of movement.

As much as to say: the obsolescence of the body that Stelarc waxes long on must be *produced.*

Outer space? Who needs it? The body is perfectly suited to its current terrestrial habitat. If anything, it is too well adapted. The revolutionary success of the human species is its own greatest threat. There are, however, existing solution-cases to the problems of overpopulation and environmental degradation. An equitable, sustainable, postcapitalist economy for one. There is no reason why the current human body-object could not find a niche in that possible future. The terrestrial body will be obsolete from the moment a certain subpopulation feels *compelled* to launch itself into an impossible, unthinkable future of space colonization. To say that the obsolescence of the body is produced is to say that it is compelled. To say that it is compelled is to say that it is "driven by *desire*" rather than by need or utility.[47]

But, in less millennial terms, isn't each little change on earth an adjustment of the functioning of the human body and its system of objects and combinatoric of possibilities? And doesn't every adjustment imply on some level an interruption of the old functioning to make an opening for the new? Isn't change always inexorably under way? Then, in a very real sense the body is always-already obsolete, has been obsolete an infinite number of times and will be obsolete countless more—as many times as there are adaptations and inventions. *The body's obsolescence is the condition of change. Its vitality is in obsolescence.* We are all astronauts. We are all moonwalkers without organs, taking small perceptual steps into the future on virtual legs (six of them, if my goggles are on right). The body without organs that Stelarc sews himself into is not so singular after all. Or rather, it is so singular, but the singular accompanies and conditions any and every particular, every action, every adjustment, and every extension of these particularities into the general. The body without organs—the reversion of thought and perception-action into pure sensation—is a constant companion of the organism, its future-double.

Operative Reason

Stelarc's art produces the hung body. Hung things have entered science and lore under the aegis of chaos theory. The focus of chaos theory are events called "bifurcation points" or "singular points." A singular point occurs when a system enters a peculiar state of indecision, where what its next state will be turns entirely unpredictable. The unfolding of the system's line of actions interrupts itself. The system momentarily suspends itself. It has not become inactive. Rather, it is in ferment. It has gone "critical." This "chaotic" interlude is not the simple absence of order. It is in fact a superordered state: it is conceived as the literal co-presence of all of the possible paths the system may take, their physical inclusion in one another. Criticality occurs when what are normally mutually exclusive alternatives pack into the materiality of the system. The system is no longer acting and outwardly reacting according to physical laws unfolding in linear fashion. It is churning over, in its system-substance, its own possible states. It has folded in on itself, becoming materially *self-referential*—animated not by external relations of cause-effect, but by an intensive interrelating of versions of itself. The system is a knot of mutually implicated alternative transformations of itself, in material resonance.[48] Which transformation actually occurs, what the next outward connection will be, cannot be predicted by extrapolating from physical laws. The suspended system is in too heightened a state of transformability. It is *hypermutable*. Hyperconnectible—by virtue of having functionally disconnected itself ("Anesthetized Body"). The system hesitates, works through the problem of its critical self-referentiality, and "chooses" an unfolding.

When scientists use words like "choice" they are of course not implying that the system reflects and uses instrumental reason to choose from an array of possibilities. But it is no exaggeration to call the system's intensive animation thought, defined once again as "the reality of an excess over the actual." The self-referentiality of the critical system is indeed that. The possible futures are present, but only in effect—incipient effect (resonance and interference, vibration and turbulence, unfoldable into an order). Possibility has, *in effect*, materialized. The matter of the system has entered a state where it does not disengage a possibility, but instead absorbs it into its animated matter. Materially present possibility, once again, is *potential*. The system's critical condition, of course, is as actual as any other state. But the self-referentiality, or infoldedness, of its criticality is not. What the self-absorbed critical system infolds is present only in potential, which doubles and animates the actual conjunction without being reducible to it.

Call a form of thought that is materially self-referential as opposed to reflective; that absorbs possibility without extensively thinking it out, or extrapolating from where it is; that embodies a superorder of superposition without disengaging an order of substitution; that infolds without extending; that does not imply a distance between successive states of a system, mediated by an intervening action, but rather their immediate proximity to each other, their inclusion in one another; that chooses according to principles unsubordinated to the established regularities of cause-effect; that poses an unpredictable futurity rather than anticipating outcomes—call that kind of thought *operative reason*, as opposed to instrumental reason. Not a purposive analysis-in-action: a hesitant self-definition in suspension. Not an extending out of matter into thought; not a doubling of perception by thought: a folding of thought into matter as such. Instrumental reason makes thoughtfully explicit what is materially implied by the criticality of operative reason. It is its unfolding or extension. Even as it doubles perception, it is already arraying futurities in extrinsic relation to each other: as mutually exclusive possibilities standing outside and against each other in principle. Possibility is extended potential—a prosthesis of potential. It is an out-worn double of the double that is potential, the thought-shadow it retrospectively projects. It pales in comparison with the felt intensity of the critical.

Now the critical point may be an interregnum between two different serial orders, two different systemic organizations with their characteristic paths of actions and reactions. Or, it may constitute a threshold between disorder and order, an entropically disordered past and a future of systemic organization. The most celebrated example of the latter case is the Bénard instability, which occurs when turbulent patterns of diffusion in a heated liquid spontaneously order into convection cells. The ordering is not predictable in terms of heat diffusion alone. In fact, according to the theory of heat diffusion it is so improbable that, in principle, it must be considered practically impossible.[49] But it effectively happens. Theorists of such "dissipative structures" explain that the self-organizing of liquid into a convection system is triggered because the instability of situation suddenly makes the liquid "sensitive" to gravity.[50] Gravity suddenly registers and resonates. The "sensing" of a force that up to that point was not pertinent to the system's transformation and had been "ignored" triggers the self-ordering. Gravity, normally a potent force of entropy, induces a locally negentropic effect: an emergence of order from disorder. Sensed, gravity has triggered or *induced* negentropy. Gravity has appeared as a negentropic inducer of hypermutability and its unfolding. Given the turbulence of the situation, the particularities of the convection system induced by the sensation of gravity are not predictable—even when or if the ordering will occur is not certain. However many times the experimenter succeeds in achieving the effect, it is always a surprise. Induction is the experimental production of the practically impossible. The "impossible" is practiced when a countereffect is produced to the normal unfolding of the natural laws in play—achieved not by contravening them, but by combining them in such a way as to create an ineradicable margin of objective indeterminacy from which a new order spontaneously arises.

This suggests a definition of operative reason as implemented by humans (in other words, as mixed with purposive analysis-in-action in an extended situation). Operative reason is the experimental crafting of negentropic induction to produce the practically impossible. It is *prag-*

matic rather than analytic. It doesn't master a situation with exhaustive knowledge of alternative outcomes. It "tweaks" it. Rather than probing the situation to bring it under maximum control, it prods it, recognizing it to be finally indomitable and respecting its autonomy. Operative reason is concerned with effects—specifically countereffects—more than causes. It deploys local interventions in an attempt to induce a qualitative global transformation: small causes with disproportionate effect, excess-effect, a little tweak for a big return. Operative reason is inseparable from a process of trial and error, with occasional shots in the dark, guided in every case by a pragmatic sense of the situation's *responsivity* (as opposed to its manipulability). Like Stelarc's art and, in spite of (or perhaps because of), its thoroughly pragmatic exercise, it is closer to *intuition*[51] than to reflective thought (hence the serviceable but inaccurate evocation of "poetry" earlier in this essay). Following another suggestion of Stelarc's, his art is more akin to *alchemy,* the qualitative science of impossible transformations, than to high chemistry or physics, quantitative sciences of elemental causes. In a more recent vocabulary, Stelarc's project is to practice art as a "minor" science.[52]

As part of that project, Stelarc's suspensions return intelligence to the degree-zero of sensation. There, thought rejoins action, the body rejoins matter, and the animate rejoins the inanimate. These no sooner rejoin than re-unfold, divergently re-extend, to enter into extrinsic and often mutually exclusive relations with one another (in keeping with and revising the combinatoric of their possibility). Suspension is the counter-gravity ground zero of differential emergence. Differential emergence from matter: the definition of *evolution.* What else would the ur-idea be? Stelarcian suspensions are a contrived induction of the conditions of evolution—that most global of qualitative transformations—an artful rehearsing of its repetition. Stelarc's project is to tweak the human body-object into a sensitivity to new forces, or neglected aspects of familiar forces, in order to induce it into a state of hypermutability which, if inventively desired and operatively extended, might bring the big result.

Multiplex

Curiously, Stelarc bristles at any suggestion that his own project has evolved. He repeatedly points out that he was already working on the idea of the suspensions at the same time he was designing the bug goggles,[53] and that the first suspensions were contemporaneous with the development of the robotic "Third Hand" that was to become the hallmark of his cyborg experiments.[54]

The nonlinear leaps between series overlapped. Their unanticipated unfoldings, the "periods" of Stelarc's art practice, are co-present dimensions: *phases* in Gilbert Simondon's sense of the term.[55] Each infolded in every other as a potential transformative extension of it. What was said of the series of suspensions applies to the larger series of his work: each event re-poses the same problem, differently. The problem is evolution. No final solution is offered to it. No particular utopic future for humankind is elaborated. No clear possibilities disengage, from which the artist would exhort his audience to choose. Instead, the same problem, the same critical condition, is replayed in multiplying variation. The same potential is rejoined, each time to different and unforeseen effect. Possibility is analytically thought-out into a combinatoric, to predictable effect. Potential is pragmatically, impossibly re-infolded in continual experimental variation. Possibility is general by nature: analyzable into a set of solution-cases disengaged from more than one particular conjunction. Potential is singular: a multiple in- and unfolding into each other of divergent futurities, only the *divergence* of which is reproducible. The particular nature of each divergent conjunction in the series is precisely what is problematic. Multiple in- and unfolding: singularity is *multiplex*. The multiplex divergence of the singular is not to be confused with the *disjunctive* simplicity at the basis of the system of possibility. The multiplex is in mutual inclusion. Possibility develops disjunctively, toward the extension of a next actual step. Multiplex potential envelops, around an intensely suspended (virtual) center.

If Stelarc's work has to do with desire, it is not desire for something in particular: no utopia. In more ways than one, it is desire without an object. It is desire as a process, purely operative rather than object-oriented: the process of reason rejoining desire.

What are the phases of Stelarc's project?

I. OPERATION: *suspension/disconnection.*
MEDIUM: *the sensible concept as sensation.*
MODE: *induction.*

This is the state in which all of the dimensions are most intensely infolded in one another. It is a degree-zero of the corporeal, in the same sense that the vacuum is the degree-zero of matter itself. The vacuum, physicists inform us, is not an absence, but an overpresence. The vacuum is the physical copresence of all possible particles, shooting into and out of existence, folding into and out of each other too fast to be instrumentally perceived with any predictive accuracy, resonating with each other in real excess over the actual. The vacuum is the operative ur-idea of material existence. It is the state of indistinction of matter with what is normally mutually exclusive of it: the abstractness of the void. Just as the degree-zero of the corporeal is the state of its indistinction with thought. The two zero-degrees are in fact facets of the same multiplex excess-over. Stelarcian sensation, or suspended animation, is the human body-object in a corporeal vacuum state. It is the operative ur-idea of human corporeal existence. In Stelarc's suspended body, humanity-particles speed in and out of existence faster than can be perceived. Ideas, dreams, pains, yearnings, visions, needs, objectnesses and organlets, intelligences and instrumentalities, begin, abort, and transform into each other. The vivid sensing by the flesh of a force previously taken for granted (gravity) induces a state of hypermutability, a hyperconnectibility that is blocked as soon as it is triggered. In sewn suspension, the limit-state of sensation, a state of intense activation and readiness is induced, but all outlet is blocked. The felt trigger-force to which the body-matter has been sensitized cannot transduce into anything in particular. The sensation is all particulars, singularly. Everything a body can do, everything a body can become: the condition of evolution. Disconnected. There is a suspension-variation in which sensation is doubled by a displaced action, as if toying with the idea of its perceptual reconnection and extension. That is the pulley suspension, where one hesitant, still countergravitational, outlet is allowed. The countergravitational function of locomotion is displaced from the legs to the arms, ensuring that the force of gravity is still uncommonly felt. The body is split, one side extending hesitantly into organic perception-action, the other side still steeped in the matter of sensation.

2. OPERATION: *suspension/connection.*
   MEDIUM: *the sensible concept as expression.*
   MODE: *transduction.*

This is when the forces absorbed by the sensitized body just start to unfold again, to extend again beyond the skin (the baseline objective extent of human body-matter, the extensive envelope of human intensity at its default setting). This dimension overlaps with the first in the suspension events. The skin itself becomes a visible expression of the trigger-force ("gravitational landscape"), which also manifests as a sound space. The resonation echoes. The extensive envelope of the intensive is reextended as far as the walls. But it goes no further because there is still no audience to walk away with the countergravitational event. Gravity has effectively transduced. It has been transformatively relayed into other forces, visibility and sound. But the relay is walled in, contained. Connection is reestablished only to be closed. The body begins to express in extension the force it was induced into sensing intensely, but the expression takes place in a communicational vacuum. The performances focusing most directly on the sensible concept as expression are the events for the "Amplified Body." "Amplified body processes include brainwaves (EEG), muscles (EMG), pulse (plethysmogram) and bloodflow (doppler flow meter). Other transducers and sensors monitor limb motion and indicate body posture. The body performs in a structured and interactive lighting installation which flickers and flares in response to the electrical discharges of the body. . . . Light is treated not as an external illumination of the body but as a manifestation of the body's rhythms."[56] Also expressive are "Hollow Body" events, in which the interior of the stomach, colon, and lungs is filmed with a miniature video camera.[57] The probes disable the default envelope of intensity by following the infolding of the skin into the body through the orifices. The extension into visibility of the body's inside reveals its sensitive-intensive, palpitating interiority to be an infolded—and unfoldable—exteriority that is as susceptible to transductive connection as any sampling of body substance. The body is hollow. There is nothing inside. There is no inside as such for anything to be in, interiority being only a particular relationship of the exterior to itself (infolding). This highlights the nonactuality of sensation. Sensation, the substance of the body, is not the presence of the flesh in its envelope, but the presence in the flesh of an outside force of futurity (in this case, a portent of the asymmetrical symbiosis of the physiological and the technological as it extends to new frontiers).

3. OPERATION: *reconnection.*
   MEDIUM: *the sensible concept as extension.*
   MODE: *possibilization.*

The body is no longer suspended. The door opens. The audience is let in. There are signs that the transductive expression wants to follow through into an actual invention, a transformative unfolding of potential into new need and utility. This phase corresponds to the prosthetic projects, like the bug goggles, the Third Hand, and the more recent Exoskeleton.[58] The body's potential is reconnected to objects that promise to be useful but in fact are not (or not yet). Possibility is just beginning to array itself before the body. The notion of prosthesis, once again, can be misleading. If it is construed as an object attachment to an organism, then the body is being treated as something already defined, as operating within a preestablished realm of possibility. In that case, its extension is limited to its prior definition: more of the same. If the extension is taken beyond the earth's orbit, then it is not a question of evolution but of *colonization:* the neoimperialism of space as the last human "frontier." But if it is remembered that the body-organism and its objects (and even matter) are mutual prostheses, then what is being extended is that *reciprocal action.* The extension, whether off-world or not, is no longer a colonization but a symbiosis. The body is opening itself to qualitative change, a modification of its very definition, by reopening its *relation* to things.

4. OPERATION: *relay.*
   MEDIUM: *the sensible concept as contagion.*
   MODE: *virtual transmission.*

So the body is no longer suspended. The door has been opened. The audience is let in, and the transduction just starts to follow through. But to what effect? Certainly not yet the desired, disproportionate effect. The audience of a Stelarc performance has not been launched off-world. But, even so, things can get spacey. The audience may be induced into a state of stupor. The performance "Fractal Flesh. Split Body: Voltage-In/Voltage Out" is a good example.[59] There is little explanation of the nature of the event: no manifestos, no introductory remarks by the artist or a commentator, just a minimal paper handout (containing a brief explanation of the performance's computer system) that doesn't seem to reach most of those present. In any event, it is too dark to read. The intent is evidently not to communicate in the sense of imparting information or interpretation. The event is basically unframed verbally, creating an air of uncertainty that quickly turns to foreboding as a nearly naked man walks silently onto the stage and is helped into a cyborgian contraption. His body is peppered with electrodes connected to the computer by wires. On his right arm is attached a robotic double, the Third Hand. An assistant starts the computer program, and the left side of the body moves. That movement is closely followed by a gestural echo from the robotic arm as it whirs in a slightly delayed response to the movements of the left flesh-arm and leg. The body goes through a dissociated dance accompanied by even stranger sound effects, verging on music but not quite. As the performance proceeds, the pace of the movements increases, and with it the rhythm of the "music." By the end, the flesh onstage is visibly exhausted, seeming to have endured a slowly intensifying pain throughout. Those in the audience who have managed to read the handout will know that the robotic arm wasn't responding directly to the left-side movements. There was a disconnect, a "splitting." The computer was plugged by electrode into the left flesh-arm and leg. The computer operator could produce a set of left side gestures in any order by pressing icons on a touch screen. A series of touch-screened gestures could be replayed continuously by activating a loop function, adding computer-generated gestural feedback. An improvise function allowed random gestures to be superimposed. Electricity transduced into organic movement. The robotic arm, however, was not remotely controlled. It was wired to right-side stomach and leg muscles, controlled voluntarily in symphony with the involuntary left-side movements (that is, as voluntarily as a body can act when most of it is given over to continuous input of remotely controlled gesture-inducing energies). Organic movement was transduced back into electricity, before reemerging again as organic movement at a new body site. This relocational transductive relay between muscle power and electricity occurred across the split between the computer's programmed gestural sequencing and the robotic arm accompaniment. What filled the interval was voluntary action. The human will was not all-directing from outside. It was doubled: it was at the terminal, partially controlling from the edge of the relay, and it was *in* the relay, folded into the split between the left and right sides of the body across which the transduction passed, controlling even more partially, obliged to respond and choreograph. The human was relegated to a position of adjacency to the relay while *at the same time* it was integrated into its very heart. There, in the split, the human will was in a kind of microsuspension, contributing to a rhythmic transduction of electromagnetic into organic forces and organic into electromagnetic: a beat at the heart of an expanded body integrating flesh, metal, and silicon in mutually prosthetic functioning, for relocation and relay.

There was no explanation of the sounds, but the parallels between its rhythm and the pace and magnitude of the gestures suggested another bodily relay. In fact, the music was generated on the basis of electrical impulses picked up from the brain, the movement of the muscles and, as in the suspensions, the flow of blood through the body. The audience, whether or not it understands the details of the plug-ins and relays, is confronted with a compelling spectacle of the body made into a literal transducer relaying between artificial and natural intelligence, human will and programmed motion, organic and mechanical movement, and electricomagnetic force and organo-mechanical force. Beautifully ghastly sound-expressions are extracted from the matter of the body. The wired body, pained, exhausted, austere, is opened to inhuman forces vibrating through its flesh. In the strangeness of its dissociated dance, so devoid of necessary function, the voluntary is relegated to local intervention, in the split. The discomfort is palpable. The onstage body's vulnerability, its constitutive openness and integratability has been communicated to the audience. Nervousness has replaced the initial uncertainty. No one speaks for awhile. Suspended and restless. When conversation resumes, a variety of responses are heard, ranging from outrage to excitement to bemusement to awe.

What has been communicated is not information or interpretation, not verbalized ideas. What has been transmitted is sensation itself, the body as sensible concept. The operation on the audience consists in inducing in them a momentary state of unhooked suspended animation: of stupor. The onstage body has effectively transduced and relayed the force of electricity, but the audience is out of the electronic loop. Sensation is repeated as an excess-effect of the reconnection of the once-suspended body. It is also doubled: once on stage in the openness and pathos of the artist's body, again in the stupor of the audience. *Stupor* is received sensation. Sensation is spun off, centrifugally, landing and reimplanting itself in the audience. Rather than reconnecting, the audience-bodies are only-feeling, in some small way entering a hypermutable state. After a moment, the spectators collect themselves and their thoughts and, as they walk away with the effects of the sensation, translate that sensation into a divergence of emotionally-charged verbal ideas. Is their verbalized reaction the same as they would have preferred before having seen the performance but in response to a description of it? Has something extraverbal happened, which has then transformatively unfolded (transduced) into phonemes? Has something changed? Will there be a difference, even a slight divergence, in the way some of the spectators—newly sensitized to the electromagnetic forces and the beating of the integrated will—live their corporeal connectibility?

The artist has tweaked. He has no mastery over the situation, no effective control over which ideas the spectators verbalize, or over how or if they subsequently connect. And he seems entirely unbothered by that fact, even pleased at the range and unpredictability of the responses. His project is induction and transduction. Meaning is incidental. What, after all, would be the point of performing, rather than reciting or writing, if meaning, the sensible concept out-thought, were the target medium of the concepts in play? "Information is the prosthesis that props up the obsolete body."[60] Meaning, whether informative, interpretive, or symbolic, props up the old body—the will-controlled body-object—over the abyss of its obsolescence. Meaning adheres the body-object and its voluntary human control to the immediate past rather than splitting it with futurity.

If the artist's project is induction and transduction, subsequent connection is the *audience's* project. Stelarc's art limits itself to being a science of indeterminate transmission: *virtual transmission*. Not meaning, not information, not interpretation, not symbolism is transmitted: only sensation, the germ of that which may eventually unfold as new possibility. What is transmitted is potential *inventiveness*. Rather than providing answers, the performance re-poses the problem of the body's reconnectibility toward change. What in particular is transmitted is by design beyond the artist's contentedly limited powers. He does, however, have a general direction in mind-body: outer space. But his transmissions will launch in that direction only if his desire is doubled many times over—only if the countergravitational compulsion animating the ur-idea of Stelarcian sensation is met, redoubled, and impossibly extended in that particular direction. Stelarc is prodding us. You can't blame a body for trying.

He is most powerfully prodding when the phases of his project combine. "Fractal Flesh" combines expressive and prosthetic elements in a new relay apparatus. This superimposition of phases is what Simondon calls a *dephasing*. In dephasing, the body, along with its objects, dissolves into a field of mutual transformation where what in extension are separate phases enter into direct contact. That field is defined less by the already established structure of the objects and organs involved than by the potentializing relay that brings them into dynamic continuity across the intervals that normally separate them, making them structurally distinct (the "splits"). The field is defined by the qualitatively transformative movements of energy *between* structural segmentations (computer/human, left side of body/right side of body, organic arm/Third Hand, control/response, and so forth). What the overall transformation is toward, aside from the question of what particular inventions, needs, and utilities might eventually follow from it, is the integration of the human body and will into an expanding *network* to such an extent that the very definition of the body (and the human) might change.

It is important to note that this kind of performance setup stages sensation collectively. After all, human bodies never come in ones. A single body evolving is an absurdity. The individual, isolated body of the suspensions was a default position of sensation, just as the skin is the default container of human intensity. And, just as the body has already extended beyond the skin into a mutual prosthesis with matter, from its first perception, so, too, is the individual body always-already plugged into a collectivity. "There is no focus on the individual. . . . [W]ords like 'I' are just a convenient shorthand for a complex interplay of social entities and situations."[61] The isolation of the suspension events was a contrivance designed to return the body to its sensation in order for it to reextend into the always-already collective on a new footing. The conditions of sensation, like those of evolution, are fundamentally collective. Simondon insists on this: the transformative field of bodily potential is "preindividual" (or better, "*transindividual*").[62] Sensation, even as applied to an artificially isolated individual, is induced by collective stagings (the artist is always assisted) and, as a connective compulsion, always tends toward transductive contagion. To return to the point where thought rejoins the body, and the human rejoins matter, is to return to the point of indistinction between the individual and the collective—which is also the point of their emergent redivergence.

The Stelarcian project truly begins to unfold when the audience is let back in. The big result it tweakingly pursues involves a reinvention of the individual in its relation to the collective. In this day and age, that involves a new kind of transductive connection between individuals, taken at least by twos, implemented through (collectively developed and deployed) technologies of communicative transmission. In other words, Stelarc's project is by nature cyberspatially oriented and was so prospectively, before the fact. The bug goggles were distant forerunners of the virtual reality helmet.

5. OPERATION: *interconnection.*
   MEDIUM: *the sensible concept as evolution.*
   MODE: *networking.*

A different dimension is reached when the audience is reinvited to participate in the performance, as it was with the bug goggles and in other early events. A member of the audience might be invited to co-control the "split body" by punching a sequence of gestures into the computer, or she might even be hooked to the electrodes and share the sensation directly. But the network dimension comes into its own with the Internet events of the late 1990s and early 2000s ("Ping Body," "Parasite," "Movatar"). The stage was set for these in "Telepolis" (1995), a re-posing of "Fractal Flesh." The idea was to hook up the computer controlling the split body's electrodes to the Internet. In practice, the fledgling World Wide Web was still too slow, so a dedicated network of modem-linked computers was substituted.[63] The basic elements were now in place. The body and the Third Arm were in Luxembourg. Other bodies in Paris, Helsinki, and Amsterdam gathered at the specially networked terminals to remotely control the body's gestures. The effects of their input were made visible to them through a video feed. The body in Luxembourg could see the faces of its part-controllers on its own screen. A visual feedback loop was thus added to the electro magnetic/organo-mechanical loop. "Look only at the movements" was now "also look at the movements." For the audience was in the loop. It had become part of the performance. The distance between the performer's and the spectator's actions is remotely abolished to the extent that it is no longer clear which is which. Sensation has unfolded into a transindividual feedback loop of action-reaction, stimulus-response. "Electronic space becomes a medium of action rather than information."[64] Action-perception is welcomed back to accompany the staging and contagion of sensation.

Since the situation is still entirely needless and useless, since it is outside established, regularized, tried-and-true action-perception circuits, this is not a full-fledged return to analysis-in-action. The performance uses instrumental reason to set up an experimental exercise in operative reason. In this mix with instrumentality, operative reason dominates. The open action-perception circuits are tried, but they are in no sense "true." For they still precede their logical possibility. (This is perhaps the meaning of Stelarc's formula "high-fidelity illusion.") The performance potentializes a material interconnection of bodies. What, if anything, will unfold from it in the way of instrumentally reasonable uses and needs is unforeseeable, a sheer futurity that will only come to pass after an indefinite series of subsequent re-posings of the same problem in varying conjunctions. What new possibilities will this serially expanding transductive activation of electronic space produce for the human collectivity? Networked, Stelarcian potential finally just begins to *repossibilize,* in an evolutionary direction.

The form in which the emergent possibilities begin to express themselves is futurist speculation. In accompanying written material posted on Stelarc's website, speculation is encouraged on the eventual uses of remote actuation. Space travel, of course, figures large. Possible uses of other Stelarcian setups are also brought into the picture. The "Hollow Body," for example, returns in a possible scenario of nanotechnological symbiosis as technology is implanted in the innermost folds of the body. Could this, combined with prostheses applied to the external envelope of the body, extend not only the spatial parameters of life beyond the earth's gravitational field but also its time parameters beyond their normal limits, making free-floating cyborg immortality a possibility as human organs are supplemented or supplanted by technological objects?[65] The fantastic solution-cases for the problems posed by Stelarcian sensation, as it just reconnects to action-perception, begin to order themselves into a future combinatoric. But these are still impossible possibilities, uses predicated on as-yet undeveloped technology. Disengaged, only-thought utilities rise like a shadowy vapor directly from the ferment of potential, skipping over the necessary intervening steps through fully fledged, instrumental-developmental action-perception. Impossible possibilities are prospective shadows. This is not a utopian moment because it does not matter, to the artist or anyone else, if anyone really takes them seriously—yet.

What is important is not the fantastic solution-cases themselves, but the new and compelling problem their speculation poses. Should these disengaged possibilities engage, should the things, objects, organs, thoughts, and anticipations they shadow come to stand by them, together with new operative and instrumental interconnections—will we still be human? Can humanity tweak itself into a new existence? The only way anyone will ever know is if the human collectivity applies itself to the development of the intervening technologies, which are then set up to sensitize and potentialize humanity-particles toward launching themselves instrumentally into their own futurity. By then, anyone (or anything) in a position to know will no longer be human. Effective knowledge of these disengaged solution-cases is humanly impossible, which is why they are necessarily the stuff of futurist speculation. In any case, the knowledge will be attained by someone or something only if there is a sufficiently shared desire among humans for the launch, a strong enough collective compulsion. It won't happen through a triumph of the will, or through an application of knowledge of outcomes, or even through natural selection. The will is unlikely to will itself to be relegated to adjacency and (insult added to injury) fully integrated into the transformative machinic relay. Reflective knowledge of evolution—all reflective knowledge for that matter—is by nature retrospective. Natural selection, for its part, is only evolution's unfolding. No, if it happens it will only be through *desire*. Desire is the condition of evolution.

When Stelarcian sensation rebegins to unfold, it is in a new countergravitational landscape in which the relations between the possible and the impossible, desire and will-directed instrumental reason, instrumental reason and reflective analysis, and instrumental reason and operative reason, have been reconfigured in an evolution-ready manner.

It needs to be emphasized that the activation of information operates through the sensitization of the human body-matter to electromagnetic *force*. More than a container of information, *cyber-"space" is a dynamic field of transduction*. Computer-assisted transductive interconnection is literally and materially a potentialization. The informational content of that connection, the meaning of the words and images transmitted, is only important as a trigger or catalyst. Information is but a local bit-player in the project of inducing a global transformation-effect whose reason is of another order. Immediately after "Telepolis" Stelarc began plans for an Internet project: "Ping Body" (1996). The momentum is rolling. A new series is underway, generating variations on itself.

This time, the body would be plugged into the network in such a way that its gestures would be controlled by the quantity of information traveling the wires:

> Instead of people from other places activating the artist, Internet data moves the body. By pinging over forty global sites live during the performance and measuring the reverberating signals, it was possible to map these to the body's muscles with the muscle stimulation system. The body does a data dance; it becomes a barometer of Internet activity. If we ping China, the signal comes back in only hundreds of milliseconds (therefore not much Internet activity there), whereas if we ping the USA, it comes back in thousands of milliseconds. The arms and legs also have sensors that produce sounds indicative of the position and velocity of the fingers and limbs. Internet activity composes and choreographs the performance.[66]

The body plugs into the *mass* of information. As a mass, information is not itself. Its content is neutralized. Information impinges directly on the body as a force, which is why voluntary control is designed out of this loop. In this variation, the emphasis is on making the *force of information* visible. It visibly expresses the evolution-readiness of the networked body. Because it makes the network an expressive medium (superimposing phase 2 on phase 5), the body is once again suspended (superimposing phase 1). It is alone under the mass of information, like the sewn body once was under the weight of rock. It feels the future force of information. The involuntary movements induced are not relayed into incipient action-perception or fed back to other bodies, as was the case in "Telepolis." The body becomes a resonating vessel for the force of information to which it is now singularly sensitized. This device encompasses a restaging of the degree-zero of sensation, tuned to the cybernetic potential of the body. It composes a virtual center for the Internet series of events.

As the transformed return of sensation illustrates once again, the dimensions of the Stelarcian multiplex are not periods in the artist's work that add up to an evolution. They are a continually varying, operative foldings into and out of each other. "Ping Body" will be followed by "Parasite" (1997), and "Parasite" by "Movatar" (2000), each enacting different phase combinations (that is to say, partial, selective dephasings potentializing qualitatively different unfoldings).[67] All of the phases and events are present, potentially and differentially, in each other. There is, however, a logical order of precedence indicated by the numbering of the phases. There is no necessity for the chronological order to follow this logical order. That it did in Stelarc's case is an accident of history, and this mainly occurred because the technological prerequisites for the network (incipient reextension phase) were simply absent in pre-cyberian 1970. But the desire was there, compulsively beginning to work itself out, waiting for objects and organs to fall into place.

It should be kept in mind that Stelarc's project has to do with performing the *conditions* of evolution. The conditions of evolution are not yet evolution. That is why Stelarc is right to resist speaking of an evolution of his project. The project cannot accurately be said to evolve, only to serially re-pose, at its farthest point just beginning to unfold. To perform the conditions of evolution is to reproblematize them. For in an immortalized cyborg future-present, natural selection would no longer be the operative principle of evolutionary unfolding. The old way of generating evolutionary solution-cases will no longer hold.

What Stelarc is projecting is a *postevolutionary* evolution of the human. Paradoxically, postevolution will only be achieved by an *actualization of the conditions of evolution,* such that what comes "first"—sensation as world-corporeal potential—also comes last, and what is infolded unfolds as such: nonobjective and asubjective, not-yet-thought and incipient action, activated and suspended, individual and collective, all rolled up together. All in one process: everything a human body can do or become (except to remain all or too human). The alchemical trick is to induce a temporal feedback loop, making the moments or dimensions of the project operatively self-referential even as it unfolds: material, qualitative autotransformation, at once local and global (multiplex), in serial succession and everywhere at a virtual center. An on-rolling infolding for an unfolding of change: the project, evolutionary in desire, is *involutionary* in its actual operation. That is why it is so thoroughly problematic.

The Evolutionary Alchemy of Reason 125

Stelarc's human body-object: involutionarily "stretched between what it never was and what it can never hope to be."[68] Suspended between the prehuman and the posthuman.

"Time to vanish."[69]

Nodally Yours (The Human)

A final warning on prosthesis, since it seemed to have established itself as the master concept in a great deal of theorizing of cyberspace and the cyborg in the 1990s. As commonly used, the term refers to the replacement of an organ with an artificial double designed to fulfill the same function. Prostheses by this definition are need and utility oriented and belong to an order of substitution. The possibilities for organic functioning precede the fabrication of the prosthesis. The actual artifact is a use-oriented image (an instrumentalized sensible concept) materializing a set of re-storable organic functions. In other words, the prosthesis is the sensible concept of a preset system of possibility. It never leaves the orbit of the organic human body-object.

The operation in play in Stelarc's project, on the other hand, has to do with *extension* rather than substitution. On the other hand: exactly. The robotic Third Hand attaches to the right flesh-arm rather than replacing it. It is a "prosthesis" in the etymological sense of the word: "to put in addition to." As an addition, it belongs to an order of superposition. The tendency of Stelarc's events is toward superposition. In the expressive events, the body is probed so that its inside is *also* an exterior. In the Internet events, the body inputs information to the computer in order to express or relay it as a force: the body places itself between information *and* force. The left side of the body receives programmed gestures fed from the machine, to which it then choreographs a circumscribed voluntary response: programmed *and* involuntary. The body relays electromagnetic movement into organic movement and back again: organism *and* machine. Computer *and* robotic arm. Infolding *and* expression. Sensation *and* incipient action-perception.

In the networked dimension, or phase 5, the serial probings, sensitizations, expressions, transductions, relays, and transmissions of the body are coaxed into copresence with each other. All of the operations are held in ready reserve as randomly accessible openings. The body as RAO *(random-*

access opening) can connect in any number of ways to itself, its objects, and other bodies. It can open, split, and reconnect at any point, inside or out. It is no longer an objective volume but an extendability. Its dimensionality has increased beyond the three of spatial presence: from the three dimensions of the voluminous it leaps to a fifth dimension of the *extensile*. This dimension is actually fractal, between dimensions. Split and extend: the basic operation used to generate fractal figures. The fractalization of the body is no metaphor. It is an operation: the posthumanizing operation.

The operation of fractalization is posthumanizing because, featured prominently among its "and's," is subject *and* object. In the Internet events, the body was acting instrumentally as a subject when it sent out meaningful information, installed remote-control terminals, and generally staged the event. But in the event, it was also on the receiving end. Information flowed back to it, not meaningfully, but felt, as a controlling force ("Ping Body"). This force of information impinged upon the body split open: the body as an operationally opened, sensitized object. The cybernetic network makes the body a subject and object simultaneously, and asymmetrically (since in its different capacities it effects different kinds of movement: voluntary and involuntary, for example). Of course, the body is always and asymmetrically both a subject and an object. But in normal human mode, it is a subject for itself and an object *for others*. Here, it is a subject and an object *for itself*—self-referentially. The one accustomed conjunction in which a human subject is also an object for itself is in reflective thought. Reflective thought aspires to self-mirroring symmetry. The networked coincidence of subject-object is neither reflective nor self-mirroring but rather operative and relaying. The "self" of this self-referentiality is of a qualitatively different kind, one that operationally includes in its being for itself other individual human body-selves as well as computers and phone lines and electromagnetism and any number of heterogeneous elements, forces, objects, organs. The body-self has been plugged into an extended network. As fractal subject-object, the body *is* the network—a *self-network*.

It was asserted earlier that the body and its objects were prostheses of *each other*, and that matter itself was prosthetic. The fractal body brings this extensile mutality to full expression. It is precisely the full expression of this aspect of the human that makes it posthuman. The self-network expresses extendability to a degree beyond the human pale. But extensile mutality is also *before* the human pale: it is a characteristic of every perceiving thing, to the extent that it is capable of change. The extension into the posthuman is thus a bringing to full expression a prehumanity *of* the human. It is the limit-expression of *what the human shares with everything it is not:* a bringing out of its *inclusion* in matter, its belonging in the same self-referential material world in which every being unfolds. The potential cyborg extensions of the human, once it has entered a hypermutably open state, are existentially unbounded. The self-network is a *worlding* of the human. The moon's the limit. Or maybe not. Having counteracted the earth's force of gravity, the posthuman body-world is in its own orbit: the *becoming-planetary* of the human.

The speculative limit is not merely the envelope of the earth's atmosphere. More than a spatial bound, the limit is a critical self-conversion point bearing on the mode of existence of the human. Modally, the limit is *self-organization*—the self-network extended to encompass all aspects of what is, by virtue of that extension, ex-human life. Thus the body never has to plug in. Wherever it goes, it is preplugged. The MIT Media Lab's dream of ubiquitous interface comes fantastically true.[70] The ex-human is now a node among nodes. Some nodes are still composed of organic body-matter, some are silicon-based, and others, like the ancestral robotic arm, are alloy. The body-node sends, receives, and transduces in concert with every other node. The network is infinitely self-connectible, thus infinitely plastic. The shape and directions it takes are not centrally decided but emerge from the complex interplay of its operations. The self-organizing network is the embodiment of operative reason expanded to fill the world. A brave new world—even if it never does get around to leaving the earth's orbit.

This is the fundamental direction in which the Stelarcian project extends intelligence: the encompassing of instrumental reason in a system of operative reason tending toward panplanetary reach. Instrumental reason is and remains highly relevant. How relevant reflective thought remains is not so certain. It is this uncertainty in particular that problematizes *agency.* The base meaning of the word "agency" in this context is the expression of intelligence in needful or useful action. Stelarc's proto–self-networking Internet events do not deny agency. Quite the contrary, they multiply it. Emergently. The extension into action has not fully unfolded. No use or need is actually fulfilled. Again, "movement" is a better term for what is happening than "action." Movement, as understood here, is in between the intense vacuum activation of sensation and extended, object-oriented action-perception. It is more forthcoming than the former, but less outgoing than latter. It is the undergoing of qualitative transformation. The Internet events catch agency in movement.

Stelarc cites four kinds of movement in operation: voluntary, involuntary, controlled, and programmed.[71] Each is in turn multiple, arising in different ways at various points in the relay system. Take "Fractal Flesh" again as an example. *Voluntary* movement figures in the setting up of the stage, the donning of the contraption, and the inputting of the computer commands, as well as in the performing body itself, as when it untangles wires, subtly changes posture to relieve fatigue, or choreographs gestures. It is most evident in the stomach-controlled movements of the Third Hand. Voluntary movement exercises reflective thought and/or analysis-in-action. *Involuntary* movement is present in the usual organic functionings of the body's autonomic nervous system, as expressed in the sound relay. It is also produced in reactions to the electrode stimulation, for example flinching in reaction to the pain or in the inability to successfully execute a willed movement due to interference of the movements induced by the electrode stimulation. The movements of the left-side arm and leg are *controlled* by the electrode stimulation. Finally, the parameters of the robotic arm's movement and the repertoire of electrode-inducible gestures are *programmed*. All of these modes of agency co-operate in the network: "already the beginnings of a symbiosis between the human and technology."[72]

Any of these movements can be modulated. For example, the computer control of arm and leg movements runs a continuum from "prompting" to full "actuation" depending on the intensity of the transmitted electromagnetic force.[73] They can also form mixes: at any level below full actuation, the body can voluntarily inflect the controlled movement by offering resistance to the stimulated movement or by following through on its momentum, extending or exaggerating it. Considered in their variations over the Internet series of events, they can in addition occupy any node in a relay system or more than one node at once. With multiple relays or feedback, the same node can exercise more than one mode of movement at the same time.

The point is that while voluntary movement is necessary, it is in no way sufficient. It takes its place in a proto–self-network whose effectivity depends on all four modes working in concert, in a combined mode of intelligent exercise that can only be characterized as operative, the most ecumenical of reasons. Of the four modes, human agency is only recognizably present in the voluntary. The hallmark of the human is spun out to a peripheral position of adjacency to the network (the computer operator) and it is integrated in the transductive relaying (the artist). The peripheralization and the integration are forms of subsumption. The integrative subsumption is the more interesting since it prefigures the destiny of the human should the network ever actually reach pan planetary scope. As integrated into the network, the human occupies a *gap* in the relay. It inhabits the "split." From the network's internal point of view, the human will is an *interrupter*. It is an irruption of transductive indeterminacy at its very heart. Whether peripheral or integrated, human agency enters the network as a local input of free variation: in other words, a variation not subordinated to the programming of the self-network. The variation is "free" in the sense that it is a given for the network, which itself expends nothing to produce it. Something for nothing: the human becomes a raw material or *natural resource* for the network. The human's two-fold "subsumption" through peripheralization and operational integration is not an obedience. If it is an exploitation, it is in the sense in which the word is used in mining and other extractive industries. Alternatively, it can be considered a *capture,* because as a raw material the human is fed into a process it isn't in a position to direct (or even digest).

Interruption of the operative principles of reason, indeterminacy, given variation: the properly human is the *unconscious* of the network. The way in which voluntary inputs are captured, transduced, and networked is a technological *symptom* of the ex-human. That symptom does not register in the network in the mode in which it is input. It is input as will, intention, meaning, but is assimilated as relay motion. The humanity of the human is symptomatically transduced from the register of reflection and meaning to that of energetic transfer. As part of the same global transformation by which the human body becomes planetary, its humanity is translated into a local force. It is only as a local force that the properly human is registered, becomes conscious (operationally present) to the worlding network. Once the speculative panplanetary self-network was up and running, all of this would even apply to the human input of computer commands or to the programming of protocols. For in a decentralized network it would only be certain program modules that would be manipulable from any given node. There would be no single point at which the network as a whole could be reprogrammed.

In the self-organizing network, the human is no longer master and no longer central. It is *subsumed*. At the limit in an integrative network there is no center or periphery, only nodes. The human is fractalized. It is dispersed across the nodes and transversed by them all in the endless complexity of relay. The human is neither "all-here" nor "all-there,"[74] neither nonexistent nor fully itself. It is part-here *and* part-there, symptomatically transduced and transformed.

It was argued earlier that the "pre-" and the "post-" coincide in the evolutionary condition. This is easy to see in the self-network. The human body-node can transduce any mode of movement at any time. Its just-past perception or exercise of agency might be the next node's about-to-be mode and vice versa. The trigger-force of electromagnetism can travel nearly instantaneously from any point in the network to any other. The past and future of any particular node have already unfolded elsewhere in the network. Not just its immediate past and future. Middling and remote pasts and futures also flicker across this web. The particular node's entire combinatoric of possibility is actually present in dispersion. Not engaged with the present—electromagnetically embodied in it. But an actual possibility is not a possibility so much as a potential. But potential is by nature infolded. These "potentials" are extended. To complicate things even more, possibilities-or-potentials of agencies that the human body-node never was nor can hope to be (for example, a computer program or a mass of information or a robotic limb) are also looming just over the next node. Possibility and potential collapse into actual conjunction. They are actualized, in mixture, in a melding of analytic thought and the forces of matter. A new mode of extended existence—*an actuality of excess over the actual*—is invented by the dispersal of agency. The dispersed co-presence of networked possibilities-potentials should not be seen as a mire of indistinction or a short-circuiting of change. It is not indistinction but an order of dispersed superposition that in fact represents a heightening of differentiation, since every node will occupy an absolutely singular conjuncture in the complex, transductive, superpositive flow. And rather than a short-circuiting of change, it is its actual embodiment: the self-organizing ebb and flow of agency-transfer makes the network a continuum of variation.

Will any of this ever happen? Should it ever happen? Doesn't this whole discussion ignore the impoverished (and most especially non-Western) bodies that will be passed over in the postevolutionary rush, consigned to abject humanity on a thoroughly trashed planet? Doesn't this beg the questions of power and inequality? These are legitimate, reflective questions to which the majority of us still-humans would probably answer "no," "no," "yes," "yes." But they are beside the problem. Not at all beside the point, but beside the problem. The problem, which Stelarc's art both expresses and exacerbates, is that the process has already begun. However far the MIT Media Lab is from achieving its dream interface, however far the Internet is from the apocalyptic possible futures speculated for it, however incompletely the new media have been implanted, however faltering is their present state of interconnection, the modal conversion of the human has sensibly begun. The Stelarcian body answers the nagging questions about it with a "yes," "yes," "not necessarily," "maybe-maybe not."

The reflective critical thinker anchors the discussion in the "no's" of will not/should not, willing a clampdown on potential in the name of justice. The experimenter in criticality starts from "yes" in the name of sensation and leaves the field wide open. The Stelarcian desire is to *affirm* the conversion, not in order to denigrate the importance of the human justice issues it incontestably raises, but rather to enable them to be re-posed and operated upon in an entirely new problematic, one that may even now be waiting for us around the next node. This experimentally open, affirmative posture can be considered a socially irresponsible approach to the problem of human evolution only if the critical thinker can answer an unhedged "yes" to this counterquestion: *If all of this doesn't happen, will there be an end to impoverishment and inequality and will the earth not be trashed?* Until that affirmation is forthcoming, there is no argument, only a clash of desires. Two desires implicating divergent modes of existence: affirmed ex-human intensity and all-too-human moralism.

5

ON THE SUPERIORITY OF THE ANALOG

The virtual, as such, is inaccessible to the senses. This does not, however, preclude figuring it, in the sense of constructing images of it. To the contrary, it requires a multiplication of images. The virtual that cannot be felt also cannot but be felt, in its effects. When expressions of its effects are multiplied, the virtual fleetingly appears. Its fleeting is in the cracks between and the surfaces around the images.

Images of the virtual make the virtual appear not in their content or form, but in fleeting, in their sequencing or sampling. The appearance of the virtual is in the twists and folds of formed content, in the movement from one sample to another. It is in the ins and outs of imaging. This applies whether the image is verbal, as in an example or parable, or whether it is visual or aural. No one kind of image, let alone any one image, can render the virtual.

Since the virtual is in the ins and outs, the only way an image can approach it alone is to twist and fold on itself, to multiply itself internally. This happens in each of the "parables" in this book. At a certain point, they knot up: infoldings and outfoldings, redoublings and reductions, punctual events falling away from themselves into self-referential encompassment, pasts projecting ahead to futures buckling back into the moment, extended intensities and intensifying extensions. The virtual can perhaps best be imaged by superposing these deformational moments of repetition rather than sampling differences in form and content. Think of each image receding into its deformation, as into a vanishing point of its own twisted versioning.[1] That vanishing into self-variety is the fleeting of the virtual—more appearingly than in the in-between and around of the single-image forms and contents, however thoroughly resequenced by cut-and-paste (combinatorics). The folding-vanishing point is the literal appearance in words—or vision or hearing—of a virtual image center.

Take the images by their virtual centers. Superpose them. You get an overimage of images of self-varying deformation: a unity of continuous separation from self. It is there that the virtual most literally, parabolically appears.

This is to say that the virtual is best approached *topologically*. Topology is the science of self-varying deformation. A topological figure is defined as the continuous transformation of one geometrical figure into another. Imagine a pliable coffee cup. Join the surfaces of the brim, enlarge the hole in the handle, and then stretch it so that all its sides are equally thick. You get a doughnut. You could then tie this doughnut into complex knots. All of the geometrical figures you can create in this way are versions of the *same* topological figure. Topological unity is, in and of itself, multiple. Of course, it is impossible actually to diagram every step in a topological transformation.[2] Practically, only selected stills can be presented. Once again, the need arises to superpose the sequencings. It is only in that superposition that the unity of the figure can be grasped as such, in one stroke. That one stroke is the virtual image center of the figure. It is virtual because you cannot effectively see it or exhaustively diagram it. It is an image because you can, for all of that, figure it, more or less vaguely, in the imagination. Imagination is the mode of thought most precisely suited to the differentiating vagueness of the virtual.[3] It alone manages to diagram without stilling. Imagination can also be called intuition: a thinking feeling. Not feeling something. Feeling thought—as such, in its movement, as process, on arrival, as yet unthought-out and unenacted, postinstrumental and preoperative. Suspended. Looped out. Imagination is felt thought, thought only-felt, felt as only thought can be: insensibly unstill. Outside any given thing, outside any given sense, outside actuality. Outside coming in. The mutual envelopment of thought and sensation, as they arrive together, pre–what they will have become, just beginning to unfold from the unfelt and unthinkable outside: of process, transformation in itself.

Whatever medium you are operating in, you miss the virtual unless you carry the images constructed in that medium to the point of topological transformation. If you fall short of the topological, you will still grasp the possible (the differences in content and form considered as organizable alternatives). You might even grasp the potential (the tension between materially superposed possibilities and the advent of the new). But never will you come close to the virtual.

Topology is a purely qualitative science. It is not empirical, if empirical investigation is meant as progressing from description to prediction. It has no predictive value.[4] Incapable of directly referencing anything other than its own variations, it is more analogical than descriptive. It is not, however, an analog *of* anything in particular. It is not an analog in the everyday sense of a variation on a model. Here, there is no model. Only infolding and unfolding: self-referential transformation. The analog is *process*, self-referenced to its own variations. It resembles nothing outside itself. A topological image center literally makes the virtual appear, in felt thought. It is more apparitional than empirical. Sensation, always on arrival a transformative feeling of the outside, a feeling of thought, is the being of the analog. It is matter in analog mode.[5] This is the analog in a sense close to the technical meaning, as a continuously variable impulse or momentum that can cross from one qualitatively different medium into another. Like electricity into sound waves. Or heat into pain. Or light waves into vision. Or vision into imagination. Or noise in the ear into music in the heart. *Or outside coming in.* Variable continuity across the qualitatively different: continuity of transformation. The analog impulse from one medium to another is what was termed in the last chapter a transduction. In sensation the thinking-feeling body is operating as a transducer. If sensation is the analog processing by body-matter of ongoing transformative forces, then foremost among them are forces of appearing as such: of coming into being, registering as becoming. The body, sensor of change, is a transducer of the virtual.[6]

Possibility, for its part, can be approached quantitatively. Probability is one of the forms the possible's quantitative expression may take. Probabilities are weightings of possibilities according to the regularity with which they might be expected to appear. Since probability approaches possibilities en masse, it approximates potential. Probability commits what René Thom calls an "imposture"[7] by expressing the potential it approximates in a way that makes it seem that by quantifying, it had made the outcome of the potential predictable, effectively converting it into the mode of possibility. It hasn't, of course. It only approaches possibility, just as it only approximates potential. The problem is that modes of inactuality are stubbornly qualitative. Quantifying conversions of them always leave a qualitative remainder. This is easily seen with probability, in the fact that it has nothing at all to say about any given conjunction. It says nothing about what will happen in any given case. It is not about particulars, let alone singularities. It targets only the general level, applying not to the event but only to an averaging of the mass of events. It concerns laws of large numbers.

Potential doesn't "apply" to the event either: it makes it. Potential was described in the last chapter as a multiplicity of possibilities materially present to one another, in resonance and interference. Their coming-together is singularly, compulsively felt, so intensely that the sensation cannot be exhausted in one go. Potential strikes like a motor force, a momentum driving a serial unfolding of events. The immanence of that forcing to each event in the series was termed a virtual center. The virtual center is like a reserve of differentiation or qualitative transformation in every event. It is the sufficient reason of the series. The virtual center never appears as such. It is insensate. It cannot be felt. It appears only in the potentials it drives and the possibilities that unfold from their driving: unfelt, it cannot but be felt in its effects. Each event in a serial unfolding is a sensible analog of that unexpressed effecting: its sensible (embodied) concept.

Both quantification and qualitative transformation, or analog series formation, involve a deactualization. Deactualizations are modes of thought, defined in the last chapter as a processual excess over the actual. They are not deactualizations in the sense that they erase or replace the actual. Rather, they double and redouble it: augment it. Quantification participates in the mode of thought commonly called instrumental reason (the thinking out of possibilities). Qualification is addressed by what was characterized in the last chapter as operative reason (the tweaking of potential). When most attentive to the virtual, qualification deforms into the topo-ontological exercise of *contingent reason* (thought bending back to participate in its own emergence from sensation; imagination, or intuition in Bergson's sense).

The actual occurs at the point of intersection of the possible, the potential, and the virtual: three modes of thought.[8] The actual is the effect of their momentous meeting, mixing, and re-separation. The meeting and mixing is sensation. Sensation stretches on a continuum from the absolute immanence of virtual center to the far end of potential, where it just extends into possibility. No actuality can be fully imaged, since it emerges from, projects into, and recedes into inactuality. Bodies and objects, their forms and contents, do not account for all of it. They do not catch the momentum. To look only at bodies and objects is to miss the movement.

136

An image of the movement of the actual's appearing—its driving, dynamic excess over itself—is an image of thought.[9] An image of thought is an imaging of the imageless. In other words, it is necessarily analogic, incomplete at any and every particular conjunction, complete only in its openness: its continuing. Topology, as a modeling of continuous transformation, can be taken as an image of thought. (For more on topology and the virtual, see chapter 8 below.)

There is another deactualization process in addition to quantification and qualification: *codification.* The digital is a numerically based form of codification (zeros and ones). As such, it is a close cousin to quantification. Digitization is a numeric way of arraying alternative states so that they can be sequenced into a set of alternative routines. Step after ploddingly programmed step. Machinic habit.

"To array alternative states for sequencing into alternative routines." What better definition of the combinatoric of the possible? *The medium of the digital is possibility, not virtuality,* and not even potential. It doesn't bother approximating potential, as does probability. Digital coding per se is possibilistic to the limit.

Nothing is more destructive for the thinking and imaging of the virtual than equating it with the digital. All arts and technologies, as series of qualitative transformations (or in Deleuze and Guattari's involuted evolutionary vocabulary, "machinic phylums"),[10] envelop the virtual in one way or another. Digital technologies in fact have a remarkably weak connection to the virtual, by virtue of the enormous power of their systematization of the possible. They may yet develop a privileged connection to it, far stronger than that of any preceding phylum. But that connection has yet to be invented or, at best, is still an inkling. It is the strength of the work of Pierre Lévy (against Baudrillard) to emphasize the participation in the virtual of earlier technologies—in particular writing—and (following Deleuze) to insist on a distinction between the possible and the potential as an integral part of any thinking of the virtual.[11] The meeting, mixing, and re-separation of the virtual, the possible, and potential concern the appearance of the actual—its emergence from an imageless interrelating. The actual is an appearance in the sense that its perception (its extension into possible action) is an effect of a process that is itself imperceptible and insensate (but moves through sensation). Equating the digital with the virtual confuses the really apparitional with the artificial. It reduces it to a simulation. This forgets intensity, brackets potential, and in that same sweeping gesture bypasses the move through sensation, the actual envelopment of the virtual.

Digital technologies have a connection to the potential and the virtual *only through the analog*. Take word processing. All of the possible combinations of letters and words are enveloped in the zeros and ones of ASCII code. You could say that entire language systems are numerically enveloped in it. But what is processed inside the computer is code, not words. The words *appear* on screen, in being read. Reading is the qualitative transformation of alphabetical figures into figures of speech and thought. This is an analog process. Outside its appearance, the digital is electronic nothingness, pure systemic possibility. Its appearance from electronic limbo is one with its analog transformation. Now take digital sound: a misnomer. The sound is as analog as ever, at least on the playback end, and usually at the recording end as well (the exception being entirely synthesized music). It is only the coding of the sound that is digital. The digital is sandwiched between an analog disappearance into code at the recording and an analog appearance out of code at the listening end.

Take hypertext. All possible links in the system are programmatically prearrayed in its architecture. This has lead some critics to characterize it not as liberating but as downright totalitarian. While useful to draw attention to the politics of the possible, calling hypertext totalitarian is inaccurate. What it fails to appreciate is that the coding is not the whole story: that the digital always circuits into the analog. The digital, a form of inactuality, must be actualized. That is its quotient of openness. The freedom of hypertext is in the openness of its analog reception. The hypertext reader does something that the co-presence of alternative states in code cannot ever do: serially experience effects, accumulate them in an unprogrammed way, in a way that intensifies, creating resonances and interference patterns moving through the successive, linked appearances. For the hypertext surfer, the link just departed from overlaps with the next. They doppler together. They are not extensively arrayed, beside and outside each other, as alternatives. Neither are they enveloped in each other as coded possibilities. They are co-present in a very different mode.

The analog process of reading translates ASCII code into figures of speech enveloping figures of thought, taken in its restrictive sense of conscious reflection. There is no thought that is not accompanied by a physical sensation of effort or agitation (if only a knitting of the brows, a

138

pursing of the lips, or a quickening of heartbeat).[12] This sensation, which may be muscular (proprioceptive), tactile, or visceral is backgrounded. This doesn't mean it disappears into the background. It means that it appears as the background against which the conscious thought stands out: its felt environment. The accompanying sensation encompasses the thought that detaches itself from it. Reading, however cerebral it may be, does not entirely think out sensation. It is not purified of it. A knitting of the brows or pursing of the lips is a self-referential action. Its sensation is a turning in on itself of the body's activity, so that the action is not extended toward an object but knots at its point of emergence: rises and subsides into its own incipiency, in the same movement. The acts of attention performed during reading are forms of incipient action. It was asserted in the last chapter that action and perception are reciprocals of each other. If as Bergson argued a perception is an incipient action, then reciprocally an action is an incipient perception. Enfolded in the muscular, tactile, and visceral sensations of attention are incipient perceptions. When we read, we do not see the individual letters and words. That is what learning to read is all about: learning to stop seeing the letters so you can see *through* them. Through the letters, we directly experience fleeting visionlike sensations, inklings of sound, faint brushes of movement. The turning in on itself of the body, its self-referential short-circuiting of outward-projected activity, gives free rein to these incipient perceptions. In the experience of reading, conscious thought, sensation, and all the modalities of perception fold into and out of each other. Attention most twisted.[13]

All of this equally pertains to inattention. Distraction, too, is accompanied by characteristic, self-referential actions: scratching, fidgeting, eyes rolling up or around in their sockets as if they were endeavoring to look back in at the brain. Every predominantly visual activity is an economy of attention and distraction, often with a pronounced tendency toward one or the other pole. Television assumes and fosters a certain inattention, as the viewing body is invited to zap channels or slip relays to other activities into the commercial slots and slow patches. Watching movies and reading books command considerably more attention, and thus tend toward the other direction. Hypertext surfing combines both modes. Link after link, we click ourselves into a lull. But suddenly something else clicks in, and our attention awakens, perhaps even with a raised eyebrow. Surfing sets up a rhythm of attention and distraction. This means that it can fold into its own process a wider range of envelopments

and reciprocities of sensation, incipient perception, and conscious reflection. This is particularly true of a structurally open hypertext environment like the World Wide Web (as opposed to closed architectures like
hypertext novels on CD-ROM or DVD or the commercial reference pack-
ages included in many computer purchases). While it is still true that
everything on the Web is preprogrammed, the notion of a dictatorship of
the link carries less weight. Search engines allow un-prearrayed linking,
and the sheer size of the Web means that it is always changing, with sites
constantly coming into and out of existence. (In 2001 it was estimated
that Web pages were being posted at a rate of eight million per day.) The
open architecture of the Web lends itself to the accumulation of analog
effects. The increase in image and sound content alongside text provides
more opportunities for resonance and interference between thought, sensation, and perception.

A crucial point is that all the sense modalities are active in even the
most apparently monosensual activity. Vision may ostensibly predomi-
nate, but it never occurs alone. Every attentive activity occurs in a synesthetic field of sensation that implicates all the sense modalities in incipient perception, and is itself implicated in self-referential action. (See
chapters 6, 7, and 8 below for more on the virtual and the interrelating of
the senses.) Each read meaning or conscious reflection that arises is en-
vironed by this synesthetic field. Since everything in the field is in incipiency and folding, it is only vaguely felt, or side-perceived, like a fringe
around formed perceptions and reflections. A determinate meaning or
clear reflection may emerge from that vagueness, but it cannot entirely
separate itself from it. (See chapter 7 below.) It remains attached to its
conditions of emergence, as by a processual umbilical cord.

When the hyperlink surfer moves from one link to the next, the conditioning synesthetic fringe of sensation moves with the flow. At the next
link, the complexion of its vagueness will have changed. One sense may
stand out more from the perceptual infusion of the always accompanying
fringe-flow of sensation. The vagueness may sharpen into a selective
perceptual focus or a clarity of thought that strikes the foreground of
consciousness in a flash of sudden interest or even revelation. Or the
vagueness may thicken into a lull or daze. Boredom. Who hasn't experienced that on the Web? The boredom often comes with a strange sense of
foreboding: a sensing of an impending moreness, still vague. Next link.
The effects doppler from one link to the next as the sense modalities

enveloped in the dominant of vision phase into and out of each other, and into and out of clear expression and reflective consciousness. The dopplering is responsible for the overall quality of the surfing process. There is an allure to that process, a pull to surf, that cannot be explained any other way. From the point of view of notable results, most hypertextual sessions are remarkably thin. If it were just a matter of the form or content of the screens taken separately, or even in a combinatoric, the experience would add up to very little. Surfing, however, like its televisual precursor, zapping, is oddly compelling. Given the meagerness of the constituent links on the level of formal inventiveness or uniqueness of content, what makes surfing the Web compelling can only be attributed to an accumulation of effect, or transductive momentum, continuing across the linkages. This accumulation of effect is to a certain degree a potentialization of the relay.

Potentialization. The mode in which the successive linkage events are co-present to each other on the receiving end of the digital processing is potential: a felt moreness to ongoing experience. Potential, it was argued earlier, appeals to an analogic virtual as its sufficient reason, as well as beckoning the possible as its thought-extension. Whatever action, perception, reflection eventuates represents a germinating of that potential. Potential, in return, is a situating of the virtual: its remaining immanent to each and every actual conjunction in a serial unfolding, to varying effect. The possibility stored in the digital coding at the instrumental basis of the process has potentialized, in a way that carries a virtual center of self-varying experience across the running of code-bound routines. The coded possible has been made a motor of transductive potential and analogic virtuality. In the actual play between the digital system of the possible, its potentializing effects, and the analogic charge of virtuality both conditioning those effects and carried by them, new thoughts may be thought, new feelings felt. These may extend into new possibilities in actual situations outside the machine and the screen experience. Seeds of screened potential sown in nonsilicon soil. Relay to the world at large.

Digital processing as such doesn't possibilize let alone virtualize. The digital is already exhaustively possibilistic. It can, it turns out, potentialize, but only indirectly, through the experiential relays the reception of its outcomes sets in motion. Those relays may even more indirectly seed as-yet uncoded possibilities: inventions (as defined in the last chapter). Whatever inventiveness comes about, it is a result not of the coding itself but of its detour into the analog. *The processing may be digital—but the analog is the process.* The virtuality involved, and any new possibility that may arise, is entirely bound up with the potentializing relay. It is in not contained in the code.

It is of course conceivable that the digital may succeed in integrating analogic process ability into its own operations. Adaptive neural nets approach this, since they are capable of generating results that are not precoded. They automatically produce unforeseen results using feedback mechanisms to create resonance and interference between routines. In other words, what is coded is recursivity—machined self-referentiality. The digital processing becomes self-modulating: the running of the code induces qualitative transformation in its own loopy operation. Evolutionary digitality. Machinic invention. There are also more literal attempts under way to integrate analog process into digital processing. These include robots powered by biological muscles produced in laboratory cultures and attempts to plug digital devices directly into living neurons. On other fronts, the sight-confining helmets of early virtual reality systems have given way to immersive and interactive environments capable of addressing more directly other-than-visual senses and looping sense modalities more flexibly and multiply into each other, packing more sensation into the digitally-assisted field of experience—and, with it, more potentialization. The notion of ubiquitous computing championed for many years by the MIT Media Lab is seeming less futuristic by the day. The idea is that inconspicuous interfaces can be implanted in everyday environments in such a way as to seamlessly and continuously relay digitally coded impulses into and out of the body through multiple, superposable sense connections, eventually developing into an encompassing network of infinitely reversible analog-digital circuiting on a planetary scale.[14] After all, the earth itself has always been the ultimate immersive environment.

Perhaps the day is not far off when the warnings that this essay began with—not to confuse the digital with the virtual—will be anachronistic. But, for the time being, the warnings hold. Certainly, if there is one day a directly virtual digitality, it will have become that by integrating the analog into itself (biomuscular robots and the like), by translating itself into the analog (neural nets and other evolutionary systems), or again by multiplying and intensifying its relays into and out of the analog (ubiquitous computing). The potential for this becoming of the digital is missed as long as the relationship between the digital and analog is construed in mutually exclusive terms, as if one entirely replaced the other. A commonplace rhetoric has it that the world has entered a "digital age" whose dramatic "dawning" has made the analog obsolete. This is nonsense. The challenge is to think (and act and sense and perceive) the co-operation of the digital and the analog, in self-varying continuity. Apocalyptic pronouncements of epochal rupture might sell well, but they don't compute. When or if the digital virtual comes, its experience won't be anything so dramatic. It will be lullingly quotidian: no doubt as boring as the Web can be.

The "superiority of the analog" over the digital alluded to in the title does not contradict this closing call to think the two together. It refers to the fact that the paths of their co-operation—transformative integration, translation, and relay—are themselves analog operations. There is always an excess of the analog over the digital, because it perceptually fringes, synesthetically dopplers, umbilically backgrounds, and insensibly recedes to a virtual center immanent at every point along the path—all in the same contortionist motion. It is most twisted. The analog and the digital must be thought together, asymmetrically. Because the analog is always a fold ahead.

6

CHAOS IN THE "TOTAL FIELD" OF VISION

The Unbearable Lightness of Seeing

For more than three decades, from the late 1920s to the mid-1960s, when the dream of a scientific psychology was still vivid, researchers became fascinated by what they called the *Ganzfeld*—the "total field" of perception. What they meant (biases in studies of perception being what they are) was the total field of vision. The idea was that if you could experimentally isolate the physical and physiological conditions of vision at their purest—at their simplest and at the same time their fullest—you would discover the elementary nature of visual perception. From there, you could successively build in levels of complexity until you had reconstituted the entire range of vision. Reduction and reconstitution. Classical scientific method.[1]

So what are the physical and physiological conditions of vision? Simply, light striking the retina. If light striking the retina is the simplest condition, then the simplest fullest condition would be white light—the simultaneous presentation of the full spectrum of color—striking the entire retina uniformly. Ingenious devices were invented to achieve this. They typically involved screens and complex diffusion setups, or goggles that were like Ping-Pong balls cut in half, which were then fit over the eye sockets and illuminated. Over the years, the devices were perfected to eliminate "inhomogenieties." The nose, for example. The nose is a particularly refractory appendage for pure vision because of its insistence on casting shadows into the eye, not to mention its adding an outside edge to monocular vision or a bloblike center to binocular vision.

Nose or no nose, the "total field of vision" was not well-disposed to reduction and reconstitution. The experimenting went on for quite long but was thoroughly forgotten in the end, because the pure field of vision, far from providing a "primitive," a clean slate or elementary building block that could be used as a solid foundation for understanding, kept leading to the most anomalous of results. Researchers simply didn't know what to do with them. The anomalousness that made the pure field of vision so inhospitable to scientific edifice-building suits it perfectly to philosophizing. In the "total field" we see vision make an experimental philosophical escape from its own empirical conditions.[2]

One of the most striking anomalies that appeared was that subjects in whom pure vision was produced found it extraordinarily difficult to express what they saw "in terms usually associated with visual phenomena."[3] After prolonged exposure (ten to twenty minutes) subjects would even report difficulty sensing whether their eyes were open or closed.[4] Vision would "blank out."[5] Pure visual experience resulted in a "complete absence of seeing." Researchers concluded that the "total field of vision" was not "a phenomenal field."[6] In other words, it was not a field of experience. What was produced by the experimental setups was less a building block of experience than an anomalous event befalling experience. The anomaly obviously pertained to experience but couldn't be said to be experienced per se: of it, but not in it.

The unexperiencing extended beyond the eyes. "Various after-effects . . . were found . . . [such as] fatigue and a feeling of great lightness of body. Motor coordination was reportedly poor, and observers had difficulty maintaining balance. Time perception was disturbed. Subjects often complained of dizziness and sometimes appeared to be intoxicated. One observer experienced temporary states of depersonalization."[7]

Activate the simplest and fullest physical and physiological conditions of vision, the most straightforward objective conditions of vision, and you not only extinguish seeing, you make people float out of their bodies and lose themselves, literally lose their selves. Under its purest empirical conditions, vision either fails to achieve itself or falls away from itself—and from the self. The empirical conditions of vision are not only not able to be held onto in experience, they prevent experience from holding onto itself.

It was felt that this embarrassing outcome was perhaps due to something that should have been obvious from the beginning: the fact that "natural" visual perception is never pure. Vision always cofunctions with other senses, from which it receives a continuous feed and itself feeds into: hearing, touch, proprioception, to name only the most prominent.

This gave researchers the idea of adding controlled stimulation in other sense modalities. Perhaps restoring vision to its naturally multimodal nexus would bring it back into the fold of experience.

The result? "Extensive hallucinations."[8] Even less hold on experience. Pure flux: delocalized and depersonalized.

Although subjects had difficulty putting what they had failed to properly experience into specifically visual terms, they were relentlessly prodded to do so by experimenters. Most described an unfocusable "cloud" or "fog" of no determinate shape or measurable distance from the eyes. Some just saw "something," others just "nothing." One acute observer saw "levels of nothingness."[9]

"Levels of nothingness" is an interesting way of describing the beginnings of differentiation in the indeterminate. Experimenters were puzzled by the variability of the descriptions. Although most participants agreed on the fogginess and described it as milky white, some insisted it was black. Questions aimed at determining whether there was any perception of form or texture, like "Do you see an object? Any edges? Anything hard? Anything slanted?," yielded statistically low results. Each of the attributes was seen by a minority of the subjects. It was as if every visual attribute could be seen by somebody, but it was quite unpredictable who would see what or why. Just about the only thing the subjects were completely unanimous on was that the unexperience was "indefinite, indeterminate or ambiguous," and specifically that there was nothing of definite size and nothing illuminated or shadowed. In other words, there was nothing that could be construed as an object.

The objective conditions of vision exclude object vision. They only afford "a tendency to see object-like impressions," such as edge and slant, that are "indeterminate with respect to depth." Neither two-dimensional nor three-dimensional. But decidedly not flat. The "fog" of pure vision, according to James J. Gibson, one of the more philosophically inclined of the investigators, was "vaguely surface-like."[10]

A vague, surfacelike field of objectlike or formlike tendency, in which all of the attributes of vision randomly appear and no sooner blank out, bar those most directly connected to determinate things.

What the participants described was a *vacuum* of vision. In physics, the vacuum is the random coming into and out of existence of all possible particles, excluding only stability. It is chaos. Pure vision, the simplest fullest empirical conditions of vision, is *visual chaos*. The levels of something-nothing seen at the point of sight's foundational extinction are the "phase space" of vision. A phase space excludes any given determinate thing, being a superposition of states that cannot phenomenally coexist. It is not phenomenal. It is an abstract space, or a spacelike abstraction. The Ganzfeld experiments produced a visual experience of the visually unexperienceable: a self-abstraction of vision. Vision at its most simple and concrete—white light on retina—is a complex presentation of its own abstraction. The closer you get to the objective, physical, and physiological bases of vision, the more vision abstracts. What began as a procedure of reduction and recombination of a field of experience ended as an exercise in its disappearance through *empirical self-abstraction*.

What this implies is that what the experiments unwittingly accomplished, rather than distilling an elementary unit, was to approach a complex limit, in the same sense in which a mathematical curve may approach a *limit*. A limit is not a boundary. It is open. It is a point that a curve infinitely approaches but never reaches. Except that it is not a point, because it can never be arrived at. The limit of a two-dimensional curve is "pointlike," just as the limit of vision, populated by bounded three-dimensional objects, is "surfacelike." The limit is in a different dimension. More precisely, it lacks determinate dimensionality so it can only be described as being "like" one of the determinable dimensionalities characterizing the movement it governs. For that is exactly what the limit does: govern a movement. The limit-point does not exist on the curve. It is abstract. It exists not on but rather for the curve. Or rather, it almost-exists so that the curve may exist. The curve moves toward the abstract limit as if its concrete existence depended on it. As it does. The limit, though abstract, is not unreal. Quite the contrary, it is existentializing. It is only by reference to the limit that what approaches it has a function: the limit is what gives the approach its effectivity, its reality. The limit is not unreal. It is virtual. It is reality-giving. Since the reality it gives is a movement or *tendency*, the limit may be called a virtual attractor (borrowing once again from chaos theory).

Vision has a *limit-field* rather than a limit-point. This visual attractor is in the peculiar situation of also *being* vision's phase space or total field (in addition to the phase space being composed of attractors such as edge and slant). In other words, as a field of experience, vision is attracted by or tends toward its own totality (Ganzfeld). That this limit-field governs a movement is indicated by the fact that the only other common feature of the participants' descriptions of the pure field of vision was motion. "A fog coming up . . . a white you could go into . . . [m]ight wander in it for hours."[11] Coming up or going into or wandering: the limit-field governs an indeterminate motion. One investigator summed up the descriptions by saying that the closest analogue was high-altitude flight in which the body loses all orientation.[12] It is worth returning to the curious fact that pure vision is *pure kinesthesis*, best described as a form of *flight*. For now, however, more about the limit.

Another analogy. A thermonuclear fusion reactor is a kind of pressure cooker melding elementary units (atomic nuclei) and producing other elementary units (heavier atomic nuclei and gamma-ray photons) as by-products. In other words, the elementary units transmute. The energy released by the transmutational reaction is so powerful that it is not containable by anything concrete that is composed of elementary particles of matter like the ones undergoing transformation. It is only containable in a magnetic field. The empirical conditions of the reaction's containment (magnetism) and triggering (pressure) do not resemble the reaction, and are not composed of its elementary units. The elementary units are givens, already in the conditioning field when everything starts to happen. The "total field" or limit-field of vision is the magnetic field. The elementary units are spontaneously arising formlike entities such as slant and edge. Each experience of vision is the instantaneous transmutation of a population of elementary visual units, which exist both before and after, but exist differently after than before their instantaneous fusion.

This analogy only goes so far. For one thing, there is no wall around the field of vision. Remove the laboratory apparatus generating the magnetic field. Vision is self-containing, or self-standing (more precisely, afloat of itself). It abstracts itself from the apparatus of the physiological body and the physics of light. Second, the open self-containment field of self-abstracting vision occupies a different dimension of reality from both what is seen and from the elementary units of the seeing (it is virtual, and they actual, in different ways). Third, the elementary units of vision do not preexist in the same way as atomic nuclei preexist fusion. They preexist more like subatomic wave particles, randomly appearing and disappearing in the rippling fog of the limit-field. Visual fusion depends on the extraction from that chaos of a determinable sampling of fusionable units.[13]

It is the movement of our bodies that operates the selection. Every

148

move we make is an existential pressure cooker bringing forth vision from the vacuum. It has long been known that vision cannot develop if the body is immobilized. This was tested in the famous (and infamous) experiments in which kittens were immobilized to find out whether they would be able to see when they grew up. They couldn't.[14] Determinate vision emerges from movement (hence the undecidability of pure vision and pure kinesthesis in the experimentally immobilized body).

By "determinate" vision is meant seeing which yields complex forms that are resolvable into constituent units (formlikes such as slant and edge) yet possess a unity of fusion that make them more than the sum of those parts: in a word, objects of perception. The formlike attributes into which objects can be resolved vary continuously according to what, in object terms, will be seen as distance, angle, and illumination. In the Ganzfeld experience, the immobilization of the body brought the continuous variation back out from under the unity. The eyes, astrain in the fog, took the leap of producing its own variations from the endogenous (self-caused) retinal firings that are always occurring and are a physiological necessity of vision.[15] The production of endogenous variations begins to explain both the vague attributes of spatiality, motion, and form reported by the experimental subjects and the striking lack of consensus about them. When the experimenters provided other-sense uptakes, the eyes strained, even harder, to respond to them as indicators of bodily movement, which always provides a dancing medley of multisense experience. The chaotic, endogenous formlikes fused into hallucinated objects.

It is therefore not enough to say that the selection and fusion producing determinate perception requires movement. It requires a coupling of at least two movements: a chaotic appearance and disappearance of spacelikes and formlikes and a movement of the body with them. The chaotic movement is not only endogenous. Its endogenous production is a default function taking over in the absence of exogenous chaos or, when it is there, subtly modulating it. What psychologists call object "constancy" is a fusion-effect of perpetual variation—at least two co-occurring perpetual variations.

The "unity" of objects over their constituents is, paradoxically, borrowed from the body's movement. Objects are the way in which the body's slowness is expressed in perceptual fusion: their unity is the sluggishness of the body's reactions relative to the chaotic movements with which they co-occur. Speedy multiplicities of chaotic appearances and disappearances, bound up with shifts in distance, angle, and illumination, not to mention endogenous firings and eye jitter (nystagmus), couple with each comparatively languid body movement. The chaotic complex repeats, with variation. Bodily reactions repeat, with less variation. The quality of the body's movement—its lag, drag, or lesser variation—is the common factor of the range of chaotic multiplicities. Every multiplicity is divisible by its reactions. The object "constancy" at the basis of cognition is not so much a persistence in existence of unitary things as it is a ratio between perpetual variations: the ratio between habit (pattern of reaction) and the sea of chaos in which it swims (doggedly holding onto itself, as its own lifeboat).[16] As Whitehead put it, "factors in our experience are 'clear and distinct' in proportion to their variability, provided that they sustain themselves for that moderate period required for importance."[17] The relative slowness of the body and the repetitions of habit are mechanisms by which factorings of experience prolong themselves in such a way as to become "important." (Sustained and sustaining—of what?: further factorings.)

It was misleading to say that object-unity was borrowed from the body, as if the body's self-sustaining functional unity preexisted its habit-forming and was projected onto the outside world. Both unities—and the very distinction between inside and outside—are fusional products of perpetual variations. What the body lends in the first instance is its *slowness*, not its presumptive unity. The unity appears "out there," in the greater-varying accompaniments to habit, as recognizably patterned by habit in such a way to reduce its complexity by a factor. The "out there" becomes an "outside" of things. The produced unity then feeds back "in." The oneness of the body is back-flow, a back-formation (as always, at a lag). The body's relative slowness returns to it, after a habitual detour, as its own objectifiable unity. Thus back-formed, the body may now appear to itself as a bounded object among others. Spatial distinctions like inside and outside and relative size and distance are derivatives of a greater "out there" that is not in the first instance defined spatially but rather dynamically, in terms of movement and variation.[18] To return to the earlier example of the fusion reaction, the dynamic "out there" is the containment vessel that on closer inspection is seen not to be "there" at all, vanishing as it does into space.

Both the bounded body and the objects it interacts with are appearances, in the sense of productions or emergences from a field that can only be characterized as "total" since it cannot be boxed in—for the very good reason that spatial distinctions derive from it. Body and objects co-emerge from an open field of variations that have none of the spatial or formal characteristics they have, or just "like-ly" have them, as a matter of habit. The "like-ness" is what habit *adds* to chaos, in the form of its own reactions. The similarity is of *the reactions* to each other—or of the automatism of habit to itself, as it repeats. Habit spontaneously patterns itself through repetition, and in so doing adds its own self-structuring to the world of chaos, in which as a result it always finds more than is really "out there": *one more* (the "*more* than the sum of its parts" of objective unity in its essential surplus over its elements; the one as the common factor that goes evenly into every multiplicity). Habit adds to reality. It is really productive. That productive capacity appeared in the multisensory Ganzfeld experiments as hallucination: a creative striving to recognize objects "out there," even under the most adverse conditions (the body's slowness having been subtracted by the immobilizing experimental setup, scuttling the rationalization).[19]

It is assuming too much to interpret the variations from which perceptual unity and constancy emerge as "interactions" of "a body" and "objects," as if their recognizable identity preexisted their chaos. Objectified body, object world, and their regulated in-between—the empirical workings of experience—arise from a nonphenomenal chaos that is not what or where they are (having neither determinate form nor dimensionality) but is of them, inseparably: their incipiency.

That ontological difference between the empirical workings of experience and their conditions of emergence is why the "total field" of vision must *befall* experience. Nonphenomenal, it makes experience fall away, or stay afloat, rather than "grounding" it in a way conducive to its flowing back on itself scientifically (to its becoming its own cognitive object). The field of vision's emergence is never an object or a body, or even a body-object interaction. It is not objectifiable. It is the always-accompanying, unentering chaos that renews. Always accompanying, but in a different dimension of reality than what emerges from it. Take-off. Unentering, ever-befalling, recessive processual dimension, inseparable from but not reducible to the empirical elements of vision, to the constancies and unities that arise with vision and from which vision no sooner takes flight. Recessive dimension: there is a remainder, after all, to the most evening and sustaining of habit-factorings. For habit and the empirical understandings which systematically extend it, the remainder is negligible. All that counts is the evening. Not so for philosophy. The recessiveness of the remainder cracks its surfacelike calm. It fractures empirical conditions from their conditions of emergence, requiring the thinking of an abyssal distinction.

If by "empirical" is meant "pertaining to predictable interactions between isolatable elements, formulatable as deterministic laws," then the conditions of emergence of vision are superempirical. They additively *include* the constancy of empirical conditions. The superempirical conditions of experience complexly include the empirical in the mode of recessive accompaniment. As experience takes off, its empirical conditions fall away. By the time the arising experience comes to ground in its empirical functioning, its remaindered conditions of emergence have already flown for the cracks. This double movement (at once simultaneous and cyclic) of rising and falling makes it impossible to distinguish the superempirical from the infraempirical. Only their distinction from the empirical stands (or constantly returns). Conditions of emergence and that which empirically emerges perpetually, reciprocally, rearisingly recede, in a rhythmic dance of becoming and return. The difference at the heart of perception is an ontological one between genesis (of the world, ever-renewed) and functioning (in the world, always again): worlding and recognition, in a mutually sustaining rhythm.[20]

The Seen and the Sat

What would the equivalent of the pure field of vision be for the sense of touch? If the field of visual experience can be described, phenomenally, as encompassing things from a distance, touch would have to do the opposite: pinpoint things in proximity. The tactile analogue of producing the total field of vision would be to isolate a point of skin and apply pressure. Generic pressure on an isolated patch of skin would be to touch what white light filling the whole retina is to sight: the production of an elementary phenomenal unit lending itself to empirical investigation. For example, you might anesthetize the whole expanse of the skin except for a single spot. The hypothesis would be that sensitivity at that spot to be highlighted, due to the absence of competing tactile stimuli, leaving you with the simplest, full experience of touch. Imagine a tickle there. Or a pinprick. They would probably be of unbearable intensity, invading your entire sense of feeling. Wouldn't isolating a patch of skin allow you to investigate pure tactile sensation and come to certain conclusions about how touch empirically functions?

Not exactly. What actually happens at an isolated skin spot is that *there is no tactile sensation whatsoever.*[21] The existence of the elementary unit of touch does not preexist the totality of the tactile surface. We think of the surface of the skin as being composed of a set of sensitive points that enter into relation with each other, allowing us to locate the things we feel by their relative positions. But, just as with vision, the units enabling position emerge from a total surface, rather than the surface being composed of preexisting units. Touch also has a limit-field, and it is just as abstract. For what is a surface before the existence of the points composing it? Indeterminate. An indeterminate totality. A surface-like indeterminate virtual totality. Tactile-attractor phase space. We can expect that there is a chaotic emergence of pressurelike and ticklelike and pricklike elements "grounding" tactility in the same self-floating way that vision empirically "grounds" itself. Touch, also, is a form of flight.

Every sense must have such a "surfacelike" or Ganzfeld all its own, entertaining unique relations of noncoincidence with its phenomenal arisings and empirical functionings. For taste, it is fat. Long thought to lack any taste at all, researchers have recently decided that its lack is a surfeit. "Fat, it turns out, doesn't just have a flavor, it has *every* flavor."[22] Whereas a sugar solution stimulates only five to ten percent of taste buds, fat stimulates ninety-five percent. "Basically, everyone can taste fat, but *no one describes it the same.* It tastes slightly sweet to me, but other people say it's bitter, and some say it's salty or slightly sour. We've done forty or fifty people now and everyone has a different way of describing it."[23] The Ganzfeld of touch remains elusively virtual, instantly withdrawing at the attempt to approach it. The virtual surfacelike of taste, for its part, actualizes to a surprising degree in a readily available substance. Fat actually envelops all of the potential variations of taste. It stands out from and above more pedestrian taste sensations like sugar, floating in its impossible fullness tantalizingly close to the insipid, a diaphanously salivary superobject. Fat is the actual double of the virtuality of taste, its empirically appearing phantom. Its concrete mystique. (What does the militantly anti-fat line followed by our contemporary culture say about its relation to the senses?)

Each sense has its field of emergence. Each such field is in a unique relation of noncoincidence with what emerges from it. In conceptualizing the senses, the way in which the emerged diverges from its emergence needs to be positively described. The virtual is too broad a word for conditions of emergence. Since virtuality is inseparable from, if not reducible to, its actual emergences, "the" virtual is always in the multiple. The follow-ups to "whether?" are "which?" and "how?" Which virtual? Under which mode of accompaniment? How appearing? How fully does the virtual range of variations actualize in any given object or substance?

Is "the" limit, then, also in the multiple?

The Ganzfeld or limit-field of vision was described as an unwalled, self-floating fusional containment bubble. Although it is unwalled, it can still be characterized as an internal limit in the sense that it concerns what, empirically, pertains to vision alone: white light on the retina. Since it isolates what solely concerns vision, it could also be called a disjunctive limit. The laboratory production of the Ganzfeld is an experimental device dedicated to the mutual exclusion of the other senses. The Ganzfeld is the limit toward which vision separates out from the other senses. Remember that the addition of a stimulus in another sense mode was incompatible with the maintenance of even those ambiguous characteristics that the limit-field could be agreed upon as having. Other-sense stimulation made the limit-field fall away (made vision most decisively take flight from its conditions)—precisely because it was no longer a "pure" field of vision but a mixed or intermodal field. The disjunctive limit of vision thus precariously neighbors a hallucinatory, intermodal (conjunctive) limit. Pure and alone, it is emergent, populated by spontaneous appearances presenting potentials for object constancy. In mixed company it is hallucinatory, populated by paradox: objects without constancy.

When else is vision not in mixed company? Not in dream, where the body is unconsciously attentive to sound and touch and the pressure of its own weight and hallucinatingly transposes that residual feed of experience into dream elements.[24] Not in waking, where movement provides a panoply of tactile, proprioceptive, auditory, and other stimuli. In no circumstances other than the most controlled and artificial laboratory conditions does vision approach "purity." Vision only actually functions in a mixed or intermodal state. It is always fed into other senses and feeds out to them. Why is sense-mixing in dreaming and laboratory Ganzfelding hallucinatory, but in waking not? The answer, of course, is movement.

The dreamer is in a naturally induced semiparalytic state. The laboratory subject is artificially immobilized. Sense-mixing in the absence of conscious movement veers toward the hallucinatory limit.

Saying that vision is never pure is just another way of underlining the nature of its disjunctive limit as a surfacelike field approached but never attained: of confirming the limit's reality as virtual. The "pure" field of vision is a virtual field. No matter how carefully an experimental setup approximates it, actual "impurities" will sneak in. For there will always already have been experience. What are the formlike emergences of the "pure" field of vision as isolated in the laboratory if not traces of past intermodal experiences straining to reactualize their ratio of constancy, to refresh already-objects they have been, to regain the world, preknown anew?

If vision is always contaminated, at the very least by multisense pastness, then the answer to the question of why waking, non-Ganzfelding bodies do not hallucinate has to be reviewed. Or rather, the blanket assumption that they do not hallucinate needs rethinking. The many mechanisms for the production of chaos outlined earlier continue outside the laboratory, throughout the day (continual variations in angle, illumination, and color, endogenous retinal firings, nystagmus, more or less "voluntary" eye movements, all manner of body movements and transports, to which might be added lapses and concentrations of attention). They persist, habitually unperceived, alongside the constancies and unities of perception that emerge from their interrelating. Vision is constitutionally double. It is doubled by its own purity or totality, as a visually unperceived from which it emerges. Paradoxically, it is only the unperceived that can in any sense be argued to be given. What is actually seen is productively added to it: *overseen*. Objects of vision are added ingredients to experience: experienced oversights or excess seeings. In a word, hallucinations. This is in no way to imply that they are unreal or simply illusory. Quite the opposite, the conclusion is that hallucination is as real as any thing. More radically, hallucination—the spontaneously creative addition of objects of perception that are not found preformed "out there"—is generative of reality (more reality). Vision gives back more to reality than it is given. It is not possible to sustain a strict distinction between perception and hallucination.[25]

The difference between what happens in a Ganzfeld and in sleep, as well as in pathological hallucinations such as those of schizophrenia, must be found elsewhere. The initial answer that movement was the differentiator can be retained if it is not thought of as providing a grounding reference to preformed reality, but quite the contrary as intensifying the *self-referentiality* of emergent experience. Movement multiplies visual and intermodal feedback loops. It enables a continuous, complexifying, cross-referencing of variations to each other—an indexing of aspects of unfolding experience to its own products and of it products to their ever-changing, unperceived field of emergence. The difference between dream, experimentally induced hallucination, and pathological hallucination from each other and from "natural" perception pertains to the kind and complexity of experience's self-referencing to its own ongoing event. The more impoverished the conditions for feedback-enabled cross-referencing, the flightier will be the creative addition of the more to reality. The danger is that, through insufficient cross-referencing, experience might overreach its own lifeboat.

If pastness is the key, would someone who had never before seen experience formlike emergences in the Ganzfeld? The first visual sensations of the congenitally blind restored to sight provide what is perhaps the only naturally occurring "pure" field of vision. Sure enough, no objectlike appearances immediately arise. The intermodal connections to the unused retina have not yet been made. "Newly operated patients do not localize their visual impressions; they do not relate them to any point. . . . [T]hey see colors much as we smell an odour of peat or varnish, which enfolds and intrudes upon us, but without occupying any specific form of extension."[26] There are as yet no objects and "no spatial dimensions."[27] "No shape to anything or distance." Only a vaguely enfolding "surface arrangement."[28] Here the "spacelikeness" or vague dimensionality of the Ganzfeld appears without the formlikes. This surfacelike "arrangement" is a "fortuitously given" chaos of color. Not even. Not even color at first—only variations of brightness, nonqualified *intensities.*[29] Constant objects and depth begin to emerge, formlike, from the surface of intensity only when the patients learn to focus their attention on fusions between vision and other senses, particularly touch and hearing, that they have already indexed to movement: when they learn to cross-reference past unsighted experience to vision. "I see it move, because I hear it," said one.[30]

Vision, as a phenomenal field fulfilling the conditions for empirical or object-based perception, actually begins less with a fusion of preexisting elements than with a prefusion—or perfusion—of the senses. The fusionable units of vision as a separable sense themselves arise from this prior level of perfusion. That is, even if they are always already there, when they will have been there *visually*, it is on the more encompassing condition of intersense fusion. Never a blank slate. Always the almost-something of prior levels of synesthetic experience.[31]

It is a simplification to present the visual limit-field as sufficient to produce vision. If the other senses have abstract surfaces or limit-fields, then these co-condition, or add containment levels, to the existentializing pressure cooker. The limit-fields of the skin and the muscles (proprioceptors), the nose (this time approached from the inside: olfactory receptors), the tongue, and the ears combine with the limit-field of vision to form the open containment field of experience. The virtual self-standing of vision actually takes place in a crowded bubble.

The interconnection of the senses was graphically illustrated by an experiment that ingeniously combined anesthetized skin and high-altitude flight. A scientist who was also an experienced pilot and had been trained to orient expertly during high-altitude maneuvers anesthetized his own ass.[32] Amazing but true: he could no longer see where he was. He could no longer orient. He had scientifically proven that we see with the seat of our pants. The interconnection of the senses is so complete that the removal of a strategic patch of tactile/proprioceptive feed makes the whole process dysfunctional.

All of this does not entirely disqualify what was said earlier about pure vision. The concept of a limit-field of vision is necessitated by the fact that in spite of the thoroughly intermodal nature of our experience we can still in some way separate out what we see from what we sit. The separation of the visual field must in some way coexist with its interconnection with other sense fields. Although "coexist" is the wrong word. "Co-attract" is better. In actuality, the senses cofunction. But for that to be possible, there must be virtual purity of each sense separately, *as well as* a virtuality governing its cofunctioning with the others: differentiation and integration go together. You can't have one without the other.

A simple example. We can see texture. You don't have to touch velvet to know that it is soft, or a rock to know that it is hard. Presented with a substance you have never seen before, you can anticipate its texture. Of course, this ability to see new tactile qualities depends on past touchings of other textures and movements providing continuous visual-tactile feedback. You have to know texture in general already before you can see a specifically new texture. But that doesn't change the fact that once you can generally see texture, you see a texture directly, with only your eyes, without reaching.

Vision has taken up a tactile function. It has arrogated to itself the function of touch. This purely visual touch is a *synesthesia proper to vision:* a touch as only the eyes can touch. This is what Gilles Deleuze has termed the "haptic."[33]

This embedding of an other-mode function in vision can be conceived as having its own phase space. In other words, virtually speaking, in addition to the disjunctive and conjunctive limits of vision, there must be another phase space, another attractor: an enveloping limit. This limit would be in close proximity to the conjunctive, intermodal limit. It would be intersense conjunction seen (from the side of vision). In other words, it would be where vision regathers itself, enveloping its own links to its sensory outside. At the extreme of intermodal conjunction, at the very point where vision's modal separation is weakest, it manages to fold back on itself to reaffirm its "purity," what only it can do. What besides sight can feel texture at a glance?

These phase spaces (and potentially many more) cofunction as differential attractors governing a self-intensifying field of experience. This total field of experience is self-intensifying in the sense that it continually folds back on itself in order to add variations on itself, as part of the same movement by which it sorts itself out: its integration and differentiation always going together, for a total field.

Vision as we experience it emerges from a tension between the movements governed by the interaction of attractors: on the one hand, a movement of visual separating-out and self-flotation, and, on the other, a movement of visual folding-in and alien-uptake. Every actual experience is at a crossroads lying intensively between the poles toward which these movements tend. Every actual experience is strung between cross-tendencies toward the limits of single-sense purity and intersense fusion. (Terms will have to be invented for uptakes by other-than-visual senses: the equivalent of the haptic for nonvisual senses.)

Every given experience is already many-mixed. It is mixed virtually in the way just described, in that it is governed by co-attraction. It is mixed phenomenally in that the elementary units of an objective plurality of the senses actually emerge, and merge, in it. And it is mixed ontologically, in that the virtual and actual mixings mix.

"Virtual mixing" is a tricky concept. Limits or virtual attractors, in and of themselves, remain recessively, superempirically untouched. It is the abstract movements they govern that mix. Separating-out/self-flotation and folding-in/alien-uptake are abstract movements *of the actual.* They are "abstract" in the special sense that they are real movements but do not begin or end at any particular, locatable points in empirical space. They are actual, but nonlocal and immeasurable. They are manner in which the virtual phases into the actual, taking form as a tension between tendencies. The limits as such must be conceived as unmixed but in enough dynamic proximity to interfere with each other in their actual effects as attractors. The recessiveness of the limits means that although they have actual effects, they lurk on a different level of reality from their effects. On that level, they are still on a different level from each other. There is a super-recessive difference between them, of which the ontological difference described earlier between the actually emerged and its emergence is distantly reminiscent. The difference between virtual limits is a proximity-at-a-distance: an interference effect registering elsewhere, like an echo in a storm drain heard at street level. This virtual condition of leveled distance in effective proximity can be termed a superposition. Superposition is what was meant by "virtual mixing." The notions of superposition and interference together expresses the idea that the virtual, or conditions of emergence, can neither be separated from nor reduced to the actual, or the conditions of empirical functioning. There is a real difference between them that depends on their coming-together on some level.[34] Without its passage into the empirical, the virtual would be nothing lurking. Without the passing of the virtual into it, the empirical would functionally die. It would coincide so even-temperedly with its own unity and constancy that it would have no ontological room to maneuver: entropic death by excess of success.

Superposition is nonspatial. But if it were spatial, it would be a depth. It is depthlike. If the phenomenal is a surfacelike mix of emergent elements fusionally afold, the virtual is a recessive or depthlike superposition of effective levels askew. The "space likeness" of the incipient phenomenal surface is an abstract echo of that virtual depth. The effectivity of the superposition—its ability to have actual effects while remaining virtual—is what is called *force*.

The Palliative of the Empirical

Force is infraempirical. No scientist has ever observed a force. Not even Newton saw gravity. Only force-effects are observable. "Force" is a word used to designate the repeatability or iterability of effects. A "force" is the set of invisible, untouchable, self-renewing conditions according to which certain effects can habitually be expected to appear. In the present context, the energy of fusion from which experience arises will be said to be the combined force of limit-attractors in tension. A perception is a force-effect. Every vision, every touch, every intermodal experience, is the event of a forced passage from the infraempirical to the added reality of the empirical, then back to the infraempirical—augmented by the event of its already having taken leave of itself (the superempirical, understood as a moment in the life cycle of the world's effectivity feeding back on itself). Every vision, every touch, every intermodal experience, passes from an unrefusable (and unobeyable) complex limit-tension, through hallucinatory grounding in objectivity, to existential flight, back to the conditions of emergence. An event, a passage: "force" is a verb.[35] Its action is unobeyable because, across its unrefusable repetition, it commands creation. Its imperative expression is the new.

The empirical, with its entropic geometry of plane surfaces and perspectival depths, with its closed forms and stable objects, is but a phase shift in this perpetual event of experience's self-renewing passage. Empirical grounding—the entropy, closure, and stability of formed perception—is provisional, but a beat in a rhythm. Its solidity is continually moved, removed, and refreshed by iterations of force.

Invisible force. Newton did not see gravity. He felt its effect: a pain in the head. The newly visioned blind do not see things. They feel a pain in their eyes. "He could not distinguish objects. The pain produced by the light forced him to close the eye immediately." The forced opening of sense experience can only figure at first as unlocalized, unspecified pain. "She couldn't even be positive these strange new sensations were coming through her eyes."[36] With more experience, the feeling of the effect comes to be identified. Reactions in different sense modes are cross-referenced. Through that cross-referencing, the feeling is consistently indexed to what have become recognizable regions of experience. The regions are distributed on either side of an inside/outside divide. The effect is now perceived as the result of localizable interactions between formed organs and objects. The experience has been determined, objectified, empiricized. Only now that it has become determinately intermodal is it experienced as a sight. The passage into empirical appearance coincides with an integration/differentiation of sense modes. With that passage, and that determination, the pain is (provisionally) assuaged.

Assuaged: the empirical is a palliative. Objects are anesthetic specifications of the growth pain of perception's passing into and out of itself. The anesthetic is the *perceived*, as distinguished from the perceiving: objects passing into empirical existence, sensation passing out of itself into that objectivity. Perceived objects are side-effects of the appearing of force, by-products of its quelling. Side-effects: because the force of emergence also continues, along with and past the empirical, into simultaneous and repeated self-abstraction from it. The "pain" also continues: simultaneous and bifurcating paths of perception's passing.

If the empirical is the anesthetic, then the pain accompanying perception's passing forcefully into itself and continuing superempirically in flight from its objective quelling—what can this be but the *aesthetic?*

The pain is the beauty (of the world emergent).

THE BRIGHTNESS CONFOUND

In my room I am surrounded by objects of different colors. It is easy to say what color they are. But if I were asked what color I am now seeing from here at, say, *this* place on my table, I couldn't answer; the place is whitish (because the light wall makes the brown table lighter here) at any rate it is much lighter than the rest of the table, but, given a number of color samples, I wouldn't be able to pick out one which had the same coloration as this area of the table.[1]

The philosopher, staring pensively at the table in front of him, begins to unsee things, things he has seen and the color of which he knows. When he looks more closely, he notices that there is a gap between what he has *seen* and his *seeing*. If he concentrates on what is actually before him at the moment of his seeing, the certainty of what he has seen dissolves. He can no longer say what color any given thing on the table is. This patch is whitish, but not white. Its brightness ("lighter") interferes with its whiteness. Looking closely, you see that color is not separate from illumination. What you are seeing is always a fusion of color and degree of brightness. The actual appearance isn't exactly "like" either color or brightness taken separately.

This inseparability of color and illumination was dubbed the "brightness confound" by an empirical researcher frustrated at his inability to explain away the anomalies of vision.[2] The "anomalies" of vision can't be brushed aside for the simple reason that they are what is *actually* being seen. The actual seeing is a singular confound of what are described empirically as separate dimensions of vision. By "singular" is meant "incomparable." The table-gazing philosopher positively despairs at the task of matching any given patch to a color standard.

The singular is without model and without resemblance. It resembles only itself. In this precise and restricted sense, what is actually seen is *absolute*: "comparable only to itself." As anyone who has dressed himself knows, "we judge colors by the company they keep."[3] It is not just that colors mutually change, or reciprocally vary, when they congregate; more radically, they become unstable and even imperceptible in isolation. What is singular about color is the *relationality* of its ever-varying appearing. There is no possibility of a fixed, one-to-one correspondence between "local physical stimuli and the perceptions they produce," despite wishful thinking to the contrary on the part of upholders of the dominant Newtonian theory of vision.[4] Colors are convivial by nature. Deprive them of company and they "blank out." "A color is an alteration of a complete spectrum."[5] The brightness confound refers to the fact that this unsplittable relationality extends to dimensions of vision foreign to color as such, foremost among them illumination or degrees and species of achromatic brightness. Color is a field, a nondecomposable relational whole, nested within a larger, achromatic field. The problem for the "objective" observer is that the boundaries of both fields are indistinct. Their fuzziness does not contradict their absoluteness. Quite the contrary, it produces it. The fringe of visual fuzz, acutely observed in all its vagueness, is what renders comparison impossible.

Absoluteness is an attribute of any and all elements of a relational whole. Except, as absolute, they are not "elements." They are parts or elements before they fuse into the relational whole by entering indissociably into each other's company, and they are parts or elements afterward if they are dissociated or extracted from their congregation by a follow-up operation dedicated to that purpose. In the seeing, they are absolute. Before after, they are relative: comparable to a standard, and by means of the standard to each other and to what they are not.

A matchable color or a measurable degree of brightness is an independent *variable*. This means that the "same" colors or degrees are perceived to appear in different situations, in various combinations. When independent variables combine, they are "extrinsically" or indirectly related, in that their gregariousness is mediated by a standard or model of comparison. What the variables are independent from is less each other—for their very nature is to combine—than any particular situation in which things "like" them occur. They are indexed more to their standardization than to their situation. Their medium is generality. Independent variables are relative to each other by virtue of their shared generality or their submission to standards of comparison.

The singular confound, on the other hand, is an absolute variation, comparable only to itself: an "intrinsic" variation or *self-variety*. Intrinsic variations co-occur with other singularities in a larger, encompassing confound. Self-varieties co-vary. Their relation is of mutual envelopment rather than extrinsic combination. They fold into and out of each other in a way that makes the transition between variations indistinct. Confound them.

It is useful to restrict the term "relation" to self-variety: the encompass-ing co-variation of singular emergences sharing zones of indistinction with each other. The brightness confound is a population of such emer-gences. Combinations of elements in extrinsic relation may be termed interaction. Interaction is relative. The comparative concept of the "rela-tive" is entirely bound up with the notion of independent variables. Rela-tivity is in fact *predicated on the possibility of a standard.* The relative co-occurs with the general or the universal. The "absolute," on the other hand, is what is resistant to generalization. It is endemic to one and only one occurrence or situation. *The absolute is absolutely situated.* The hitch is that since the "situation" is resistant to standard and measure, it retains a character of transitional indistinction. The absolutely "one and only" is by nature vaguely demarcated. The situation is struck with nonlocality. Only when its "elements" are wrenched from their singular situation does the absolute become generalizable. It was perhaps inaccurate to say that the relational whole was "unsplittable." It is more that it is splittable but at the price of becoming something other than it is (a generality). The absolute is a processual moment between emergence and dismantling extraction. *The absolute is not a Platonic ideal.* It is the very moment of the actual: its unsplitness.

The dismantling of the absolute is the activity of the empirical: *reduc-tion* of the whole to the variable sum of its dissociated parts. The reductive dismantling of relation is termed "analysis." The emergence of relation is not the opposite of analysis. The opposite of analysis is "synthesis," which is another word for "construction." Synthesis is an inverse movement inseparable from analysis. It makes a necessary contribution to the opera-tion of reduction: it is the variable summing of the dissociated parts. Synthesis contributes to reduction by constructing the backdrop of generality, the summation against which the reduced elements appear as addable, or as independently combinable, dissociated from their absolutely situated appearing. In nonscientific arenas, a combination of elements against a general backdrop is called *context*. In scientific contexts, it is called objectivity. Context and objectivity are operations of de-*situation*. Relational appearing of the kind occurring on Wittgenstein's table is neither analysis nor synthesis. It is *catalysis*. It is a fusional production of a primacy of relation. For, in the company of the confound, the "parts" disappear into their reciprocity. The relating takes priority over any possible separation between combinable "terms." Relation takes autonomy from its terms. Absoluteness is the autonomy of a relational whole with respect to its parts. The relation determines the parts, not the other way around.[6]

In the standard Newtonian empirical analytic, color is said to have three dimensions, each in one-to-one correspondence with a physical characteristic of light. The "dimensions" are independent variables. These are understood to combine in any given context to specify an act of vision. A variable, as just described, is an operation upon a relation: an extraction and making ready for recombination. In other words, a variable is a transformative process. When a variable is given a name, becoming a substantive like "hue," it is easy to treat the process as a part. The "conceived separately" slips into "conceived as existing separately." The extracted variable is mistaken for an objective part. This slippage from process to part, from relation to term in relation, is called *hypostasis*.

Hypostasis is an endemic danger to empirical thought, placing it in secret collusion with idealism. Idealism occurs when "elements" of relation are separated out as variables, then substantivized as parts, and finally hypostasized as general entities like the hues represented on color wheels. Where and when is the "white" I have seen on the color wheel? Not here on this table right now. If I look closely, I can't make the match. Standard "red" or "blue" or "white," separate from vagaries of illumination, are seen anytime in principle, but nowhere in particular. Anytime and nowhere: the elements of the empirical are timeless and spaceless. What earns these abstract entities the name "objective" is exactly that: they can be used as the basis for comparative judgment in any context, independent of situation. The "hue" on a color wheel may not be on the table, but de-situated it is matchable enough to be used to test color blindness or brain damage, for example. In anybody, at any place, at any time.

This diagnostic de-situation gives the empirical its formidable practical power. Diagnosing a condition is the first step toward "correcting" or "improving" it. But empiricism's practical power is also its philosophical weakness. The clinical or experimental context produces a backdrop of generality. It does this simply by building an *assumption* of comparison into the situation. It produces standardization by assuming its possibility and institutionalizing the assumption. Anomalies that do not conform to the applied standard, or do not follow standardizable deviations from it (identifiable "deficiencies" or "diseases"), are thrown out, discounted as "exceptions." Statistics is the methodological instrument for identifying and discounting exceptions. Statistical method squeezes out the singular in a pincer movement between the general the discounted. It closes the circle between the assumption of the standard and its practical production. The singular is left out of the loop. Philosophical thought pries open the circle in order to spiral back to the singular. Its "object" is the exception. Anomaly is its friend.

The divisions and dimensions of Euclidean space are the prototype of hypostasis. A mythical account of their extraction would imagine a manipulable experiential patch laid between two other experiential patches. If that relation is conserved beyond the minimum perceivable interval, the two patches and the patch between them can be considered, for all intents and purposes, as more or less static relative to each other. The first relatively static patch, the thing between, can then be taken out of that situation and laid beside a second pair of things. This repeat lay-beside allows the second pair to be compared to the first pair. The thing that moves from one pairing to the next, from one situation to the next, is now a protostandard: a de-situated thing, or object. The object no longer appears for and as itself but only for comparison. All that needs to be done now is for the comparison object to be divided into units. Once divided into units, the standard is not only de-situated but dematerialized. Its units add up to a fully abstract standard. An ideal entity. Space is now constructed of spaceless entities.

Folding that abstraction back onto matter, applying it to things again, enables the reproduction of uniform comparison objects. Behold, "the" yardstick. Any yardstick can be used to select comparable objects for specific uses. For example pieces of wood can be selected as in conformity with each other and with the standard, for use in building. The generality of the standard is transferred to the lengths of wood, which become comparable elements of construction. They, too, lose their singularity, since they now have value only for their uniformity or resemblance to each other. De-situation. Dematerialization. Proliferation of idealization. What presents itself to the carpenter is less *this* wood than "a" *two-by-four:* "the" two-by-four as it appears in the present context, so statistically like every other in any other useful context of construction. The singularity of wood-appearing now appears as a *class* of objective elements similarly ready-to-hand as particular instances conforming to a model. Primacy is now not with relation but with resemblance.

Instead of repeating the measurement to compare multiple objects, now repeat it against the same object from different approaches. Divide the approaches into units—in this case angles. Select right angles sharing a base but repeating a different line of approach. Put the units from the yardstick on each of the resulting axes. Presto, you have the Cartesian coordinate grid defining the three dimensions of Euclidean space.

The same operation that was applied to the conservation of relation in the experiential confound can be transferred by analogy to alteration and passing away. The outcome is time, divided into standard and standardizing units that are like snapshots of transition. Stills. Like spatial cross-sections of what has come to pass. Time is now constructed of timeless elements modeled on the spaceless elements of space. As Henri Bergson argued, linear time is a retrospective spatialization of transition. The philosopher confounded by his table returns logically to the moment before the separating out of space and spatialized time from what actually appears. The experiential confound includes not only color and illumination. More exciting—or more disturbing, depending on your perspective—its fusion extends to space and time themselves.

In addition to hue, the standard hypostases of the experiential confound that have entered the scientific thought of vision are brightness and saturation. Like all independent variables, these dimensions of vision are general abstractions. They are not what is actually seen. They are abstract tools for seeing something else, which does not present itself directly to the investigator's experience (color blindness, brain damage, and so forth). They are abstract entities serving for inductive analysis.

"One specific illumination," writes David Katz, "is not associated with one specific surface color. Surface colour and illumination constitute, rather, an indissoluble unity. . . . To every visual field with a particular illumination there belongs a *particular* [read "singular"] white, a *particular* grey, etc., and we cannot arbitrarily replace these by the same colors in other degrees of pronouncedness. When one illumination with its corresponding colors becomes associated with another illumination with its corresponding colours, the process is purely external, for the one illumination with its colours *emerges from the other, and merges back into it;* they are both indicators and bearers of each other." Singularity and emergence, against extrinsic relation. Unmediatedly. "The impression of illumination forces itself immediately upon one, more so than do the colours of individual objects. . . . [T]here is *a non-derived, non-inferred primary impression of illumination* of the visual field, which from the point of view of experience is *genetically prior* to the experience of the individual colours of the objects which fill the visual field."[7] Before objective vision: a chaos of hue confounded with other dimensions of visual experience. The brightness confound is just an "impression" of illumination, because it resembles the illumination we see after the emergence of color as little as it resembles colors themselves. It is color borne by proto-brightness, and illumination borne by proto-hue. "Bearers of each other": mutual conveyance toward objective emergence. Given this mutuality, the "brightness confound" could equally be called the "color confound." The brightness confound refers to the emergent indissolubility of color and illumination. The broader term "experiential confound" extends this indissolubility to other sense modes, as well as to space and time.

What the philosopher unsees is what a baby sees: a brightness confound enveloped in an experiential confound. "The newborn's senses are intermingled in a synesthetic confusion. . . . [E]nergy from the different senses, *including the proprioceptive sense of his or her own movement,* is largely if not wholly undifferentiated." Including proprioception: the specialized sense of spatial perception. Although "wholly undifferentiated," from the present perspective, would do better as "differentiated as a whole" (appearing as a relation). Because the experience is not undifferentiated. In fact, it is the direct perception of *integral differentiation* (a field, a moving fusion). What is perceived is wholly and only *change.* The infant "responds to changes in energy . . . ignoring modality of input."[8] The infant perceives only transition, unspecified as to sense. Given that the spatial sense is one of those unspecified, the transition is without beginning and end points: relation without its terms. Termless, relation does not objectively appear. It can only appear as a whole and *energetically:* as an unspecified (if not undifferentiated) *intensity* of total experience.[9]

The disorienting "brightness" into which color melts, with illumination, to form the brightness confound reappears on the level of the experiential confound as a total, floating intensity specific to no particular sense mode—not just "intermodal" (combining sense modes) but *amodal* (fusing the senses). Philosophy, as distinct from empirical inquiry, is amodal energetic thought, concerned with fusional intensities before partitive objectivities. The intense confound it unseeingly sees is itself leveled, with a divergent symmetry from one level to the next. Levels upon levels within levels: time within space within color within illumination, a color confound within an intermodal brightness confound within an amodal experiential confound, vision within proprioception within vision. Reciprocating levels, fractally self-standing, on no ground other than their own self-repeating complexity. No beginning, no end. Just event, just William James's "streaming." Darwin:

> I carefully followed the mental development of my small children, and I was astonished to observe in . . . these children, soon after they reached the age in which they knew the names of all the ordinary things, that they appeared entirely incapable of giving the right names to the colors of a color etching. They could not name the colors, although I tried repeatedly to teach them the names of the colors. I remember quite clearly having stated that they were color blind. But afterwards this turned out to be an ungrounded apprehension. When I told this fact to another person, he told me that he had observed a rather similar case.[10]

Words are invisible yardsticks. Children are still too close to the confound to match what they are seeing by wordly measure. Their perception is not diseased or deficient. Just philosophical. Wittgenstein, or the philosopher-child. In the seeing, things retain a synesthetic tinge of singularity. Their elements settle only slowly into general classes divided according to sense mode and inculcated through conventional language, language used as an abstract standard of comparison. Color is of particular interest because it is the last objective "element" to hypostasize by meeting the measure of words. That the adult philosopher can unsee the protoscientific, linguistically assisted objectivity of things indicates that the confound continues into and through adulthood. It is not a stage or phase superseded by the sense-mode separation enabling of intermodal articulation. It is an ongoing ingredient of experience, tinging or "fringing" all appearing. The singular streaming of integral experience accompanies its analytic separation into speakable parts, or *"particulars."* The analytic extraction of particulars goes hand in hand with a synthetic articulation into classes or categories: the ideal wholes into which the particulars abstractly combine and from which they divide. The linguistically assisted objectivity of things is their conventionally constructed, unacknowledged ideality. The particular and the general are the two dimensions of the ideal. They co-occur with language.

Katz's vocabulary in the quote above needed correcting because what we see is not a "particular" white inseparable from a "particular" degree of brightness. The particular is part and parcel of the general. What we are seeing is the *singularity* of a confound. We are seeing the fusion; we are seeing the inseparability; we are seeing the integrity of before-after differentiations. Like the newborn, we directly perceive the relation. Then again, there is what we *have seen*. We have seen the particular and the general pronounced in marriage, in abstraction of actual relation. The singularity we are seeing still keeps them silent company. It quietly haunts them both, tingeing and fringing them with the relationality they have lost. We directly perceive the lost relation as a *side-perception,* crowded out to the fringe by the ceremonial application of terms of conformity. Crowded out from the convivial circle but always ready to spiral back in to assert its adult autonomy from standardized interaction.

The haunting singularity of the experiential confound leaves its side-perceived mark even on the conventionally used language. Lexically, few languages systematize colors in anything approaching the order of a color wheel. In fact, "many languages of the world do not have color-referring terms as such. They may, however, have words that are used to describe the appearance of things in terms of what we would identify as color. These words are often context-dependent."[11] By "context-dependent" is meant that other axes of distinction intersect indissociably with that of color. In other words, other-sense appearings confound with color. The most salient of these are texture and taste. To take a much discussed example, in Hanunóo (a Polynesian language), distinctions between dryness and wetness, indicative of degree of succulence, is a fundamental dimension of color judgment. Here, both texture and taste fuse with color. Also entering in are amodal perceptions. These are directly processual, pertaining to change of quality (such as weakening or fading).[12] There is no need to travel to exotic linguistic landscapes to find this kind of example. You just need to think of the names of crayons and paints in English, or the vocabulary of interior decorators, to confirm the necessity of synesthetic or amodal dimensions to the definition of color. Color per se "is not linguistically salient unless made so. . . . Colors . . . as we know them are the product of language under the influence of culture."[13] But even cultures that have abstracted color from the confound most single-mindedly and have systematized color relations most extensively cannot maintain the reduction efficiently beyond a few basic or "primary" terms. The synesthetic and the amodal exploit the invisible transitions between primaries to creep back into the most well-policed reduction. Their fringed reentry makes the primaries themselves appear much less the model, three-dimensional, objectivities they are presented as being: "What is there in favor of saying that green is a primary color, not a blend of blue and yellow? . . . How do I know that I mean the same by the words 'primary colors' as some other person who is also inclined to call green [much less "wet"] a primary color? No —here language-games decide."[14]

"Confusion" about color is not endemic to non-European languages. Classicists were thrown into an uproar a century and a half ago when it was suggested that ancient Greek "failed" to make the kind of color distinctions modern Europeans consider so obvious and basic.[15] The thought that European culture's Greek forebears were so "primitive" as not to know the difference between "black" and "purple" or "bright" and "white" was too much for the Victorian mind to bear. It was hypothesized, in their defense, that the poor folk were color-blind. But of course the Greeks were not deficient. Just philosophical. In the classical color vocabulary "no real distinction is made between chromatic and achromatic."[16] The Greek lexicon concerns the brightness confound more than color per se. "Within each [vocabulary] group the terms did not differentiate in virtue of hue but were either used indifferently as synonyms or differentiated in respect of brightness and intensity."[17] This focus on the brightness confound is already reduced in relation to the Hanunóo concern with the full experiential confound. But it is in no way unusual. In fact, it is more the rule than the exception.

A heroically misguided attempt to establish the universality of "basic color terms" found languages in which there were only two such terms. These did not separate hue from degree of brightness, corresponding to black/dull and white/brilliant.[18] There were no cases of languages with two basic "color" terms which did not confound the chromatic and the achromatic in just this way. Even in the most "advanced" vocabularies, there were always points where distinctions of lightness/darkness impinged on hue. Perhaps most significantly, the only "systematic error" was the "premature appearance of grey" in the supposedly linear progression from "primitive" two-term languages to "advanced" multiterm, technicolor languages.[19] Goethe's anti-Newtonian phenomenology, as well as Klee's artistic vision, sees color as enveloped in and emerging from gray, in the fuzzy transitional zones of moving edge and shadow.[20] Interesting: a "universal" system of color terms including cultures without terms for colors, haunted through and through by achromatic anomaly, and making a systematic Goethean "error" concerning gray and the emergence of color. One wonders if the premature gray was really on the temples of the researchers.

None of this should be taken to mean that the extraction and separation of color from the confound and its standardization are not real or do not work. They work and they are real. They just don't work everywhere all of the time, in spite of their empirical mission to do so. Their reality is that of an extractive event or process of differentiation selectively applied by collective mechanisms of language and culture to a philosophically, phenomenally, and artistically persistent confound. The word "confound" should not be considered to carry the negative connotations so often attributed to it by empirical research. It should be taken in its etymological meaning: simply, "found together." James's "conflux" could be substituted for "confound" in order to avoid the pejorative connotations.[21] In Deleuze and Guattari's vocabulary, the conflux is a "block" of experience. Their term, which foregrounds the fusional aspect, is used most often in the compound "childhood-block."[22] The term carries no connotations of regression or primitiveness. Deleuze and Guattari are careful to stress that the "childhood" block is an accompanying dimension of emergence contemporaneous to every age. They might just as well have called it a "philosopher-block." It is as much a becoming-philosopher of the child as a becoming-child of the philosophically seeing adult.

Confession of a scientist: "Any color perception in real life is accompanied by a number of appearance characteristics that we ruled out rather rigidly as outside the subject of color. To the observer in any given situation, these other characteristics are often of greater importance than the color. . . . Color is simply one frame of reference."[23]

If . . .

If artists follow Wittgenstein, the Hanunóo, Goethe, and Klee in not "rigidly ruling out" whole domains of confounding but absolutely real visual and synesthetic experience, then their treatment of form is significantly altered. Color is no longer separable from form, as a less real or less interesting "secondary quality." Color can no longer be discounted (or celebrated) as subjective or whimsical ("decorative"), as it often was in modernism and postmodernism. It is experienced as being as fundamental as form. Color, illumination, form, three-dimensional space, and linear time all *emerge*, and emerge together, reciprocally, differently each time, from a many-more dimensioned, self-varying confound.

If the singular confound is self-varying, then making something of it or doing something with it requires the artist to yield to its self-activity. The artist's activity does not stand outside its "object" and operate upon it, as some alien matter. Doing so automatically converts the variation into a reductive combination of manipulable independent variables. Yielding to the complexity of variation, the artist's activity *joins* the confound, through experienced zones of synesthetic and spatiotemporal indistinction. The artist's activity *becomes* one of the encompassed variations of the confound. The artist can still act. But her action is more an experimental tweaking of an autonomous process than a molding of dumb matter. The artist's joining the confound helps catalyze a particular co-emergence of color, illumination, form, and space-time. This is still a "creative" process—all the more so because it modulates an actual emergence. It brings a singular variation out into integral, unfolding expression. For Klee (as for Cézanne and Guattari),[24] this bringing into singular expression, this unfolding of the confoundingly enveloped, is the literal creation of a world: art as cosmogenesis. From an aesthetic direction as different from Klee's and Cézanne's as they are to each other, recall Monet's buildings and flowers, emerging from nothing, or from the vague and insubstantial "envelope"[25] of a brightness confound appearing for itself as formless fog and in foggy forms—inseparable from variations of color—as a fuzziness of edge, an openness of outline rendering it impossible to recognize the painting's "elements" taken separately, or viewed in a way that extracts them from their relational whole—a whole world captured at the moment of its emergence from the unform.

If artistic activity is a catalysis, then it is not a "construction." Construction takes already extracted variables and recombines them. Protestations to the contrary, constructivism operates entirely within the one framework of objectivism. Its "relativism" is more a confirmation than a counterindication of this. The subjectivism of relativism is complementary to science's objectivism. It just shifts the emphasis. Objectivism is secretly founded upon the generalizing extraction of spaceless, timeless units or inert particles of abstracted matter. It thus requires an even more abstract center of activity ("the subject," however "decentered"—the more the better in fact) to manipulate the inertness and generality. The subject is not inert. It is a pure activity responding to the inertness of matter. The subject expresses its activity by lending it to matter, "independently" making it move and vary (creative "freedom": the "ideal" proper to art). The subject's activity is as spaceless as the ideal matter it freely and unconfoundingly ("critically") manipulates. But its activity operates in time. It adds time back into matter ("historicizes" or "recontextualizes"), as if the singularity of situation that was generalized away to begin with can be added back in and cobbled back together ("constructed") by yet another layer of generalizing abstraction. "Relativism" is when the emphasis shifts from the activity of standardization that produced the abstract entities in the first place to their critical and historicized cobbling back together—as a natural extension of the first activity. Art as an autonomous process of bringing an enveloping self-variation into its own truly singular expression is a catalytic fusion. Catalysis involves *resituating* variation—a very different proposition from contextualizing things. Klee called this "composition" in contradistinction to "construction."[26] Composition is less a critical thought project than an integrally experienced emergence. It is a creative event.

If construction recombines found (already extracted) elements or fragments, and composition involves the unfolding of an absolutely singular worlding relational whole, *then* before hackles raise too high, it is important to specify that the whole never actually exists. It always moves to the edge or recedes infinitely into the shadows. It isn't an outline or boundary, but an indeterminate fringing. It is not a closure or framing or subsumption. It is the openness of closed form, form continually running into and out of other dimensions of existence. Although the relational whole does not appear outside an actual, situated expression of it, it is not reducible to its situation. It is too confoundingly fuzzy, too impossibly overfull with mutually conveying dimensions of experience emerging into and out of each other, too self-varyingly plastic to be actual. Neither reducible to nor separable from any given situation: nonlocality. The nonlocal relationality, the integrality of the creative event, is *virtual.* Only the terms of the relation are actual. The virtual whole is a transformational or *transitional fringing* of the actual. It is like a halo of eventness fuzzifying solidity of form and thus confounding closure. It is the "aura" of newness surrounding and suffusing what actually emerges. Newness: what is comparable only to itself. Only a theory willing to re-entertain the notion of the absolute can approach the virtual.

If all emergent form brings its fringe of virtuality with it, then no particular medium of expression has a monopoly on the virtual. Every medium, however "low" technologically, really produces its own virtuality (yes, even painting). "Digital art" is in no way synonymous with "virtual reality." What matters is the "how" of the expression, not the "what" of the medium, and especially not the simple abstractness of the elements that the medium allows to be combined.

If digital art is not synonymous with virtual reality, then it is missing the point to consider all things digital "new" and "virtual." In fact, virtual reality in the narrow sense has generated more than its share of old-fashioned reductive activity. Even the supposedly liberating paradigm of the "rhizome," as commonly construed, repeats the founding gesture of empirical reduction. It takes a multidimensional experiential process and reduces it to a spatial configuration. Once again, transition is spatialized. Then time and change are added back in as the movement of the subject (cursor) through abstract (cyber) space. The problem is that the backdrop against which that movement takes place remains general (which is not exactly the same as abstract—the virtual is abstract yet singular). The digital "architecture" framing the movement typically does not itself move. This is the case for example in a closed hypertext environment, where all the possible permutations preexist the "change" added by the subject's movement and remain untouched by it. Unchanged change? Open hypertext environments (like the World Wide Web) and "interactive" (relational) environments with transmutational or evolutionary potentials built in need really new virtual concepts. Or new really virtual concepts capable of grasping *process* unencumbered by reductive spatial or even spatiotemporal framings. They need philosophy.

But that does not mean that they necessarily need *philosophers.* For the art of catalyzing a relational emergence is philosophy in action. The conceptual newness is there, in the event, *enacted*. Art, as "composition," is enacted philosophical thought. Explicit theorizing may be of help. But it is not by any stretch a necessity. As the popular rhizome suggests, it is often a hindrance.

With that, I will return to my table. (I wonder if it changed when I wasn't unseeing it.)

STRANGE HORIZON

Buildings, Biograms, and the Body Topologic

In architecture, computer-assisted topological design technique is no longer a novelty. With the required software and hardware now accessible, paperless studios and offices are less the exception than they once were. However, with growing familiarity have come inklings of discontent. There is a common drift to many of the reactions voiced at lectures, conferences, and in the classroom. It seems to be a widely held opinion that the abstractness of the digital space of topology contradicts the spatial reality of bodies and buildings. We do not live in non-Euclidean space, the objection goes. Why then are you foisting mutant geometries on us that don't correspond to anything real? Topological architecture is just too abstract. It can't connect to the body as we experience it. Besides, you can animate architectural design practice as much as you like. You still end up with a building that isn't going anywhere. It's all a sham. Design techniques based on continuity and movement rather than static form betray themselves in the fixity of their final product. If you're so stuck on continuity, where's the continuity between your process and its product? It's all very pretty, but why should we, your public—livers-in and passersby buildings—why should we care?

What if the *space of the body is really abstract?* What if the body is inseparable from dimensions of *lived abstractness* that cannot be conceptualized in other than topological terms? The objections that topological architecture is too abstract and doesn't connect at all with the body would dissipate. Conversely, the question of how precisely the process continues in the product would become all the more pressing. Topological architecture would need to do more than it has up to now to develop a response. After all, its very effectiveness as a design method is in the balance. The answer may well disappoint partisans of concreteness incarnate. It may turn out that computer-assisted topological design technique has inadequately addressed the question of its end-effectiveness because *it is not abstract enough* to be a fitting match for the abstract resources of "concrete" experience.

The Argument from Orientation

It is with some chagrin that I confess to having sat contentedly in my temporary office at the Canadian Centre for Architecture for no less than two months looking at the wrong street out the window. I was looking east onto rue St. Marc. But I was seeing north onto rue Baille. I am sad to report that there is no resemblance between the two scenes. Something that was seriously disorienting me was happening in the time it took me to get from the side entry of the building to the door of my office. But that's just the half of it. The something seriously disorienting that was happening as I snaked my way through the corridors overpowered the evidence of my eyes. It was completely overriding the clear-as-day visual cues available to me out the window of my office. The sudden realization that my north was everyone else's east was jarring. True, I hadn't paid much attention to the scene. But I wasn't just not paying attention. When it hit me, I had the strangest sensation of my misplaced image of the buildings morphing, not entirely smoothly, into the corrected scene. My disorientation wasn't a simple lack of attention. I had been positively (if a bit vaguely and absent-mindedly) seeing a scene that wasn't there. It took a moment's effort to replace what positively hadn't been there with what plainly was. When you actively see something that isn't there, there is only one thing you can call it: a hallucination. It was a worry.

Thinking about it, I realized that I could make my way to and from my office to the building's exit without error, but, if I had been asked to sketch scenes from the corridors or to map the route, I couldn't have done it with any accuracy. I had precious little memory of the way—yet I navigated it flawlessly. Correction: I had precious little *visual* memory of the way. I must have been navigating on autopilot using some form of basically nonvisual memory. If I put myself mentally through the paces of exiting, instead of seeing passing scenes I felt twists and turns coming one after the other with variable speed. I was going on a bodily memory of my movements, one of contorsion and rhythm rather than visible form. There is in fact a sixth sense directly attuned to the movement of the body: proprioception. It involves specialized sensors in the muscles and joints. Proprioception is a self-referential sense, in that what it most directly registers are displacements of the parts of the body relative to each other. Vision is an exoreferential sense, registering distances from the eye.

It appears I had been operating on two separate systems of reference: a predominantly proprioceptive system of self-reference operating in the tunnel-like bowels of the building and a predominantly visual system of reference for the vistas outside. The two systems were not calibrated to each other—or they hadn't been until my moment of hallucinatory truth before the window. Their respective spaces of orientation had been non-communicating, like qualitatively different monads of experience. The idea that this is not as unusual a situation as my initial concern had suggested came to me in the subway on the way home. If you have ever ridden a subway, it is likely that you have had a similarly jarring experience when surfacing to street level.[1]

That must be it. The paucity of visual cues in tunnel-like places like corridors and subways requires a backup system to take over from the usual way of orienting: using visible forms grouped into fixed configurations to make what psychologists call cognitive maps. I had a happy ride. Until I thought about how I had just gotten where I was. My memory of getting from the exit of the building to the subway stop just moments before was virtually blank. Not quite (not again!): twists and turns in rhythm. Yes, again, I had been on autopilot. I had gotten to the train by habit, and it was evidently my proprioceptive system of reference that seemed to be the habitual one, window or tunnel, vista or no vista. Clear visual images of forms in mapped configurations now seemed the exception. Landmarks I remembered. Sporadically. Rising into the light from rhythms of movement, as from an unseen ground of orientation, in flux.

Close your eyes and try to make your way to the fridge. Your visual memory of the rooms and the configurations of the furniture will start to fade within seconds. But chances are you will "intuitively" find your way to the food with relatively little difficulty. Especially if you're beginning to get hungry. If you think about it, we all go about most of our everyday lives on habitual autopilot, driven by half-conscious tendencies gnawing at us gently like mild urban hungers. Orienting is more like intuitively homing in on the food with your eyes closed than it is like reading a map.

Something is rotten on the shelf of spatial-experience theory. Cognitive maps, built on the visual basis of generic three-dimensional forms in Euclidean geometric configurations, aren't all that they are advertised to be. As a general explanation of orientation, they are past their "use by" date. The way we orient is more like a tropism (tendency plus habit) than a cognition (visual form plus configuration).

Research in spatial orientation has been stumbling in the same direction. Recent studies assumed the traditional cognitive model, based on "reading" visual cues embedded in the forms and configurations of objects. It was found, however, that the brain's ability to orient increased the *emptier* the space. The conclusion was that humans orient more by the "shape of the space" than the visual characteristics of what's in it.[2] But what is the shape of empty space? Indeterminate—except for the rhythm of movement through it, in its twistings and turnings. The studies were suggesting that the proprioceptive self-referential system—the *referencing of movement to its own variations*—was more dependable, more fundamental to our spatial experience than the exoreferential visual-cue system. Self-referential orientation is called "dead reckoning," after the nautical term.[3] It is known to be the basis of many animals' abilities to orient. It is a key element, for example, in the homing pigeon's well-known feats of navigation. Its role in human orientation has significant implications for our understanding of space because it *inverts the relation of position to movement*. Movement is no longer indexed to position. Rather, position emerges from movement, from a relation of movement to itself. Philosophically, this is no small shift.

It takes little reflection to realize that visual landmarks play a major role in our ability to orient. Landmarks stand out, singularly. Most of us would be capable of pasting them together into a visual map. But to do that, you have to *stop* and think about it. It takes effort—an effort that interferes with the actual movement of orientation. *Cognitive mapping takes over where orientation stops.*

The way landmarks function in the actual course of orientation is very different from reading a map. They are what you habitually head for or away from. They trigger *headings*. Vectors. Landmarks are like magnetic poles that vectorize the space of orientation. A landmark is a minimal visual cue functioning to polarize movement's relation to itself in a way that allows us habitually to flow with preferential heading. The vectorial structuring effected by landmarks gives the space of orientation a *qualita-*

tive dimension, expressed in tropistic preference. The cognitive model assumes that visual cues are somehow used to calculate distances, as if our brains were computers preprogrammed in inches and feet. Isn't it more plausible instead that our bodies are habituated in steps? And that steps relate more directly to other steps than they do to conventional feet? The computational fiction is a natural outgrowth of the assumption that we effectively move through and live in a static, metric or quantitative, Euclidean space. I for one don't count my way around town. A qualitative space of moving, step-by-step self-reference accords better with my navigationally competent (if at times cognitively challenged) sense of where I am.

Landmarks rise up visibly from a nonvisual sea of self-related movement. They refer more directly to the self-referencing of the movements surrounding them than to each other. Fundamentally, each landmark stands alone with its associated coursings. What they mark most directly is a *monad* of relation, a patch of motion referencing its own self-variations (the multiple headings it carries). Landmarks and their associated patches of qualitative relation can be pasted together to form a map, but only with an additional effort that must first interrupt the actual course of orientation. It is in a second moment, in an added operation, that the quantifiable cognitive product is fed back into the space of movement. This can indeed increase the flexibility and precision of a body's orienting. But it remains that cognitive mapping is secondarily applied to the experience of space, or the space of experience. This makes it an *overcoding*—a certain way in which experience *folds back on itself.* It is very uncommon, a limit-case rarely attained, that we carry within our heads a full and accurate map of our environment. We wouldn't have to carry maps on paper if we had them in our brains. No matter how consciously overcoding we like to be, our mappings are riddled with proprioceptive holes threatening at any moment to capsize the cognitive model (like the empty quarters filled with sea monsters on medieval maps). No matter how expert or encompassing our cognitive mapping gets, the monstrous sea of proprioceptive dead reckoning is more encompassing still. We are ever aswim in it.

The very notion of cognitive overcoding implies that we orient with two systems of reference used *together.* The contradiction between them is only apparent. Pragmatically, they cofunction. Visual cues and cognitive mappings function as storage devices allowing us more ready reaccess to less habituated proprioceptive patches. They also serve as useful correctives, when we find ourselves hallucinating buildings that positively aren't there. The reverse is also true: proprioceptive orienting can act as a corrective to visual awareness. When we are momentarily lost, the buildings in front of us are in plain view. They may be strangely familiar, but we still can't place ourselves. Oddly, the first thing people typically do when they realize they are lost and start trying to reorient is to look away from the scene in front of them, even rolling their eyes skyward. We figure out where we are by putting the plain-as-day visual image back in the proper proprioceptive sea-patch. To do that, we have to interrupt vision, in the same way visual awareness interrupts proprioception. The alarmingly physical sense we feel when we realize we are lost is a bodily registering of the disjunction between the visual and the proprioceptive. Place arises from a dynamic of interference and accord between sense-dimensions.

Our orienting abilities, then, combine the resources of two different dimensions of experience. The places we plainly see as we go about our daily lives are products of a cooperation between two sense systems. A *synesthetic* system of cross-referencing supplements a systemic duality, exoreferential and self-referential, positional and moving, Euclidean and self-varyingly monadic. Synesthetic cooperation links these dimensions to each other, always locally—specifically, where we are lost. Cross-sense referencing forms a third hinge-dimension of experience. This "lost" dimension of experience is where vision's conscious forms-in-configuration feed back into the vectorial tendency-plus-habit of proprioception, and where proprioception feeds forward into vision. Where we go to find ourselves when we are lost is where the senses fold into and out of each. *We always find ourselves in this fold in experience.*

An aside: If the positioned sights we plainly see always result from synesthetic interference and accord, was there really a difference in nature between the sight I positively saw that wasn't there out my window, and the one I laboriously replaced it with? Weren't they just two sides of the same coin: the interference side and the accord side? If every effectively placed experience is a synesthetic production, it becomes difficult to maintain that there is a difference in nature between hallucination and perception. Isn't it just a pragmatic difference, simply between cross-referenced and not cross-referenced? It would stand to reason that there would be a kind of continental drift naturally affecting proprioceptive experience patches due to their self-referential, monadic operation. Their mode of *reality* demands it. Isn't getting lost, even seeing things that aren't there, just a momentary grounding in an impractical dimension of reality? It is the encompassing reality of what we really experience in a spatial way that gets lost if we try to limit our understanding of space too narrowly to vision in its exoreferential single-sense functioning and the associated Euclidean geometry of form-in-configuration. In Euclidean vision, where we always find ourselves is what gets lost.

Look at things from the proprioceptive side. Its elements are twists and turns, each of which is already defined relationally, or differentially (by the joint nature of the proprioceptors), before entering into relation with each other. That makes the relation entered into among elements a double differentiation. The elements fuse into a rhythm. The multiplicity of constituents fuses into a unity of movement. The resulting patch is a self-varying monad of motion: a dynamic form figuring only vectors. Although effective, the dynamic form is neither accurate nor fully visualizable. It is operatively vague, a vector space not containable in metric space. It is a qualitative space of variation referenced only to its own movement, running on autopilot. It is not a space of measure. To get a static, measurable, accurately positioned, visual form, you have to stop the movement. This capsizes the relation between movement and position. Now position arises out of movement. Static form is extracted from dynamic space, as a quantitative limitation of it. An exact vector space feeds its self-variational results into the limitative conditions of quantitative, Euclidean space, populated placidly by traditional geometric forms plottable into configurations.

Doesn't this sound familiar? Doesn't the proprioceptive experience-patch sound an awful lot like a topological figure in the flesh? Doesn't the way it all shapes up sound a lot like the way Greg Lynn describes computer-assisted design—starting with differential parameters that automatically combine to govern unities/continuities of self-varying movement, ending only when the program stops running, leaving a Euclidean form as a static witness to its arrested dynamism?[4] Doesn't topological design method digitally repeat what our bodies do noncomputationally as we make our way to and from our workstations? Then, when we watch the program run, aren't we doing it again, slumped before the screen? Are we not immobily repeating our body's ability to extract form from movement? When we stare, barely seeing, into the screen, haven't we entered a "lost" body-dimension of abstract orientation not so terribly different from the one we go to when we roll up our eyes and find ourselves in the fold?

The proprioceptive dimension of experience was described as one of two experiential dimensions. But the two were also described as folding into each other. That folding of the Euclidean and non-Euclidean into and out of each other is itself understandable only in topological terms. This hinge-dimension between quantitative and qualitative space is itself a topological figure—to the second degree, since topology already figures in it. It is a topological hyperfigure. The non-Euclidean, qualitative, and dynamic is more encompassing than the Euclidean, quantitative and static, by virtue of this double featuring. Simply, to put the two together you have to make a move between them. You have to fold experience back on itself. You have to twist one of its dimensions into the other and cross-reference them both to that operation. This means that all orientation, all spatialization, is operatively encompassed by topological movement—from which it derives in the first nonplace.

The space of experience is really, literally, physically a topological hyperspace of transformation.

A Note on Terminology

"Topology" and "non-Euclidean" are not synonyms. Although most topologies are non-Euclidean, there are Euclidean topologies. The Möbius strip and the Klein bottle are two-dimensional Euclidean figures.[5] The distinction that is most relevant here is between topological transformation and static geometric figure: between the process of arriving at a form through continuous deformation and the determinate form arrived at when the process stops. An infinite number of static figures may be extracted from a single topological transformation. The transformation is a kind of superfigure that is defined not by invariant formal properties but by continuity of transformation. For example, a torus (doughnut shape) and a coffee cup belong to the same topological figure because one can be deformed into the other without cutting. Anything left standing when the deformation is stopped at any moment, in its passage through any point in between, also belongs to their shared figure. The overall topological figure is continuous and multiple. As a transformation, it is defined by vectors rather than coordinate points. A vector is *transpositional:* a moving-through points. Because of its vectorial nature, the geometry of the topological superfigure cannot be separated from its duration. The figure is what runs through an infinity of static figures. It is not itself determinate, but determinable. Each static figure stands for its determination but does not exhaust it. The overall figure exceeds any of its discrete stations and even all of them taken together as an infinite set. This is because between any two points in Euclidean space, no matter how close, lies another definable point. The transformation joining the points in the same superfigure always falls *between* Euclidean points. It recedes, continuously, into the between.[6] The topological superfigure in itself is the surplus passing-through between Euclidean spatial coordinates. Logically, it is not sequential, even though it is oriented (vectorial). It is recessively *transitional.* In this essay, the word "non-Euclidean" is used as a convenient shorthand for a space of this kind: one that cannot be separated from its duration due to a transitional excess of movement. "Non-Euclidean" is a good-enough nontechnical term for dynamic or durational "spaces" that do not fit into the classical Euclidean (actually Cartesian) intuition of space as a triple-axis, coordinate box that contains things. In this view, widely thought to correspond to our everyday experience, time is an independent variable adding a fourth, formally distinct, dimension to the traditional three of space. Topologically speaking, space and time are dependent variables. They are not formally distinguishable. They cannot be separated from each other without stopping the process and changing its nature (Euclideanizing it). The relation of the dimensions of space to that of time is one of mutual inclusion. This mutual inclusion, and the strange logical and especially experiential effects associated with it, is what is termed a "hyperfigure" or "hyperspace" for the purposes of this essay. It may be noted in passing that even a Euclidean topological figure may generate a surplus-effect, although in a more static vein. The Möbius strip and the Klein bottle are two-dimensional figures whose folding and twisting on themselves create three-dimensional effects. The "effects" are real, but not part of the formal definition of the figure. They are in the figure as it is really experienced, adding another *quality* to it, precisely in the way it stands out from its formal limits. They are extraformal stand-out or pop-out effects. The word "hyperspace" may also be applied to experiential surplus-dimension effects of this kind, whatever the geometry. Experience itself may be defined as a hyper-

dimensional reality: as the "being" of the excess of effect over any determinate spatial configuration. As the following argument from synesthesia
asserts, the "shape" of experience can be considered to be a one-sided
topological figure: an abstract (recessive/pop-out) "surface" for the reception, storage, and reaccess of qualitative hypereffectivity that can only
be approached head-on.

The Argument from Synesthesia

The hinging of the proprioceptive on the visual in the movement of orientation is a synesthetic interfusion. It is not the only one. Each side, for
example, enters into its own synesthetic fusion with the tactile: a determinate, positioned sight is a potential touch; the tropism of proprioceptive
twisting and turning is assisted by past and potential bumps and the tactile feedback from the soles of our feet. There are many other synesthetic
conjunctions, involving all the senses in various combinations, including
smell and hearing. Clinical synesthesia is when a hinge-dimension of
experience, usually lost to active awareness in the sea change to adulthood, retains the ability to manifest itself perceptually. In synesthesia,
other-sense dimensions become visible, as when sounds are seen as colors. This is not vision as it is thought of cognitively. It is more like other-
sense operations at the hinge with vision, registered from its point of view.
Synesthetic forms are dynamic. They are not mirrored in thought; they
are literal perceptions. They are not reflected upon; they are experienced
as events. Synesthetes who gain a measure of willful control over them still
perceive them as occurrences in the world, not contents of their heads.
They describe summoning them into perception, then moving toward or
around them. Synesthetic forms are used by being summoned into present perception then recombined with an experience of movement. And
they are useful. They serve as memory aids and orientation devices. Since
they work by calling forth a real movement-experience, they retain a
privileged connection to proprioception. This is not cue-based, form-
and-configuration vision. Although synesthetic forms are often called
"maps," they are less cartographic in the traditional sense than "diagrammatic" in the sense now entering architectural discourse.[7] They are lived
diagrams based on already lived experience, revived to orient further

experience. Lived and relived: *biograms* might be a better word for them than "diagrams."

It is worth paying close attention to how synesthetes describe their "maps." The biograms are usually perceived as occupying the otherwise empty and dimensionless plane between the eyes and objects in the world. This liminal nonplace has been characterized as "peri-personal." It lies at the border of what we think of as internal, personal space and external, public space. The appearance of the biogram is borderline in time as well. It is accompanied by a feeling of "portentous" déjà vu: an already-past pregnant with futurity, in present perception.[8] This makes experiencing the biograms, in the words of one synesthete, dubbed MP in the literature, like "seeing time in space"—a good way of describing an event.[9] They have a feeling of thickness or depth to them, like a "flexible moving 3 dimension." But the depthlikeness is vague enough that they can still be likened to diaphanous "slides" projected on an invisible screen. They retain a *surface* character. The "maps" MP draws at the researcher's request do not satisfy her. Her biograms are not plainly visible forms. They are more-than visual. They are event-perceptions combining senses, tenses, and dimensions on a single surface. Since they are not themselves visual representations, they cannot be accurately represented in mono-sense visual form. Oddly, although they appear in front and in the midst of things, the biograms are "larger than my visual range, like looking at the horizon." They are geometrically strange: a foreground-surround, like a trick center twisting into an all-encompassing periphery. They are uncontainable either in the present moment or in Euclidean space, which they instead encompass: strange horizon.

Since they are determinately positioned neither in time nor space, their presence can only be considered a mode of abstraction. They are real—really perceived and mnemonically useful—abstract surfaces of perception. Since they continue indefinitely, in order to bring up certain regions the synesthete has to move around, into, or away from them. She doesn't *actually* walk, of course. The movement, though really perceived and mnemonically useful, does not measurably take place in Euclidean space. It is an *intensive* movement, occurring in place (as at a workstation or with rolled-back eyes)—or more accurately out-placed, in the event. This is an *abstract movement on an abstract surface*.

The synesthete uses her biograms, for example, to keep track of birthdays. On the birthday biogram, each region stores a conjunction between a date, a name, and a color. When she has to recall a birthday, she will use the color as a landmark, and when she approaches the properly colored region, the name and date will appear. The shape and sound of the letters and numbers are stored in the colors, diaphanously merged into them as in a dissolve, or like strands "woven together" in a patch of fabric. They are accessed by a reverse dissolve that is like "pulling out threads." Shape, sound, and language: of a fabric with color.

MP has a unique biogram for everything she needs to remember. The biograms are "not connected in any way." They are like separate monads of abstract lived experience. Except that in their strange twisting between foreground and horizon each loops back at a certain point into darkness. Each biogram arcs in multicolored mnemonic glory from a sea of shadow. What lies in the darkness at the end of the rainbows? The answer comes without the slightest hesitation: *other people's minds.*

Biograms cannot be described without resorting to topology: centers folding into peripheries and out again, arcs, weaves, knots, and unthreadings. Face it. That is to say, you are always facing it. Wherever you are, whoever you are, whatever day or year it is, the biogram is *in front* of you. The synesthetic form of experience is *faced,* in something like the sense in which writing is handed.[10] Except that a left has a right, and this front doesn't have a back (yet it still has shadow?). This means a biogram is a *one-sided topological surface*—really, strangely, usefully.[11] This is not a metaphor. If there is a metaphor in play, isn't it rather the mathematical representation that is the metaphor for the biogram? The biogram is a literal, graphically diaphanous event-perception. It is what is portended when you remember seeing time in space.

Synesthesia is considered the norm for infantile perception. The theory is that it becomes so habitual as to fall out of perception in the "normal" course of growing up. It is thought to persist as a nonconscious underpinning of all subsequent perception, as if the objects and scenes we see are all "threads" pulled by habit from a biogrammatic fabric of existence.[12] Synesthetes are "normal" people who are abnormally aware of their habits of perception. "Normality" is when the biogram recedes to the background of vision. Biograms are always in operation. It is just a question of whether or not their operations are remarked.

For all perceivers, the biogram is the mode of being of the intersensory hinge-dimension. Its strange one-sided topology is the general plane of cross-reference not only for sights, sounds, touches, tastes, smells, and proprioceptions, but also for numbers, letters, words, even units of grammar. On that plane, the learned forms that are usually thought of as restricted to a "higher" cultural plane re-become perceptions. *Practice becomes perception.* The cognitive model has it that "higher" forms are associative compounds built up from smaller sights and sounds as from elementary building blocks. But the workings of synesthetic biograms show that the higher forms feed back to the "lower" perceptual level. They enter the general dissolve, on a level with the elementary, fused into the surface, interwoven components of the fabric of life. This makes it impossible to apply to "raw" experience distinctions such as "higher" and "lower," "perceptual" and "cognitive," or even "natural" and "cultural." There is no "raw" experience. Every experience takes place in the already-taken place of higher and lower, where they join for the future. Every experience is a portentous déjà vu at a hinge.

The relevant distinction is between involuntary and elicited. Or rather: this is the relevant connection. Biograms are described as having an odd status: they are *"involuntary and elicited."*[13] They retain the surprise of the déjà vu even for clinical synesthetes who can summon them forth and consciously navigate them for future heading. Eliciting with future heading is not the same as willing. Biograms remain their own creatures even for proficient synesthetes. They maintain a peri-personal autonomy from psychological or cognitive containment. They cannot be entirely owned personally, since they emerge from and return to a collective darkness. But they can be tamed, induced to appear and perform feats of memory. They are less like a static image on a projector screen than a live circus act, performed in a ring that lies center stage and encircles the tent.

Clinical synesthetes have trained synesthesia to perform on signal. They have perfected the trick of consciously eliciting involuntary, intersense connection as a way of invoking memory. Vision is typically used as a plane of general cross-reference. It is on the abstract surface of color that everything fuses in a way that allows a single thread to be pulled out again as needed, before returning to the fold. All the other senses, and any and every "higher" form, are gathered into color, together with the three dimensions of space and time. It is as if all the dimensions of experience were compressed into vision. This is why the topology of the biogram is so strangely twisted. It is not due to any lack, say of cognitive organization or of Euclidean accuracy. There are simply too many dimensions of reality compressed into vision. It can't hold them all in discrete, determinate, harmonious form and configuration. It buckles under the existential pressure.

The biogram is not lacking in order. It is overorganized, loaded with an excess of reality. It is deformed by experiential overfill. It is a *hypersurface*. Its hyperreality explains why it is so stubbornly abstract. Since it cannot concretely hold everything it carries, it stores the excess fused in abstraction, ready for useful reaccess. In other words, the hypersurface of synesthetic experience is "real and abstract" in precisely the way Deleuze describes the *virtual:* as an intense, torsional coalescence of potential individuations. Pulling out a thread, or decompressing a differential strand of the fusional weave of experience, involves actualizing a virtuality. That is why the synesthetic perception is always an event or performance pulling determinate form and function out of a larger vagueness, like a rabbit from a one-sided hat.

It was argued earlier that there was no essential difference between perception and hallucination, both being synesthetic creations. The feedback of "higher" forms and their associated functions onto the biogrammatic hypersurface expands the list. There is no fundamental difference between perception, hallucination, and cognition. It was also argued that the separation between the natural and the cultural was not experientially sustainable. In view of this, is it so far-fetched to call the unseen out of which biograms arc "other people's minds"? Not particular other people's minds, of course. The other of them all: an other of particular mindedness from which everyone's individuated perceptions, memories, and cognitions emerge and to which they return in a twisting rhythm of appearance and dissolve: a shared incipiency that is also a destiny. What is the other of mindedness? From what does all individual awareness arise and return? Simply: matter. Brain-and-body matter: rumbling sea for the rainbow of experience. The synesthetic hypersurface refracts the activity of matter through many-dimensioned splendor into color. It is the hinge-plane not only between senses, tenses, and dimensions of space and time, but between matter and mindedness: the involuntary and the elicited.

Reaccessing the biogram and pulling a determinate strand of organized experience from it is to reapproach the point where the materiality of the body minds itself. It is to catch the becoming-minded of the movements of matter in the act. It is to re-perform the memorial trick of experience pulling itself rabbitlike out of the black hat of matter. This is quite an ontogenetic contortion. It involves a hyperreal looping between the impersonal and the peri-personal. Any personal strand is pulled out of that non- to near-personal loop as the grande finale. After which there is nothing to do but introduce the next abstract act.

That the personal is the finale distinguishes this synesthetic onto-genesis of experience from phenomenological approaches. For phenomenology, the personal is prefigured or "prereflected" in the world, in a closed loop of "intentionality." The act of perception or cognition is a reflection of what is already "pre-" embedded in the world. It repeats the same structures, expressing where you already were. Every phenomenological event is like returning home.[14] This is like the déjà vu without the portent of the new. In the circus of synesthesia, you never really know what act will follow. The rabbit might turn into a dove and fly away. Experience, normal or clinical, is never fully intentional. No matter how practiced the act, the result remains at least as involuntary as it is elicited. Under the biogrammatic heading, the personal is not intentionally prefigured. It is rhythmically re-fused, in a way that always brings something new and unexpected into the loop. The loop is always strangely open (with just one side, how could it ever reflect itself?).

What if topological architecture could find ways of extending the "diagrams" it designs into "biograms" inhabiting the finished product? What if it could find ways of embedding in the materiality of buildings open invitations for portentous events of individuating déjà vu? Might this be a way of continuing its topological process in its product?

To do this would require somehow integrating logics of perception and experience into the modeling. Processes like habit and memory would have to be taken into account. As would the reality of intensive movement. Ways of architecturally soliciting an ongoing eliciting of emergent forms-functions at the collective hinge of perception, hallucination, and cognition would have to be experimented with. Techniques would have to be found for overfilling experience. The methods would have to operate in a rigorously anexact way, respecting the positivity of the virtual's vagueness and the openness of its individual endings. Never prefiguring.

In a way, architecture could even surpass synesthetes like MP by finding ways of building-in nonvisual hypersurfaces. There is nothing wrong with color, light, and darkness. Rainbows of experience are good. But imagine the startling effects that might be achieved by using proprioception as the general plane of cross-referencing. Imagine how positively, qualitatively moving that would be. Practices of architecture allied with experimental art, like the "reversible destiny" architecture of Arakawa and Gins or the "relational" architecture of Rafael Lozano-Hemmer, might have much to contribute. Technologies that can be twisted away from addressing preexisting forms and functions toward operating directly as *technologies of emergent experience* could be favored. Imagine if these were to become infrastructural to architectural engineering. What better place to start than with the much-touted "new media," approached not only as design tools but as architectural elements as basic as walls and windows? Could architecture build on the ability of digital technologies to connect and interfuse different spheres of activity on the same operational plane, to new effect? This is a direction in which the work of Lars Spuybroek, among others, is moving.[15]

The Argument from the Facedness of Experience

Whether you are clinically synesthetic or not, wherever you are, you are ever facing the continuation of your experience. You are always heading onward. It is relatively easy to say where any given form or configuration that comes into focus along the way is located. But where is the heading itself? That is the same as asking where is the ongoing of experience? It is not in any recognized thing or place. It is in them all, but in each under a different heading. Experience, as it happens, is in difference-of-heading before it goes in any determinate direction. The space of continuing experience is a pure or absolute space of differential heading: an indeterminate vector space infusing each step taken in Euclidean space with a potential for having been otherwise directed. The whole of vector space is compressed, in potential, in every step. Taking into consideration the feedback of higher forms discussed above, our concept of this intensive vector space of experience must be broad enough to encompass headings toward qualitatively different planes (habit, memory; vision, proprioception; color, language).

The Argument from Doubling

In synesthesia, remembering is a perceptual event. It is a reactivation of a biogram for purposes of reaccess. If an event-perception is faced, then when a biogram is reaccessed isn't the synesthete facing a previous facing? Hasn't experience doubled back on itself like a Möbius strip? The exemplary experience of the most renowned synesthete in the literature, A. R. Luria's patient S., supports this (exemplary because S.'s synesthesia was so intense that he enjoyed total recall).[16]

S.'s biograms were very different from MP's. No two synesthetes generate the same dynamic forms. S.'s were built explicitly on a shifting proprioceptive ground. They came in "walks." He would store biograms as "objects" deposited at a particular turn along a meandering walk. There they would remain as mnemonic landmarks that would come into sight when approached. When an object became visible, the component sense-threads could be pulled apart to yield an astounding range of determinate word and number memories that had been woven into them. The walks themselves were biograms of a configurational kind. They were composed of a number of synesthetic objects stored in vicinity to one another. They had to be reaccessed in order, following the proprioceptive twists and turns of the walk. Each object-form had a background, for example a wall or corner or other feature. These figure-ground landmarks combined into whole itinerant geographies. To find a memory, S. would have to enter the right geography and then move ahead proprioceptively, cross-checking against his mnemonic progress against visual landmarks until he reached the one he needed to unthread. The eventfulness of the biograms is illustrated by the fact that he could make mistakes. Significantly, the mistakes were not cognitive errors. They were tricks of perception. For example, he might accidentally store a bright biogrammatic object against a white wall, and when he passed that way again he might overlook the memory because it blended in.[17] The involuntary had failed to be elicited.

To simplify matters, he would sometimes use a familiar scene as a template for a new biogrammatic geography. For example, he might take his bedroom and store synesthetic objects under the bed, in the closet, and in all the drawers and corners. Whether based on a found geography like his bedroom or entirely constructed, a biogram is a previously experienced vector-space. When S. faced one of his biograms, he was facing his own previous presence. This facing was usually implicit, or virtual. When he recalled a biogram, he didn't usually see himself facing it the last time. Otherwise he would be facing a potentially infinite regress of himself as he repeatedly reaccessed. There were, however, times when he did encounter his former facing in the biogram.[18] The folding back of the facedness of experience on itself is a virtual biogrammatic operation which, like the biograms themselves, can actualize in conscious visual form. Perhaps schizophrenia involves a continual, involuntary awareness of the double-facedness-to-infinity endemic to experience?[19] At the other extreme, "normal" perception would be habitual unawareness of it. Isn't what we call "cognition" a deceitful simplification of the virtual regress of reaccess into a plainly available present "reflection"?

The biogram is a perceptual reliving: a folding back of experience on itself. ("He revived the situation in which something had registered in his memory.")[20] Each biogram, then, is a virtual topological superposition of a potentially infinite series of self-repetitions. A biogram doubles back on itself in such a way as to hold all of its potential variations on itself in itself: in its own cumulatively open, self-referential event. Synesthetic experience becomes monadic in the vicinity of a biogram. Facing a biogram, we are *looking forward to our own past* and *looking past into the future,* in a seeing so intense it falls out of sight. ("He would close his eyes or stare into space.")[21] Experiential vector-space time-loops. Each new present, each event-perception, is a differential repetition of that spatiotemporal loop-the-loop: different if only by virtue of being an "again," darkly.

It is often argued that architecture should allude to history. How pale that clear-eyed ambition seems faced with the twisted intensity of the biogram. If architecture were to make its mission to build in biogrammatic triggers or elicitation devices rather than contenting itself with all-too-cognitive "citations," it would have outgrown its moniker as a "spatial art." It would have become not just metaphorically historical, but a literal technology of time. It would be as directly an art of time as of space, concerned with eliciting their continuous looping into and out of each other, in mutual reaccess and renewal.

The Argument from Recursion

To the continuing chagrin of cognitive theory, the time-loop of experience has been experimentally verified. In famous studies in the 1970s, Benjamin Libet demonstrated that there is a half-second delay between the onset of brain activity and conscious awareness of the event.[22] Cognitive scientists and theorists of consciousness have worried over this because, in brain terms, a half second is a very long time. This is a long incipiency of mindedness in brain matter. All kinds of things might be going on in autopilot as perception and reflection are taking off from chemical and electrical movements of matter. Thought lags behind itself. It can never catch up with its own beginnings. The half-second of thought-forming is forever lost in darkness. All awareness emerges from a nonconscious thought-o-genic lapse indistinguishable from movements of matter.

One of the things that happens in the lapsing is a fiction. Libet determined that thought covers up its lag: the awareness is "backdated" so that each thought experiences itself to have been at the precise time the stimulus was applied. Thought hallucinates that it coincides with itself. So, the simplest perception of the simplest stimulus is already a fairly elaborate hoax, from the point of view of a theory of cognitive authenticity that sees truth in plain and present reflection. To accept the implications of the Libet lag, cognitive theory would have to accept that its own model is an even more elaborate hoax: a sophisticated version of thought's self-coinciding, matter aside. The cognitive model would have to recognize that it, too, has been a matterful hallucination, on the half-second installment plan.

The conclusion has to be that the elementary unit of thought is already a complex *duration* before it is a discrete perception or cognition. Further, it is a duration whose end loops back to its beginning. It is a recursive duration.

The complexity of this recursive duration only started to emerge later. Libet found that stimuli applied during the thought-o-genic lapse could affect the outcome. You'd think that a stimulus applied at a quarter second would have to wait until three-quarters of a second were up to make its mark. It would come in orderly succession after the half-second awareness emerging from the first stimulus. That way you'd get a reasonable succession of discrete perceptions or cognitions, even though each would still be a bit of a cheat by virtue of having backdated itself. The backdating would just be a quantitative peccadillo, a simple, measurable lag that we might find it in our cognitive selves to forgive our brains for. But if the intervening stimulus affects the outcome of the first, then things get much less reasonable. If a later stimulus can modulate an earlier one before it becomes what it will have been, the recursive durations start to meld together. Experience smudges. You get a *thirdness:* a supplemental effect not reducible to the two stimuli's respective durations considered separately. You get a supernumerary difference, a qualitative difference arising from the interrelation of recursive durations. To put it bluntly, you get a relational time-smudge. A kind of hypertime. Think about it. Since any lapse of time is infinitely divisible, and at every instant there must be some kind of stimulus arriving through one sense channel or another, if you try to fill in what happens in the half-second lapses of awareness, things get downright hallucinogenic. Say at .01 seconds a second loop begins even before the half-second loop that began at .00 has had a chance to run its course. At .02 seconds another begins, but at .015 seconds there will have been an intervening beginning, and also at .0125. You're left with an infinite multiplication of recursively durational emergent awarenesses, madly smudging each other. You get an exponentially self-complicating relational mess.

The only way to sort it out is to posit a double system of reference, with each doublet effectively enveloping an experiential infinity. Each recursive duration must be posited as leading to a discrete awareness. Except that only a very few of the teeming swarm actually make it to awareness. The others subsist nonconsciously. These are Leibniz's infinitesimally "small perceptions," each a monad unto itself.[23] In other words, the bulk of discrete perceptions and cognitions remain virtual. Our lived experience swims in an infinite cloud of infinitesimal monadic awarenesses: micro-awarenesses without the actual awareness, gnats of potential experience.[24]

Every awareness that achieves actual expression will have been in some way modulated by the swarm from which it emerged. But the modulatory effect is in principle separable from what the result would have been had the recursively durational monad not smudged. This "would have been" discrete of actual awareness can potentially be accessed, if experience folds back on itself, cross-references, and pulls on the right strand to extract an associated form from the fusional smudge. The effective discreteness of an awareness is an active creation of experience doubling back (on its already recursive duration) and extractively self-referencing.

Every first-time perception of form is already, virtually, a memory. Perception is an intensive movement back into and out of an abstract "space" of experiential previousness.

The supplemental fusion-effect that can be cross-referenced-out for present purposes belongs to a second experiential infinity. Every virtual gnat of awareness will have potentially modulated every other, if ever so slightly, actually or not. Thus there co-subsists with the swarm of potential forms/configurations an infinity of qualitative relational differences. This second virtual infinity is infinitely larger than the first, since each member of the cloud of discreteness potentially has an infinity of microperceptions to smudge with, and each smudge can smudge again, indefinitely. The relational infinity is not only larger than the first, discrete infinity, but also differs in nature. It is composed of productive interferences, or in-between effects (affects). Accordingly, it comprises a continuity of transitions rather than a collection of discrete elements. It is differentiated as a continuous variation.

We have seen this double system of reference before. The discrete perceptions/cognitions that are actually extracted provide the elementary building blocks for compound forms and configurations. They feed into metric, Euclidean space and the present of linear time associated with it. The relational, variational continuum pertains to a qualitative space that can only be described topologically. Its recursivity cannot be ignored, so it is as immediately a nonlinear temporality as it is a non-Euclidean space.[25]

The two systems virtually co-subsist and actually cofunction. Normally, the relational continuum actually appears only in its modulatory effects. It is backgrounded or peripheralized by forms and configurations taking center stage, cross-referenced-out by their attention-grabbing extraction. But it is insistent. It always finds a way to reenter the scene. It appears, for example, in the settled cloud of sawdust covering the floor of the circus ring, swarming but ignored beneath the stand-out movements of the featured performers. And in "peripheral vision," the kinesthetic-proprioceptive commotion ringing every determined act of viewing with a barely noticed, synesthetic, color and light show. Or as a white wall that a synesthetic object accidentally blends back into.[26]

Architects do not have to choose between the two systems of reference, as if one is more real than the other. The challenge is to design for both simultaneously: to build discrete forms in functional configurations, but in ways that newly reaccess the infinities of experiential potential, discrete and continuous, from which they were extracted. Building for the historically positioned here and now is to be satisfied with too little: a gnat of design. The challenge is to build *also* for the recursive duration. To see discretely in present time and determinate space—but also to "see time in space," necessarily more vaguely (and creatively), in direct future-past relation: in continuing modulation. Don't mediate. Modulate.

The Argument from the Feedback of Higher Forms

It was asserted earlier that practice becomes perception. In other words, compound forms of result feed back to the thought-o-genic level, where they fuse with more "elementary" or gnat-like components of experience, toward a new emergence. Words, numbers, and grammars recursively-durationally smudge as messily as anything. They reenter the relational continuum. This means that no matter how conventional or even stereotyped they may be, they never really go stale. They are odd fruits of experience that go "raw."

Corroboration for this has been found in studies of blind-sight. Blind-sight is nonconscious visual perception usually due to brain injury. People with blind-sight may consider themselves totally blind. Put an object in front of them, and they will insist that they see nothing. But if you ask them to reach out for the object, their hand goes straight toward it and their fingers open exactly far enough to grasp it. They do see, but nonconsciously. Their visual awareness remains virtual. (The success of their grasping stands as a testament to the effective reality of the virtual.)

The traditional explanation of this phenomenon has been that "higher" cortical functions were damaged, but that "lower" functions embedded deeper in the "reptilian" brain were still intact. This convenient interpretation was shattered by the discovery that people with blind-sight can also *virtually read*. This was demonstrated in patients who were partially blind-sighted but retained a reduced field of normal vision. The experimenter would flash a word with more than one meaning in the sighted field. Then a word associated with one of its meanings would be presented in the blind field. For example, "bank" would flash into sight, followed by a flash of either "money" or "river" in blind-sight. It was found that the word presented to the patient's blindness would color their interpretation of the word they could see.[27] An unconscious perception involving highly developed cognitive skills was *modulating* conscious awareness. A practiced meaning had become a nonconscious perception capable of positively coloring the conscious production of more meaning (interpretation). This loop between "primitive" perception and "higher" cognition has been observed in undamaged brain function. One of the most startling findings has been that a single neuron is capable of recognizing a face.[28]

The feedback of "higher" functions undermines the deconstructionist mistrust of "naive" or "natural" perception. In deconstructivist architectural theory, this mistrust has often translated into an aversion to any talk of direct perception, shunned in favor of mediated readings. But, if social operations like recognizing a face or cultural operations of literate interpretation can dissolve back into direct perceptions, there is nothing to worry about. If there is never any possibility of raw experience to begin with, there is nothing to bracket or deconstruct. The most material of experience, the firing of a single neuron, is always-already positively sociocultural. Conversely, and perhaps more provocatively, *reading ceases to be a practice of mediation.* We are capable of operating socially and culturally directly on a level with matter.

It all becomes a question of modulation. This is a pragmatic rather than critical issue: how, concretely, can the virtual feedback of higher functions be used to remodulate experience? How can unmediated inflections of sociality and literate interpretation be embedded in the direct experience of the built environment? How can cultural signs be encouraged to rematerialize, to feed back into a "smallness" of perception on a level with the movements of matter? How can the literate become literal and the literal literate in two-way, creative interference? Most of all, how can this involuntary but elicited looping be accomplished *openly* and without moralizing—without the arrogance of deceit, the preciousness of conceit, or the imposition of an authorial "voice" or "vision" aimed at grounding a sea-tossed world?[29]

The Argument from Change

We tend to think of our bodies as being contained in a three-dimensional space as in some kind of box. Things are in the boxed present, which skips along from moment to moment, as from one point on a line to the next. The past is simply a point somewhere behind on the line, and the future is just a point ahead. Past and future are nothing more than presents in succession. Nothing exists outside of the march of the boxed-in present.

The problem is that if the body were all and only in the present, it would be all and only what it is. Nothing is all and only what it is. A body present is in a dissolve: out of what it is just ceasing to be, into what it will already have become by the time it registers that something has happened. The present smudges the past and the future. It is more like a doppler effect than a point: a movement that registers its arrival as an echo of its having just past. The past and future resonate in the present. Together: as a dopplered will-have-been registering *in* the instant as a unity of movement. The past and future are in continuity with each other, in a moving-through-the-present: in transition.

It is not the present that moves from the past to the future. It is the future-past that continually moves through the present. How could it be otherwise? If the body were all and only in the here and now, unlooped by dopplerings, it would be cut off from its "was's," not to mention its "would have been's" and "may yet be's." How could a body develop habits and skills? Are these not pastnesses primed in the present for the future? How could a body remember? To remember something we have forgotten, must we not somehow return to the pastness in which it lies dormant, in order to pull out its thread of presence again? Most of all, how could a body change? Where would it find change if it did not have the resources for it already within itself?

A body does not coincide with its present. It coincides with its *potential*. The potential is the future-past contemporary with every body's change.

The basic insight of Henri Bergson's philosophy, taken up by William James and later Gilles Deleuze, is that past and future are not just strung-out punctual presents. They are continuous dimensions contemporaneous to every present—which is by nature a smudged becoming, not a point-state. As Deleuze repeatedly notes, the present would never "pass" if it didn't have a dimension of "passness" or pastness to fold aspects of itself into as it folds out others into what will have presently been its futurity. Past and future are in direct, topological proximity with each other, operatively joined in a continuity of mutual folding. The present is the crease. The moments of time are dimensions of each other's unity of movement into and out of each other. They are co-operating dimensions of transition. A body does not coincide with the discretely cognizable point of its here and now (remember the Libet lag). It coincides with the twisted continuity of its variations, registered in an endless doppler loop.

The point is that *the idea that we live in Euclidean space and in linear time excludes the reality of change.* The things with which mindful bodies interact, involuntarily and otherwise, also change. As do the buildings they live in or with. Things, too, coincide with their potential. Anything that endures varies. Anything that varies in some way carries the continuities of its variations. The difference between minds, bodies, and objects are perhaps not as essential as philosophies stuck on the subjective-objective divide make them out to be. Perhaps it is not the presence or absence of any supposedly essential properties, for example consciousness or life, that distinguishes a mind from a body from an object. Perhaps they are distinguished modally, by their ways of carrying variation: by their different dopplerings of potential (different "speeds").

A thing cannot be understood without reference to the nonpresent dimensions it compresses and varyingly expresses in continuity. The formula is by now familiar: these dimensions are abstract yet real. They are virtual. Logics of presence or position that box things in three-dimensional space strung out along a time line just don't doppler. Logics of transition are needed: qualitative topologics.

The Argument from Outer Space

"Diverse astronomical observations agree that the density of matter in the cosmos is only a third of that needed for space to be Euclidean."[30] Attempts to study the size and shape of the universe have largely given up on Euclidean geometry, in favor of non-Euclidean hyperbolic topologies.[31] Some strange twistings are required to account for the "lost" matter, the "dark" matter that stubbornly fails to show (insistence of the void). Strange void-related twistings also show up in the vicinity of a black hole, where events of cosmic scale funnel directly back into the quantum soup in contravention of Euclidean gradations of scale. Understanding black holes and dark matter will have to wait for a "theory of everything": a model connecting relativity (itself based on Reimannian geometry) to quantum mechanics. The most promising candidates are topological "superstring" theories, in which the world is described as a spaghetti of multidimensional, continuous strands in unimaginable contortions.

Two of the greatest mysteries of cosmology are questions every child asks: if everything is in the universe, then what is the universe in? And, where was the world before the big bang, and how long was it there? The first question is a logical consequence of the assumption that space is Euclidean, like a box containing things. The second is an equally logical consequence of the assumption that time is a line with a beginning and end, running through or alongside space. It is clear that no glimmer of a solution is possible working with these assumptions. Some recent scientific efforts to solve these cosmically childlike questions have gone so far as to suggest topological models where space loops so twistedly that it ends up back in time. For example, the outer edge of the universe might not be an edge at all, but a recursion where the limits of space loop back to the irruption of time, from which space unfolded in the first place. Certain modelings of what occurs inside a black hole also feature a space-time fold. It has been hypothesized that matter funneling into a black hole is converted into a soup of virtual particles, called tachyons, moving backward in time.

Whatever the final answers—if they are ever arrived at—odds are that the descriptions of upper and lower limits of material existence, and the weird sinkholes bunching its fabric, won't be based on a Euclidean geometry or linear notion of time. The universe is not just a bigger box. It could well be a giant version of a Libet lag: not the box to end all boxes but the monad to outloop all monads. (Is our every Libetian awareness then a modest echo of a cosmic dynamism?)

The Argument from Inner Space

The body is composed of a branching network, decreasing in size right down to the level of molecular tubes at the mitochondrial scale. Geometrically, a body is a "space-filling fractal" of a "fourth" dimensionality, between a two-dimensional plane and a three-dimensional volume.[32] "Our skin obeys the laws of three dimensions . . . but our internal anatomy and physiology is living in a four-dimensional spatial world" (the three of enveloping Euclidean space plus the "fourth" fractal dimension of internal branching).[33] A body lives in three dimensions only at the envelope of the skin. The "Euclidean" space of the body is a *membrane*.

The membrane isn't closed. It folds in at the mouth, ears, nostrils, eyes, anus, urethra, vagina, and pores. The mouth connects through the stomach and intestines to fold back out the anus. This is one leaky "box." It's closer to a Klein bottle: a two-dimensional topological figure. Even the skin isn't really three-dimensional. It just acts as if it were. It creates a three-dimensional closure effect by regulating movements into and out of the space-filling fractal it twistedly envelops. Biologically, it's all an act, a complex nutritive, excretive act: circus of the body. We do not live in Euclidean space. We live *between* dimensions.

Might it still be argued that even if we do not live in Euclidean space, we certainly build in it? Fair enough: we build in Euclidean space in the same sense that we eat in it. To build is to produce a closure-effect by regulating movements in and out (and fractally all around). A building is a membrane.

Regulating movements is a question of scale and speed. An architect or engineer is not concerned with the swarming micromovements of matter occurring in insane velocity at the molecular level of the materials used in construction. All that concerns her is that at a certain level those unpredictable movements settle into a dependable patterning. It is the undependable movements' *aggregation* that can be depended upon: their manner of massing. The solidity of a brick is a mass mannerism, a crowd phenomenon: a *molar* relational effect.

When you place a brick against a brick, you are not rubbing hard matter up against hard matter. The electrons and nuclear particles making up the molecular aggregates are separated by voids many orders of magnitudes larger than they are. A brick is as sparse as a little universe. Nothing actually touches. The brick's "surface" is pitted by emptiness. Nor is there anything solid within each atom. Subatomic innards are a quantum soup of intense, virtual events, some occurring faster than the speed of light (quantum tunneling), some enjoying experimentally verified recursive causality (complementarity). The effective stability of the brick emerges from the interrelation of those intensive, incorporeal movements. The quality of hardness is a surface-effect defined by what the holding-together of the brick's fused elementary constituents lets pass, captures, or blocks. It is a regulated regime of movement. The "surface" itself is nothing other than this relational effect of hardness, or regime of passage. The effect is relative to the nature of the movement that comes to pass, its scale, and speed (a gamma ray would neither find it hard nor treat it as a surface to bounce off).

When you place a brick next to another brick you are not placing matter against matter. You are placing effect against effect, *relation against relation*. You are building a conglomerate economy of movement. You are hinging molar stabilities to build larger molar stability. What we think of as Euclidean space is a mutual holding in relational stability of incorporeal event-spaces, relative to kind of movement, scale, and speed. Incorporeal: abstract. Euclidean space is the *relative concreteness of the abstract*. It is a certain kind of abstract-surface hinge-effect.

When you place bricks together to build four walls and then put a body inside, something similar is happening. The memories, habits, and tropisms the body carries with it in the associated, intensive event space of incorporeal or abstract movement evoked repeatedly in this essay, constitute an aggregate of relation. All the goings-on and passings-by around the building constitute another aggregate of relation: a sea of movements, each of which has a potential effect on the body, capable of modulating which determinate threads are pulled from the relational continuum it carries. Which threads the body reexpresses is regulated by the modulatory sense-interferences that the walls, doors, and windows—not to mention screens and speakers—let pass. Certain tendential headings, perceptions, and cognitions are backgrounded, peripheralized, or blended out by the synesthetic economy of movement-across that is regulated by the architectural regime.

A building is a technology of movement—a technology of transposition—in direct membranic connection with virtual event spaces. It functions topologically, folding relational continua into and out of each other to selective, productive effect. It functions abstract-concretely to inflect determinations of potential experience. A building is an experiential supermodulator device: a modulator of modulations. It is a way of placing relation against relation, toward inflected variation. Its three-dimensional closure effect is a regulated coupling between virtual seas of relation, swarming and smudgeable. We build in Euclidean space when we design the kind of aggregate hinge-effects between swarmings and smudgings of experience that shake out in favor of maximum stability of cognitive result ("there's nothing like home": recognition). To build in Euclidean space is to build in predictability.

Is it possible, in addition, to build for newness, for the emergence of unforeseen experiential form and configuration, inflected by chance? We know that it is possible to design topologically. This essay has argued that we live topologically. But can we also build topologically?

To build topologically would be to accept that the body's ultimate innards are as effectively incorporeal, as really abstract, as the atom's. The body's innards are not just the stomach and intestines. As vitally as food, a life feeds on habits, memories, and tropisms. The living body's "ultimate" innards are the proprioceptive habits on a level with muscle fiber. They are the microsocial skills on a level with a single visual neuron. They are enculturated memories lying at the crossroads of sense channels coursing through the flesh. They are the pattern of preferential headings hinging on all of the above, which we somewhat grandly call our "personality." The body *is* the holding-together of these virtual innards as they fold out, recursive-durationally, in the loopy present, in determinate form and configuration, always provisional because always in becoming.

The arguments presented in this essay all make the same point: that the life of the body, its lived experience, cannot be understood without reference to abstract-real processual dimensions. These cannot be contained in Euclidean space and linear time. They must be topologically described, using an array of concepts specially honed for the task: continuous variation, intensive movement, transpositionality, event, durational space, recursive-duration, modulation, qualitative effect, biogram, and feedback of higher functions, to name just a few.

This is not to say that there is one topological figure, or even a specific formal non-Euclidean geometry, that corresponds to the body's spacetime of experience or some general "shape" of existence. Topologies, like Euclidean geometry, are modeling tools. Each echoes an aspect of the world's dynamism (and share of stability). Each repeats, on screen or in thought, an intensive mode of movement that is really of this world. Each is capable of bringing to formal expression certain dimensions of the infinitely twisted life of the body and the cosmos. No one model can lay claim to a final "reflection" of or "correspondence" to reality. It is simply not about reflection or correspondence. It is about *participation*. Differential participation. In what way does a given geometry's effective resonance with intensive movements in the world allow us to extend them, in our orientations, memories, and brain-lagged awareness, toward their (and our) creative variation? How can geometry make a qualitative difference in the world?

Once again, these are pragmatic rather than critical issues. It's a question of appropriate technology. Choosing a geometry to design with is to choose potential modulations not only of the designed form but, through its device, of people's lives. It was not the purpose of this essay to suggest particular design methods, aesthetics, or "ideal" end effects. It was only to suggest that new paths might be found by letting go of the sterile opposition between the abstract and the concrete and its fellow-traveler, the subjective and objective. To do this, it is necessary to take another look at perception and lived experience and even broach such tired topics as consciousness. The fear that this will inevitably fall into a domesticating, self-satisfied subjectivism-in-spite-of-itself, like that preached by phenomenological architecture, is not justified. All you need to do to avoid that path is, quoting Deleuze and Guattari: *look only at the movements.*[34] It has been suggested that extending the concept of the diagram into the biogram might be a vector worth pursuing. Formal topologies are not enough. The biogram is a *lived* topological event. It is *onto-topological.* It is the event of experience folding back on itself for its own furtherance, its continuing becoming. Onto-topological means *ontogenetic.* The biogram is experience reaccessing its powers of emergence, for more effect. It is the existential equivalent of lifting oneself up by the bootstraps: ontogenetic and *autopoietic.*

Look only at the movements—and they will bring you to matter. The perspective suggested here displays a tropism toward realist materialism (without reflection: especially not "pre-"). At virtually every turn in the discussion, dynamics that seemed "subjective" to the extreme made a literal end run back to impersonal matter. The end run of mindedness back to matter always somehow coincided with its emergence from it, the exemplary case being Libet's feedback loop between the dawning of perceptual awareness and the ever-present previousness of movements of brain matter capable of coloring experience without themselves becoming aware. Accepting this insistence of the material and impersonal (the "involuntary") *in* bootstrapped personal experience distinguishes the current account most sharply from phenomenological approaches. Its claims both to realism and materialism paradoxically depend on it— paradoxically, because the "backdating" of matter-driven consciousness is also an argument that there is no essential difference between perception, cognition, and hallucination. This is a realist materialism with a paradoxically creative edge, summed up in the mantra: involuntary *and* elicited. The involuntary and elicited no-difference between perception, cognition, and hallucination can in turn be summed up in a single word: *imagination*.

This is also where topological architecture is carnally challenged and proves inadequately abstract. It does well with the involuntary, in the form of chance variations programmed into the topological form-generating software. It does much less well with the elicited. Putting the two together is necessary for grasping the minded body's mode of reality, which can be evoked by any number of necessary oxymorons: modulated self-decision, creative receptivity, induced self-activity, laboriously orienting autopilot, ever-present lapse. Use your imagination: no single logic, geometric or otherwise, is flexible enough to encompass the concrete abstractness of experience in all its ins and outs. Just as the body lives between dimensions, designing for it requires operating between logics. To be sufficiently abstract, topological architecture needs to welcome the translogical. A translogic is different from a metalogic. It doesn't stand back and describe the way multiple logics and the operative levels they model hold together. It *enters* the relations and tweaks as many as it can to get a sense of what may come. It is pragmatic. It imaginatively enters the fabric of transition and pulls as many strands as it can to see what emerges. It is effective. Rather than metalogical, it is supermodulatory.

It is not that architecture does not already go about its business like this, in a certain regulatory manner, if not always fully cognizant of the strange horizon of that relational fact, and at times even in outright denial of it (as when it proudly deconstructs positively absent structures, or privileges determinations of history over potential becomings, or cutely cites when it could be effectively tweaking, or boringly domiciles the world in its own supposed prereflection). If architecture pursues extending diagrams into biograms it will become more what it has always been: a materialist art of qualitative body modulation, a translogical engineering of matter gone mindful. Its buildings will also be more what they are. More modulatory. More flexibly membranic. More intensely lived between more relational dimensions brought concretely into abstract-surface proximity. How such an onto-topological architecture will develop, if it does, certainly cannot be prereflected. It will unfold experimentally. Or not.

To be determined.

TOO-BLUE

Color-Patch for an Expanded Empiricism

It's very simple. The researcher asks a subject to match the blue of a certain friend's eyes. The friend, of course, is absent. The procedure is repeated with the black of the subject's hat, the red of his own lips, the brown of the bricks of the house he lived in. The idea is to test the effect of memory on color constancy. The researcher is David Katz, working in the first decade of the twentieth century.[1]

It isn't really that simple. As an uncontrolled experiment, unaccounted for variables entered in. All of the things Katz asked to be color-matched were intimate everyday objects and could thus be expected to be charged with layers of interest and affect. What was being tested, then, was less memory than the cofunctioning of affect with memory. Further, Katz assumed that language was operating neutrally. The word "blue" is assumed to play the role of a transparent designator of what two particular things have in common, a pair of eyes in the world at large and a test patch in the laboratory. Language is assumed to be a medium of commonality in two senses. First, in the sense that it is posited to harbor a generality capable of effectively subsuming two particulars. Second, in the sense that the experimenter and the subject are assumed to have equal access to its operations of neutrality, or to stand in the same relation to "blue" as deployed in the laboratory. The word is used by the experimenter to stage a match or mismatch. The role Katz assigned to language is standardizing: to deploy and guarantee a standard of comparison in order to test a response against it.

Under the circumstances, however, the experimenter and the subject do not stand in the same relation to "blue." There is an asymmetry in their relation to the word, due to the asymmetry of their respective stances in the laboratory context. Language is playing a primarily standardizing function only for the experimenter. For the subject, it is primarily operating as a trigger—for affect and memory. So what Katz has staged is a cofunctioning of language, affect, and memory. From his stance as experimenter, this *complex* cofunctioning appears *simply* as a one-to-one correspondence (or lack thereof) between a present test patch and a past perception. Katz hasn't reduced experience to another level, for example physiology or the physics of light. But he has extracted a simplicity from a complexity of experience. He has extracted a narrow correspondence effect from a more encompassing asymmetry. What he has done is perform a reduction of experience operating on the level of experience itself. This kind of endo-reduction of experience might be argued to characterize the Gestalt approach to experimentation, of which Katz was an important forerunner.

You could say that this is bad science and dismiss it out of hand. Or, you could say that it is proto-science or perhaps semi-science, and ask what precisely it semi-did and proto-how. For Katz's procedure does constitute a kind of empirical investigation, and it did generate a repeatable result with some claim to factuality. The semi-fact is: under these circumstances, a match does not take place. What does the generation of this factoid allow one to think about the cofunctioning of language, memory, affect, asymmetrical social relations, lived complexity, and produced simplicity? If you resituate the factoid in that encompassing cofunctioning, the stakes change. The problem for the traditional scientist would be how to convert the factoid into a full-fledged fact: to verify it. This would involve purifying the experiment of uncontrolled variables. Language, affect, and social position would have to be neutralized to the greatest extent possible. In other words, ways would have to be found to make memory and color perception approach the physiological limit of bare brain functioning. This is a more severe reduction than Katz's. It is no doubt possible to carry out and would quite possibly yield something of value, perhaps to neurophysiology, which down the line might in turn prove profitable, for example, to medicine, by supplementing its diagnostic or therapeutic techniques.

But there are other ways of approaching the situation than barebraining it. For one thing, you could try to *think* it. Again, you could resituate the factoid in its encompassing *cofunctioning* and ask what that cofunctioning demands or allows one to think. The question is no longer whether the "fact" is truly a fact or how it might profitably become one. The question bears on the encompassing cofunctioning from which the fact or factoid, such as it is, was *generated*. In other words, what is at stake is no longer factuality and its profitability but rather *relation* and its *genitivity*. The question is: what new thoughts does this nexus of productively experienced relation make it possible to think? This is a philosophical question. This is the positive problem of the philosopher. Included in it is the further question: under what circumstances and to what effect might that new-thought relationality and genitivity be extracted from this nexus of experience and inserted into others, variationally? That is the pragmatic problem of the philosopher (or the pragmatic moment of the philosopher's positive problem). In this second moment philosophical method segues into ethics and politics, just as scientific method relays in periodic fashion into technique and its capitalization.

Now it just so happens that the way in which Katz's subjects positively produced their mismatch is quite telling. They "almost always" selected a color that was "too bright to match a bright object," "too dark to match a dark object," and "too saturated to match an object which is known to have a distinct hue." The cofunctioning of language, memory, and affect "exaggerates" color. The exaggeration, Katz remarks, results from the "absolute striking character" of certain "color-peculiarities." The remembering of a color is not effectively a reproduction of a perception, but a transformation or becoming of it. Matching, it would seem, is not inherent to the mechanism of color memory. Testing a correspondence between a past perception and a present one is what the *experimenter* does with the memory he is given. He takes the memory-color generated by his subject and submits it to a test of identity. He tests it for standard. What the subject does, it turns out, exceeds the standard. While the experimenter is representing standards, the subject is surreptitiously trucking with singularity. He or she is exaggeratedly conveying an "absolutely striking peculiarity of color." The memory of the friend's eyes is in some way *too* "blue": excess. The remembered color exceeds the testable meaning of the word. In the name of color constancy, the subject has expressed a singular and excessive becoming of color. Between "blue" used as the trigger for the production of a memory, and "blue" used to test the identity of that memory, something extra has slipped in, which the color-word, as the common property of the experimenter and the subject, does not designate. The too-blue of the friend's eyes dodges the standardizing language that triggers and tests it. It is spoken or written only negatively, as a miss. It is on that basis that it enters language, in the experimenter's reporting of the test results, and becomes generally available for conscious elaboration. A normative deployment of language has provoked the production of a singular excess of meaning. Then, in a second moment of reporting about the production, that deployment brings the excess-over-itself into itself. Language is operating simultaneously to standardize (reduce) and convey (express) an ineffable singularity of experience.[2]

If, in the interval between triggering and testing by "blue," the subject is not doing what the experimenter is doing—setting up a correspondence between a past and present perception—then what exactly is he or she doing with color? Or is that even the right question? Isn't the question rather: What is color doing to the subject? For the subject is not even aware of the excess she is producing until the experimenter reports the results. Until then, she is left in the belief that she has made the match. The exaggeration that she effectively produces is the result of some "absolutely striking" peculiarity of color. The subject has been singularly struck by color. Color has *struck*, and without either the subject or the experimenter willing it so, it has exceeded. It has gone over the instituted line, pushed past the mark set for it by the laboratory setup, as unwilled as it is unmatched by its human hosts.

This pushiness is what Hume called the "vivacity" of an "impression."[3] It attests to a *self-activity* of experience. When color is interrogated by language, it displays a self-insistent dynamism that commands itself to the instituted context, into which it breaks and enters, delivering itself to the questioning. This self-delivery or ingressive activity of experience is neither a common property of the language acts that end up expressing it nor the sole property of any of the language users involved. The excess of color slips into language *between* the experimenter and the subject. *It belongs to their joint situation.* More precisely, it *enters* their situation. It is an impersonality of experience that makes social ingress. It becomes personal, when the subject is confronted by another with evidence of his exceptional miss and has to own up to it. *The color experience is not fundamentally personal.* It is more accurate to say that it becomes personalized, and that it does so only in the playing out of a very particular situation enveloping a social asymmetry: the differential in status and power between the roles of the experimenter and the subject. *Experience becomes personal socially.* This is attested to by the fact that its pushiness, as personalized, is struck by the social asymmetry. The produced excess is personally owned up to only by the "subject." The experimenter keeps a distance from this owning. He cleaves to the neutralizing, standardizing operation of language as reportage. For him, the excess appears as an "object" of experience, however unexpected. The "subjectivity" of the experimentee emerges in cofunctioning with "objectivity," maintained against surprise, at a different pole of the same asymmetry. The emergence of the subjective, in this personal sense, and the maintenance of the objective are co-results of the same event.

The event lies at the intersection of at least two (and in reality many more) process lines. One is the adoption and imposition by the experimenter of the institutional setup of the experiment, as defined linguistically, architecturally, and on any number of other interlocking levels. Call this the *context.* Context preexists. The possibility of maintaining objectivity in the face of surprise comes from the context's relative stability as a more or less determinate given. The second process line is the self-insistence of an autonomy of experience. Reserve the term *situation* for the event of an autonomy of experience pushing into and moving across a context. The color singularity, by virtue of its self-motivating experiential autonomy can, in and of itself, be considered a kind of impersonal subjectivity. The owned subjectivity with which the experimentee leaves—the public memory of having personally misremembered—is a contextual expression of the insurgent, impersonal subjectivity that is the singularity of color. The personal and impersonal poles of subjectivity lie at two ends of the same process line. At the beginning of the line, a self-activity pushes in from outside. By the end, that vivacity has settled into a stable structural coupling that gives it reportable meaning, as the asymmetrical opposite of the objective. Except that there is no beginning, because the insistent singularity is immemorial, arriving, as far as this context is concerned, out of nowhere. The beginning is an *indeterminate givenness,* which by virtue of its indeterminacy cannot be said exactly to have preexisted. But neither can it be expected to end. The next time the subject remembers his friend's face, those familiar eyes will still be too-blue. Think of Frank Sinatra. The structural capture of the vivacity of color coexists with its continued autonomy: dead, objectified . . . *but still.*

Headline: "Sinatra Remembered Can't Match Old Blue Eyes."[4]

Although the singularity of experience has no assignable beginning or end, it does pass thresholds, arriving unbidden into a context, then settling in and no sooner slipping out to seek ingress elsewhere. Its traveling across thresholds from situation to situation may prove to have a periodicity that, if followed, provides a more ample expression of its self-activity. Upon that expression a speculative narrative can be built. The narrative is "speculative" because even though the ambulation it follows exhibits a periodic consistency, at each departure the singularity disappears into itself, into its own pure activity (uncontextualized and intersituational). The next arrival is always across the threshold of that subjective indeterminacy. This makes thoroughly reliable prediction impossible. It is the philosopher's job to tell the story of that impossibility.

There is a certain slippery eternity to the color's experienced singularity. Nothing is subtracted from experience when the singularity appears asymmetrically in a given context as a standard-beholden "object" of investigation. Something is added. What has happened is that a reportable (and thus intentionally repeatable, institutionally controllable, stabilizable) structural coupling has been added to a traveling autonomy (an unintended, automatic repetition). In any case, *experience continues*. Experience is an additive "form of transition," a continual motion of intersecting process lines: a co-motion (commotion) of mutual nonexclusion.[5] As William James puts it, experience never stops "streaming," and its streaming snowballs.[6]

The snowballing is transformative. The singularity of color struck the prepared context, yielding an unexpected result, and the context structurally struck back, capturing the result for control purposes. The "impression" was mutual. It is this mutuality of transformation that makes it possible to hold, without a hint of contradiction, that the color was produced in context *and* eternally "insists" on itself, in pushy independence.[7] The blue belonging to the situation is both "constructed" by the context, which in large part is language determined, *and* insists or persists outside linguistic determination (*ex*-ists). Constructed *and* self-standing: far from being an indictment of "reality," as an antispeculative "science warrior" of the Alan Sokal variety might have it, the philosophical story I have just told suggests a human definition of it. The real is that which expresses itself in language upon forcibly breaking-and-entering from an immemorial outside. Again, in James's words, the "ultimate fact" is the certainty of a "really-next-effect" whose nature cannot entirely be foreseen: an indefinite ever "more" that "fringes" every determinate context with a timeless margin of chance and newness.[8] Reality is not fundamentally objective. Before and after it becomes an object, it is an inexhaustible reserve of surprise. The real is the snowballing *process* that makes a certainty of *change*. To be expected: the arrival of the new, the uninvited ingress of the singular. Produced and eternal, constructed and self-standing, unaccountably old and ever-changing, captive to context and eluding it, verified and storied, sitting true and in fictive travel to a future context—sci-fi (*sci-phi*). The fable of the real.

Katz's color-singularity appears in and to the context structurally stabilized as an object of discourse susceptible to subsequent verification by fine-tuning the experimentation. It is in the same stroke that singularity enters discourse and is structurally stabilized as a proto- or semi-scientific object. The object has a life cycle. It passes from the "ultimate fact" of its unexpected arrival to the status of a "factoid" that is felt to be (and can be) meaningfully discussed but requires further investigation to determine precisely what manner of object it is and what is to be done with it. In certain contexts, such as Katz's, the factoid has a distinct calling to mature into a verified "bare" fact. The life cycle of the object is from active indeterminacy, to vague determination, to useful definition (tending toward the ideal limit of full determination). What we call *common sense* is the field of the factoid. *Anecdote* is its characteristic content as a genre of thought. Not all objects complete their life cycle, passing from the status of factoid to bare fact. However, *all bare facts are born factoid*. Every new object of science emerges from a "mangle" of practice in which the specialized procedures and discourses of science, confronted with an ingress of reality and drawing upon all available resources to grapple with it, remix with common sense and anecdote operating inside and outside the laboratory and passing freely across its walls. A factoid that cannot, will not, or hasn't yet matured remains a mangled object of anecdotal discourse or *gossip*—as it is, again, after it matures, in addition to being a scientific object and to the precise extent to which it is noteworthy. Gossip is the archaeology of science. It does not belittle or criticize science to point out this kinship. After all, it is no mean feat to transform the vagueness and changeability of anecdote into a dependable fact. All of technique rests on that transformation.[9]

When the feat has been accomplished, a life cycle has been completed. A stream of experience has, in James's and Whitehead's vocabularies, reached a "terminus."[10] It is important to reiterate that a "terminus" of experience is not necessarily a beginning or an end. It can be a threshold: the object has an afterlife. A technical object continues to evolve, but within the bounds of its definition. It changes but not noticeably enough to merit a new official name. If it does jump the bounds of its nominal identity, it is because an event has transpired. Something new has arrived in the world. In a very particular context, a new singularity has irrupted, making the context a genitive situation again. "More" has come. A new life: more to reality.

The birth of a new technical object is never a linear progress. It is knotty, a mangle-prone emergence across a threshold of surprise. A new cycle begins, from active indeterminacy, to vague determination, to "full" determination (nominal identity deployed within a conventional sphere of practical dependability). The life of a technical object must always pass through the stages of ultimate fact of experience (rupture/irruption/ threshold of existence) and merely-talked-about factoid (semi-objective elaboration) before finally baring itself through experimentation (ver- ification/profitable deployment). For this reason, the history of science is never linear and never pure of context and situation. The history of science cannot be contained in "intellectual history." It is always "dirtied" by an unavoidable genealogical link to chance event, common sense, and gossip. In short, recounting its story, describing its effective form of tran- sition, demands a broadly Foucauldian genealogy of the kind practiced by Bruno Latour and supported philosophically by Isabelle Stengers. As both authors emphasize, that genealogy must include "transversal" link- ages to nonscientific spheres of practice (especially commercial and gov- ernmental, most crucially concerning questions of regulation and fund- ing) as well as to proto- or semi-scientific spheres. These latter may not be as formalized as what is recognized as Western science, but they are far more elaborated and dependable than common sense and gossip. They attest that there are many degrees of reality or forms of transition populat- ing the interval between factoid and bare fact. Each degree has its own contextual habitat, conventions of technique, and modes of transmission from one more or less controlled context to the next. There are degrees of factuality, corresponding to species of science. Gestalt is one such spe- cies. As are "traditional knowledges." And informal, "alternative," or "folkloric" knowings of many kinds. These species coexist, co-adapt, and mutually influence one another. In short, there is a global *ecology of knowl- edge practices.*[11]

These are some ways of thinking about the singularity of experience from the angle of its loquacious capture for objectivity and technique. But what of its reserve? What of its self-insistent stillness? What of its eternally mercurial subjectivity? Talking about that dimension of the situation requires a different story, with different protagonists, following other lines of process entwined with the one just traced.

The color blue figured in Katz's experimental situation in divergent capacities. It was a *differential object*. Along one axis, or in one of its differential dimensions, it was a matched standard assignable by common consensus to things other than itself and to which it equally inhered: a retina and a test patch. It figured as an *attribute* (or common property incumbent in standardized language use). It was also an asymmetrically owned mismemory that was assumed to be knowable but whose exact nature was yet to be determined by follow-up experimentation. In this dimension, it was a multivalent *content*, at once of inalienable personalized memory and of a public discourse of knowing capture. When we speak of "an" object or thing, what we are referring to is a complex interweaving of attributes and contents as subsumed under a nominal identity (a name). "An" object subsumes a multiplicity that evolves situationally. Every object is an evolving differential: a snow balling, open-ended variation on itself.

But there is more to the object than attributes and contents. There was the Sinatra dimension: ole too-blue eyes. This was the axis of escape along which the differential object "blue" slipped quietly away from its own growing objectivity. The "too" of the blue was an excess marking the certainty that a line of experiential self-activity or impersonal subjectivity that has made ingress into the situation will overspill it, going on to enter other situations, across other thresholds of indeterminacy. The excess was a reserve of recurrence in the situation, vaguely palpable but not definable or confinable. It was the direct presence, in the collective experience, of a "more" of experience: the presence of process.

It was stated earlier that the object owes this elusive excess to an accumulation of familiarity and fondness that the triggering of the friendly memory automatically brought out. But that is not the whole story. As it transpires, the excess of blue is owned by the experimentee only retrospectively. It makes ingress in excess of its expressibility as a personal feeling. The "excess," then, is less the quantity of feeling than the surprising manner in which the feeling preceded itself into the context: it is the contextual *precession* of ownable feeling. That is why the excess is not simply a quantity of feeling, however great. It is a *qualitative* surplus over any quantity of personal feeling. It may well not have come about without an antecedent accumulation of familiarity and fondness. But it is not reducible to that personal "investment." This is all the more apparent when it is considered that the ingress of the excess was rigged into being by the experimental setup.[12] Too-blue is collectively contextualized as a content of a personal life. As a discursively defined content, it is a retrospective, collective, contextual artifact. As a discursive content, it comes to be. As excess, it continues. It runs through this containment, jumping to the next contextual rigging. Its precession proceeds apace. The excess is the *quality* of continuing activity by which the differential object "blue" escapes its contextual containment—its objectivity.

Reserve the term "emotion" for the personalized content, and *affect* for the continuation. Emotion is contextual. Affect is situational: eventfully ingressive to context. Serially so: affect is *trans-situational.* As processional as it is precessional, affect inhabits the passage. It is pre- and postcontextual, pre- and postpersonal, an excess of continuity invested only in the ongoing: its own. Self-continuity across the gaps. Impersonal affect is the connecting thread of experience. It is the invisible glue that holds the world together. In event. The world-glue of affect is an *autonomy of event-connection* continuing across its own serialized capture in context.

The true duality is not the metaphysical opposition between the subject and object. Subject and object always come together in context. They tightly embrace each other in their reciprocal definition in discourse, as the owner and the ownable of conventional content. The true duality is between continuity and discontinuity (trans-situation and context). This is not a metaphysical opposition. It is a processual rhythm, in and of the world, expressing an ontological tension between manipulable objectivity and elusively ongoing qualitative activity (*becoming*). Much useless theoretical fretting could be avoided by deflecting issues customarily approached by critiquing or deconstructing the subject-object "divide" onto pragmatic inquiry into modes of *continuity* and *discontinuity.* These also are in embrace. Their embrace is operative, not metaphysical or definitional. It is a contemporary proverb that walking is controlled falling. Continuity embraces discontinuity as walking includes falling. The momentum of walking is the excess of its activity over each successive step. The ongoing quality of walking is that trans-step momentum. Each next step is momentous, in its own little way: it is the event of a caught fall. The catch renews the walking's functional context. The rhythm of falling and catching organizes an indefinite series of varying contexts for the walking-event's continuation.

There are other connecting threads besides affect. The interlocking pre-given levels mentioned earlier as defining the context also have their lines of continuity. These are levels of conventionalized discourse and institutional practices like architecture that are heavily discourse-delimited (following Foucault's analyses). Discursive and institutional practices manage a certain regularity and predictability in the passage from context to context. This contextual continuity is in a different mode from the affective. It pertains to nominal identity. Identified subjects and objects are considered, in principle, to cross the affective gap between contexts essentially unchanged. It is admitted that they appear in the successive contexts in which they figure under continual modification, but the change is understood as occurring within acceptable bounds of recognizability and predictability. This gives their progress the appearance of an ordered, even necessary, evolution (or *history*). The bounds of recognizability and predictability are already implicit in the nominal identities: already discoursed upon and institutionalized, already in place, social givens. Any as-yet unidentified irruptions that may occur are prechanneled toward recognition and prediction. They are grasped, pushiness aside, from the docile anger of their *identifiability* as objects or subjects. Their nomination may be a work (or walk) in progress, requiring experimentation, but their contextualization, their eventual induction into already operating discursive and institutional practices of regularization, is a foregone conclusion. The foregoneness of the conclusion is called the march of *discovery*. After all, what is there to history but contexts progressively falling into order?

Besides context? There is situation. There is the unbiddenness of qualitative overspill. There is self-activity qualitatively expressed, presenting an affective order that is not yet "yours" or "mine." There is event. There is anomaly. There are jilted expectations.

All of this can be conventionally dispatched by cleaving expressive quality along an assumed subject-object divide. A share of the liveliness that the quality presents may be apportioned to objects as properties or attributes ("blue" to color patch and eyes). This share is deemed useful, because its apportionment is verifiable (match-testable) and thus manipulable. The remainder will fall to the subject side, where it may be dismissed as merely personal, lacking in dependable function and in many contexts even of general interest. Affective "exaggeration" is now contained. One share has been functionalized, the remainder relegated to the tawdry status of a private "emotion." The subjective share is conventionally considered arbitrary: fluff to be discarded. Or, in extreme cases, to be dealt with by the appropriate professionals.

A passing note: this is where capitalism exceeds objectivity and capitalism's own constitutive links to the technologized knowledge-products of "hard" science. Even something that is by definition dysfunctional can still be made profitable. Capitalism's genius is not so much its fostering and feeding off of the "rationalization" of the world accompanying the emergence and dissemination of technology. To valorize technology, all it has to do is extract more value from an already recognized value: a surplus-value from a use-value. Its true genius, and its tenacious staying power, has to do with its capability of absorbing the qualitative remainders of that rationalization: extracting surplus-value from uselessness. This profit conversion of the functionally residual is the fundamental growth industry of contemporary ("late" or "postmodern") capitalism. Capitalism fosters and feeds off both sides of the affective divide. It should be noted that on both sides, capitalism *goes for excess:* surplus-value. The surplus-value extracted from both sides of the cleavage is formally identical. In a certain sense, *capitalism restores the unity or continuity of excess self-activity.* Capital doesn't just valorize technology. It is itself an abstract technology of excess, as qualitative in its operations as it is quantitative; as subjectively restorative, in an impersonal, maniacal kind of way, as it is objectively destructive ecologically. But that is another story. Back to the more restrained story under way.

Affective cleavage, utilitarian triage, subjective remaindering. The overall effect is to enclose experience in the *determination* of regularized context. Situation submerges. The gap of uncontained affect disappears from view. The world's vivacious charge of indeterminacy recedes into the unperceived from which it came. The world's processual openness, its self-activity, recedes at the same rhythm. Now it really does appear that the only activities in the world are the regularizations of discourse and institution. "Truth," some will say: finally, things are usefully named, disciplined to mean what they are and to act how they mean. "Construction," others will retort: all a ruse of power. But "self-standing *and* constructed"? The "and" will not stand. Enter the reign of the excluded middle.

Context. History. March of technical knowledge. Useful—if a bit dead. If instead of cleaving the affective line of continuity you cleave to it, if you include the middle of the impersonal, insurgent connecting thread of every "too," the world takes on a different hue. The line of uncontained affect reinjects unpredictability into context, re-making it eventful. Affect is vivacity of context: situation. Affect enlivens. Its vivacity, ever on the move from situation to situation, strings context-orderings together in eventfulness, holding them together from the angle of what new and unpredictable enters into them. Its context-rocking trans-situational drift is the life-glue of the world—a world capable of surprise (surplus-value of being).

It was stated that uncontained affect was a quality of self-activity. The too-blue that was actually perceived was a contextual expression of it. This is "quality" in a sense closer to the everyday notion of it, as a property attributable to an object or, failing that, something that can still be personally contained. The quality is an integral expression of the world's amalgamated liveliness. It always retains at least a tinge of that liveliness, even when it is propertied or personally contained in a collectively rigged conscious perception available for discursive elaboration. A quality, by nature, is a perceptible expression of uncontained affect. It always retains a sense of openness—if your sensing and speaking retains an openness to it. Ultimately, the question is not "Whose?" Whose mistake, whose mismatch, whose truth? The question is "Of what?" Answer: *the world's.* Altogether and openly.

A quality is a perceptual self-expression, an expressive self-perception, of the world's holding-together: its affective self-adhesion. This is a given. We all adhere, impersonally, in a *lived belief* in the world's continued holding-together across its gaps. This belief is "lived" because it is prior to any possible verification, having been always-already experienced by the time it is tested. It is a surplus belief that evidences itself, appropriately, in exaggeration. As a kind of belief that enters conscious awareness only in surprise, it can never itself be the object of a recognition.

Is it accurate to say that it "enters" consciousness? *Is it not its coming-as-a-surprise that constitutes consciousness?* What are recognized object attributes and owned emotions if not old surprises to which we have become more or less accustomed? Aren't the perceived unity and constancy of the object and of the subject—co-snowballing differentials both—just habitual, even institutionalized, exaggerations? Is recognition anything more than the habit of no longer seeing what's new? Is scientific and technical knowledge radically skewed against newness, for all its rhetoric of discovery?

Belief, as "ultimate fact" of experience, is in the world's continued ability to surprise. It is our automatic adherence to the world's adherence to its own autonomous activity. Those ole eyes are blue. This is true. But blue needs more than eyes for seeing. It needs relation—a sight in itself. Altogether, now:

> The sense-awareness of the blue as situated in a certain event which I call the situation, is thus exhibited as the sense-awareness of a relation between the blue, the percipient event of the observer, the situation, and intervening events. *All nature is in fact required.*[13]

A quality is an actual presentation of lived relation. World-glue made visible. See it, be surprised, live it and like it (or not). But don't just emote it. Above all, don't take it personally.[14]

The exaggerated "too" qualifying experimental blue expressed something besides world-glue: an "absolute striking color-particularity" or *singularity*. Objectively, color is traditionally said to comprise three dimensions: brightness, saturation, and hue. Each time Katz asked one of his experimental subjects to make a match, one of these dimensions pushed itself so forcibly into experience that it falsified the match. Both the chosen test-patch and the retina were blue. But they weren't true blue. The memory was a patch of a different color from the verifiable attribute. The experience isn't reducible to the objective truth of it. Or, the truth of the experience isn't reducible to its objectification (and personification). What "more" is there? The answer is the same as before: situation. Let's re-answer the question, humoring objectivism by cleaving more closely to its side of things.

What is there besides the objective ingredients of color? Is it an affront to objectivism to say that there is, in addition to the ingredients, their interaction and its effect? In a word, their event. The event of blue's appearance has something the ingredients themselves don't have: an ability to do without them. The event of the interaction has a certain independence vis-à-vis its ingredients. It can repeat in the absence of any *particu-*

lar set of them. *Any* particular set will do. The ingredients and their interaction are generally necessary for the event of color. Their repeated objective presence—their re-production—defines the *general conditions* of the event. But there is no general event. There is only *this* event, and *this* one, and *this* other one—none of them exactly alike.[15] Each event is unique. It only stands to reason, then, that the event's general conditions do not fully account for its repetition, as it happens: different at each iteration.

The problem is that the general conditions only account for what is necessary for the event to happen. In any event, contingencies creep in. The necessary ingredients are always accompanied by contingent ingredients. The accompaniment of the necessary by the contingent is so unfailing that the surplus of ingredience introduced by contingency must be considered as necessary as the necessities. The singularity of the event is not in contradiction to its generality. The singularity is in necessarily contingent excess over the generality. It is an unfailing ingredient surplus, above and beyond the appearing object's possibility of being certified as a true case of its general category—a singularity above and beyond its particularity as a representative of a class defined by the reproducible presence of certain standard objective properties. The general, necessary conditions define the event as belonging to a recognizable class of events. The singular, contingent ingredients give it its uniqueness, its stubbornness in remaining perceptibly itself in addition to being a member of its class—its quality. The event retains a quality of "this-ness," an unreproducible being-only-itself, that stands over and above its objective definition.

Both the test patch and the remembered retina were certifiably blue. This much is true. But there was a singular excess in the retinal memory. This excess of effect was not attributable to any colored object. It was attributable to the uncontrolled conditions of the memory's emergence in *this* experimental situation. This much "more" is also true. The interaction of the objective dimensions of blue was *interfered* with and *modulated* by a previousness of familiarity and fondness: by an unconsciously ingredient emotional charge. This affective modulation was as effectively conditioning of the memory-color's emergence as the objective properties of the light that might be scientifically confirmed as have been reflected by the friend's retina. Affective modulation was the color's condition of anomaly. Anomalous is precisely how the blue really appeared.

The *real* conditions of *this* repetition of blue included not only its conditions of reproducibility, its objective conditions, its conditions of possibility for being a particular case of a general rule, but also its conditions of anomaly.[16]

The interfering charge of affect invested itself in one objective dimension of color. It made that dimension stand out excessively: absolutely strikingly. In that surplus standing-out, the affect itself was brought out, for all to know, in the form of a miss. The contingency of the affect's selective ingredience was contextually *expressed* in a surprise modulation of the collective effect of the objective conditions. The expression of the affect is what made the color unmatchably, mistakably "lively," imbued with *life directly, qualitatively perceived,* amiss in conventional discourse.

The example of memory-color can easily be misconstrued as necessitating just the kind of foundational subject-object split that has repeatedly dismissed as irrelevant here. Even if it is acknowledged that the affect in play was impersonal, it can still be argued to have resided in an unconscious of emotional content contained in a single human brain. To construe the situation this way would be to ignore the insistence of the "more." Every event, of whatever kind, carries conditions of anomaly. There is always a really-perceived miss in every context. There is always something really amiss in contextualized language use. No anomaly, no this-ness: it's as simple as that. The necessary "more" than objective ingredient is never subjective in the narrow, personalized sense, even when it has to do with emotion. Emotion was able to make the difference (between particularity and singularity) because it made ingress: because it was operating trans-situationally, in the gap between its entering the experimental context and its leaving the contexts of previous friendship. It effectively interfered and modulated because it was operating pre-expressively, in the affective manner in which it precedes itself. It had proceeded to phase back into affect.[17]

The fact that emotion figures in any capacity is likely to disqualify this account in many eyes. If there is emotion involved, how could it seriously be argued that the excess is not subjective in a most banal sense? An example from chaos makes the same point without the involvement of anything personal: that there is a something more than objective ingredients and their interaction that is contingently necessary to the reality of a happening.

In Ilya Prigogine and Isabelle Stengers' analysis of the Bénard stability, a liquid chaotically dissipating heat that enters it at certain rate suddenly self-organizes into an ordered population of convection cells. The transition from chaotic disorder to dynamic order occurs when the dissipative system suddenly "senses" the force of gravity. Up until that point, the influence of gravity is negligible. Suddenly, the dynamic between the liquid's molecules makes them "sensitive" to gravitational interference.[18] They have acquired the collective ability to be *affected* by gravity. In response to that newly sensed interference, the interaction changes in nature, passing a threshold from chaotic disorder to turbulent order. A qualitative difference has singularly struck the liquid.

The molecular ingredients were not initially open to gravitational influence, either taken individually or en masse (as a collection of discrete elements). It was their *interacting* that opened them to qualitative change. It was their coming-together dynamically, their unity in movement, that "sensed" gravity and allowed it to interfere—and that also made "more" of the interference than a simple negativity or "perturbation." The ingredients' coming-together extracted from gravity a surplus-value of being, an excess of effect: an emergence of order, a belonging-together in the same event of global qualitative change.

Call the openness of an interaction to being affected by something new in a way that qualitatively changes its dynamic nature *relationality*. Relationality is a global excess of belonging-together enabled by but not reducible to the bare fact of having objectively come together. Relationality cannot be accounted for by the objective properties of the actual ingredients in play considered as discrete elements. It cannot even be reduced to the interactions that might logically be predicted according to those properties. The order-out-of chaos effect was entirely unexpected by science: a major surprise. In fact, by classical standards, the probability that it could happen is vanishingly close to zero. It is as good as impossible.[19] Yet it happens. Its practically impossible occurrence is and will remain outside the purview of classical laws of nature. This is so even though the "something new" that interferes with the liquid is as old as can be: an already operating, scientifically established, general necessity (the previousness of the force of gravity to any interaction of any physical system). The liquid, it must be emphasized, in no way contradicts the objective laws of nature. Rather, it adds a surplus ordering effect to their already-in-operation. It is that surplus of effect that is the "something new." The sensing of gravity by the liquid's interaction *adds* effect to its old-as-can-be objectivity rather than in any way contradicting objective causality. Relationality is the potential for singular effects of qualitative change to occur in excess over or as a supplement to objective interactions. Relationality pertains to the *openness* of the interaction rather than to the interaction per se or to its discrete ingredients.

The reality of self-organizing relational events in nature requires an expanded notion of causality. In addition to classical, linear causes, operating locally in part-to-part connections between discrete ingredients, there are relational causes operating directly upon the coming-together of the ingredients—on their dynamic unity. This kind of cause may be termed a quasi cause, since it concerns openness rather than determination and dynamic unities rather than parts. It is best thought of as a global surplus of effect, a kind of booster effect, rather than as a "cause" in any traditional sense of the word.

The quasi cause is the condition of newness or anomaly. Classical, linear cause pertains to the generally predictable context within which newness irrupts. The laws of classical causality express the "conditions of reproducibility" of the event in general, or as a particular instance of its general class (in this case, the class of dissipation events). Quasi cause must be added to account for the "conditions of repetition" of the event as singular, qualitative transition (dissipative self-ordering). Classical cause concerns context; quasi cause concerns situation. Classical cause is reactive or, in other words, active-passive (stimulus-response; action-equal reaction). Its effects are quantifiable and under controlled conditions are regularly dependable. Quasi causality is sensitive-affective, or creative (adding a surplus-value to response). It expresses a global ability to sense and be affected, qualitatively, for change. It injects a measure of objective uncontrol, a margin of eventfulness, a liveliness. Objectively causal conditions are general conditions of possibility. Quasi causality is practically "impossible." But chaotic self-organizations not only happen, they can be repeatedly induced. What they cannot be is faithfully reproduced. There is always an element of unpredictability making it uncertain whether the effect will actually transpire in any given case and, if it does occur, whether it will be the same or whether a different terminus or "attractor" will have spontaneously "captured" the system.[20] That is why "laws of chaos" are not classically determinist and, consequently, must be expressed as laws of probability.

Although the mathematical modeling of chaotic ordering events is probabilistic, the reality of the events they model is not. In science, probability is conceptualized in terms of differently weighted but equally co-present logical possibilities. Quasi causality concerns something very different: practically absent material *potential*. A potential does not preexist its emergence. If it doesn't emerge, it's because it wasn't really there. If it does, it really only just arrived. Potential is an advent. It is the contingency of an event in the future imperfect: "will have" (precessive processing). It just will have come, that's all there is to it. Always, just: a hint of eternity arriving. Before coming, it will have been objectively indeterminate. Really. Not a calculable co-presence of already-possibilities: a *virtuality*.[21] The virtual is not quantifiable. Quasi causality expresses a real, material reserve of unpredictable potential; a virtual "always just will have" in excess of the possible; a nonobjectifiable kernel or qualitative remainder of self-producing impossibility in matter, anomalously apt to irrupt in even the most closely controlled contexts. Surprise. Matter boost. In effect, uncaused. Self-creative activity in and of the world.[22]

This inverts the relation between the general/particular and the singular. Singularity is no longer a particular case inexplicably, and uninterestingly, deviating from its general rule. Rather, the general rule of law generates particularity by limiting singularity. The excess of singularity is primary. Scientific discourse missed spontaneous self-organization and the primacy of singularity for so long because of the controls it classically imposes on its experimental contexts. Self-organization, like emotion, was actively ruled out. The qualitative expression of self-organization was hampered by the assumption informing classical scientific discourse that only a controlled context, in other words closed context, could generate useful results. A closed context is one in which energy is largely conserved (input equals output). Unexpected ingresses of activity are laboriously barred. Likewise, dissipation is minimized. It's all rigged. And it's true. Closure and control—the rule-generated limitation of the particular experimental context to what appears quantifiable under the sign of equality, to the exclusion of lopsided qualitative anomaly—this is indeed necessary to ensure maximum reproducibility of results. But that is exactly the point: the limitation narrows the results to the reproducible, or to bounds of the possible. To approach potential, other assumptions and other riggings are necessary which welcome ingress and dissipative activity: other truths.

Taking into account the quasi causality of relational causality contingently necessary to self-organization involves a willingness to find in matter itself the incipiency of distinctions more comfortably restricted to the human cultural level: context/situation, quantitative/qualitative, subject/object (creative/reactive), sensation/affect (global openness to change). Most especially the latter. There are few things all chaos theorists agree upon. One of them is that chaotic self-ordering depends on a "sensitivity to initial conditions," no matter how far the system has drifted from its initial terminus. What is this continued openness to being affected by a previousness of process? Is not this enduring "sensitivity" a connecting thread of affect meandering impersonally through the world? World-affect: life-glue of matter.

This liquid detour enables a further clarification of the notion of affect. From the point of view of a given context, affect is the quasi-causal openness of a characteristic interaction under way in that context to a sensing of "something new," the arrival or irruption of which is expressed in a global qualitative change in the dynamic of the interaction, to sometimes striking effect.[23] Applying this to Katz's experiment, it becomes all the clearer that the "affect" in play was not so much the personal "familiarity and fondness" already felt by the experimentee for the owner of the eyes of blue. These were already operating emotions, personalized contents. The affect was more accurately the openness of the context to an anomalous expression of those emotions.

The previousness of the emotions triggered the uncontainment event. But their trigger ability did not inhere in them alone. Considered alone, as already constituted, they are discrete ingredients among others, but unwanted. They were determined to play a triggering role by the interactive setup of the experimental context. Their power to enter the context absolutely-singularly-strikingly was due as much to the nature of the interaction under way in that context as by any property they may retrospectively be recognized as already having had. They were determined, by the context, to be undetermined, for the context. Their role as event-catalyzers was rigged by their contextual unwanting. In many nonscientific contexts of everyday life, the same eyes would be no more than musty, old part-friends, incapable of the least surprise. It was the scientific will to exclude emotion from this situation that gave it its irruptive power. No longer in the context of the friendship from which it came, unauthorized entry into the experimental context, the emotion was thrown back into the gap of indeterminacy of the in-between of contexts. It was re-virtualized. The attempt at an interactive exclusion of emotion's in-gredience gave it a relational right of return. The flip from regulated interaction-in-context to relational-resituating-event hinged on an un-willed *return of the removed:* revenge of the re-virtual. Nothing in the prepared logic of the context could account for the excess of effect with which the uninvited return expressed itself. The shock of the re-virtualized's return thus figures in the context as an autonomy from it: a mode of self-activity. In better-controlled scientific contexts, the rela-tional effect of emotion would have been successfully ruled out. All result-ing activity would then have duly appeared as a predictable effect of knowing context control, attributable by cognitive right to the subject who organized the controls, while at the same time being recognized as a property of matter ("discovery"). In a sense, integrating quasi causal efficiency or relationality makes for a more materialist (if less objective) account than that of science. It acknowledges organizing self-activity as a rightful expression of matter. Matter appears as a self-disclosing activity rather than as a passive object of discovery: a singularly self-disclosing activity passing through context, rather than a general object of discovery whose disclosure at the hands of science is contained in context.

Everything that contributes to how an interaction goes—including what it laboriously isn't, what it attempts to exclude, its attempted mode of closure—is in some capacity ingredient in the surplus-effect of its open-ness. The asymmetry of language use, the differential of power, the con-ventions of scientific experimentation and the rigorousness of their ap-plication (or lack thereof), the architectural norms of the laboratory, all of these levels of previous determination positively contributed to the affec-tivity of the Katz color context, to its situation, by working to close con-text, attempting to hold potential effects at a remove. The affect that runs into and through the context cannot be pinned on a single ingredient. It may well be that a certain too-lively element stands out in a catalytic or event-inducing capacity, giving it a privileged role in forcing open the context, in the threading of affect through the world's in-betweenness. But the openness itself is not attributable to that ingredient alone or to any particular property of any determinate class of ingredients (emotional or otherwise). Only directly relational notions, such as quasi cause, inter-ference, modulation, catalysis, and induction, are embracing enough to begin to grasp the effective reality of affect in and of the material world: always in contingent return, at a necessary remove.

The still-suspect status of chaos theory in the eyes of the established scientific disciplines may have everything to do with its verging on ideas considered more "properly" to be of the province of philosophy: relationality, affect, creativity, and virtuality. The whole difference between science and philosophy fits into the gap suggested above between probability and potential, the possible and the virtual. Chaos theory approaches that gap, coming close enough to intuit that there is something on the philosophical side, but steadfastly refusing to make the leap. It approaches the qualitative limit of science, taking painstaking probabilistic care *not* to cross over. It is not the only science to make the approach. Quantum physics and cosmology have for many decades tread on territory dangerously close to the virtual and the anomalously relational. It has already been a century since Jules-Henri Poincaré introduced "resonance" into Newtonian physics, in connection with the infamous forerunner of chaos theory, the "three-body" problem.[24] Thermodynamics made the approach only three decades ago, with the arrival of Prigogine's "dissipative structures" (of which the Bénard instability is just one example). The very notion of catalysis comes from chemistry, which has also had to contend with qualitative events of self-organization in such phenomena as "chemical clocks." More recently still, biology and brain science have found themselves in steady approach to relational thresholds.[25] Even acoustics is currently laboring under the nonlinear shock of "stochastic resonance" and the surplus of effectiveness it brings.[26] The list could go. Everywhere, for example, there is an operative "field," from embryology to relativity, relationality is nigh.

Every science, as its observations accumulate and its paradigms complexify, may be expected to approach the qualitative limit of relationality. The virtual is a limit of objectivity which sciences approach *from within* their own operation. It is the immanent, philosophical limit of science, one every science must and does approach as it multiplies its ability to integrate variables, moving from general laws to greater and greater particularity, coming within striking distance of the singular, in flirtation with event. But it is also a limit sciences must refuse to cross if they are to remain scientific. Which is to say objective. Which is to say dealing with specifiable objects in their discreteness, and then producing dependably reproducible results across a range of actual contexts in which the specified objects may figure (attributing to each particular object in a class general properties that more or less predictably define their conditions of possibility, or functional parameters of emergence and lawful interaction); then formalizing those peer-reviewed results in quantitative terms. To fail to recoil at the relational limit is to risk becoming philosophical.

Horror. We know how high an opinion many scientists have of philosophy. Just how widespread and vehement the hostility is can only be taken as an indication that the slide toward relationality is a proximate danger from which science must dramatically save itself. Turn back, yes. Perfectly understandable where there is a will to science. But why such horror? Is the surplus of hostility toward philosophy really necessary? Or is it an excess of effect? Has philosophy ever really been in a position to threaten science from without? Psychoanalysis tells us that horror is always at an other within. But that is yet another story. The materially indeterminate protagonist of this story may be nonconscious, but it is not Freud's unconscious. This is not about personal fantasy. This is a story of the real and the empirical and of the really, empirically "removed." The "return of the repressed" is another matter.

The "real": there's the rub. The philosophy-bashing that has become such a blood sport among some scientists justifies itself on the grounds that nonanalytic philosophy ("French" for short) and its poor cousin, cultural theory, are antirealist. This is not the place to rehearse all the reasons why indeterminate is not the same as "arbitrary"; why relational is not the same as "relative"; and why contextual irruptions of the qualitatively new are not reducible to "cultural constructions." The rebuttals could also go on as indefinitely as the list of horrors thought to have been carried to American shores by the contagion of what it pleases some to call the latter-day "French disease." Instead of entering into a tit for tat on these charges of degenerative thought-disease, I would like simply to suggest that philosophy, art, and even cultural studies, are *empirical enterprises* in effective connection with the *same reality* science operates upon, generating results with their own claim to validity. The astonishingly workable results science regularly generates gives it a well-earned claim to realism and validity. But it does not give it a monopoly on them. This argument is perhaps best developed using the resources of the only homegrown *American* philosophy: pragmatism.

William James had another name for pragmatism: radical empiricism. What makes his empiricism "radical" is that it considers relations to be givens of experience. According to James, relations are no less fundamentally given, no less directly given, than discrete objects and their component properties.[27] That they are directly given means that they are directly perceived. Relation is immediately perceived *as such.* A relation is not a secondary product of association. According to the association theory adopted by classical empiricism, what is given in experience are collections of discrete, unconnected appearances or "sense data." Their connection is added by a subsequent mental operation (following an inductive logic). James counters this, arguing that relationality is already in the world and that it registers materially in the activity of the body before it registers consciously. This is the sense of his famous dictum that we do not run because we are afraid, but that we are afraid because we run. We become conscious of a situation in its midst, already actively engaged in it. Our awareness is always of an already ongoing participation in an unfolding relation. It is only after we have stopped running and can look back that we are clearly cognizant of what it was that set us dashing. *Participation precedes recognition.* From this point of view, the surprise coming-to-consciousness of the too- of Katz's blue is much less the anomaly. It is in fact the norm. Awareness always dawns as a fright, surprise, pain, or shock, of varying intensity, from the mildest (most habituated) to the severe.

Participation precedes recognition: *being precedes cognition.* The separately recognizable, speakable identities of the objects and subjects involved in the unfolding event come into definition only retrospectively.[28] In the event, they are inseparable from the immediacy of the relation. Their coming-together precedes their definition. And it is their definition that culminates the event: only after it has run its course can the situation be fully contextualized, accurately determined to have been a particular case of a certain general class of happening. Coming-together, or belonging-together, takes logical and ontological precedence over discreteness of components and, in particular, over the subject-object separation. Subject and object are embedded in the situational relation in a way that cannot be fully determined in advance. As long as the event is ongoing, its outcome even slightly uncertain, their contextual identity is open to amendment. In other words, they are embedded in the relation as the real potential to be exactly what they will have effectively become when the event will have run its course. Their identities figure virtually.[29] Chances are, when all is said and become, that the subjects and objects involved will be largely what they were in previous definitions. Largely the same but with some difference—if only by virtue of their having come to be themselves *again*. They will be at least as different as last is from next.

The point is that the being that precedes cognition is always actively engaged in a defining actualization of potential. It is a being in becoming. As such, it carries a certain vagueness. The vagueness is the way in which potential presents itself in the unfolding of experience. The degree of vagueness corresponds to the margin of uncertainty in the situation. It carries over into the actual outcome of the event as the difference the event will have made in the identities of the subjects and objects that have come together in it: their share of newness. The vague is the newness, the "nextness" of what will be again—but already, as it is under way. It is the difference in the *process* of repetition. It is the perception of continuation. It is what relation looks like in action. This is not the kind of vagueness that can be reduced to a simple lack of information. It is constitutive. It is existential. It is a being on the way to identity (again). Every experience, as it happens, carries a fringe of active indetermination. Experience under way is a constitutionally vague "something doing" in the world. Something-doing is a participation that is logically and ontologically prior to its participants: the doer and the done in their separate, contextualized identities. It is a coming-together prior to the divisibility of its own components. A being-in-relation prior to the cognitive terms of the relation.[30] Something-doing is what was described earlier as "lived belief." The difference it makes as it unfolds in context is experienced as a quality of liveliness striking the context as a whole. Objective "properties" are knowing containments of the lively. With the right organizing effort the "something" doing the new can almost always come to be defined as an added class of object with its own particular complement of properties. The vague is open to determination.

If being-in-becoming precedes cognition, then the determining procedures of science jump in at a certain point in the world's already-under-way-again. Scientific endeavor begins in the afterstrike, at the point when enough distance from the situation's liveliness can be taken that it becomes practical to *suspend lived belief*. The inaugural gesture of science is the suspension of lived belief.

If scientists are heroes in a horror story, as some of the most militantly antiphilosophical like to think, then what they do starts when the running stops. Science kicks in when the frightened protagonist has dashed far enough ahead that he can *look back* and wonder what he saw. Alien? Mutant? Philosopher? I didn't recognize it. But I feel safe now. Time to plan. I rig things so that I may come to recognize it. I track it, bait it, eventually trap it. Then I pinch it, probe it, and in the end dissect it. Laboriously, bit by bit, I cobble together an identity for it. The next time a monster is sighted, I run *toward* it, with newfound confidence. Now I know. I can recognize it. I can say whether the next one is the same as the last. I apply the identity I produced to test my recognition: match or mismatch. I eagerly share my observations. Others using the same methodology confirm my findings. The results of the investigation are reproduced and verified. Now preventive measures can be taken to save the planet from invasion.

There is one catch in using this horror story to retell the philosophical story this essay set out to narrate. Philosophically, the world is the monster. The monster is not an invasion from outer space, it's an ingress from immanence: an emergence from or surprising self-disclosure of the world's already-in-process. The flight is of course also in the world. What scientists do when confronted with the world's relational surprises is more like running in place than running away. It consists in cleaving to a limited, and limitative, trajectory. When a surprise arrives, the scientist is already looking back. Her store of accumulated knowledge, the availability of techniques and methodologies, and the corroborating company of her peers places her immediately in a posture of confidence. The surprise has been converted into an anticipation of recognition: this shall be known, following these steps. . . . Scientific method is the institutionalized maintenance of sangfroid in the face of surprise. Properly scientific activity starts from a preconversion of surprise into cognitive confidence. Science takes off from an a priori posture of recognizability: a knowledge-ready precontextualization of any and every situation. From there it runs through reproducibility of results to utility (saving the world from its own lack of boundary control). In the best of all possible worlds, it continues past making-useful, or functionalization, to the point of profitability. At profitability, science passes a threshold. Now it is science that becomes something new: capitalized technique; technologization, with all its spin-offs. Beyond functionalization lies intensive capitalization (which, as we saw, entertains a privileged connection to the patently useless and unabashedly excessive that is as foreign to scientific activity, as it officially defines itself, as philosophy is).

Science confidently jumps into the world's ongoing downstream of relation and stops shy of its excessive expressions of self-activity as it appears in and through context. Scientific recognition is not extended to excesses of effect such as too-blue, except to the extent that they are containable in an old identity or if a new class of nominal identity can be produced to render its monstrosity recognizable after all. Otherwise, they are discounted as irrelevant and even lacking in reality. The trajectory of science stretches from the worldly step just after quasi cause to the step before quality; from just after unquantifiable potential to just before the supernumerary expression of excess reality; from just after the virtuality of having-been-already-in-relation to just before extra-being, amiss in the orderings of conventional discourse; from just after the ingress of affect to just before its missed, qualitative expression jumps context.

It was said earlier that every mode of knowing was a "process line" running between "termini." It was also said that affect or relationality was the immanent limit of science's processing ability. It is now apparent that science also has an outside limit, in what has been termed "quality." If we take "empirical" in its etymological meaning as "experienced," and if we accept that relation is directly if impersonally experienced, and if we remember that consciousness is a verbose staging of the missing-in-discourse of also-sensed quality, then it becomes evident that science is operating in a restricted empirical field. It is choosing a limited itinerary between carefully policed processual termini: recognizability and func-tionalization (determinable factoid and fully determined bare fact). It cannot surpass these limits. Where it surpasses itself is in the afterlife of its own products: the many eventful spin-offs attendant to the dissemination and implantation of the capitalizable techniques it "discovers" into the world's every available relational niche. Where science continues is into the world-imperialist movement of capital. Through capitalization it flows back into a trans-situational world-tide of manic self-organizing activity reunifying excess-effect in an impersonal-subjective mode again. In a way, capital is the "return of the removed" most successfully haunt-ing science. You need only listen to the vehemence of the protestations that scientific research remains "pure" in spite of the ubiquity of cor-porate financing to understand both how much of a danger capital rep-resents to science's self-definition and how integral it is to science's continuation. The more vigorous the attempts to remove capitalist modu-lation of research, whether by wishful thinking, vociferous protest, or increased vigilance in the application of the scientific method, the more strenuously it returns, by virtue of the thoroughly "mangled" relational situation of science.

Processually, science is defined by two limits it cannot cross in principle and one threshold it cannot but cross to the precise extent to which it succeeds at its own self-assigned task of functionalization. Continually crossing its threshold, it becomes self-consciously other than itself in a way that enables it to do more of what it does best, as a portion of the profit that its successes generate is fed back in as research funding. Pointing out science's self-limitations is not an accusation. It is in fact an acknowledgement of its ability to define itself as self-organizing process. Pointing out that it crosses a threshold of becoming-other that sets in motion a feedback effect of corporate complicity is not necessarily an accusation either. It is a realistic reminder that the rightful autonomy of science is not a "purity" or watertight enclosure but an "autonomy of connection" subject to modulation (no autonomy is ever a purity of disconnection—other than that of death). Science generates results by imposing controls designed to close its contexts as much as methodologically possible. But the results of its own method, the very effects its closure enables it to produce, flow back around to create a qualitative global situation that makes reopening ingress into, and interferes with, its every contextual exercise. You don't need to visit many laboratories to discover that funding looms large in scientific gossip. In spite of all of this, pointing out the limitations and thresholding of science is a roundabout way of testifying to its processual staying power—its ability to remain its own activity even in connection with ineluctable processes whose operative bounds encompass it.[31]

Another way of stating the processual parameters of scientific activity is to say that it trips in at the first glimmers of particularity as it emerges from the singularity of the event and carries through to the point that a general, quantitative formulation of the particular's conditions of possibility is developed (within a structurally stabilized, institutionally guarded subject-object/knower-known framework). This implies two things. First, if you allow a role in your story of the real for singularity on the one hand and for its expression in quality on the other, then you are confronted with an *expanded empirical field*. The classically empirical assumptions and methods of science operate selectively in a limited range of empirical reality. The question then arises as to what modes of knowing can connect with the regions of empirical reality that science studiously leaves out and to what effect the connections can be made. Second, it becomes hard to argue that science has a monopoly on understanding nature. In fact, it can be argued that science *misses nature by design.* From the very beginning, science operates in investigative contexts that are highly culturally, socially, and economically predetermined. Anything unforeseen that transpires has made forcible ingress. From the moment a newness irrupts, procedures already ready-at-hand clamp down for the knowing capture. The scientific process line thus inaugurated is a cofunction of the cultural-economic-social predeterminations and the determinability of the ingressive. What is the qualitatively transformative force that makes social ingress? Is it not nature? What is nature "in itself" if not the world's dynamic reserve of surprise? The "real"? *Nature in itself is the actively indeterminate.* The moment it begins to come out of itself, it has made social ingress. Scientific activity begins at a point at which nature has made social ingress and is already on the road to some form of determination. As Bruno Latour strenuously argues the "raw" objects of science are already nature-culture "hybrids."

Science is not the only nature-culture mix that begins at this same point. Habit does also: habits contracted by the body (as basic as looking or reaching). "Normal," everyday knowing begins at exactly the same point science does. Every ingress meets a habitual reception. The "surprise" that has been repeatedly invoked in this essay is the effect of a miss in habitual reception. The cognitive miss or mismatch is preceded by a precognitive failure to recognize. The processing of the ingress event begins to trifurcate at that point where recognizability becomes an issue. Following one path, it runs into common sense, anecdote, and gossip. These are practices of language whose job is to rehabituate the shocking: to give it at least an air of recognizability (if not always usefully making it understood). This terminally factoidal route is the discursive equivalent of a collective sigh of relief. Following a second path, the ingress runs into more cognitively elaborated, but still more or less informal, knowledge practices producing semi-facts that in their own context have a recognized use-value. Finally, it may take a turn down the royal road of science, toward the cognitive sanction of full and formal factual determination: official recognition. Habit lies at the hinge of nature and these divergent process lines of culture. Habits are socially or culturally contracted. But they reside in the matter of the body, in the muscles, nerves, and skin, where they operate autonomously. Although they are contracted in social/cultural context, they must be considered self-active autonomies: spontaneous self-organizations that operate on a level with movements of matter. But, in that case, can't the self-organizations of matter described by chaos theory also be considered habits? Aren't they inhumanly contracted habits of matter? Habit is at the matter-hinge between nature and culture. But where is the hinge? Is there a difference in kind or only a difference in mode or degree between the inhuman habits of matter and the human ones?

There are incipiencies of cultural hinge-activity everywhere in "nature," in even the brutest matter. The border between nature and culture is actually unassignable. This is why science must impose so strict a procedural cutoff point at a certain level: that of recognizability in specific, controlled social/cultural contexts lending themselves to certain regulated modes of discursive elaboration. As a matter of fact, the cutoff point is an indistinct gradation: a continuum. Science may be able to suspend the liveliness of lived belief, but it cannot suspend habit. And it cannot acknowledge that it cannot suspend it. The *nature-culture continuum* is the ultimate "removed" of science: the material heritage or "archaeology" science cannot acknowledge if it is to place itself confidently on the all-knowing-human-subject side of a divide from the natural "object." Because it cannot acknowledge it, it leaves itself open to modulation by the removed's return. For example, in the form of capitalist interference. Capital's power to make ingress into even the most closed scientific contexts rides on its ability to operate more and more directly with and upon the nature-culture continuum, as the capitalized technique more and more intensively rejoins the self-organizing levels of matter, the very levels at which nature contracts its incipiently cultural, inhuman habits (biotechnology being the most obvious example but by no means the only one).[32]

If the border between nature and culture is actually unassignable, then what authorized the preceding reference to nature "in itself"? The key is "actually." If nature is the actively indeterminate, then "in itself" it is virtual. But there is still a problem: the virtual does not exist. It comes into being, as becoming. Its "nature" is to come to be: to make ingress. Its ingress injects potential into habitual contexts. Nature is not really the "given." It is the giving—of potential. The giving always holds back from what it gives, so that it does not exhaust itself and can come to give again.

Nature always holds itself in iterative reserve. Its continually repeated holding-in-reserve might be considered an "in-itself." Except that "it" is not. "It" is not an object but a reserve of relation, a surplus reserve, for the giving. In the end, nature is not well described as an "in-itself." It is an *of-itself*. It is a partitive, giving always *of* itself—of relational potential—while holding back a remainder on which to draw again. "Of-itself"—and "more." This is Spinoza's "naturing nature": nature as an inexhaustible, impersonal reserve of giving self-activity. Naturing nature is "subjective" nature, if that word can be used in a sense prior to the actual distinction between subject and object: a radically inhuman "subjectless subjectivity" as endlessly generous in its giving as capitalism is manic in its taking (if capitalism culturally rejoins nature, it is with a change of polarity). Something's doing in the expanded field.[33]

Nature is partitive. Science (like every actually determining process) is limitative. The expanded empirical field within which science sets its limits broadens to include relation. As argued earlier, the real world is not reducible to its necessary conditions, or conditions of possibility or reproducibility. The "real conditions" of any event include anomalous or necessarily-contingent quasi-causal efficiencies. Call necessary conditions *requisites*. Call everything that effectively enters the event but cannot be reduced to requisite part-to-part causal interactions between discrete ingredients an *accompaniment*. This is Whitehead's plea for an expanded empiricism:

> Everything perceived is in nature. We may not pick and choose. For us the red glow of the sunset should be as much part of nature as are the molecules and electric waves by which men of science would explain the phenomenon. . . . The real question is, When red is found in nature, what else is found there also? Namely, we are asking for an analysis of the accompaniments in nature of the discovery of red in nature.[34]

When too-blue is found in the laboratory, what else is found there? This essay began by asking for an analysis of the accompaniments in nature-culture of the self-disclosure of excess liveliness in the laboratory.

"What we see," Whitehead concurs, "depends on light entering the eye." Light is a requisite of vision. But there's a hitch: "we do not perceive what enters the eye." "The wave theory of light is an excellent well-established theory; but unfortunately it leaves out color as perceived."[35] Whitehead is referring in particular to effects that can only be explained relationally. The classic examples are color complementarity, colored shadows, and spectral halos. These are whole-field effects irreducible to part-to-part interaction between discrete elements.[36] The objective color-dimensions of hue, saturation, and brightness that can be defined in terms of wavelength properties of light cannot account for the full range of real color-experience. The scientific truth of light accounts very well for the possibility of color in general. But the reality of color extends to objectively impossible effects of relationality as they figure in *this* perception and *this* one. . . and *this* other one. By shunning those singular quasi-causal effects, science usefully limits its empiricism. It pays a price for that functionality: the glow. The glow does not exist for it. The unique color-quality of a sunset does not exist for the scientific observer. But then what can you do with the glow of *this* sunset anyway? Just wonder at it.

Wonder. This is where philosophy comes in. Philosophy is the activity dedicated to keeping wonder in the world.[37] It has its job cut out for it, drowning as we all are in a techno-sea of utility and profitability. Philosophy, then, starts with accompaniment: the perceived effects of relational quasi causality.[38] It starts with the glow. Or the "too-" of the blue. Understood specifically as whole-field effects. That is philosophy's first terminus, the point of departure of its process line. It works back from there, "against the stream of perception" as Bergson used to say, toward relationality "in itself"; toward the virtual. Philosophy is a labor of decontextualization. It distills singularity from its contextual expression. It subtracts the relation from its actual terms. After it has distilled the relation, philosophy goes on to connect the singularity with another similarly decontextualized singularity, distilled from other contextual expressions. Its second terminus, its point of arrival, is the connection between singularities. Philosophy makes virtual connections: pure *linkage* without the links.[39] Its process line is for the production of trans-situational linkage, or *affect*. This is what Deleuze and Guattari mean by "consistency." A philosophical concept, they say, doesn't have an object. It has only consistency: pure holding-together (minus the held). Its "object" is the gap between contexts into which the world's self-activity recedes as it pushily continues across on the way to a next ingress. The activity of philosophy is the thinking of the reserve of context-rocking potential. It is the activity of rejoining the resituating movement of the new—through a decontextualizing countercurrent of thought. It is human thought endeavoring to flow back on nature's self-activity.

Running counter as it does to the actuality of contexts, philosophy is an *antihistory*. It is the affirmation of the trans-situational potential that runs through history and is contained in it, but never without remainder. Its not-an-object is the indeterminate excess of self-active, connective potential continuing through and renewing history. Without that potential-injecting transconnective flow, history would only be able to repeat its own bare fact. It would be self-identical. Unmodulated. It would simply lack the relational resources to qualitatively self-differ in its order of repetitions. In other words, it wouldn't be history at all. It would be all order. Stasis. Nothing doing. Philosophy runs antihistorical in order to flow back on the *life* of history's iterative self-ordering: its eventfulness. Philosophy's nonobject is change. It is the counterthinking of the new.

Philosophy engages with history to attain its *nature:* the reserve of surprise lurking inhumanly in history's gaps of renewal.[40] Philosophy is nature philosophy by vocation. It is *nature philosophy* when it is doing what no other knowledge practice cares to do, when it goes where no other can go due to the self-policed limits it processually observes. It was just asserted that nature is as a matter of fact the immanent limit of scientific knowledge. Philosophy operates at that immanent limit. It continues where science turns back. As the references to history implies, the "science" whose immanence concerns philosophy must be broadly defined. "Soft" sciences modeling themselves in key ways on the "hard" sciences are included. "Social" or "human" sciences that aspire to be quantitative or, even if they describe themselves as "qualitative," that claim any form of predictive validity for their results; that claim to produce verifiable truths about actual contexts; that operate with notions of causality privileging part-to-part interaction between ingredient elements; that think of their elementary units of description as having determinate properties prior to the event of their coming-together; that see themselves as usefully expressing what is necessary to the world; that consider thought to begin with conscious object-recognition; in short, that adopt a classically empirical view of reality, whether implicitly or explicitly—these are included. Philosophy wonderingly parts company with them all.

What philosophy tries to articulate are *contingencies:* potential relational modulations of contexts that are not yet contained in their ordering as possibilities that have been recognized and can be practically regulated. Philosophy's back-flow is to a point of pre-possibility. It is a form of *contingent reason* whose nonobject is the practically *impossible*. The impossible is not the opposite or simple negative of the possible. It is the indeterminate but positive potential for possibilities to be added to particular contexts. This can only occur through a qualitative excess-effect of the kind discussed earlier with reference to the Bénard instability. The impossible is potentialized when interactions sense themselves open: when, to use Derrida's term, an unpredictable margin of "play" strikes a singular coming-together, for more (or, to use the vocabulary suggested at the opening of this essay, when relation and genitivity go together). What actually takes effect as the situation plays out its potential is the *emergence* of a possibility. What has transpired is that a potential has actualized. A positive indeterminacy has come to be a determinate possibility. Actualized potential may be automatically captured by habit and from habit may pass into language to become one of the acquired attributes and contents whose discursive dissemination predetermines context. An actually captured potential is an acquired possibility: a recognized permutation captured in matter and functionally contained in an already operating order. Possibility is function-ready enculturated nature, from the iterative moment of its first emergence.

Just as science pays a price for recoiling at its relational limit, philosophy pays a price for following its own vocation to approach it. Since philosophy only allows itself a virtual nonobject, it is an utterly *speculative* undertaking. Its moving against the grain of nature's cultural expression is a highly artificial movement of thought. It is an utterly contrived thought-fiction. Specifically, since its fiction concerns impossible objects, it is a *fable*. The nature it rejoins is frankly fabulatory. It is prefunctional. Thus attaining it is a supremely useless gesture. Philosophy makes itself useless to the exact extent to which it succeeds at its self-chosen task. It is the glow of understanding (without the *actual* understanding). The sunset of practical reason—with an uncanny resemblance to its dawning.

A philosophical concept can make no claim to correspond to anything real. But it can claim to *be* something real. The "empirical" was taken earlier in its etymological meaning of "experienced." James was cited as having argued that relations are directly sensed alongside their actual terms and, in a way, irreducible to them. For James, relation is directly sensed as a "fringe" of ongoing, a residue of potential or newness marginally accompanying every determinate perception (the virtual as it actually presents itself). Philosophy is the movement of thought to the virtual fringe of things. It is the labor of making relation "more" sensible, of making the "more" of relation sensible, in a movement occurring purely in thought, logically prior to the point at which relation has actual terms. Its terminus of departure is quality, the virtual as actually presented in the fringing of given contexts. Its terminus is the reserve expressed by that "moreness." In other words, philosophy rigs thinking to make singular connections in fictional *anticipation* of their actualization. It is fabulously portentous (which is why it was earlier implied to be close to science fiction, which as a genre specializes in straddling the divide between hard science and speculative philosophy). The portentousness is *thought itself becoming sensible:* however systematic or precise its logic of consistency or pure linkage is, philosophy's nonobject remains ontologically vague, vague by nature. Philosophical thinking, even (especially) the most rigorous, is a conceptual *groping* of potential-to-be.[41]

Katz's experiment drew attention to the fact that the dawning of consciousness is always collective and expectant—that experience becomes personal socially, when something absolutely-strikingly-singular has irrupted in context in way that is just asking to be determined. Awareness dawns in a collective, expectant reception of something whose entry into context has preceded its possibility of being determined. Expectant reception: wonder. Consciousness dawns amiss in wonder. In a very real sense, any act of wonder is already a philosophical act. Wonder is prephilosophical in the same way that habit is prescientific. Science formally prolongs habit (the reception of the new in an a priori mode of recognition). Philosophy speculatively prolongs wonder (the remainder of surprise persisting across its a priori capture by habit). The thoroughly collective nature of any event of consciousness authorizes Deleuze and Guattari to say that although the prolonged wonder of philosophy has no object it still has a subject of sorts. Philosophy addresses its thought-sensed nonobject to the collectivity capable of determining it. That collectivity is as anticipated as the potential self-activity dawning for it. Philosophy addresses itself to a *community to come.* Or, as Giorgio Agamben says, a coming community: a community in potential ingress.[42] Philosophy has no object, but it has a virtual subject. It is portentous but never predictive, for it must wait for the coming, collective determination of the community. Philosophy is forever in suspense. In many societies, philosophy is practiced as the most intensely solitary thought-activity to which a body can lend itself. This only pushes it deeper into collective suspense. The farther it recedes bodily from its subject, the more intensely it approaches it virtually.

Philosophy is gloriously useless. But it can feed into useful activity. If science makes recognizability useful by preparing closed contexts, it stands to contingent reason that by preparing an openness of contexts to each other, the potential portented by philosophical speculation may actualize, adding determinate possibility to the world. This would involve tweaking the regulated connection between contexts, their already ordered interaction, in such a way as to reopen their coming-together to a relational quasi causality. The result would be an excess self-organizing effect, as the intercontextual order readjusts itself around the shock of the new, possibilizing the surplus of potential that has vaguely presented itself by contracting the new habits and discursive contents, even new discourses, that will determine what will have been when all is said and become. This amounts to a whole-field modulation of the nature-culture continuum—a qualitative shock to the world-historical system (or at least a connectively autonomous region of it). The groping of philosophy will have given way to pragmatic tweaking, a hands-on experimentation in contextual connectivity. The modulation that occurs will not resemble the pure, virtual linkage produced by the countercontextual movement of philosophical thought. When it reenters the contextual realm, the consistency of the concept will be necessarily inflected by the grit and friction of the already-actual outside philosophy. What the effect will turn out to be will be functionally determined as contextual orderings already in operation adjust their comings-together under its ingressive impetus: as they *resituate* themselves. By its very (ontologically vague) nature, a philosophical concept is incapable of serving as a model of resemblance for actual objects and interactions. It can take actual effect only in self-differing. There is only one word for the activity of using philosophy's offer of resituating self-difference to produce global self-organizing effects: *politics*.

Politics is philosophy continued by other means. Correction: an exploratory politics of *change* is philosophy pursued by other means—a radical politics equal to the "radicality" of the expanded empirical field itself. Radical politics is an inherently risky undertaking because it cannot predict the outcome of its actions with certainty. If it could, it wouldn't be radical but reactive, a movement dedicated to capture and containment, operating entirely in the realm of the already possible, in a priori refusal of the new. Radical politics must tweak and wait: for the coming, collective determination of the community. Its role is to catalyze or induce a global self-reorganization: tweak locally to induce globally (to modulate a slogan). Speaking of slogans, repeat this one: "be realistic, demand the impossible." Under what conditions could that be a formula for a *political empiricism?*

It is precisely when nature philosophy becomes politically useful that it ceases to be itself. Just as science crosses a threshold when it feeds into technological "progress," so, too, does philosophy when it lends itself to radical politics. Agreeing with Foucault, Deleuze says that a philosophical concept may be a "tool." But it becomes a tool only after it has been picked up by nonphilosophical hands actually engaged in collective experimentation. Philosophy needs nonphilosophy to make an actual difference in the world. Nonphilosophical context is the point of departure to which philosophy differently returns. This is the pragmatic problem of the philosopher referred to earlier.[43]

Philosophy can be useful even when kept at arms length. Even to science. It was asserted earlier that chaos theory is an instance of science approaching its immanent, relational limit. When it first emerged, chaos theory went through a heady period of public basking in the philosophical glow. But almost immediately it pulled back. Most scientists engaged with chaos theory have precious little patience for the philosophical preoccupations still very much in evidence in the current work of some of its founders (in particular, Ilya Prigogine). The scientists who recoil at the danger of becoming-philosophical are hard at work at the task of bringing chaos theory back into the scientific fold in as unambiguous a fashion as possible. This involves formally quantifying the uncertainty factor inherent to self-organization and building on that formal basis some manner of reproducibility of result or predictive value. Functionalizing chaos in this way is a challenge. The only way to quantify chaotic self-organization, given its native uncertainty, is in terms of probability. The return of chaos theory to the scientific fold requires learning how to make probability useful in a dependable way. This is already occurring in a number of scientific domains, and, in not a few cases, results are already reaching the stage of technologization. But isn't the unexpungability of probability a niggling philosophical issue tagging along with chaos theory even as it returns to its fold? Probability is a mathematical expression of the practically impossible. Its formal insistence in scientific modeling is an unacknowledged testament to the world's relationality: to the "many-body" reality that interactions between discrete elements tend naturally toward an openness of outcome expressed in qualitative leaps in mode of activity. However rigorously scientific chaos theory manages to become, it will still carry a philosophical afterglow, radiation burn of the virtual.

It was stated earlier that every science tends inexorably toward its immanent limit of relationality, from which it must periodically pull back in order to remain its own activity. This applies to "soft" sciences as well as "hard." All science is philosophically modulated at a distance, from within its own self-defined process line, following its own self-professed movements of approach and repulsion. Science suffers a fatal attraction to philosophy. It needs philosophy, like a poison that leaves you stronger if you survive it. Philosophy needs science too, in its own way. Philosophy starts from accompaniment (whole-field effects). Accompaniment is what tacitly remains after the requisites are scientifically spoken for. Accompaniment and requisition are reciprocal. This means that philosophy depends for its starting point on science's power to define its own contents. Philosophy, modest activity that it is, gets the leftovers. It doesn't complain though, so wondrous are the sunset scraps. This is to say that nature philosophy must be as scientifically savvy as it can be if it is not to "miss" its own qualities. It cannot afford to maintain a simply negative or critical stance toward science. It must remain informed of where the bounds of ordered interaction and its functional reproduction have been scientifically set.

Science and philosophy are symbiotic activities. They naturally, continuously feed into each other, in different ways. Science definitionally modulates philosophy's point of departure. Philosophy modulates science across its horrified recoil at its point of no return. Science and philosophy processually complement each other, even in times of declared "war." There are not "two cultures." There two (actually many) process lines plying the same nature-culture continuum. Both "sides" should accustom themselves to the idea of sharing their reality. In any case, that is what they are already engaged in.

The empirically real was defined by its basic etymological meaning of "sensed" or "experienced." To be sensed or experienced is the same thing as having effects: registering a difference elsewhere. The measure of the empirical field is *effective reality:* the ability to make a difference. The point was made that there is a necessarily contingent surplus of effect over cause. Deterministic *causal reality* only covers a portion of the empirical field. Any activity that is capable of producing effects has a claim to empirical reality and to a mode of validity corresponding to its manner of effecting: to a certain truth-value. That truth is the *power* to produce effects is the pivotal insight of pragmatism.

Philosophical speculation has just as much a claim to empirical truth as science does. It just has a different claim to it. A philosophical concept is true to the extent that it can help catalyze change in a movement of ceasing to be its useless self. Its truth is in giving itself up—something science will never countenance for its own part. The real issue between philosophy and science is not the relativity of truth. It is the *plurality of absolute truths.* By "absolute" is meant simply "without resemblance, comparable only to itself." Each process line of knowledge plies a unique trajectory through the empirical field, bringing different dimensions of its ceaseless self-activity to pragmatic expression in a way specific to that line. The "success" of the effects a process line produces can only be judged by its own performative criteria: its way of making "something doing" something done and determinate. One process line cannot judge another. Process lines can interfere with each other. They can modulate each other. They can capture each other's effects and convert them into more of their own. But they cannot judge each other because they are doings immersed in the empirical field, not "reflections" of it. There is no neutral outside of shared empirical reality in which to stand in final judgment of its divergent coursings. What a process line of knowledge production does "corresponds" only to its own activity. When one claims to judge another's truth, it is trying to impose its own activity where it isn't doing. It is not engaging in a noble act of impartial knowing. It is declaring an imperialist war of cognitive cleansing. The "judgment" is tantamount to an interdiction of existence based on a refusal of empirical difference: this becoming should be mine or should cease; its effects should not be here or how they are; there is not enough room in this empirical reality for the both of us—so get out of my world. This kind of gesture is an attempt to substitute *moralism* for politics. For if process lines can only really interfere with, modulate, and capture each other's effectiveness, then their interaction is always political: a catalysis, battle, or negotiation. Morality attempts to cover up the political reality with an annihilating fiction of one true way of doing something.

A common way of going about this is in the name of a universal "we" that is a thinly disguised assertion of a restricted "we's" exclusive right to existence based on monopoly access to the "laws" or "principles" "behind" empirical reality. A strange "empiricism," isn't it, that claims to act exclusively on behalf of law or principle? What are laws and principles if not *beings of reason?* Any knowledge practice that posits laws behind empirical reality in fact constitutes a strange mix of rationalism and empiricism. Both Hume, the inventor of empiricism, and C. S. Peirce, the inventor of the pragmatism further developed by James, argued that nature does not follow laws. *Laws follow nature.* What nature does is generate surprises and contract habits. Laws come after.[44] They formally model the already contracted habits of nature in a way that makes them humanly useful. The "laws" of nature are functional end-products of science. They do not "correspond" as such to anything "behind" nature. Nature only goes one way: into *this* world. It has no determinate behind. Laws are human, contextual creations: effective fictions fit for useful service. This is in no way to suggest that scientific laws do not have *general* validity. They are laboriously tailored for validity in as broad a range of contexts as possible. None are valid in all contexts (even Newton's foundational laws are valid only at a certain scale, for energy-conservative systems). But scientific laws are generally true to the extent possible. Their inbred tendency is to extend themselves to every possible context. However generally they extend, their well-established truth does not exhaust the truth of a single one of its applicable contexts. Simply because every context is struck by singularity. Generality and possibility are not the only things doing. It is precisely by general *extension* that laws miss the really-felt *intensity* (vivacity) of events.

If laws are effective fictions, it appears that philosophy is not the only fabulator. It is just the most "radical" in its fabulations. The most fabulous thing about law-giving science is that it so easily substitutes the models that it itself so laboriously produces for the more encompassing reality in connection with which it produces them. That reality is necessarily more encompassing simply because it includes the scientist's activity of formulating laws. Science, like every activity, is in the world. Science cannot claim to speak for an "in-itself" out the far side of the empirical reality science itself is immersed in. Claiming the privilege of an outside perspective on the world is religion's fictitious job. It, too, labors extremely hard to maintain its stance. Science is really only in a position to claim for itself a *share* of nature's surprise-giving "of-itself." A most powerful share but a share nonetheless. If it takes its claims too far for "of-ness," it is at the price of becoming-theological—whether it cares to admit it or not.

Case in point: the classical-empiricist fundamentalist Edward O. Wilson states what would appear to be the consensus view of "science warriors" outraged at the current "excesses" of humanities disciplines. He invokes a universal "we" sharing the "common goal of turning as much philosophy as possible into science." Franco-diseased philosophy and its co-carriers of plague, "postmodern" art and cultural studies, he is confident, will "wink out in the dimensionless dark" like "sparks from fireworks."[45] Their demise will be the soon-to-be-released "theory of everything": the reductive law to end all thought-infraction. The empirical science defended by warriors like Wilson and Alan Sokal (with far less intellectual engagement than Wilson) is a sometimes viciously moralizing *rationalist empiricism* which, aspiring to a supreme principle, slips into a becoming-theological even when, as in Wilson's case, it is self-avowedly atheist. The tacit becoming-theological of rationalist empiricism is not so implicit in other scientist's writings. The most revered guru of rationalist empiricism is Stephen Hawking. He claims outright that when science has finally completed the difficult construction of the Theory of Everything "we" will finally "know the mind of God."[46] TOE: Where empirical scientists turn podiatrists of the soul.

By Wilson's own contradictory admission, the glowing "dimensionless" darkness that horrifies him has at least three dimensions: philosophy, art, and cultural studies. To bring this philosophical story to a close, it will be necessary to consider very briefly how the other two dimensions of nonscientific "darkness" process reality.

Philosophy operates at the immanent limit of science, "downstream" of its beginning terminus in recognizability, approaching nature's of-itself. What operates beyond science's outside limit, its end terminus in reproducibility? This is the empirical region of quality, understood as the actual expression in context of the vivacious excess of virtuality or relationality. A quality presents the pushy self-activity of life on the move: the remainder of ingressive potential too ongoing to be exhausted by any particular expression of it. The process line most directly concerned with the qualitative expression of self-transforming life-activity is art.

Mention has already been made of one "artist": Frank Sinatra. His Katzian eye-color makes him a good place to start. Sinatra is arguably more of a turning point in popular culture than Elvis or The Beatles. It was in fact Sinatra who made the artistic connections that subsequent icons modulated in their own way. Artists, like philosophers, make connections. But rather than connecting singularity to singularity the artist connects quality of excess to quality of excess. Sinatra connected the too-blue of his glancing eyes to the too-mellifluous of his oscillating voice. Then he connected the too-mellifluous of his voice to the subtly too-smooth of his gestures. He connected qualities by seamlessly linking movements of his body into a carnal melody. The interlinkage constituted a composition of qualities that sensibly repeated the linguistic content of the lyrics. The perceived overall quality of the performance meant romance—again. It *meant* romance and *expressed* a singular way of moving through the world: *My Way*. What was expressed through the words and gestures was a way of circulating through the offstage world. The movement between contexts notably included heterosexual romance but was not reducible to it. It also included the homosociality of the interracial "Rat Pack" and rights of entry into the White House and Mafia hangouts. These were all a part of the Sinatra mystique. The connection between embodied qualities Sinatra performed was intimately associated with a surprising way of connecting contexts that in principle (according to the conventionally accepted order of circulation of that era) should be kept carefully segregated: blacks and whites, the presidency and sex, romance and corruption, politics and organized crime.

Sinatra's popularity has a double content. It was a lyrical double articulation. It connected a performative body-melody (itself a connection of qualities) to a way of connecting contexts. The contexts were connected simply by moving the body-melody through them. Both articulations of content were marked by excess. The body-melody meant romance. Love: the driving quality of a person's self-activity that cannot be contained without remainder in any particular domestic context (even in monogamist terms, where love still figures as a kind of qualitative life-glow, a global excess of desired and desiring effect in essential surplus over the banal actuality of life's conjugal details). The moving of the melody between contexts expressed an excess liberty of movement: a greater degree of circulatory freedom than conventionally allowed for.

In the connection of connections—or *composition*—the eyes winked supreme. Everything was summed up in them. All of the content of the performance, linguistic, carnal, and circulatory, was contracted into that ineffable quality of blue. Sinatra's blue eyes gathered all that he performed into a *face*. In other words, it embodied it in a personal way, "my" way. Sinatra's too-blue expressed a life, a singular life. It expressed this life as personal *and* shareable. Sinatra's fans could bask in his personal life-glow. They could feel the quality in every recess of their swooning, finger-snapping bodies. They could try to carry the glow into their own circulation through life's contexts. Sinatra's too-blue expressed the singularity of a life as a potentially shareable (heterosexual) lifestyle. His way of connecting lyrical movements of language to bodily movement to contextual circulations was just that: the creation of a style. However low-brow it might be by many standards, his singing was a bona fide artistic endeavor because it created a powerfully effective new style. The genius of his style was to *personalize a composed singularity of vital movements in a way that it could collectively spread.* He made his own liveliness collective by force of personality—so forcefully that it became literally contagious. Popular song had become a technique of lifestyle *contagion.* Sinatra lyrically reinvented heterosexuality as a popular culture virus.

This is the mode of connection that the popular music of the 1960s drew upon and modulated. It was not actually that large of a step, in spite of the contrasting political and social polarity of the "Movement." The rebellious performers of the 1960s took the musically composed lifestyle contagion Sinatra invented to greater excess. Their stylistic expressions added degrees of freedom to the anticonventional circulation between offstage contexts. They intensified the style of popular music, contracting so many degrees of movement into their straining eyes that they would glaze over in connective overdose or roll Iggy Pop frenetic. But the basic structure was the same: sharing in a collective quality of life-movements personally summed up in the iconic face of the performer. The contagion at issue was not an imitation as such, even in Sinatra's case. Few fans of Sinatra, if any, took his life as a literal model for theirs. Very few actually hung out presidentially with packs of human rodents. Under the felt sameness of expressed too-blue quality was an assumed difference in the kinds of contexts that could be connectively lived. The effective sharing of the felt quality did not preclude major differences in the actual offstage movements. This differential between expressed quality and actual movements was consciously played upon and widened during the 1960s, when "imitating" an icon came to be experienced as a liberation not only from conventional orders of circulatory context connection but from fealty to all models of behavior—even the icon's. The same differential widened yet again a decade later with punk (after which the affective economy of popular music underwent another transformation in the course of which the lifestyle link was weakened).

Popular art is a collective technology of vitality. Its continued reliance on personalization and its emphasis on shareability means that it retains a connection to common sense, however stretched. However "counter-cultural" or "sub-cultural" it gets, popular music is still playing personally with collective "imitation" effects. What is often dismissed as "avant-garde" art involves the creation of styles that refrain from presenting their qualitative expression as personal (arguing that it is first and foremost critical or cosmic), that try to expunge the sense of sameness from the compositions (claiming inimitable singularity), and that cut off or undermine the smoothness of the connections between levels (movements of language; bodily movements; movements between actual contexts). The compositional strategies of avant-garde or "serious" art *disjunctively conjoin* the movement levels that popular art endeavors to connect seamlessly. It sometimes has a tendency to present itself as a "pure" activity opposite in nature from mere popular artistry. In fact, like all activity, it is always impure. Its unacknowledged impurity consists in being an operation on popular artistry. Avant-garde artists have a reputation for being hyperaware of the vagaries of popular lifestyle "statements." They have to be close to popular culture in order to know how to disarticulate it. All-too-popular life-stylized artistry is the avant-garde "removed" that ineluctably returns. When "serious" artists neglect to not personalize the styles they create, or when their work is personalized in spite of their best efforts, their art turns into "high" art. All the excess falls back on the personalization, which greatly intensifies because it doesn't have the outlet of collective contagion and thus carries little or no effective differential, little or no variational connectivity between actual contexts (other than between the contexts of the gallery, museum, and salons of the wealthy). In high art, excess of creative personality ("genius") is converted directly into capitalist surplus-value.

Popular art, for its part, has no complexes about its own capitalist feed-forward. When avant-garde art gets "high" on society and feeds into capitalist circulation, it rejoins popular art—and scientific technologization. Witness the role of technology turnover in renewing artistic expression: from analog to digital media; from vinyl to CD to the Internet and

MP3; at each turnover there is a new and intensified threshold of profit-making stylistic circulation. Capital is the shared threshold of science and art. (What, by the way, is the relation between capital and philosophy? Both have been described as supremely useless and as reconstituting excess-unities of linkage or circulation. How near and how far! Is the relation between philosophy and capital a parody? A simulation? Is contemporary capitalism the farce of philosophy's second historical coming?)

The processings of science run usefully from recognizability to reproducibility. The processing of philosophy runs uselessly from accompaniment (actual qualitative expression) to relationality (virtual connection between singularities). Those of art cleave to actual qualitative expression, running from quality to quality in a way that envelops actual movements (in a composition that can be either seamless or disjunctive, contagious or off-putting). Philosophy and art bookend science, working from opposite scientific termini. Both art and philosophy, unlike science, are concerned with the eventful expression of singularity. Philosophy presents singularity as virtually expressing (surplus-giving relation, or situation). Art re-presents it as actually expressed (contextual excess or remainder). They both present the singular as the qualitatively transformative movement it is: as *affective* rather than as objectified. But they present it in different modes. Philosophy presents affect as thought-sensed; art, as sensationally performed.

There is one process line in the expanded field that has not been spoken for: from relationality to expressed quality. This is a more ample movement, beginning before the scientific limit of recognizability and continuing past its limit of reproducibility. This is a broad sweep running from philosophy to art, through a middle region that is shared, in passing, with science. If a process line succeeded in following this path, there would be nothing prohibiting it from then turning around and taking the same path in reverse, going from expressed quality to relationality. A process line of this kind would make a bidirectional sweep across the entire nature-culture continuum. Imagine the powers of contrivance, the fabulatory skill, necessary to pull that off. Imagine the ire of science, so easily horrified, at a more ample movement trespassing on its empirical territory, even in passing. A process line of this kind would be most fraught—and filled with its own unique potential. It might even be in a position to draw political effectiveness from its movements, perhaps serving in some way as an arbiter in the mutual interferences, battles, and negotiations between philosophy, science, and art. It would distinguish itself from both art and philosophy by taking their political middle as its eventual terminus. Unlike the other process lines, it would circle around to having only that one terminus. Its movement would be a bidirectional orbit around the terminus of the political middle. What would distinguish it from other political movements would be its base in cultural institutions such as the university, museum and gallery, think tank, and research center.

This process line could well be cultural studies. But it isn't. Cultural studies has missed its processual boat because it has not had the audacity to sweep far enough in either direction. As it is widely practiced, cultural studies falls short of singularity at both limits because it clings to the notion that *expression is of a particularity.* It realizes that expression is always collective. But it takes the collectivity as already constituted, as a determinate set of actually existing persons (in common parlance, a constituency). This contains expression: it restricts its movement to the manifestation of a content considered to be generally applicable to a collection of particular persons, to an established category or class of human. It treats expressed qualities as general attributes or properties shared by the members of a class by pregiven "right" (in principle if not in fact). This misses surplus-giving relation and the qualitative excess of liveliness overspilling every determinate expression. It misses the relational comingness of the community and the qualitative contagion of collective life-movement. It misses the impersonal or overpersonal excesses of ongoing transformation. It generally-particularly misses change: hence the obsession with change that has haunted cultural studies from the beginning.

Practiced in this way, cultural studies lacks processual specificity. Containing expression in properties belonging to general classes of beings is science's activity. To the extent that cultural studies generally construes expression to be of a particularity, it begins to pass a threshold toward science: the "soft sciences." In recent years, a strong current within cultural studies has in fact pushed it toward more sociological or classically empirical historical methods. Politically, this missing of expression has pushed cultural studies away from whole-field modulation ("radical" intervention) toward advocating regulation in the generally perceived interests of the particular: in short, toward liberal government policy designed to give existing constituencies what is theirs by right. The current most forcefully advocating this turn is the wing led by Tony Bennett whose "post-marxist" aim is to remake cultural studies as "cultural policy studies." The title of one of Bennett's recent books says it all: *Culture: A Reformer's Science*.[47]

There is always room for expansion in the empirical field. The more process lines, the merrier. The point is not to decry these developments, which are doubtless capable of positively producing self-validating effects. The bifurcation of cultural studies does not present a problem for the expanded field unless it plays out in a way that subtracts from the field what cultural studies could be if it pushed itself to its farthest limits and circled back to the political, anomalously modulated simultaneously by philosophy and art. When cultural studies veers toward social science or policy studies, it passes a threshold. It ceases to be its own becoming, becoming something else again. It relinquishes its self-activity.

Were it to push its self-activity into a more ample orbit instead, it might realize its dream of making a unique contribution to political change. There is a potential role for practices of knowledge attentive to particularity but not limited by its already-constituted contents and attributes. Not being or having a determinable constituency helps. The much maligned "isolation" of so-called "tenured radicals" is potentially a tremendous political resource. It means that in fact they "represent" no one—in the best case scenario, not even themselves. People burdened with that label are often highly uncomfortable with the privilege attached to their cultural-institutional base. This makes them outward-looking in the hope of connecting with other, qualitatively different lifestyles or forms of life: the more ongoingly transformative the better. This habit of looking wistfully away drives a wedge between their objective interests as members of a constituted class and their affective tendencies. The resulting differential is not unlike that between the linguistic level of popular artistic expression and the level of contextual circulation. Except that it lacks contagiousness—to the great relief of the practitioners of radical cultural studies themselves. The last thing they would want is for everybody to become professors like they are. Residually marxist rhetoric aside, *class interest is the removed of radical cultural studies* (which, like all processual removals, returns to haunt). What is potentially unique about cultural studies is its institutional calling to *substitute affect for interest,* more or less vague affective tendency for sharp class self-defense. This is also not something they would want everyone to do. There are acute

254

contextual differences in many people's lives that make general defenses of particular interests or rights a vital necessity. The removal is self-referential: pertaining only to the self-activity of cultural studies.

If radical cultural studies semiartistically refuses to set itself up as a model of any kind, yet lacks powers of contagion, how can it be effective? What mode of validity can it possibly achieve for itself? Consider that the expanded empirical field is full of mutually modulating, battling, negotiating, process lines liberally encouraged to develop and sharply express self-interest across their collectively remaindered, ongoing transformations. The anomaly of an *affectively engaged yet largely disinterested* process line could conceivably be a powerful presence if it were capable of conveying its (masochistic?) removal of self-interest. The reciprocal readjustments always under way in the empirical field make the pursuit of politics an *ecological* undertaking, whether it thinks of itself that way or not. This essay began by invoking an ecology of knowledge practices. It is now clear that this is a *political ecology*.[48] The "object" of political ecology is the coming-together or belonging-together of processually unique and divergent forms of life. Its "object" is symbiosis, along the full length of the nature-culture continuum. The self-disinterest of cultural studies places it in a privileged position to side with symbiosis *as such*. What cultural studies could become, if it finds a way of expressing its own processual potential, is a political ecology affectively engaged in symbiosis-tending. This is what was meant earlier by acting as an "arbiter." But the word arbitration is not quite right. To retain its singular mode of self-activity, political ecology would have to refuse steadfastly to wield decision-making power, or to act as a moral judge. It would find a quasi-causal role for itself, as one modulating instance among others, but different by virtue of its "masochism"—its taking the *risk* of neither defending its own interests nor claiming to represent anyone else's, in general or particular.[49] Deleuze uses the word "intercessor" for this disinterested but affectively engaged political risk-taking role.[50]

A political knowledge-practice that takes an inclusive, nonjudgmental approach to tending belonging-together in an intense, affectively engaged way is an *ethics*—as opposed to a morality. Political ecology is an amoral collective ethics. Ethics is a tending of coming-together, a *caring for* belonging as such.

All of this assumes that cultural studies is destined to be political. What else could it be, when it does what it can do the best that it can? When it fulfills the potential amplitude of its connectively autonomous movement? Faulting cultural studies for being political is like faulting science for being useful (or philosophy for being speculative). If it wants to live up to its potential, cultural studies has to be as proudly, loudly political as philosophy is glowingly useless. Exactly how that more ample movement will develop, including the extremes of philosophy and art in its orbit, passing through middling science and liberalism without becoming them—that is for a coming cultural studies community to determine. It is not for a useless philosopher to say.

Of course, cultural studies is not the only potential ethically-tending process line.[51] There are any number of other ethics. Every process line described in this essay is endlessly proliferative in its self-variations. The key to an expanded empiricism is additivity. There is always enough room in this world for qualitatively "more." More modulation. More belonging. Only those who say there isn't room to share nature's giving ever more culturally of-itself deserve to be told to get out. There is only one general principle in ethics: no process line has the God-given "right" to tell another to "wink out." Constituencies interested in annihilation should be graciously encouraged to go first to show how it is done: to make an example of themselves by "winking" out before they do ecological harm to other forms of life. Ethics is exemplary.

NOTES

Introduction: Concrete Is as Concrete Doesn't

1 Michel Foucault, "The Discourse on Language," trans. Rupert Sawyer, in *The Archaeology of Knowledge* (New York: Pantheon, 1982), 231.

2 For a useful recent collection of essays exploring contemporary Bergsonian perspectives, see John Mullarkey, *The New Bergson* (Manchester: University of Manchester Press, 1999). On Zeno's arrow, see Bergson, *Creative Evolution*, trans. Arthur Mitchell (Mineola, N.Y.: Dover, 1998), 308–10.

3 "Concrete is as concrete doesn't" is a phrase from the Sheryl Crow song "Solidify"—a rare instance of a Bergsonian pop lyric—from *Tuesday Night Music Club* (Universal/A&M, 1993).

4 "The subject-term must always include the predicate-term. . . . [W]hen the predicate is not contained expressly in the subject, it must be contained in it virtually." G. W. Leibniz, "Discourse on Metaphysics," section 8, in *Philosophical Writings*, ed. G. H. R. Parkinson, trans. Mary Morris and G. H. R. Parkinson (London: Everyman Library, 1995), 18–19.

5 On the miraculation of "forces and agents" see Gilles Deleuze and Félix Guattari, *Anti-Oedipus: Capitalism and Schizophrenia,* trans. Robert Hurley, Mark Seem, and Helen R. Lane (Minneapolis: University of Minnesota Press, 1983), 10–11. In Deleuze and Guattari, the concept is restricted to paranoid formations. Here, it is taken in a broader sense, as applying to any "quasi-causal" efficiency (defined in chapter 9).

6 Gilbert Simondon, *L'individuation psychique et collective* (Paris: Aubier, 1989). For an excellent introduction to Simondon's work, see Muriel Combes, *Simondon: L'individu et collectivité* (Paris: PUF, 1999).

7 On the critique of possibility, see Bergson, "The Possible and the Real," *The Creative Mind* trans. Mabelle L. Audison (New York: Philosophical Library, 1946).

8 Deleuze's terms for incorporeal materialism are "superior empiricism" or "transcendental empiricism." The word "transcendental" may trouble some readers. For Deleuze, transcendental refers to the ontogenetic difference between emergence and the emerged. Giordano Bruno had a word for something like an incorporeal materialism that is even more troubling: *magic*. Some of his formulations, however, sound disjunctively contemporary to those of

this essay, including the cardinal idea that body comports an incorporeal dimension. "The void is not a bodiless space, but a space in which diverse bodies succeed one another in mutual movement; hence the continual movement of parts of a body toward parts of another body, across a continuous, uninterrupted space, as if the void was the mediator between two plenitudes," *De la magie*, trans. Danielle Sonnier and Boris Donné (Paris: Allia, 2000), 33. The distance between Bruno and our modernity (or postmodernity) is narrowed somewhat by his definition of magic as the "alloying of knowledge and the power to act" (12). This authorizes a *pragmatic* understanding of magic. There is good reason to do this. It allows us to forego a debunking attitude to "premodern" variations on European thought, and more importantly to contemporary nonmodernities, both within the West and in non-Western cultures around the globe. A reconciliation with the "magical thinking" belittled by the combined forces of enlightenment humanism, scientific rationalism, and psychoanalysis is a project of Jane Bennett's in *The Enchantment of Modern Life: Crossings, Energetics, and Ethics* (Princeton: Princeton University Press, 2001). A pragmatic approach to magic enables a reconciliation that is not articulable as a return to an "irrationalism"—the simple opposite of the opposition to magic. The doctrine of irrationalism is a condescending back-formation: the negative project of what "we," the "enlightened," proudly see ourselves to be. The ethnopsychiatry of Tobie Nathan is perhaps where a rapprochement between "modern" and "premodern" (or as Bruno Latour would say "nonmodern") modes of thinking and being has been achieved in the most thoroughly pragmatic and nonjudgmental manner. Nathan achieves this by bracketing the category of "belief." This is a gesture that ritual studies and the ethnography of religion would do well to emulate. See Tobie Nathan, *Fier de n'avoir ni pays, ni amis, quelle sottise c'était* (Paris: La pensée sauvage, 1999), and Tobie Nathan and Isabelle Stengers *Médecins et sorciers* (Le Plessis-Robinson: Synthélabo, 1995).

9   Ian Hacking, *The Social Construction of What?* (Cambridge, Mass.: Harvard University Press, 1999), 103–108.

10   The idea of "process" as a nature-culture continuum of variation is a major thread running throughout Deleuze and Guattari's *Anti-Oedipus*. Deleuze and Guattari's philosophy of nature, as developed throughout their work, has a close kinship with A. N. Whitehead's "process philosophy."

11   As a general rule, in this volume "perception" is used to refer to object-oriented experience, and "sensation" for "the perception of perception," or self-referential experience. Perception pertains to the stoppage- and stasis-tending dimension of reality (and by extension to the second-order movement of retroduction derived from it, associated with the production of possibilities). Sensation pertains to the dimension of passage, or the continuity of

immediate experience (and thus to a direct registering of potential). Perception is segmenting and capable of precision; sensation is unfolding and constitutively vague (the "fringe" William James saw as accompanying the streaming of experience). Perception enables quantification; sensation is only ever qualitative. Perception is exoreferential (extensive); sensation is endo-referential or self-referential (intensive). It should be noted that this usage departs sharply from the customary usage in experimental psychology and analytic philosophy, where "sensation" is synonymous with "sense-datum." A sense-datum is understood as a discrete stimulus or passive sensory input constituting an elementary unit of experience. Sense-data link together to form perceptions. In the perspective advanced here, experience cannot be built up from a linkage or association between discrete elements. Continuity is as "elementary" as discreteness, relation as primordial as individuation. There is also, in every experience at whatever level, a dimension of activity (if only by virtue of the coming-together of continuity and discreteness—think quantum). This disqualifies any fundamental reliance on stimulus-response or input-output models, as well as any simple active-passive framework.

12 Leibniz, "Paris Notes," quoted in *G. W. Leibniz's* Monadology: *An Edition for Students,* ed. Nicholas Rescher (Pittsburgh: University of Pittsburgh Press, 1991), 78.

13 This idea of the contemporaneousness of the past and the present is a signature concept of Bergson's *Matter and Memory,* trans. Nancy Margaret Paul and W. Scott Palmer (New York: Zone Books, 1988). Tendency is also a crucial Bergsonian concept, especially as developed in *Creative Evolution.*

14 This is the spatium of Deleuze's *Difference and Repetition,* trans. Paul Patton (New York: Columbia University Press, 1994), 230–32.

15 Baruch Spinoza, *The Ethics,* IIP1, 3, in *The Collected Works of Spinoza,* vol. 1, ed. and trans. Edwin Curley (Princeton: Princeton University Press, 1985), 458–62. See Gilles Deleuze, *Spinoza: Practical Philosophy,* trans. Robert Hurley. San Francisco: City Lights, 1988), 123–24, and Deleuze and Guattari, *A Thousand Plateaus: Capitalism and Schizophrenia,* trans. Brian Massumi (Minneapolis: University of Minnesota Press, 1987), 260–65.

16 William James, *Essays in Radical Empiricism* (Lincoln: University of Nebraska Press, 1996).

17 Giorgio Agamben, *The Coming Community,* trans. Michael Hardt (Minneapolis: University of Minnesota Press, 1993), 9–10.

18 Giordano Bruno, *De la magie,* 33.

1 The Autonomy of Affect

1   Hertha Sturm, *Emotional Effects of Media: The Work of Hertha Sturm*, ed. Gertrude Joch Robinson, Working Papers in Communications (Montreal: McGill University Graduate Program in Communications, 1987), 25–37.

2   The thesis on the waning of affect in Jameson's classic essay on postmodernism powerfully raised the issue of affect for cultural theory. "The Cultural Logic of Late Capitalism," in *Postmodernism; or, The Cultural Logic of Late Capitalism* (Durham, N.C.: Duke University Press, 1991), 1–54. The most sustained and successful exploration of affect arising from subsequent debates is Lawrence Grossberg's *We Gotta Get Out of This Place: Popular Conservatism and Postmodern Culture* (New York: Routledge, 1992). The present essay shares many strands with Grossberg's work, including the conviction that affect has become pervasive rather than having waned. Differences with Grossberg will be signaled in subsequent notes.

3   Grossberg slips into an equation between affect and emotion at many points, despite distinguishing them in his definitions. The slippage begins in the definition itself, when affect is defined quantitatively as the strength of an investment and qualitatively as the nature of a concern (82). This is done in order to avoid the perceived trap of asserting that affect is unformed and unstructured, a move which Grossberg worries makes its analysis impossible. It is argued here that affect is indeed unformed and unstructured, but that it is nevertheless highly organized and effectively analyzable (it is not entirely containable in knowledge but is analyzable in effect, as effect). The crucial point is that form and structure are not the only conceivable modes of differentiation. Here, affect is seen as prior to or apart from the qualitative (understood in terms of determinate properties), and its opposition with the quantitative, and therefore is not fundamentally a matter of investment. (If a thermodynamic model applies, it is not classical but quantum and far from equilibrium; more on this later.)

4   The reference to conventional discourse in Spinoza is to what he calls "universal notions" (classificatory concepts that attribute defining structural properties to things and obey the law of the excluded middle) and "transcendental notions" (teleological concepts explaining a thing by reference to an origin or end in some way contained in its form). *The Ethics*, IIP40S1, in *The Collected Works of Spinoza*, vol. 1, ed. and trans. Edwin Curley (Princeton: Princeton University Press, 1985), 475–77.

5   The retrospective character of attributions of linear causality and logical consistency was analyzed by Henri Bergson under the rubric of the "retrograde movement of truth." See *The Creative Mind*, tr. Mabelle L. Audison (New York: Philosophical Library, 1946), 27–28, 107–25.

6   John Horgan, "Can Science Explain Consciousness?" *Scientific American,* July

1994, 76–77 (emphasis added). See Benjamin Libet, "Unconscious Cerebral Initiative and the Role of Conscious Will in Voluntary Action," *Behavioral and Brain Sciences* 8 (1985): 529–66. Libet's essay is followed by a lengthy dossier of responses from the field.

7 See in particular *Matter and Memory*, tr. N. M. Paul and W. S. Palmer (New York: Zone Books, 1988).

8 Félix Guattari's last book explores the intersection between his work, solo and with Deleuze, and chaos theory. *Chaosmosis: An Ethico-Aesthetic Paradigm*, tr. Paul Bains and Julian Pefanis (Bloomington: Indiana University Press, 1995).

9 In recognition of intensity as emergent qualitative difference, beginning in chapter 2 below the vocabulary around *quality* and *intensity* with which this chapter opened will begin to mutate. The term "quasi-qualitative" will be used to distinguish intensity, as a signifying or organizational difference-in-the-making, from already emerged, already defined, determinate qualities. By chapter 9, the vocabulary will have shifted significantly. Intensity will take over the label of qualitative and, to make room for this, determinate qualities will be relabeled "attributes" or "properties." This shift is necessitated by a changed context foregrounding the distinction between quantitative and qualitative, rather than, as in this chapter, the distinctions between intensity on the one hand and signification and functional organization on the other. The ways in which intensity as such feeds forward into conscious perception and levels of organization—its modes of actual appearance—will be treated in chapters 6, 7, and 9.

10 For more on the "feedback of higher functions," see chapters 8 and 9.

11 See Gilbert Simondon, *L'individu et sa genèse physico-biologique* (Paris: PUF, 1964), in particular chapter 2 (an analysis of the chemistry of crystallization). Throughout his work, Simondon carries out a far-reaching critique of concepts of form and structure in philosophy and the natural and social sciences. For more on phasing and dephasing, see chapter 4 below.

12 Gilbert Simondon, *L'individuation psychique et collective* (Paris: Aubier, 1989), 99. For more on germinal form, see chapters 6 and 7. For more on ways of conceptualizing the unstructured differentiation of the field of emergence, see chapters 3 and 8.

13 On proprioception and affect, see chapter 2 below. On synesthesia, see chapters 6, 7, and 8. On virtual perspective, chapters 2 and 8.

14 A connection could be made here with the work of Walter Benjamin on shock and the circulation of images. Susan Buck-Morss quotes from Benjamin's *Arcades Project* on the "monadological structure" of "dialectical images." This structure is a "force-field" manifesting a nonlinear temporality (a conflict between "fore-history" and "after-history" in direct connection with one another, skipping over the present without which the conflict would nevertheless

not take place: "in order for a piece of the past to be touched by present actuality, there must be no connection between them"). "Dream-World of Mass Culture: Walter Benjamin's Theory of Modernity and the Dialectics of Seeing," in *Modernity and the Hegemony of Vision*, ed. Michael Levin (Berkeley: University of California Press, 1993), 312.

15 For a brilliant analysis of affect in terms of intensity, vitality, synesthesia ("amodal perception"), and nonconscious sense of self, see Daniel Stern, *The Interpersonal World of the Infant: A View from Psychoanalysis and Developmental Psychology* (New York: Basic Books, 1985). In the remainder of this book, distinctions will be made between affect, perception, and sensation in an attempt to flesh out some of these points.

16 Simondon, *L'individuation psychique et collective*, 149.

17 See in particular, *Difference and Repetition*, trans. Paul Patton (New York: Columbia University Press, 1994), 271–72, and Deleuze and Guattari, *A Thousand Plateaus*, trans. Brian Massumi (Minneapolis: University of Minnesota Press, 1987), 141. For more on self-referentiality and the indistinction of the human, artificial and invented, see chapters 4 and 9 below.

18 Deleuze discusses perception, the brain, and matter in *Cinema 1: The Movement-Image*, trans. Hugh Tomlinson and Barbara Habberjam (Minneapolis: University of Minnesota Press, 1986), chapters 1 and 3 (in relation to Bergson). Deleuze and Guattari make the connection between the brain and chaos in their conclusion to *What Is Philosophy?*, trans. Hugh Tomlinson and Graham Burchell (New York: Columbia University Press, 1994).

19 David Bohm and B. J. Hiley, *The Undivided Universe* (London: Routledge, 1993).

20 The main difference between this perspective and that of Lawrence Grossberg is that his approach does not develop a sustainable distinction between implicate and explicate orders (between virtuality and actuality, intension and extension). Although Meaghan Morris does not use the term affect, her analysis of the function of the TV screen brings her approach to the mass media into close philosophical affinity with the one being developed here. In "Ecstasy and Economics (A Portrait of Paul Keating)," she describes the screen image as triggering a "phase of empowerment" that is also a "passage" and "transport," not between two places but between a place and a nonplace, an "elsewhere": "the screen . . . is not a border between comparable places or spaces. . . . What visibly 'exists' there, 'bathed' in glow, is merely a 'what'—a relative pronoun, a bit of language, that relation 'your words describe.' " That relation is a "sociable disjunction." Morris, *Too Soon, Too Late: History in Popular Culture* (Bloomington: Indiana University Press, 1998), 90.

21 Simondon, *L'individuation psychique et collective*, 156.

22 Having conceded the ambivalence of the terms *immanence* and *transcendence*,

at many points in this book "immanence" will nevertheless be championed, for strategic reasons pertaining to the history of Western philosophical and political thinking and also following Deleuze. The "productively paradoxical" procedure adopted to deal with the problems Simondon signals, and to avoid the danger of spatialization, will be to inflect the notion with timelike concepts of process and self-reference (the immanent understood not as an immanence to something, but of the belonging of a process to its own potential to vary) while retaining a connotation of spacelikeness (the immanence of process as a "space" proper to change as such). For more on spatiotemporal inflections of immanence, see in particular chapters 2, 8, and 9.

23 Oliver Sacks, *The Man Who Mistook His Wife for a Hat* (London: Picador, 1985), 76–80.

24 On these and other topics, including gory detail of Reagan's crumblings, see Kenneth Dean and Brian Massumi, *First and Last Emperors: The Absolute State and the Body of the Despot* (New York: Autonomedia, 1992), and chapter 2 below. The statement that ideology—like every actual structure—is produced by operations that do not occur at its level and do not follow its logic is simply a reminder that it is necessary to integrate infolding, or what David Bohm calls "implicate order," into the account. This is necessary to avoid capture and closure on a plane of signification. It signals the measure of openness onto heterogeneous realities of every ideological structure, however absolutist. It is a gesture for the conceptual enablement of resistance in connection with the real. Ideology is construed here in both the commonsense meaning as a structure of belief, and in the cultural-theoretical sense of an interpellative subject positioning.

25 On mime, see José Gil, *Metamorphoses of the Body*, trans. Stephen Muecke (Minneapolis: University of Minnesota Press, 1998), 101–104.

26 For one account of how this larger field functions, see Gilles Deleuze, "Postscript on Control Societies," in *Negotiations, 1972–1990*, trans. Martin Joughlin (New York: Columbia University Press, 1995), 177–82. See also Brian Massumi, "Requiem for Our Prospective Dead: Towards a Participatory Critique of Capitalist Power," in *Deleuze and Guattari: New Mappings in Politics, Philosophy, and Culture*, ed. Eleanor Kauffman and Kevin John Heller (Minneapolis: University of Minnesota Press, 1998), 40–63.

27 The concept of transduction is taken, with modifications, from the work of Gilbert Simondon.

28 In addition to the quotes in Buck-Morss cited in note 12 above, see in particular "On the Mimetic Faculty," in Walter Benjamin, *One Way Street* (London: Verso, 1985), 160–63. See also Michael Taussig, "Tactility and Vision," in *The Nervous System* (New York: Routledge, 1992), 141–48. Mikhail Bakhtin also develops an analog theory of language and image, in which synesthesia and the

infolding of context discussed earlier in this essay figure prominently: "The Problem of Content, Material, and Form in Verbal Art," in *Art and Answerability: Early Philosophical Essays by M. M. Bakhtin,* ed. Michael Holquist and Vadim Liapunov, trans. Vadim Liapunov and Kenneth Brostrom (Austin: University of Texas, 1990), 257–325. For more on the analog, see chapter 5 below.

29 Bohm and Hiley use a holographic metaphor to express the monadic nature of the "implicate order" as "enfolded" in the explicate order. *The Undivided Universe,* 353–54. See chapter 8 for more on monadism.

30 Robert Heilbroner and Lester Thurow, *Economics Explained: Everything You Need to Know about How the Economy Works and Where It Is Going* (New York: Simon & Schuster, 1994), 138: "Behind [currency], rests the central requirement of faith. Money serves its indispensable purposes as long as we believe in it. It ceases to function the moment we do not."

31 Ibid., 151.

2 The Bleed: Where Body Meets Image

1 Ronald Reagan and Richard B. Hubler, *Where Is the Rest of Me?* (New York: Elsevier-Dutton, 1965; reprint Karz Publishers, 1981), 78.

2 Reagan and Hubler, *Where Is the Rest of Me?,* 78–79.

3 On nonlinear continuity, and the paradoxical necessity of conceiving it from certain approaches as monadic (as enveloping a disjunctive multiplicity, in something like the way quantum phenomena are wavelike or particulate depending on how they are approached), see chapter 8 below.

4 This is close to what Raymond Ruyer calls *"survol absolu."* There is no adequate translation for the term. Here "absolute over-sight" might be the best rendering, although there is a hint of "over-flight" (except that the "over" is in). Ruyer defines it as "existence-together as primary form" (113) of consciousness, at a lived point of indistinction with sensation and perception. In oversight "solid bodies are opened onto a fourth dimension," which he characterizes as an "absolute surface" of relation (96) that constitutes a "transspatial domain." Raymond Ruyer, *Néo-finalisme* (Paris: PUF, 1952), 95–115. For more on the notion of an absolute surface, see chapter 8 below. Deleuze and Guattari make extensive use of the concept of Ruyer's *"survol"* in *What Is Philosophy?,* trans. Hugh Tomlinson and Graham Burchell (New York: Columbia University Press, 1994), where it is translated as "self-survey" (probably the best general translation of the term).

5 Reagan and Hubler, *Where Is the Rest of Me?,* 4.

6 Reagan and Hubler, *Where Is the Rest of Me?,* 4–5.

7 Reagan and Hubler, *Where Is the Rest of Me?*, 5–6. Subsequent quotes are from page 6.

8 For analyses of Reagan's amputational propensities, see Michael Rogin, "Ronald Reagan, the Movie," in *Ronald Reagan, the Movie and Other Episodes in Political Demonology* (Berkeley: University of California Press, 1987), 1–43, and Kenneth Dean and Brian Massumi, "Postmortem on the Presidential Body, or Where the Rest of Him Went," *First and Last Emperors: The Absolute State and the Body of the Despot* (New York: Autonomedia, 1992), 87–151.

9 In chapter 9 below, a distinction will be made between "context" and "situation." A situation is an empirical context grasped from the point of view of the eventful washing-through it of an ongoing movement of transformation. In other words, the term situation will be used to refer to the potentialization of a context.

10 The concept of quasi corporeality is akin to what José Gil calls the "infra-linguistic" in *Metamorphoses of the Body*, trans. Stephen Muecke (Minneapolis: University of Minnesota Press, 1998). Gil's "infra-linguistic" and the notion of "the body without an image" advanced here are local appropriations, in the context of anthropology and media theory respectively, of the idea of "the body without organs" developed by Gilles Deleuze and Félix Guattari in *Anti-Oedipus*, trans. Robert Hurley, Mark Seem, Helen R. Lane (Minneapolis: University of Minnesota Press, 1983), and *A Thousand Plateaus*, trans. Brian Massumi (Minneapolis: University of Minnesota Press, 1987).

11 The proprioceptive system was first systematically described by Charles S. Sherrington. See Sherrington, *The Integrative Action of the Nervous System* (New Haven: Yale University Press, 1906), especially 129–32, 336–49. See also William James on feelings in the joints and muscles, *Principles of Psychology*, vol. 2 (1890; reprint, New York: Dover, 1950), 189–203. For more recent summaries of the scientific understanding of proprioception, see Jean-Pierre Roll, Régine Roll, and Jean-Luc Velay, "Proprioception as a Link between Body Space and Extra-personal Space," in *Brain and Space*, ed. Jacques Paillard (New York: Oxford University Press, 1991), 112–32; Jacques Paillard, "Motor and Representational Framing of Space," *Brain and Space*, 163–82; and V. S. Gurfinkel and Yu S. Levick, "Perceptual and Automatic Aspects of the Postural Body Scheme," *Brain and Space*, 147–62.

12 For more on proprioceptive mapping or diagramming and its relation to vision, see chapter 8 below (on "biograms").

13 Physiologically, what is termed "viscerality" here pertains to the *enteric nervous system*. This is a neuronal network in the gut which "functions independently of control by the brain or spinal cord." Although it is not controlled by the brain—directly, autonomously processing unconscious perceptual stimuli—its operations have conscious effects. It communicates indirectly with the brain

through peristaltic contractions of the bowel, which are felt proprioceptively, and through hormonal releases which alter mood. The independent functioning of these "gut feelings" was first noted in 1899, but were forgotten by physiology until the late 1980s. The enteric nervous system provides one of the physiological bases for the autonomy of affect discussed in chapter 1. It empirically describes one of the ways in which our body thinks with pure feeling before it acts thinkingly. On thinking-feeling, see chapter 4 below. For a brief overview of the enteric nervous system by its contemporary rediscoverer, see Michael D. Gershon, "The Enteric Nervous System," *Encyclopedia of Neuroscience*, vol. 1, ed. George Adelman (Boston: Birhauser, 1987), 398–99. The quotes above are on page 389. For more extended coverage, see Gershon, *The Second Brain: A Groundbreaking New Understanding of Nervous Disorders of the Stomach and Intestines* (New York: Harper, 1999). What is specifically of interest in the context of this essay is the functioning of "viscerality" in relation to shock. The enteric nervous system does not only respond to sudden shock but also to stress (which might be thought of as slow-motion shock). It is however in shock that its effects are most noticeable.

14 Steven Shaviro develops a theory of film spectatorship revolving around concepts of "passion," an axis of "tactile" vision that is elsewhere than in identity, mimesis, and contagion, to which this account is deeply indebted. See *The Cinematic Body* (Minneapolis: University of Minnesota Press, 1993), in particular chapter 1, "Film Theory and Fascination." See also Shaviro, *Passion and Excess: Blanchot, Bataille, and Literary Theory* (Tallahassee: Florida State University, 1990).

15 In chapter 9 below, the "quasi-" will be dropped from "quasi-qualitative." "Quality" is called upon to do double duty, denoting a "property" as well as the infra-empirical intensity of which properties are the objective expressions. This doubling of vocabulary occurs frequently in this book. It is necessitated by the project of grasping things at the level of their emergence (also the point of their re-infolding in potential) where they are not yet or no longer what they will have become, as well as in their actual structuring. In this essay, the prefix "quasi-" is used to signal the emergent level. In other essays, the adjective "pure" is often employed for the same purpose ("pure quality," "pure relation," "pure sociality," etc.).

16 The mesoperceptive and synesthetic nature of proprioception has been noted by researchers working from the "ecological school" of perception studies founded by James J. Gibson. "In absolutely every instance of tactile perception a [proprioceptive] awareness of one's body *stands between one and awareness of the tactile object.*" Brian O'Shaughnessy, "Proprioception and Body Image," in *The Body and the Self*, José Luis Bermúdez, Anthony Marcel, and Naomi Eilan (Cambridge: MIT Press, 1995), 176; my emphasis. The same argument can

be made for all of the exteroceptive senses. An important proviso is that the in-betweening "awareness" is normally nonconscious. On the synesthetic nature of proprioception, see Marcel Kinsbourne, "Awareness of One's Body: An Attentional Theory of Its Nature, Development, and Brain Basis," op. cit., 213. The role of synesthesia was emphasized by Paul Schilder, who developed the concept of "body image" in psychology. See Schilder, *The Image and Appearance of the Human Body: Studies in the Constructive Energies of the Psyche* (New York: International Universities Press, 1950), 36–38. The visual bias and representational model underlying the concept of "body image" in the line of thinking about the body initiated by Schilder is questionable from the perspective developed here, which asserts the need to conceptualize the body without an image (to which vision contributes but does not overall lend its model of linear perspective and static form).

17 On the equation of phantasm (simulacrum) and event, see Gilles Deleuze, *Difference and Repetition* (New York: Columbia University Press, 1994), 124–28, and *The Logic of Sense*, translated by Mark Lester with Charles Stivale, edited by Constantin V. Boundas (New York: Columbia University Press, 1990), series 21 and 30, and appendix 3 (on Klossowski).

18 This phrase was suggested by Meaghan Morris's analysis of the way in which another leader "generates Being by Seeming." See "Ecstasy and Economics," *Too Soon, Too Late: History in Popular Culture* (Bloomington: Indiana University Press, 1998), 158–94. The present essay is written in tacit dialogue with Morris's beautiful and thought-provoking essay on then-Treasurer of Australia (subsequently Prime Minister) Paul Keating.

19 *New York Times Magazine,* 6 October 1985, 32.

20 For a detailed analysis of the presidential functioning of Reagan's (quasi-corporeal) body in relation to the televisual apparatus, see Dean and Massumi, *First and Last Emperors.*

21 Michel Foucault, "The Discourse on Language," trans. Rupert Sawyer in *The Archaeology of Knowledge* (New York: Pantheon, 1982), 231. Quoted in Steven Shaviro, *The Cinematic Body,* 25.

22 The assertions that repetition is always of the different and that "only differences resemble" are developed at length in Gilles Deleuze, *Difference and Repetition.* See in particular 152–57.

23 The ideas that the world is an interrelation of movements, that stasis is a movement-effect, that there is no object or subject of movement separate from the movement, and that subject-object relations (and thus positionality) are effective "illusions" arising from "arrests" or "gaps" in movement form central theses of the philosophy of Henri Bergson. For a useful summary, see Bergson, "The Perception of Change," in *The Creative Mind,* trans. Mabelle L. Audison (New York: Philosophical Library, 1946), 153–86. For a neo-Bergsonian anal-

ysis of film, see Gilles Deleuze, *Cinema 1: The Movement-Image*, trans. Hugh Tomlinson and Barbara Haberjam (Minneapolis: University of Minnesota Press, 1986), in particular chapter 1 ("Theses on Movement") and 2 ("The Movement-Image and Its Three Varieties"), 1–11, 56–70.

24 Reagan's impact was still headline news twenty years after his inauguration as president: "As Reagan Turns 90 His Impact Grows," *USA Today*, 1 February 2001, 1–2. During the 2000 presidential campaign, the *New York Times* published, within two weeks of each other, articles analyzing how *both* candidates were claiming the Reagan mantle: "Bush's Words Resound with Echoes of Reagan," 2 October 2000; "For Gore, A Page from the Reagan Playbook." Déjà vu? Not really. It's more that the office of the president itself is now Reaganly déjà-rigged.

3 The Political Economy of Belonging and the Logic of Reason

1 Michel Serres, *The Parasite*, trans. Lawrence R. Schehr (Baltimore: Johns Hopkins University Press, 1982), 224–34; Bruno Latour, *We Have Never Been Modern*, trans. Catherine Porter (Cambridge, Mass.: Harvard University Press, 1993), 50–55; Pierre Lévy, *Becoming Virtual: Reality in the Digital Age*, trans. Robert Bononno (New York: Plenum, 1998), 151–53.

2 Chapter 4 below will further develop the distinctions in play here between perception, sensation, and action, as well as the concept of transduction. The remixing of reflective elements in sensation and perception is what was termed in chapter 1 "the feedback of higher forms." For more on this concept, see chapter 8. In chapter 9, the notion of the part-subject is reinvestigated (without using the term) in relation to color.

3 Félix Guattari, *Chaosmosis: An Ethico-Aesthetic Paradigm*, trans. Paul Bains and Julian Pefanis (Bloomington: University of Indiana Press, 1995), 10–31.

4 Recall Reagan's problem with perspective in chapter 2. The "reflective" space of the referee's decision-making is a variety of Reagan's "mirror-vision." Here, suspension, the referee's stopping of the action, is depotentializing and establishes the space of reflection or mirror-vision. For Reagan (and in chapter 4 for Stelarc) suspension is potentializing and establishes a space of transformation. As with most concepts in this book, "suspension" has no identity as a concept. What it is depends on what it does (i.e., what kind of unfolding it interrupts and to what effect). In other words, the concept of suspension is itself relational: it is nothing outside its situated enactments. No identity, only variations. As explained in chapter 9, this way of employing concepts belongs to a pragmatic philosophy: a concept (any phenomenon) is what it does, and therefore can only be evaluated according to its effects. It has no inherent meaning or truth-

value. This kind of pragmatism is a correlate of the "exemplary" method advanced in the introduction. None of the concepts in this book should be taken to be generally applicable (since they aim for the singular). By the same token, differences between occurrences of the same concept should not necessarily be taken as contradictions (but rather as a positive capacity for variation).

5   The link between the Super Bowl and domestic violence is itself violently contested. In 1993, a debate was triggered in the media (and still rages today on the Internet) when the liberal media watchdog group Fairness and Accuracy in Reporting (FAIR) announced the connection, based on anecdotal evidence and a single statistical study ("The Impact of Professional Football Games upon Violent Assaults on Women," G. F. White, J. Katz, and K. E. Scarborough, *Violence and Victims* 7, no. 2 [1992]: 157–71). Conservative Republicans, "pro-family" lobby groups, and men's and fathers' rights groups immediately went on the offensive, denouncing FAIR, in often extreme language, for spreading "anti-male" feminist propaganda. Many mainstream women's and public health interest groups subsequently distanced themselves from the issue. Sports associations around the United States worked to delink professional sports from domestic violence by organizing annual funding drives on Super Bowl Sunday for public interest groups addressing issues of violence toward women. Their efforts were somewhat marred by an ill-timed series of highly publicized arrests of prominent sports figures on charges of domestic violence. Overall, however, the counterattack was highly successful. The Super Bowl Sunday story was widely republicized in the media as a "hoax" and is now a favorite entry on lists of "urban myths," although enough anecdotal evidence still surfaces from time to time to keep the issue alive for some. (The anecdotal evidence often takes the form of reports of large spikes in the number of calls to local crisis centers on Super Bowl Sunday; see the web page of the American Academy of Family Physicians, http://www.aafp.org/981200ap/quantum.html). The point of bringing up this issue is not to enter the debate on whether there is an empirically provable causal link between professional sports and violence against women. The outpouring of verbal aggression provoked by the mere suggestion that there was a link is enough to establish the theoretical point in question here: that what the mass-media transmit is not fundamentally image-content but event-potential. A mediatized event has the potential to transfer into new domains, and when it does it repeats its eventfulness, with a change in its nature. The intensity of the Super Bowl debate alone shows that the transmission of certain sports events potentializes them for a qualitative change from intra-gender competitive play to an inter-gender battle around issues of dominance.

6   Giorgio Agamben, *Means without End,* trans. Vincenzo Binetti and Cesare Casarino (Minneapolis: University of Minnesota Press, 2000), 59, 82–83.

7   In the vocabulary of chapter 9, they are catalytic converters of "contexts" into "situations."

8   On the concept of control, see Gilles Deleuze, "Postscript on Control Societies," *Negotiations, 1972–1990*, trans. Martin Joughin (New York: Columbia University Press, 1995), and Brian Massumi, "Requiem for Our Prospective Dead: Towards a Participatory Critique of Capitalist Power." In *Deleuze and Guattari: New Mappings in Politics, Philosophy, and Culture,* ed. Eleanor Kauffman and Kevin John Heller (Minneapolis: University of Minnesota Press, 1998), 40–63.

4 The Evolutionary Alchemy of Reason: Stelarc

1   Stelarc, "Portrait robot de l'homme-machine," interview with Jean-Yves Katelan, *L'Autre journal* 27 (September 1992): 28.

2   Stelarc, "The Body Obsolete: Paul McCarthy Interviews Stelarc," *High Performance* 24 (1983): 14–19; James D. Paffrath and Stelarc, *Obsolete Body/Suspensions/Stelarc* (Davis, California: JP Publications, 1984).

3   Paffrath and Stelarc, *Obsolete Body*, 134; Stelarc, interview with Martin Thomas, special issue on *Electronic Arts in Australia,* ed. Nicholas Zurbrugg, *Continuum* 8, 1 (1994): 389; personal conversation with the artist, December 1995.

4   Stelarc, interview with Martin Thomas, 379, 383; Stelarc, interview with Jean-Yves Katelan, p. 27.

5   Interview with Jean-Yves Katelan, p. 27; Paffrath and Stelarc, *Obsolete Body*, 8.

6   Ken Scarlett, "Early Performances: Japan/Australia," in Paffrath and Stelarc, *Obsolete Body*, 20.

7   Stelarc, interview with Jean-Yves Katelan, 26.

8   "Event from micro to macro and in between," 1970; "Helmet no. 3: put on and walk," 1970; described in Anne Marsh, *Body and Self: Performance Art in Australia, 1969–1992* (Melbourne: Oxford University Press, 1993), 25–26, and Stelarc, "The Body Obsolete: Paul McCarthy Interviews Stelarc," 15.

9   Henri Bergson, *Creative Evolution*, trans. Arthur Mitchell (Mineola, N.Y.: Dover, 1998), 11–12, 96–97, 188.

10 Bergson, *Creative Evolution*, 48–49.

11 On the direct experience of moreness in transition ("the immediate feeling of an outstanding *plus*"), see William James, *Principles of Psychology,* vol. 2 (1890; reprint, New York: Dover, 1950), 151–52; James's emphasis.

12 Chapter 6 below ("Strange Horizon") makes some suggestions on how this hypercomplex order might be conceptually approached.

13 "The world does not exist outside of its perceptions," Gilles Deleuze, *The Fold:*

Leibniz and the Baroque, trans. Tom Conley (Minneapolis: University of Minnesota Press, 1993), 132. If the proliferation of "poles" has become confusing, a simple distinction will help. The poles of perception, thought, and sensation concern the ongoing of *process* (the rolling of the already more of the world into a nextness). The poles of the body and the thing concern a *structuring* of that process as it goes on (the germ of subject-object relations). To say with Deleuze and Leibniz that the world does not exist outside of its perceptions (that it is "not all in" them) is to say with Whitehead that it is composed of sensation (the actual registering of the potential more of which perception is not all; its tending, pending envelopment in each connection). "Feeling" is Whitehead's term for what is called sensation here: "the philosophy of organism attributes 'feeling' throughout the actual world. . . . [W]hen we observe the causal nexus, devoid of interplay with sense-presentation [that is to say, pending perceptual reconnection], the influx of feeling with vague qualitative and 'vector' definition [tending] is what we find," *Process and Reality,* ed. David Ray Griffin and Donald W. Sherburne (New York: Free Press, 1978), 177. It is important to note that the usage of "sensation" here departs from its usage in psychology and analytic philosophy, where it is synonymous with "sense-presentation" or "sense-datum." In the present vocabulary, both of these terms are associated with "perception" which, as this quote from Whitehead asserts, is different from feeling/sensation. As Whitehead remarks, and as we will see later in relation to Stelarc's suspension events, sensation as such involves a "voiding" of perception. Sensation, it will be remarked parenthetically below, is itself a continuum stretching between extremes or poles of its own. One is pure sensation (pure potential), experience as radically voided of perception as possible. The other is the point at which sensation just starts to recede from perception (still mixed potential). The continuum of sensation fills intervals of *destructuring,* since sensation is where experience falls away from perception, action, and thinking out. As we will see, these intervals of destructuring paradoxically carry the momentum for the ongoing process by which thought and perception are brought into relation toward transformative action.

14 Bergson, *Creative Evolution,* 161: "All the elementary forces of the intellect tend to transform matter into an instrument of action, that is, in the etymological sense of the word, into an *organ* . . . inorganic matter itself, converted into an immense organ by the industry of the living being."

15 Bergson, *Creative Evolution,* 206: "neither does matter determine the form of the intellect, nor does the intellect impose its form on matter, nor have matter and intellect been regulated in regard to one another by we know not what preestablished harmony, but that intellect and matter have progressively adapted themselves one to the other in order to attain at last a common form."

16 Marsh, *Body and Self,* 25–26.

17 Stelarc, "The Body Obsolete," 18.

18 Stelarc, Artist's statement in "The Function in Art and Culture Today," *High Performance* 11 (Spring/Summer 1988): 70; Stelarc and Paffrath, *Obsolete Body*, 8.

19 Stelarc, interview with Jean-Yves Katelan, 28.

20 Artist's statement, 11, 70.

21 Stelarc and Paffrath, *Obsolete Body*, 17.

22 Ibid., 66.

23 Marsh, *Body and Self*, 66.

24 Henri Bergson argues that this is in fact what always happens. The possible is always a retrospective projection, he argues, and its forward-looking operation is a trick of consciousness (undoubtedly another example of the time-slip capacities of consciousness, in addition to the Libet lag analyzed in chapters 1 and 6). Stelarc's practice, then, would be a *making felt* of the retrospective nature of possibility. See Bergson, "The Possible and the Real," *The Creative Mind,* trans. Mabelle L. Audison (New York: Philosophical Library, 1946), 107–25.

25 Paul Virilio, "Rat de laboratoire," *L'Autre journal* 27 (September 1992): 32, and Paul Virilio, *The Art of the Motor,* trans. Julie Rose (Minneapolis: University of Minnesota Press, 1995), 109–19.

26 Stelarc and Paffrath, *Obsolete Body,* 100.

27 Ibid., 16, 21, 117, 120; Stelarc, Paolo Atzore, and Kirk Woolford, "Extended-Body: Interview with Stelarc," *C-Theory* (1995), http://www.ctheory.com.

28 Stelarc, interview with Rosanne Bersten, *Internet.au* (1995): 35. On transduction, see Gilbert Simondon, *L'individu et sa genèse physco-biologique* (Grenoble: Millon, 1995), 30–33, 231–32. See also Muriel Combes, *Simondon: Individu et collectivité* (Paris: PUF, 1999), 15–20.

29 Stelarc and Paffrath, *Obsolete Body,* 8, 66.

30 Ibid., 20.

31 Ibid., 144.

32 Ibid., 16.

33 Ibid., 21.

34 Ibid., 57. See also "The Body Obsolete," 16.

35 Gilles Deleuze and Félix Guattari, *A Thousand Plateaus,* trans. Brian Massumi (Minneapolis: University of Minnesota Press, 1987), 149–66.

36 Stelarc, "The Anaesthetized Body" (n.d.), www.stelarc.va.com.au/anaesth/anaesth.html; Stelarc, "From Psycho to Cyber Strategies: Prosthetics, Robotics, and Remote Existence," *Canadian Theatre Review* 86 (Spring 1996): 22.

37 Ibid. "Distraught and disconnected the body can only resort to the interface and symbiosis"—into the next series.

38 Stelarc and Paffrath, *Obsolete Body,* 59.

39 Interview with Martin Thomas, *Continuum* 8, 1: 383.

40 Stelarc and Paffrath, *Obsolete Body*, 147.

41 Ibid., 105.

42 Ibid., 153.

43 James, *Principles of Psychology*, vol. 2, 174n.

44 For more information on these projects, see Stelarc's official Web site, www. stelarc.va.com.au.

45 Deleuze and Guattari, *A Thousand Plateaus*, 282. What is described here as an infolding that rejoins a virtual center immanent to every event in a series of transformations is what Deleuze and Guattari call "involution." They call the intensive movement of involution "absolute movement," and assert that evolution occurs through involution (267).

46 Bergson, *Creative Evolution*, 218–20.

47 Stelarc, Artist's Statement, 11, 70.

48 "Internal resonance is the most primitive form of communication between different orders of reality; it comprises a double process of amplification and condensation," Simondon, *L'individu et sa genèse physico-biologique*, 31n. See also p. 25.

49 Ilya Prigogine and Isabelle Stengers, *Order Out of Chaos: Man's Dialogue with Nature* (New York: Bantam, 1984), 142–43.

50 Prigogine and Stengers, *Order Out of Chaos*, 163–65; Prigogine and Stengers, *Entre le temps et l'éternité* (Paris: Fayard, 1988), 59–60.

51 Stelarc and Paffrath, *Obsolete Body*, 153; Bergson, *Creative Evolution*, 186–95; Bergson, *The Creative Mind*, 126–53.

52 Deleuze and Guattari, *A Thousand Plateaus*, 361–74.

53 Stelarc, "The Body Obsolete," 15.

54 "The Third Hand is a human-like manipulator attached to the right arm as an extra hand. It is made to the dimensions of the real right hand and has a grasp-release, a pinch-release, and a 290-degree wrist rotation (CW & CCW). It is controlled by EMG signals from the abdominal and leg muscles. This allows individual movement of the three hands. Electrodes positioned on four muscle sites provide the control signals. By contracting the appropriate muscles you can activate the desired mechanical hand motion. After many years of use in performances the artist is able to operate the Third Hand intuitively and immediately, without effort and not needing to consciously focus. It is possible not only to complete a full motion, but also to operate it with incremental precision. It is not capable though of individual finger movements. The Third Hand is effective as a visual attachment to the body, sometimes mimicking, sometimes counter-pointing the movements of the actual hands. Amplifying the motor sounds enhances these small hand motions," Stelarc Official Web site, www.stelarc.va.com.au/articles/index.html.

55 Simondon, *L'individu et sa genèse physico-biologique*, 23, 229–30; Combes, *Simondon*, 10–15.

56 Stelarc, "Amplified Body," Stelarc official Web site, www.stelarc.va.com.au.

57 Stelarc, "Interview with Martin Thomas," *Continuum* 8, 1: 388.

58 "Exoskeleton is a . . . pneumatically powered 6-legged walking machine with a tripod and ripple gait. It can move forwards, backwards, sideways (left and right), sway, squat, stand-up and turn. . . . The body is positioned on a turntable so it can rotate on its axis. . . . The 6 legs have 3 degrees of freedom each. The walking modes can be selected and activated by arm gestures. An exoskeleton wraps around the upper torso embedded with magnetic sensors, which indicate the position of the arms. Small gestures are magnified into large strides—human arm movements are transformed into machine leg motions. Human bipedal gait is replaced by an insect-like traversing of space. The body also is extended with a large 4-fingered manipulator, which has 9 degrees of freedom. Compressed air, relay switches, mechanical sounds and signals from the machine and manipulator are acoustically amplified. Choreographing the movements of the machine composes the sounds," Stelarc official Web site, www.stelarc.va.com.au/articles/index.html.

59 Performed at Saw Gallery in Ottawa, September 1995.

60 Stelarc, "From Psycho to Cyber Strategies," 19.

61 Stelarc, "Interview with Martin Thomas," 381, 389.

62 Simondon, *L'individu et sa genèse physico-biologique*, 29; Combes, *Simondon*, 47. See also chapter 3 above.

63 Stelarc, conversation with the author, Melbourne, 28 September 1996.

64 Stelarc, "High-Fidelity Illusion," Stelarc official Web site, www.stelarc.va.com.au.

65 Stelarc, "Interview with Martin Thomas," 391.

66 Stelarc Official Web site, www.stelarc.va.com.au/articles/index.html.

67 In "Parasite" the visual feed is no longer expressive but becomes operative, part of the incipient action-perception loop: "A customized search engine was constructed to scan the www live during the performance to select and display images to the body through its video headset. Analyses of the JPEG files provide data that is mapped to the muscles through the Stimbox [the computer control console first used in 'Fractal Flesh']. The body is optically stimulated and electrically activated. The images you see are the images that move your body. You become sustained by an extended and external nervous system of search engine software code and Internet structure. In these performances the body is in effect telematically scaled-up to perceive, and perform within a global electronic space of information and images," Stelarc official Web site, www.stelarc.va.com.au/articles/index.html.

Here is Stelarc's project statement for "Movatar":

An exoskeleton for the arms is being constructed that will be in effect a motion prosthesis allowing four degrees-of-freedom for each side. This would produce a kind of jerky, GIF-like animation of the arms. Embedded with accelerometer, proximity and tilt sensors, this will be an intelligent, compliant servo-mechanism which will allow interaction by the dancer, interrupting the programmed movements—stopping, starting, altering the speed and inserting selected sampled sequences. Now imagine that this exoskeleton is the physical analogue for the muscles of an intelligent avatar. Attaching the exoskeleton means manifesting the motions of a virtual entity. It is an avatar imbued with an artificial intelligence that makes it somewhat autonomous and operational. It will be able to perform in the real world by accessing a physical body. So if someone wears the device and logs into the avatar it will become a host for an intelligent virtual entity—a medium through which the motions of the avatar can be expressed. A phantom possesses a body and performs in the physical world. And if Movatar is a VRML entity based on a Web site then anyone anywhere will be able to log into it. And from the point of view of the intelligent avatar it would be able to perform with any body, in any place either—sequentially with one body at a time or simultaneously with a cluster of bodies spatially separated, but electronically connected to it. A global choreography conducted by an external intelligence. What would be interesting would be a kind of dance dialogue by a combination of prompted actions from the avatar and personal responses by the host body. The experiences would be at times of a possessed and performing body, a split body. Not split vertically left and right as in the Internet performances, but split horizontally at the waist. The pneumatically actuated exoskeleton motions of the prosthesis are able to make the upper torso of the body perform in precise and powerful ways whilst the legs can perform with flexibility and freedom. The avatar would be able to determine what is done with the body's arms, but the host would be able to choose where and for what duration it could be done. The issue is not one of who is in control of the other but rather of a more complex, interactive performing system of real and virtual bodies. Movatar would be best described as an inverse motion capture system. And since sounds generated by the body would be looped back into the avatar's program to generate a startle response, Movatar would have not only limbs but also an ear in the world." From the perspective of the present essay, the "phantom" Stelarc refers to is not the avatar itself but rather the entire network that sustains its effects—the network is the "external intelligence," acting as much through the avatar as through the wires and the human bodies it integrates. The network is the machinic subject of the movement, whose principle lies in the prosthetic mutuality of all its elements as they enter into operative continuity with each other.

68 Stelarc and Paffrath, *Obsolete Body,* 153.
69 Ibid., 70.
70 Nicholas Negroponte, *Being Digital* (New York: Alfred A. Knopf, 1995).
71 Stelarc, "Portrait robot," 27, 26.
72 Ibid.
73 "Stimbod," Stelarc official Web site, www.stelarc.va.com.au.
74 Ibid.

5 On the Superiority of the Analog

1 Gilles Deleuze, *Francis Bacon: Logique de la sensation* (Paris: Éd. de la Différence, 1981), 15–18.
2 C. S. Peirce, *Reasoning and the Logic of Things,* ed. Kenneth Laine Ketner (Cambridge, Mass.: Harvard University Press, 1992), 2, 71–72, 246–68. See also Deleuze, *Francis Bacon,* 65–71, and Deleuze and Guattari, *A Thousand Plateaus: Capitalism and Schizophrenia,* trans. Brian Massumi (Minneapolis: University of Minnesota Press, 1987), 91, 140–42, 510–13.
3 See Gilles Deleuze, *Kant's Critical Philosophy,* trans. Hugh Tomlinson and Barbara Habberjam (Minneapolis: University of Minnesota Press, 1984), 17–18, 50–52, and *Difference and Repetition,* trans. Paul Patton (New York: Columbia University Press, 1994), 320–21.
4 René Thom, interview, *Le Monde,* 15549 (22–23 January 1995).
5 Deleuze, *Francis Bacon,* 73–81; Gilbert Simondon, *L'individu et sa genèse physico-biologique* (Grenoble: Millon, 1995), 263–68; Muriel Combes, *Simondon: Individu et collectivité* (Paris: PUF, 1999), 20–24.
6 In chapter 9 it will be argued, using an example from chaos theory, that no rigid distinction between the living body and inorganic matter is sustainable. Sensation is in the world, which carries its own charge of vitality. The difference between the sensitive capacities of organic and inorganic matter is of transductive mode and degree. It is not a difference in kind.
7 René Thom, interview.
8 In a similar vein, in chapter 8 (in the section entitled "The Argument from Inner Space") it will be argued that the solidity of actual matter and spaces is an emergent property of "a mutual holding in relational stability of incorporeal event spaces."
9 Gilles Deleuze and Félix Guattari, *What Is Philosophy?,* trans. Hugh Tomlinson and Graham Burchill. New York: Columbia University Press, 1993.

10 Deleuze and Guattari, *A Thousand Plateaus*, 406–407, 409–410.

11 Pierre Lévy, *Becoming Virtual: Reality in the Digital Age*, trans. Robert Bononno (New York: Plenum, 1998).

12 William James, "The Feeling of Effort," *Collected Essays and Reviews* (New York: Russell and Russell, 1969), 151–219.

13 This account of reading is akin to Bakhtin's early account of poetic speech. The speaker, he writes, "sees, hears, evaluates, connects, selects even though there is no actual exertion of the external senses." All of this occurs in "nonactuality," with "only the tension corresponding to this movement." That movement is essentially the "feeling of the activity of connecting": "relational self-activity," "living self-sensation of activity." This expansive, living charge of nonactuality is enveloped in the actual "feeling of verbal activeness": the "feeling of generating the signifying sound." "Included here are all the motor elements—articulation, gesture, facial expression, etc." In reading, the motor elements are reduced to a minimum and short-circuited by being turned in on the body. Reading is prompted, suspended speech: a short-circuiting of communication. The suspension increases the degree of envelopment of the actual in the nonactual and vice versa (intensifies the connection with the virtual). The reader is drawn even further into Bakhtin's intensely activate "inner body" by dint of passivity. The "inner body" is what was termed the "body without an image" in chapter 2. Reading can be considered another way of "rigging" the body without an image. What is unique about developments like the World Wide Web is that they activate the body without an image in a way that intensifies *extensively*—in a manner that is *distributed* across the series of links. The hypertext reader doesn't tarry, she surfs, accumulating effects in the continual move from one to the next rather than by burrowing into the experience of any particular way station. A reader of a poem will tarry over a passage, furrowing his way into level after level of enveloped sense. In hypertext, those levels are laid out horizontally and their envelopmental layering is an effect of movement (dopplering). Digital technologies are capable of bringing the intensity of the virtual into extension: of *actualizing the virtual as such* to an ever increasing, and increasingly expansive, degree. (This is the "actuality of the excess over the actual" referred to at the end of chapter 4.)

Part of the uniqueness of digital technologies is their ability to make intensity *boring* (a potential inherent in extension, even extensions of the virtual). This is evident in video gaming: how more intensely boring can an activity get? What we are experiencing in this transitional period to fuller implantation of digital technology in the social field is the onset of the *everydayness of the virtual*. The banalization of what were once avant-garde artistic strategies is part of that transition. These include strategies of performance (art as event rather than enduring object) and accelerated image turnover and recombination (epitomized by the once-shocking but now also intensely boring MTV aesthetic). Television has in fact been the vector for these "digital" transformations (their preparatory precursor). It was the first mainstream medium to restructure itself in a way that institutionalized a primacy of event over content (a development that came into full expression in the 1980s). Television is a serialization of events that are as forgettable as they are spectacular. Those two attributes go together: it is the self-erasing of each event by its inherent forgettability that leaves a clean slate for the next spectacular event in the series. Spectacularized banality becomes the momentum motoring the process. The quotes from M. M. Bakhtin are from "The Problem of Content, Material, and Form in Verbal Art," in *Art and Answerability: Early Philosophical Essays by M. M. Bakhtin*, ed. Michael Holquist and Vadim Laipunov, trans. Vadim Liapunov (Austin: University of Texas, 1990), 309–15.

14 Nicholas Negroponte, *Being Digital* (New York: Alfred A. Knopf, 1995).

6 Chaos in the "Total Field" of Vision

1 Experimentation with the Ganzfeld began with the work of German psychologist W. Metzger. The Gestalt psychologists took up the concept, which later passed into the general domain of American experimental psychology. For a Gestalt treatment, see Kurt Koffka, *Principles of Gestalt Psychology* (New York: Harcourt, Brace, 1935), 110–28. It will become clear that the directions developed here diverge sharply from the Gestalt paradigm, while benefiting from its practitioner's experimental ingenuity. Gestalt theory centers perception on figure-ground relations composing actually existing functional wholes whose dynamic is equilibrium-seeking. Here, the conditions of perception are considered to be nonfigurative and to concern movement and limit-states more than centerings; any wholeness is virtual, and the dynamic is far from equilibrium. For a valuable critique of Gestalt theory, see Raymond Ruyer, *La conscience et le corps* (Paris: PUF, 1950), 85–96, and *Néo-finalisme* (Paris: PUF, 1952), 67–71. Although the Gestaltists were interested in the Ganzfeld precisely because it seemed to offer a primitive Gestalt or total "configuration," since it was conceived in terms of purity, or in psychological terminology "homogeneity," it still qualifies as a scientific reductionism. The defining characteristic of the Gestalt reduction is that it is to a field rather than to a simple function or fundamental element. Gestalt reduces experience to a preorganized kernel of itself rather than to atomistic ingredients whose operating principles are to found at other levels, for example the biophysical (from which the Gestaltists segregated the psychological by means of a parallelism). The Gestalt method might be characterized as an *endoreduction* of experience. It

is Gestalt's heroic combination of "wholism" (emphasis on germinal self-consistency) and experimentalism that makes it a fertile ground for reflection (if ultimately unsatisfying, philosophically).

2   The *Ganzfeld* did not entirely fade away after experimental psychology lost interest in it. It relocated itself. In the mid-1960s it became a concern of experimental artists concerned with the conditions of perception (in particular Robert Irwin and James Turrell). Still later it entered the annals of parapsychology. A World Wide Web search of the term will uncover hundreds of sites dedicated to it. From a New Age perspective, the Ganzfeld's uncertain empirical status, the phenomenal liminality described in this chapter, is wishfully interpreted as a threshold to a "deeper," collective consciousness. A great deal of parapsychological research has been done to establish that Ganzfeld states increase receptivity to direct mind-to-mind thought transfer (the ultimate in wireless communication—don't be surprised if your next Nokia is made with Ping-Pong balls). The Koestler Parapsychology Unit of the University of Edinburgh (http://moebius.psy.ed.ac.uk/t_index.html) organizes and assesses double-blind experiments to test claims of extrasensory perception, with an ongoing focus on the Ganzfeld. The unit's director, Robert Morris, claims statistically significant results for certain ESP-detecting Ganzfeld experiments. For an interview with Morris on this topic, see "Tales of the Paranormal," *New Scientist*, 3 March 2001, 46–49. Morris's claims are of course contested by other researchers. For a review article reporting negative results for Ganzfeld trials, see Julie Milton and Richard Wiseman, "Does Psi Exist? Lack of Replication of an Anomalous Process of Information Transfer," *Psychological Bulletin* 125 (1999): 387–91.

3   Walter Cohen, "Spatial and Textural Characteristics of the *Ganzfeld*," *American Journal of Psychology* 76 (1957): 409.

4   Lloyd L. Avant, "Vision in the Ganzfeld," *Psychological Bulletin* 64, no. 4 (1965): 256.

5   Cohen, "Spatial and Textural Characteristics," 409–10.

6   Avant, "Vision in the Ganzfeld," 256.

7   Ibid., 247.

8   Ibid.

9   James J. Gibson and Dickens Waddell, "Homogeneous Retinal Stimulation and Visual Perception," *American Journal of Psychology* 65, no. 2 (April 1952): 268.

10 Ibid., 267–70.

11 Gibson and Waddell, "Homogeneous Retinal Stimulation," 268.

12 Avant, "Vision in the Ganzfeld," 246.

13 The "formlike" or "objectlike" emergences of the Ganzfeld can be assimilated Gilles Deleuze's Leibnizian "inflections," for which he adopts Bernard Cache's term "objectile" in *The Fold: Leibniz and the Baroque*, trans. Tom

Conley (Minneapolis: University of Minnesota Press, 1993), 14–20. The objectile, in turn, can be assimilated to the *clinamen,* or minimum material deviation (empirical drift, or self-fall-away) from which the world emerges according to Lucretius. Gilles Deleuze, *Difference and Repetition,* trans. Paul Patton (New York: Columbia University Press, 1994), 184, and Gilles Deleuze and Félix Guattari, *A Thousand Plateaus,* trans. Brian Massumi (Minneapolis: University of Minnesota Press, 1987), 361, 489–90. Deleuze himself swerves from Lucretius's atomism. In his account both of the objectile and the clinamen, phenomenal emergence is credited less to the pre-givenness of elements than the ever-renewed event of their fusional variation (articulated in the first case in relation to Simondon's theory of modulation, and in the second borrowing the model of differential composition from calculus). From the point of view of that event, the elements in play are never determinate givens. They are "determinabilities," grasped from the angle of their capacity for becoming (their virtuality). It is for this reason that when Deleuze and Guattari reach for the elemental level, a concept of "virtual particles" in dialogue with quantum physics is not far behind. On determinability, see Deleuze, *The Fold,* 89, and *Difference and Repetition,* 85–87. On the chaotic vacuum and virtual particles, see Gilles Deleuze and Félix Guattari, *What Is Philosophy?,* trans. Graham Burchell and Hugh Tomlinson (New York: Columbia University Press, 1993), 118, 153. Although the elements of vision always precede it, they are not "givens" in the usual sense, because they only figure (and ground) as transmuted, always already and again. The before of perceptual fusion is ideal. *Nothing,* no content, no structure, *is given to vision.* Nothing except the event of its reiterative renewal. The only "given" is the transformational *process* that is vision-becoming. To say that vision is empirically "self-abstracting" or "self-standing" is to say that its becoming is self-giving, or "autopoietic," in Guattari's "hijacked" sense of Varela and Maturana's term: not "a subjectivity given as in-itself, but with processes of the realization of autonomy," Félix Guattari, *Chaosmosis: An Ethico-Aesthetic Paradigm,* trans. Paul Bains and Julian Pefanis (Bloomington: University of Indiana Press, 1995), 7. See also Humberto Maturana and Francisco Varela, *The Tree of Knowledge: The Biological Roots of Human Understanding* (Boston: Shambhala, 1992), 47–52, and *Autopoiesis and Cognition: The Realization of the Living* (Dordrecht: D. Reidel, 1980), 63–123. By "autonomous" is meant emerging *with* its elements (in their transmutational midst) *as* that fusional event, taking off from empirical conditions. This essay's developing preoccupation with synesthesia should not be interpreted as being contradiction with its intention to carry out a meditation on the autonomy of seeing.

14 Richard Held and Alan Hein, "Movement-Produced Stimulation in the De-

velopment of Visually Guided Behavior," *Journal of Comparative and Physiological Psychology* 56, no. 5 (1963): 872–76.

15 Denis Baylor, "Colour Mechanisms of the Eye," in Trevor Lamb and Janine Bourriau, eds, *Colour: Art and Science* (Cambridge: Cambridge UP, 1995), 120, and C. L. Hardin, *Color for Philosophers: Unweaving the Rainbow* (Indianapolis: Hackett, 1986), 12–13.

16 Perceptual constancy is a continuing conundrum to empirical researchers, who have failed to find a convincing physiological basis for it. The prevailing theory is that the brain averages variations in brightness in different regions of the visual field and uses this calculation to identify object boundaries, size, and shape. This kind of ratio theory is undermined by a problem comparable to the famous "Three-Body Problem" in physics: it breaks down when there are more than two regions involved (Hans Wallach, "Brightness Constancy and the Nature of Achromatic Colors," in Mary Henle, ed. *Documents of Gestalt Psychology* [Berkeley: University of California Press, 1961], 125). What visual field, outside the laboratory, is so controlled as to have fewer than three regions of variation in color and brightness? The model is flawed because it assumes both a computational model of brain functioning on top of a representational one (the perceptual apparatus as receiving and in some way mirroring, then processing, determinate features of an already-formed outside) and disregards the fundamental necessity of multiple registers of movement to perception. Nystagmus is another kind of endogenously produced chaotic movement. It is the continual micro-jitter of the eye. The combination of this "saccadic tremor" and voluntary eye movements "have the effect that contours in the image are constantly crossing the receptor elements of the retina. Not too much is known of the actual effect of this but it is certain that it plays a large role in contour perception and it appears to be a necessary condition for vision" (Ralph M. Evans, *The Perception of Color* [New York: John Wiley and Sons, 1974], 22). It is difficult to see how a representative model can be maintained in the face of the multiple scramblings and variations endemic to the physiology of perception. For more on the problem of perceptual constancy, in particular regarding color and brightness, see chapter 7 below.

17 Alfred North Whitehead, *Modes of Thought* (New York: Macmillan, 1938), vii.

18 This is the *spatium* (the intensive depth of sensible experience) of Deleuze's *Difference and Repetition*, 231, 266.

19 On the creativity or spontaneously productive capacities of habit, see Deleuze, *Difference and Repetition*, 70–82, 96–97.

20 On the simultaneous rising and falling of the *"sans-fond,"* the groundless ground, see Deleuze, *Difference and Repetition*, 28–29, 151–52, 229–30, 272–75.

21 Raymond Ruyer, *La conscience et le corps*, 62.

22 Burkhard Bilger, "The Flavor of Fat: Debunking the Myth of the Insipid Lipid," *The Sciences* (November/December 1997), 10 (emphasis added).

23 Bilger, ibid., quoting neuroscientist Timothy A. Gilbertson (emphasis added).

24 Henri Bergson, "Dreams," *Mind-Energy: Lectures and Essays*, trans. H. Wildon Carr (London: Macmillan, 1920), 84–108.

25 In the psychological literature, the addition of visually experienced object unity to what is empirically given to vision is called "amodal completion," a concept pioneered by Albert Michotte. A prime example of amodal completion is the fact that after an event people will systematically report having seen objects or parts of objects that were hidden behind obstacles. Perception fills itself in, in a perfectly functional mode of hallucination. According to Michotte, amodal completion is the very mechanism of object perception. Their perceived constancy and unity depends on it. All objects, then, are hallucinated: perceptual filler. The "amodal" is the point at which perception at the same time completes itself and shades back into an experiencing of the imperceptible—in other words, thought. In amodal completion, perception is caught in the act of feeding back into its conditions of emergence. Philosophically, the already thorny problem of synesthesia or intermodal perception broached in this essay pales in comparison to the problem of amodal perception and its relation to thought. The amodal is a place only philosophy can go. It is where philosophy must take over from, and take leave of, psychology. Michotte's classic essay on amodal completion is included in Georges Thinès, Alan Costall, and George Butterworth, eds., *Michotte's Experimental Phenomenology of Perception* (Hillsdale, N.J.: Lawrence Erlbaum, 1991).

26 M. von Senden, *Space and Sight: The Perception of Space and Shape in the Congenitally Blind before and after Operation*, trans. Peter Heath (London: Methuen, 1960), 129.

27 Ibid., 135.

28 Ibid., 130.

29 Ibid., 130, 135. This is the "brightness confound" of chapter 7 below.

30 Ibid., 137.

31 A paean to synesthesia from a classic text in the development of psychology and perception studies: "We should not forget that every sensation is generally synesthetic. This means that there does not exist any primary isolation between the different senses. The isolation is secondary. We perceive and we may with some difficulty decide that one part of the perception is based upon the optic impressions. The synesthesia, therefore, is the normal situation. The isolated sensation is the product of an analysis. . . . Perception is synesthetic," Paul Schilder, *The Image and Appearance of the Human Body: Studies in the Constructive Energies of the Psyche* (New York: International Universities Press,

1950), 38–39. Although in *actual* perception the separation of the senses may be "secondary," philosophically the fusion and separation must be considered co-primary, since the *potential* for each conditions the actual exercise of both. The philosophical task it describes is the virtual conditions for the senses' operating separately-together.

32   Richard D. Walk and Herbert L. Pick, eds., *Intersensory Perception and Sensory Integration* (New York: Plenum Press, 1981), 181.

33   Gilles Deleuze, *Francis Bacon: Logique de la sensation,* vol. 1 (Paris: Editions de la Différence, 1981), 99, and Deleuze and Guattari, *A Thousand Plateaus,* 492–99. It is useful to note that Deleuze makes special usage of the term "haptic" which departs from its standard definition, widespread in the empirical literature, as a synonym for "tactile."

34   This conceptual tension is expressed in Deleuze's work as an oscillation between the Bergsonian model of the virtual (the many-leveled inverted cone) and the radically "flat" model of the "absolute surface" borrowed from Ruyer. Ruyer argues that perception operates empirically by virtually entering into an absolute proximity with all of the elements in its actual field. He calls this virtual co-presence in actual perception "self-survey" (*survol*), emphasizing that it requires no "supplemental" dimension. These models, which in Deleuze's thinking flow into the notion of the *spatium* (the intensive depth of sensible experience) and the "plane of consistency" (the nondimensionality of thought) respectively, should not be seen as contradictory but rather as mutually complicating. There is no need to choose between them (any more than there is a need to choose between thinking and feeling). A Deleuzian approach to the virtual requires creatively combining them.

35   The substantive grammatical form of the word "force" encourages the unfounded assumption that the "conditions" of a phenomenon's emergence constitute a subject or agent "behind" its appearing. "A quantum of force is equivalent to a quantum of drive, will, effect—more, it is nothing other than precisely this very driving, willing, effecting, and only owing to the seduction of language (and of the fundamental errors of reason that are petrified in it) which conceives and misconceives all effects as conditioned by something that causes effects, by a 'subject,' can it appear otherwise. . . . [T]he popular mind separates the lightning from its flash and takes the latter for an *action,* for the operation of a subject called lightning . . . [b]ut there is no 'being' behind doing, effecting, becoming; the 'doer' is merely a fiction added to the deed—the deed is everything," Friedrich Nietzsche, *On the Genealogy of Morals,* trans. Walter Kaufmann (New York: Vintage, 1967), 45. "Whether we ought to say that a force *is* an acceleration, or that it *causes* an acceleration, is a mere question of propriety of language. . . . [I]f we know what the effects of force are, we are acquainted with every fact which is implied in saying that a force exists,"

C. S. Peirce, *The Essential Peirce: Selected Philosophical Writings*, vol. 1, ed. Nathan Houser and Christian Kloesel (Bloomington: University of Indiana Press, 1992), 136. It is a convenience of language that has embedded itself in empirical thinking to separate the conditions of the experienced event from its effects. Conditions of effective emergence are not separable from what actually emerges, even if philosophically they must be conceived of as ontologically different from them (as virtual). The philosophical problem is to conceive of experience as effectively self-conditioning. On perception as a force-effect, see Deleuze, *Francis Bacon*, 39–42.

36 von Senden, *Space and Sight*, 130.

7 The Brightness Confound

1 Ludwig Wittgenstein, *Remarks on Colour*, ed. G. E. M. Anscombe, trans. Lindal L. McAlister and Margarate Schättle (Oxford: Basil Blackwell, 1978), III, 95: 28.

2 Marc H. Bornstein, "Chromatic Vision in Infancy," in *Advances in Child Development and Behavior*, vol. 12, ed. Hayne W. Reese and Lewis P. Lipsitt (New York: Academic Press, 1978), 132.

3 John Mollon, "Seeing Color," in *Colour: Art and Science*, eds. Trevor Lamb and Janine Bourriau (Cambridge: Cambridge University Press, 1995), 149.

4 Ralph M. Evans, *The Perception of Color* (New York: John Wiley and Sons, 1974), 7.

5 Jonathan Westphal, *Colour: Some Philosophical Problems from Wittgenstein*, Aristotelian Society Series, vol. 7 (Oxford: Basil Blackwell, 1987), 84.

6 For more on relation vs. interaction and situation vs. context, see chapter 9 below.

7 David Katz, *The World of Colour*, trans. R. B. MacLeod and C. W. Fox (London: Kegan, Paul, Trench, Trubner & Co., 1935), 294, 41 (emphasis added).

8 Daphne Maurer, "Neonatal Synaesthesia: Implications for the Processing of Speech and Faces," *Synaesthesia: Classic and Contemporary Readings*, eds. Simon Baron-Cohen and John E. Harrison (London: Routledge, 1997), 227, 237.

9 Note well: "Kinesthetic contributions are unconscious and cannot be deliberately deconfounded." Marcel Kinsbourne, "Awareness of One's Body: An Attentional Theory of Its Nature, Development, and Brain Basis," in *The Body and the Self*, eds. José Luis Bermúdez, Anthony Marcel, and Naomi Eilan (Cambridge: MIT Press, 1995), 213. The proprioceptive sense of the muscles and joints and the labyrinthine sense of the inner ear are the dedicated components systems of kinesthesia.

10 Charles Darwin, "Biographical Sketch of a Young Child," *Kosmos* 1 (1877): 367–76.

11 John Lyons, "Colour and Language," Lamb and Bourriau, *Colour: Art and Science*, 223.

12 Harold C. Conklin, "Hanunóo Color Categories," in *Language in Culture and Society*, ed. Dell Hymes (New York: Harper & Row, 1964), 191.

13 John Lyons, "Colour and Language," Lamb and Bourriau, *Colour: Art and Science*, 223.

14 Wittgenstein, *Remarks on Colour*, I, 6: 2–3.

15 W. E. Gladstone, "Homer's Perceptions and Use of Colour," *Studies on Homer and the Homeric Age*, vol. 3 (Oxford: Oxford University Press, 1858).

16 Maurice Platnauer, "Greek Colour-Perception," *The Classical Quarterly*, 15, nos. 3/4 (1921): 162.

17 P. G. Maxwell-Stuart, *Studies in Greek Colour Terminology*, vol. 1 (Leiden: E. J. Brill, 1981), 4.

18 Brent Berlin and Paul Kay, *Basic Color Terms: Their Universality and Evolution* (Berkeley: University of California Press, 1969), 23–25. For a useful critique of Berlin and Kay, see John A. Lucy, "The Linguistics of 'Color,'" in *Color Categories in Thought and Language*, eds. C. L. Hardin and Luisa Maffi (Cambridge: Cambridge University Press, 1997), 320–46.

19 Ibid., 45.

20 Johann Wolfgang von Goethe, *Theory of Colors*, trans. Charles Lock Eastlake (Cambridge, Mass.: MIT Press, 1970); Paul Klee, *Notebooks*, vol. 1, *The Thinking Eye*, trans. Ralph Manheim (London: Lund Humphries, 1961).

21 William James, *Essays in Radical Empiricism* (Lincoln: University of Nebraska Press, 1996), 107–108.

22 Gilles Deleuze and Félix Guattari, *A Thousand Plateaus*, trans. Brian Massumi (Minneapolis: University of Minnesota Press, 1987), 293–94.

23 Evans, *The Perception of Color*, 209.

24 Joachim Gasquet, *Joachim Gasquet's Cézanne* (London: Thames and Hudson, 1991); Félix Guattari, *Chaosmosis: An Ethico-Aesthetic Paradigm*, trans. Paul Bains and Julian Pefanis (Bloomington: University of Indiana Press, 1995).

25 René Huyghe, ed., *Impressionism* (NY: Chartwell, 1973), 139.

26 Klee, *The Thinking Eye*, 92.

8 Strange Horizons: Buildings, Biograms, and the Body Topologic

1 Sandra Buckley analyzes the differences, cultural and experiential, between ground-level movement through architectural spaces and underground movement in "Contemporary Myths of the Asian City," *(In)Visible Cities: From the*

Postmodern Metropolis to the Cities of the Future, ed. Robert Sergent and Pellegrino D'Acierno (New York: Monticello Press, forthcoming).

2   See Russell Epstein and Nancy Kanwisher, "A Cortical Representation of the Local Visual Environment," *Nature,* vol. 392 (9 April 1998), 598–601. For a popular press account of Epstein and Kanwisher's work on adult brain functioning during orientation tasks, see "A Positioning Unit of Sorts in the Brain," *New York Times,* 28 April 1998, B13: "The experiments dovetail with work on rats and human infants showing that when they get lost, it is the shape of the space, rather than the objects in it, that are used to get reoriented."

3   For an overview, see Ariane S. Etienne, Joëlle Berlie, Joséphine Georgakopoulos, and Roland Maurer, "Role of Dead Reckoning in Navigation," *Spatial Representation in Animals,* ed. Sue Healy (Oxford: Oxford University Press, 1998), 54–68. Most animals combine landmark recognition with dead reckoning. Studies of the ant's ability to orient have shown that dead reckoning (or "path integration") predominates in learning phases and that landmark use takes over for known territory. This accords with the argument developed here for human orientation: that the process of orienting differs in nature from the "mapped" application of its cognitive products, which function as a kind of visual shorthand for the more encompassing sensorimotor process from which they derive. See B. Schatz, S. Chameron, G. Beugnon, and T. S. Collett, "The Use of Path Integration to Guide Route Learning in Ants," *Nature* 399 (24 June 1999), 769–72.

4   Greg Lynn, *Animate Form* (New York: Princeton Architectural Press, 1999), and *Folds, Bodies, and Blobs: Collected Essays* (Brussels: La Lettre Volée, 1998).

5   Bernard Cache, in "A Plea for Euclid," provides an excellent account of the topological resources of Euclidean geometry available for architectural design. *ANY (Architecture New York),* 24 (1999): 54–59. The present essay, however, diverges sharply from Cache in its assessment of the importance and usefulness of non-Euclidean conceptions. For a primer on the geometry of the Möbius strip and the Klein bottle, see Richard Courant and Herbert Robbins, *What Is Mathematics? An Elementary Approach to Ideas and Methods,* 2d ed., rev. by Ian Stewart (Oxford: Oxford University Press, 1996), 259–64.

6   "Movement in itself *continues* to occur elsewhere: if we serialize perception, the movement always takes place above the maximum threshold [in the superfigure's passing-through] and below the minimum threshold [recessively] in expanding or contracting intervals [microintervals]. . . . Movement has an essential relation to the imperceptible; it is by nature imperceptible," Gilles Deleuze and Félix Guattari, *A Thousand Plateaus,* trans. Brian Massumi (Minnesota: University of Minnesota Press, 1987), 280–81. Another word for "imperceptible" is "abstract."

7 *ANY (Architecture New York),* 23 (1998), special "Diagram Work" issue, ed. Ben van Berkel and Caroline Bos.

8 On the peri-personal and déjà vu, see Richard E. Cytowic, "Synaesthesia: Phenomenology and Neuropsychology," *Synaesthesia: Classic and Contemporary Readings,* ed. Simon Baron-Cohen and John E. Harrison (Oxford: Blackwell, 1997), 20, 23.

9 The case of MP is described in Richard E. Cytowic, *Synesthesia: A Union of the Senses* (New York: Springer-Verlag, 1989), 217–27.

10 For diagrammatic renderings of this facedness, see Cytowic, *Synesthesia: A Union of the Senses,* figures 7.9–7.17, pp. 202–209.

11 Raymond Ruyer: Experience is "a surface with just one side. . . . If the sensible surface could be seen from two sides, it wouldn't be a sensation, but rather an object. . . . [I]t's an 'absolute surface' relative to no point of view outside of itself." *Néo-finalisme* (Paris: PUF, 1952), 98–99.

12 See Daphne Maurer, "Neonatal Synaesthesia: Implications for the Processing of Speech and Faces," in Baron-Cohen and Harrison, eds., *Synaesthesia: Classic and Contemporary Readings,* 224–42, and John Harrison, *Synaesthesia: The Strangest Thing* (Oxford: Oxford University Press, 2001), 13–22, 212–21. For a theory of developmental psychology consistent with the view that infant perception is synesthetic and that synesthesia persists unconsciously as a stratum of adult experience, see Daniel Stern, *The Interpersonal World of the Infant: A View from Psychoanalysis and Developmental Psychology* (New York: Basic Books, 1985). The theory of the synesthetic basis of infant perception was most influentially advanced by Eleanor J. Gibson, *Principles of Perceptual Learning and Development* (New York: Appleton-Century-Crofts, 1969). For a series of essays on empirical investigations into the functioning of synesthetic perception in infants, see David J. Lewkowicz and Robert Lickliter, eds., *The Development of Intersensory Perception: Comparative Perspectives* (Hillsdale, N.J.: Lawrence Erlbaum, 1994), 165–370. On the limitations of "intermodality," see chapter 6 above.

13 Cytowic, "Synaesthesia: Phenomenology and Neuropsychology," 23.

14 The notion of intentionality is often used as a way of establishing an identity between the structure of the world and the structure of the subject in the world. The insistence on such an identity is a tacit assumption of a divide. An objective-subjective split is backhandedly enshrined in this way of thinking. A mediating instance is then required to bring the two realms back into harmony. The senses are assigned to the job. In architectural phenomenology, a building becomes a "metaphor" "reflecting" for the senses the identity-structure shared by the subject and the world. Architecture is called upon to express, and reinforce in concrete, that ideal fit. Its "mission" is to concretize the

"integrity" of being-in-the-world: close the loop. The whole process revolves around identity and an ultimately normative ideal of authenticity. The ideal is suspiciously domestic (Heidegger's "house of being" is just around the corner). This is how Juhani Pallasmaa puts it: "The timeless task of architecture is to create embodied existential metaphors that concretize and structure man's being in the world. Architecture reflects, materializes and eternalizes ideas and images of ideal life. . . . Architecture enables us . . . to settle ourselves in the world. . . . Our domicile becomes integrated with our self-identity. . . . Architecture is the art of reconciliation between ourselves and the world, and this mediation takes place through the senses." The "mental task" of architecture, Pallasmaa continues, was best formulated by Frank Lloyd Wright: "What is needed most in architecture today is the very thing most needed in life— Integrity. Just as it is in a human being, so integrity is the deepest quality in a building. . . . If we succeed, we will have done a great service to our moral nature." It all adds up to a high-minded moralism. This is sharply at odds with any form of architectural experimentalism, whose rallying cry would not be to close the loop, but to loop-the-loop; not to ground in the "authentic" but to dizzy with potential (remembering that position arises from intensive movement, rather than extended movement departing from pre-position). Pallasmaa, *The Eyes of the Skin: Architecture and the Senses* (London: Academy Editions, 1996), 50–51. In the perspective of this essay, there is not an identity between the subjective and objective or between the world and experience: there is a continuity that mutually includes each side of the divide in the same self-differentiating reality.

15 Arakawa and Madeleine Gins, *Reversible Destiny* (New York: Guggenheim Museum, 1997). Take "reversible destiny" as "re-incipient life" (experience returning to the point of matter-minded ontogenesis). On "relational architecture," see Rafael Lozano-Hemmer, *Alzado Vectorial. Arquitectura Relacional No. 4/Vectorial Elevation. Relational Architecture No. 4* (Mexico City: National Council for Culture and the Arts, 2000). Take "relational" to mean "intensively cross-referencing disparate planes of experience." For an overview of the work of Lars Spuybroek see Spuybroek, *Deep Surface* (Rotterdam: NOX, 1999) (exhibition catalogue, Exhedra Gallery, Hilversum). See especially "Off the Road: 103.8 MHz," a description of a housing project and noise barrier in Eindhoven. The aim of the project is to create a "zone of transition" (using among other devices a sound processing feedback loop between the houses and the cars passing by on the highway) that sets up a "resonance" between "bits and bricks," air-"waves and ground." This activates the in-between as an operator of relation rather than leaving it a passive boundary. The "zone of transition" is an airborne, abstract holding-together in addition to (rather than in opposition to, or simply breaking down) the concrete holding-apart

of discrete, down-to-earth divisions demanded by the need for a highway noise barrier.

16 A. R. Luria, *The Mind of the Mnemonist: A Little Book About a Vast Memory* (Cambridge, Mass.: Harvard University Press, 1968).

17 Luria, *Mind of the Mnemonist*, 35.

18 For example, see ibid., 108.

19 See Luria's discussions of S.'s "split I," ibid., 149–60.

20 Ibid., 63.

21 Ibid., 10.

22 217–40. See in particular Benjamin Libet, "Unconscious Cerebral Initiative and the Role of Conscious Will in Voluntary Action," *Behavioral and Brain Sciences* 8 (1985): 529–66. For a good presentation and summary of the issues raised by Libet's work, see Tor Norretranders, *The User Illusion: Cutting Consciousness Down to Size*, trans. Jonathan Sydenham (New York: Viking, 1998), 213–50. For considerations of the implications of Libet's work for cultural theory, see William Connolly, "Brain Waves, Transcendental Fields, and Techniques of Thought," *Radical Philosophy* 94 (March/April 1999), and chapter 1 above.

23 Gottfried Wilhelm Leibniz, preface to *New Essays in Human Understanding*, in *Philosophical Writings*, ed. G. H. R. Parkinson, trans. Mary Morris and G. H. R. Parkinson (London: Everyman, 1995), 153–58.

24 These are related to the normally unperceived "objectlikes" and "spacelikes" of chapter 6.

25 Walter Benjamin's early essays develop a philosophy of experience that dovetails in many ways with the one advanced here. For the early Benjamin, experience is a supplemental abstract-excess (recessive/"pop-out") surface of "legibility" best described in topological terms, as enveloping a double infinity: "A given surface of legibility (or set of conditions for possible experience) is supplemented by the speculative claim that these conditions are themselves but one of an infinite set of possible surfaces or conditions of experience. The speculative configuration is both folded into and exceeds the particular surface of legibility, allowing Benjamin to conceive of a double infinity: the transcendental infinity of possible marks on a given surface (or perceptions within a given framework of possible experience) and the speculative infinity of possible bounded but infinite surfaces or frameworks of experience," Howard Caygill, *Walter Benjamin: The Colour of Experience* (London: Routledge, 1998), 4. The "speculative infinity" is what is termed the "virtual" here, in its largest extension. For reasons that cannot be adequately dealt with in the present framework, this "surface" as virtually construed is better understood to be "limited" rather than "bounded." A limitation is not necessarily the same thing as a boundary. On reading, see the next argument (on the feedback of higher forms).

26 On the white wall of perception, see Deleuze and Guattari's comments on the work of Isakower, Lewin, and Spitz on the relation between vision and proprioception, in *A Thousand Plateaus*, 169–70. On the background as a "groundless ground" that rises into vision and, in rising, recedes, see Deleuze, *Difference and Repetition*, trans. Paul Patton (New York: Columbia University Press, 1994), 28–29, 151–52, 229–30, 272–75.

27 David Corcar, "Out of Sight, Into Mind," *New Scientist* (5 September 1998), 41. For the classic account of blindsight, see L. Weiskrantz, *Blindsight: A Case Study and Implications* (Oxford: Oxford University Press, 1986).

28 Itzhak Fried, Katherine A. MacDonald, and Charles L. Wilson, "Single Neuron Activity in Human Hippocampus and Amygdala during Recognition of Faces and Objects," *Neuron* 18 (May 1997): 753–65. "Some neurons maintained a record of previous stimulus response that was more accurate than the person's conscious recollection," 753.

29 Pallasmaa, among many others, exalts the traditional view of architecture as ground: "The sense of gravity is the essence of all architectonic structures and great architecture makes us aware of gravity and earth. Architecture strengthens the experience of the vertical dimension of the world," *The Eyes of the Skin*, 47. Compare Greg Lynn's arguments for an architecture of "lightness": "When defined by the qualitative relations between particularities of matter rather than by the relation of various masses to a single ground form, a multiplicity of potential architectural gravities emerge," *Folds, Bodies, and Blobs*, p. 100. See also John Rajchman, "Lightness," *Constructions* (Cambridge: MIT Press, 1998), 37–54.

30 Jean-Pierre Luminet, Glenn D. Starkman, and Jeffrey R. Weeks, "Is Space Finite?" *Scientific American* (April 1999), 94.

31 On hyperbolic models of the universe, see Luminet, Starkman, and Weeks, op. cit., and Roger Penrose, *The Large, the Small, and the Human Mind* (Cambridge: Cambridge University Press, 1997), 21–49.

32 Geoffrey B. West, James H. Brown, and Brian J. Enquist, "A General Model for the Origin of Allometric Scaling Laws in Biology," *Science* 276 (4 April 1997): 122–26. In all organisms "essential materials are transported through space-filling fractal networks of branching tubes," 122.

33 Geoffrey West, quoted in Roger Lewin, "Ruling Passions," *New Scientist*, 3 April 1999, 39.

34 Deleuze and Guattari, *A Thousand Plateaus*, 281.

9 Too-Blue: Color-Patch for an Expanded Empiricism

1 David Katz, *The World of Colour*, trans. R. B. MacLeod and C. W. Fox (London: Kegan, Paul, Trench, Trubner & Co., 1935), 164. (The first German edition was published in 1911.)

2 "The general case of conscious perception is the negative perception, namely, 'perceiving this stone is not grey.' The 'grey' then has ingression in its full character of a conceptual novelty, illustrating an alternative." Alfred North Whitehead, *Process and Reality*, eds. David Ray Griffin and Donald W. Sherburne (New York: Free Press, 1978), 161.

3 David Hume, *A Treatise of Human Nature*, intro. and ed. Ernest C. Mossner (London: Penguin, 1969), 147 (book 1, chapter 8).

4 *Montreal Gazette*, 29 May 1999, Arts and Entertainment section, D4.

5 The term "form of transition" is Alfred North Whitehead's. See *Modes of Thought* (New York: Free Press, 1963), 82, 89.

6 Experience "grows by its edges. . . . [T]he unity of the world is on the whole undergoing increase. The universe continually grows in quantity by new experiences that graft themselves upon the older mass," William James, *Essays in Radical Empiricism* (Lincoln: University of Nebraska Press, 1996), 87, 90. On James's famous "stream of thought," see ibid., 95, and *The Principles of Psychology*, vol. 1 (1890; reprint, New York: Dover, 1950), 224–90.

7 On "insistence" and the "eternity" ("Aion") of the singular event, see Gilles Deleuze, *Logic of Sense*, trans. Mark Lester with Charles Stivale, ed. Constantin V. Boundas (New York: Columbia University Press, 1990), 21–22, 165–67. Deleuze's account in *Logic of Sense* of the kinship between eternity and event in the genesis of sense can be linked conceptually to Whitehead's "eternal object" ("essence" in the vocabulary of *Logic of Sense*).

> An eternal object can be described only in terms of its potentiality for "ingression" into the becoming of actual entities; and its analysis only discloses other eternal objects. It is pure potential. The term "ingression" refers to the particular mode in which the potentiality of an eternal object is realized in a particular actual entity, contributing to the definiteness of that actual entity. . . . This definition can be stated more generally to include the prehension of an eternal object by an actual entity; namely, the "positive prehension" of an entity by an actual entity [or actual occasion] is the complete transaction analysable into the ingression, or objectification, of that entity as a datum for feeling, and into the feeling whereby this datum is absorbed into the subjective satisfaction [the doubling into "datum" and "satisfaction" is the object/subject "divide" discussed later on in the present essay]. . . . Qualities, such as colors, sounds, bodily feelings, tastes, smells, together with

Notes to Chapter Nine 291

perspectives introduced by extensive relationships, are the relational eternal objects whereby the contemporary actual entities are elements in our constitution. This type of objectification has been termed "presentational objectification." (Whitehead, *Process and Reality*, 23, 52, 61)

8   James, *Essays in Radical Empiricism*, 67–73.
9   Andrew Pickering, developing Bruno Latour's concept of the "actor-network," analyzes scientific practice as a "mangle" in which "human and material agency are reciprocally and emergently intertwined," with "existing culture constitut[ing] the surface of emergence" of the scientific object. *The Mangle of Practice: Time, Agency, and Science* (Chicago: University of Chicago Press, 1995), 21. See Latour, *Science in Action: How to Follow Scientists and Engineers through Society* (Cambridge, Mass.: Harvard University Press, 1987). The scientific objects of Latour's scientific actor-networks are "invention-discoveries" that have "a simultaneous impact on the nature of things and on the social context" while "not reducible to the one or the other." *We Have Never Been Modern*, trans. Catherine Porter (Cambridge, Mass.: Harvard University Press, 1993), 5.
10 On "termini" see James, *Radical Empiricism*, 56–63. On termini and the development of "bare facts," discussed in relation to color, see Alfred North Whitehead, *Concept of Nature* (Cambridge: Cambridge University Press, 1964), 12–13. What are called "bare facts" here are "bare objectives" or "entities" in Whitehead's vocabulary, "ultimate fact" corresponds to Whitehead's "fact." "Factoid," for its part, is meant to resonate as much with Bruno Latour's "factish" (*faitiche*) as with Whitehead's own intermediate term, "factor." See Latour, *Petite réflexion sur le culte moderne des dieux faitiches* (Le Plessis-Robinson: Synthélabo, 1996); and Isabelle Stengers, *Cosmopolitques*, vol. 1, *La guerre des sciences* (Paris/Le Plessis-Robinson: La Découverte/Synthélabo, 1996), chap. 2, 30–49. "Factish" is a development of the concept of the "hybrid object" from Latour's earlier work (see *We Have Never Been Modern*, chapters 1 and 3). The distinction between "bare fact" and "ultimate fact" is comparable to Deleuze's distinction between "bare repetition" and the "singular subject" of repetition in *Difference and Repetition*, trans. Paul Patton (New York: Columbia University Press, 1994), 23–25, 84.
11 Stengers, *Cosmopolitiques*, vol. 1, chap. 3, pp. 51–72. In all of her work Isabelle Stengers pays special attention to "minor" knowledge practices: experimental and theoretical projects that in retrospect take on new significance (precursors in physics and chemistry to contemporary sciences of irreversibility and self-organization), paths not taken (the practices of hypnosis from which Freudian and Lacanian psychoanalysis turned away), and new hybrid formations (the ethnopsychiatry of Tobie Nathan). On hypnosis, see Isabelle Stengers and

Léon Chertok, *A Critique of Psychoanalytic Reason: Hypnosis as a Scientific Problem from Lavoisier to Lacan*, trans. Martha Noel Evans (Stanford: Stanford University Press, 1992), and Stengers and Chertok, *L'Hypnose, blessure narcissique* (Paris: Editions des Laboratoires Delagrange, 1990). On ethnopsychiatry, see Tobie Nathan and Isabelle Stengers, *Médecins et sorciers* (Le Plessis-Robinson: Synthélabo, 1995).

12 On contextual rigging and affect, see chapter 2 below.

13 Whitehead, *Concept of Nature*, 152 (emphasis added).

14 Taking adhesion in the world personally and emoting on the connectedness of things is characteristic of New Age philosophy.

15 "This," here, is James's "that": " 'Pure experience' is the name I gave to the immediate flux of life which furnishes the material to our later reflection with its conceptual categories. . . . [Pure experience is] a *that* which is not yet any definite *what*, tho' ready to be all sorts of whats; full both of oneness and of manyness, but in respects that don't appear . . ." (93–94). "If we take conceptual manifolds, or memories, or fancies, they also are in their first intention mere bits of pure experience, and, as such, are single *thats* which act in one context as objects, and in another context figure as mental states" depending on how they are taken up and toward what "termini" those processual uptakes lead (15). Their status as subjective or objective are results of the uptake. " 'Pure experience' . . . is only virtually or potentially either subject or object as yet. For the time being, it is plain, unqualified actuality, or existence, a simple *that*" (23). "Its unity is aboriginal, just as the multiplicity of my successive takings is aboriginal. It comes unbroken as *that*, as a singular which I encounter; they come broken as *those* takings, as my plurality of operations" (105). All quotes from James, *Radical Empiricism*.

16 On real (singular) conditions of emergence versus general conditions of possibility, see Deleuze, *Difference and Repetition*, 284–85.

17 This is an instance of the "feedback of higher forms" that in some way or another always blurs any attempt to police distinctions between levels (especially of cause and effect). This processual recycling makes it impossible to maintain terminological distinctions, such as that earlier suggested in this essay between affect and emotion, in any final way. It is as important to grasp the processual oscillation between terms as it is to assert their distinction. In the approach advanced here, clarity of distinction serves as a springboard for dynamic reconnection and never as an end in itself. The reconnection constitutes an added distinction. Where a duality is asserted it is always meant to function additively, as a first step in a multiplication of distinctions following processes of feedback or other forms of relational modulation. "Multiply distinctions" is the methodological rallying cry of the approach advocated here. The "feedback of higher forms" is discussed in chapters 1 and 8 above.

The work of Gilbert Simondon provides a precedent (brackets translate the passage into the vocabulary of this book):

> Affectivity precedes and follows emotion [emotion feeds back into affect]. . . . Emotion implies the presence of the subject to other subjects or to a world that places the subject in question as a subject [it is naturally relational and socially problematic]. . . . [E]motion assumes affectivity, it is the point of insertion of an affective plurality in a unity of signification; emotion is the meaning [becoming-content/attribute] of affectivity. . . . [W]e should not speak of affective states, but rather of affective exchanges, of exchanges between the preindividual [nature] and what is individuated in the being of the subject [its contextualized personhood, or individuality]. Affectivo-emotivity [the subjective process line from uncontained affect to its personalized expression] is a movement between indeterminate nature and the here and now of actual existence [the irruption of the event]; it is what makes the indeterminate in the subject mount toward [be expressed in] the present moment which incorporates it in the collectivity [co-constituted with the subject's individuality]. . . . Positive affective states mark the synergy of constituted individuality [the personal terminus of the subjective process line] and the actual movement [the emergence and ongoing of the process line] through which the preindividual is individualized. . . . Affectivity and emotivity are apt to undergo quantum reorganizations; they proceed by sudden leaps according to degrees [periodically disappear into themselves, into their own intensity or singularity], and obey a law of thresholds. They are the relation between the continuous and the discontinuous [they are the world-glue connecting disparate contexts]. . . . [T]he reality of affective-emotive movement is that of a relation that has, with regard to its own terms [termini], a self-positing value [it is self-active and self-affirming, even as it ends]. (Simondon, *L'individuation psychique et collective* [Paris: Aubier, 1989], 98–99, 106–107 [order of the passages modified])

18   Ilya Prigogine and Isabelle Stengers, *Entre le temps et l'éternité* (Paris: Fayard, 1988), 59–61, and Prigogine and Stengers, *Order Out of Chaos: Man's Dialogue with Nature* (New York: Bantam, 1984), 163, 165.

19   "One may conclude that the probability of such a phenomenon of self-organization occurring is practically zero." Prigogine and Stengers, *La nouvelle alliance: Métamorphose de la science* (Paris: Gallimard, 1986), 214–15. The corresponding passage in *Order Out of Chaos* (which differs significantly from the French edition) is on p. 142.

20   The "bifurcation point" of chaotic ordering is when a newly-felt global "sensitivity" produces an undecidability between two or more outcomes. On this

point in relation to the Bénard instability, see Prigogine and Stengers, *Order Out of Chaos*, 165.

21 On the distinction between the possible and the virtual, see Deleuze, *Difference and Repetition*, 211–15, and chapters 4 and 5 above.

22 To summarize: classical scientific laws pertain to linear, part-to-part connections between discrete elements whose interactions can be predicted on the basis of their individual properties. They are locally deterministic. "Laws" of chaos pertain to whole populations of elements whose collective behavior cannot be extrapolated from their individual properties. They are not deterministic in the sense of being able to predict the outcome of any particular interaction. That is why they are necessarily formulated as laws of probability. Ilya Prigogine forcefully argues the necessarily probabilistic nature of laws of chaos, at the quantum level as well as on the macro level of thermodynamic systems. He also insists that the margin of indeterminacy that imposes the need for probabilistic treatment is not simply due to unavailability of complete information. It is, he says, a natural reality: a positive potential in matter, which is one with its capability of evolving (in particular, it might be added on a Bergsonian note, its ability to evolve life, to become alive). See Prigogine, *Les lois du chaos* (Paris: Flammarion, 1994), and Prigogine and Stengers, *The End of Certainty: Time, Chaos, and the Laws of Nature* (New York: Free Press, 1997). On life: "It is certainly true that life is incompatible with Boltzmann's [probabilistic] order principle but not with the kind of behavior that can occur in far-from-equilibrium conditions" like those of the Bénard instability. "Life, far from being outside the natural order, appears as the supreme expression of the self-organizing processes that occur." Prigogine and Stengers, *Order Out of Chaos*, 143, 175.

23 The crucial distinction between situation and context required a terminological doubling with regard to concepts of qualitative activity (affect and emotion). So, too, with concepts of receptivity. Reserve "sensation" for the impersonal experience of something new globally registering in a context. Use "perception" for the determination of constituent elements, or parts retrospectively experienced as composing the actual context. Perception is structural or interactive (subjective-objective, in reciprocal definition). Sensation is eventful or processual. Perception is exoreferential (pertaining to recognized part-to-part connections understood as external to the knowing subject). Sensation is *self-referential:* pertaining to the context's relation to itself (change) and encompassing of the structural coupling of the subjective and the objective ("autonomous" rather than subjective-objective). These distinctions are developed in chapters 3, 4, and 5 above.

24 For a history of the "three-body" (or "many-body") problem and an intro-

duction to its scientific offspring, see Florin Diacu and Philip Holmes, *Celestial Encounters: The Origins of Chaos and Stability* (Princeton: Princeton University Press, 1996).

25 Ecology is perhaps most predisposed to relation, since it explicitly defines interactive contexts as its object of study. But even what has historically been the most willfully reductive of the biological sciences, molecular biology, is being relationally challenged by concepts like "endosymbiosis" introduced by the work of Lynn Margulis (for an overview, see Margulis and Dorion Sagan, *What Is Life?* [London: Weidenfeld and Nicholson, 1995], 90–117). The trends in brain science are clearly toward treating brain functions as network events involving differential populations of cells interconnected by complex patterns of feedback. Neurons' collective responses may be induced by a discrete stimulus, but always displays a systematicity (a global excess of effect due to feedback) that forbids any strictly linear causal model.

26 The stochastic resonance effect is "surplus" or excessive because it concerns the ability of *subthreshold* signals to be perceived, or to induce a "switching event" in the receiving system: "the signal, by itself, never has sufficient amplitude" to "deterministically" cause a change in the system's state (1385). And yet it does, due to a singular interaction between signal and noise. Stochastic resonance, which replaces linear causality with near-relational concepts involving "noise" (chaotic indeterminacy of signal), interactive "amplification," "threshold," and global or systemic "modulation," has implications far beyond acoustics. It has particular significance for brain science, where it adds a level of nonlinear causality functioning *on the level of the single neuron*, even prior to the consideration of the collective behavior of populations of cells. For overviews, see Frank Moss, David Pearson, and David O'Gorman, "Stochastic Resonance: Tutorial and Update," *International Journal of Bifurcation and Chaos* 4, no. 6 (1994), 1383–97, and Kurt Wiesenfeld and Frank Moss, "Stochastic Resonance and the Benefits of Noise: From Ice Ages to Crayfish and SQUIDS," *Nature* 373 (5 January 1995): 33–36.

27 "The relations that connect experiences must themselves be experienced relations, and any kind of relation experienced must be accounted as 'real' as anything else in the system," *Essays in Radical Empiricism*, 42. See also pp. 16n, 25, 71–72, 110. "Radical" empiricism takes into account the "superempirical" dimensions of experience mentioned in chapters 2 and 6.

28 "Subjectivity and objectivity are affairs not of what an experience is aboriginally made of, but of its classification," James, *Essays in Radical Empiricism*, 141.

29 "We are virtual knowers . . . long before we were certified to have been actual knowers, by the percept's retroactive validating power," James, *Essays in Radical Empiricism*, 68.

30 The way Deleuze formulates this is that "relations are external to their terms."
   He begins to develop this concept in his first book on Hume: *Empiricism and
   Subjectivity: An Essay on Hume's Theory of Human Nature,* trans. Constantin
   Boundas (New York: Columbia University Press, 1991), 66, 101. Gilbert Simondon's phraseology is "the terms of the relation do not preexist it": *L'individu et sa genèse physico-biologique* (Paris: PUF, 1964), 17, 274. Foucault's way
   of making the same point for the contents of language is that "discursive
   relations are not interior to discourse . . . yet they are not relations exterior to
   discourse . . . they are, in a sense, at the limit of discourse; they offer it objects
   of which it can speak, or rather (for this image of offering presupposes that
   objects are formed [or, in the language of this essay, determined] independently of discourse), they determine the sheaf of connections [*rapports*] that
   discourse must establish in order to speak of this or that [particular] object, in
   order to deal with them, name them, analyze them, explain them, etc. These
   relations [*relations*] characterize not the particular language [*langue*] used by
   discourse, nor the circumstances [contexts] in which it is deployed, but discourse itself as a practice [process line]." Foucault, *The Archaeology of Knowledge,* trans. A. M. Sheridan (New York: Pantheon, 1972), translation modified.
   Finally, William James: "Relations are feelings of an entirely different order
   from the terms they relate," *The Principles of Psychology,* 149.
31 This relational perspective differs sharply from the debunking attitude some
   practitioners of cultural studies have adopted, for whom "techno-science" is a
   term of abuse marking a complicity that invalidates science as a whole. The
   problem is precisely that they look at science "as a whole" rather than as a
   process (one that is strictly self-limited and precisely *because of that* displays a
   continuing openness). The hyphen in "techno-science" is used less as a plus
   sign than as an implicit equal sign. The theory and politics of making an equation is very different from those of making a connection, however inexorable
   that connection is seen to be (however necessary its situational contingency).
   A radical empiricism continuously multiplies processual distinctions rather
   than making judgmental equations that implode the world's additivity.
32 On the "subsumption of life under capital," see Brian Massumi, "Requiem for
   Our Prospective Dead: Towards a Participatory Critique of Capitalist Power"
   in *Deleuze and Guattari: New Mappings in Politics, Philosophy, and Culture,* ed.
   Eleanor Kauffman and Kevin John Heller (Minneapolis: University of Minnesota Press, 1998), 40–63.
33 The concept of "subjectless subjectivity" is from Raymond Ruyer. See Paul
   Bains, "Subjectless Subjectivities," *A Shock to Thought,* ed. Brian Massumi
   (forthcoming). On "naturing nature," see Deleuze, *Spinoza: Practical Philosophy,* trans. Robert Hurley (San Francisco: City Lights, 1988), 92–93. Keith
   Ansell-Pearson cautions that Deleuze's appropriation of this Spinozist con-

cept is strongly influenced by his reading of Bergson. Ansell-Pearson, *Germinal Life: The Difference and Repetition of Deleuze* (London: Routledge, 1999), 12, 36–37.

34 Whitehead, *Concept of Nature*, 29, 41. James makes a similar point, with an affective inflection appropriate to the approach adopted here: "real effectual causation . . . is just what we feel it to be," *Essays in Radical Empiricism*, 185.

35 Whitehead, *Concept of Nature*, 27, 46.

36 The classic study of relational color effects remains Johann Wolfgang von Goethe, *Theory of Colors*, trans. Charles Lock Eastlake (Cambridge: MIT Press, 1970). See also chapter 7 above and Brian Massumi, "The Diagram as Technique of Existence," *ANY (Architecture New York)* 23 (1998): 42–47.

37 "Philosophy begins in wonder. And, at the end, when philosophic thought has done its best, the wonder remains," Alfred North Whitehead, *Nature and Life* (Cambridge: Cambridge University Press, 1934), 96.

38 Is it stretching things too far to construe Deleuze and Guattari's analysis of philosophy and "friendship" as a way of talking about accompaniment? See the preface to *What Is Philosophy?*, trans. Hugh Tomlinson and Graham Burchell (New York: Columbia University Press, 1994), 1–12.

39 On the concept of pure linkage (*liaison*) "at a distance" from the actual elements linked, see Raymond Ruyer, *La conscience et le corps* (Paris: PUF: 1950), 46–47, 61, 94–95.

40 On the inhuman or "nonhuman" as a potential, in relation to historical orderings and language, see Alan Bourassa, "Language, Literature, and the Nonhuman," *A Shock to Thought: Expression after Deleuze and Guattari*, ed. Brian Massumi (London: Routledge, forthcoming). The notion that historical potential inhabits event-gaps ("ruptures" or "cesuras") in its actual order is central to the philosophy of Michel Foucault: "The event is not of the order of bodies. Yet is in no way immaterial; it is on a level with materiality that it takes effect, that it is effect; it has its locus and consists in the relation, coexistence, dispersion, intersection, accumulation, and selection of material elements. . . . Suffice it to say that the philosophy of the event should move in the paradoxical direction of a materialism of the incorporeal. . . . [I]t is a question of cesuras that break open the moment and disperse the subject in a plurality of possible positions and functions [this is the "subjectless subject" alluded to earlier; in the present framework, potential might be substituted for possible]. . . . [W]hat must be elaborated—outside philosophies of the subject and of time—is a theory of discontinuous systematicities" [holdings-together in the gaps of ongoing between contexts] privileging neither "mechanical causality" nor "ideal necessity" but instead welcoming contingency. Foucault, *L'Ordre du discours* (Paris: Gallimard, 1977), 58–61.

41 Chapter 4 above develops similar ideas in relation to the art work of Stelarc.

42 Giorgio Agamben, *The Coming Community,* trans. Michael Hardt (Minneapolis: University of Minnesota Press, 1993). Deleuze and Guattari also link philosophy to a "people to come" in *What Is Philosophy?,* 109.

43 On philosophy as providing a conceptual "tool box," see Gilles Deleuze and Michel Foucault, "Intellectuals and Power," in Foucault, *Language, Counter-Memory, Practice,* ed. Donald Bouchard (Ithaca: Cornell University Press, 1977), 205–17. On philosophy's necessary relation to nonphilosophy, see Deleuze and Guattari, *What Is Philosophy?,* 40–41, 218.

44 James found a characteristically pithy way of phrasing this: "Nature exhibits only changes, which habitually coincide with one another so that their habits are discernible in simple 'laws,' " *Essays in Radical Empiricism,* 148. For Peirce on laws of nature as habits of matter, see *The Essential Peirce,* vol. 1, ed. Nathan Houser and Christian Kloesel (Bloomington: University of Indiana Press, 1992), 223–24, 277–79.

45 Edward O. Wilson, *Consilience: The Unity of Knowledge* (New York: Alfred A. Knopf, 1998), 12, 44.

46 Stephen Hawking, *A Brief History of Time* (New York: Bantam, 1988), 175. See also Paul Davies, *God and the New Physics* (London: Penguin, 1983): "Science offers a surer path than religion in the search of God," 229.

47 Tony Bennett, *Culture: A Reformer's Science* (Sydney: Allen and Unwin, 1998). For a critique of Bennett's approach, see Meaghan Morris, *Too Soon, Too Late: History in Popular Culture* (Bloomington: University of Indiana Press, 1998), 227–31.

48 On political ecology, see Félix Guattari, *Chaosmosis: An Ethico-Aesthetic Paradigm,* trans. Paul Bains and Julian Pefanis (Bloomington: Indiana University Press, 1995), 119–35, and *The Three Ecologies,* trans. Ian Pindar and Paul Sutton (London: Athlone, 2000).

49 The concept of creative risk is central to Isabelle Stengers's model of an ecology of practices, as developed in *Cosmopolitiques* and elsewhere.

50 Unhappily translated as "mediator." See Deleuze, "Mediators," *Negotiations, 1972–1990,* trans. Martin Joughin (New York: Columbia University Press, 1995), 121–34.

51 For a consonant approach starting from an institutional base in political science rather than cultural studies, see William Connolly, *The Ethos of Pluralization* (Minneapolis: University of Minnesota Press, 1995).

WORKS CITED

Agamben, Giorgio. *The Coming Community.* Trans. Michael Hardt. Minneapolis: University of Minnesota Press, 1993.
——. *Means without End.* Trans. Vincenzo Binetti and Cesare Casarino. Minneapolis: University of Minnesota Press, 2000.
Ansell-Pearson, Keith. *Germinal Life: The Difference and Repetition of Deleuze.* London: Routledge, 1999.
Arakawa and Madeleine Gins. *Reversible Destiny.* New York: Guggenheim Museum, 1997.
Avant, Lloyd L. "Vision in the Ganzfeld." *Psychological Bulletin* 64, no. 4 (1965): 246–58.
Bains, Paul. "Subjectless Subjectivities." *A Shock to Thought: Expression after Deleuze and Guattari,* ed. Brian Massumi. London: Routledge, forthcoming.
Bakhtin, M. M. "The Problem of Content, Material, and Form in Verbal Art." In *Art and Answerability: Early Philosophical Essays by M. M. Bakhtin.* Ed. Michael Holquist and Vadim Laipunov. Trans. Vadim Laipunov and Kenneth Brostrom. Austin: University of Texas, 1990.
Baron-Cohen, Simon, and John E. Harrison, eds. *Synaesthesia: Classic and Contemporary Readings.* London: Blackwell, 1997.
Baylor, Denis. "Colour Mechanisms of the Eye." In *Colour: Art and Science,* eds. Trevor Lamb and Janine Bourriau. 103–126.
Benjamin, Walter. *One Way Street.* London: Verso, 1985.
Bennett, Jane. *The Enchantment of Modern Life: Crossings, Energetics, and Ethics.* Princeton: Princeton University Press, 2001.
Bennett, Tony. *Culture: A Reformer's Science.* Sydney: Allen and Unwin, 1998.
Bergson, Henri. *Creative Evolution.* Trans. Arthur Mitchell. Mineola, N.Y.: Dover, 1998.
——. *The Creative Mind.* Trans. Mabelle L. Audison. New York: Philosophical Library, 1946.
——. *Matter and Memory.* Trans. Nancy Margaret Paul and W. Scott Palmer. New York: Zone, 1988.
——. *Mind-Energy: Lectures and Essays.* Trans. H. Wildon Carr. London: Macmillan, 1920).

Berlin, Brent, and Paul Kay. *Basic Color Terms: Their Universality and Evolution.* Berkeley: University of California Press, 1969.

Bermúdez, José Luis, Anthony Marcel, and Naomi Eilan, eds. *The Body and the Self.* Cambridge: MIT Press, 1995.

Bilger, Burkhard. "The Flavor of Fat: Debunking the Myth of the Insipid Lipid." *The Sciences* (November/December 1997), 10.

Bohm, David, and B. J. Hiley. *The Undivided Universe.* London: Routledge, 1993.

Bornstein, Marc H. "Chromatic Vision in Infancy." In *Advances in Child Development and Behavior.* Vol. 12. Ed. Hayne W. Reese and Lewis P. Lipsitt. New York: Academic Press, 1978.

Bourassa, Alan. "Language, Literature, and the Nonhuman," *A Shock to Thought: Expression after Deleuze and Guattari.* Ed. Brian Massumi. London: Routledge, forthcoming.

Bruno, Giordano. *De la magie.* Trans. Danielle Sonnier and Boris Donné. Paris: Allia, 2000.

Buckley, Sandra. "Contemporary Myths of the Asian City." *(In)Visible Cities: From the Postmodern Metropolis to the Cities of the Future.* Ed. Robert Sergent and Pellegrino D'Acierno. New York: Monticello Press, forthcoming.

Buck-Morss, Susan. "Dream-World of Mass Culture: Walter Benjamin's Theory of Modernity and the Dialectics of Seeing." In *Modernity and the Hegemony of Vision.* Ed. Michael Levin. Berkeley: University of California Press, 1993.

Cache, Bernard. "A Plea for Euclid." *ANY (Architecture New York)* 24 (1999): 54–59.

Caygill, Howard. *Walter Benjamin: The Colour of Experience.* London: Routledge, 1998.

Cohen, Walter. "Spatial and Textural Characteristics of the *Ganzfeld.*" *American Journal of Psychology,* 76 (1957): 403–10.

Combes, Muriel. *Simondon: Individu et collectivité.* Paris: PUF, 1999.

Conklin, Howard C. "Hanunóo Color Categories." In *Language in Culture and Society,* ed. Dell Hymes. New York: Harper and Row, 1964.

Connolly, William. "Brain Waves, Transcendental Fields, and Techniques of Thought." *Radical Philosophy* 94 (March/April 1999).

——. *The Ethos of Pluralization.* Minneapolis: University of Minnesota Press, 1995.

Courant, Richard, and Herbert Robbins. *What Is Mathematics? An Elementary Approach to Ideas and Methods,* 2d ed., rev. by Ian Stewart. Oxford: Oxford University Press.

Cytowic, Robert E. "Synaesthesia: Phenomenology and Neuropsychology." In *Synaesthesia: Classic and Contemporary Readings,* ed. Simon Baron-Cohen and John E. Harrison. London: Blackwell, 1997.

——. *Synesthesia: A Union of the Senses.* New York: Springer-Verlag, 1989.

Darwin, Charles. "Biographical Sketch of a Young Child." *Kosmos* 1 (1877): 367–76.

Davies, Paul. *God and the New Physics*. London: Penguin, 1983.

Dean, Kenneth, and Brian Massumi. *First and Last Emperors: The Absolute State and the Body of the Despot*. New York: Autonomedia, 1992.

Deleuze, Gilles. *Cinema 1: The Movement-Image*. Trans. Hugh Tomlinson and Barbara Habberjam. Minneapolis: University of Minnesota Press, 1986.

———. *Difference and Repetition*. Trans. Paul Patton. New York: Columbia University Press, 1994.

———. *Empiricism and Subjectivity: An Essay on Hume's Theory of Human Nature*. Trans. Constantin Boundas. New York: Columbia University Press, 1991.

———. *The Fold: Leibniz and the Baroque*. Trans. Tom Conley. Minneapolis: University of Minnesota Press, 1993.

———. *Francis Bacon: Logique de la sensation*. Paris: Editions de la Différence, 1981.

———. *Kant's Critical Philosophy*. Trans. Hugh Tomlinson and Barbara Habberjam. Minneapolis: University of Minnesota Press, 1984.

———. *The Logic of Sense*. Trans. Mark Lester with Charles Stivale. Ed. Constantin V. Boundas. New York: Columbia University Press, 1990.

———. *Negotiations, 1972–1990*. Trans. Martin Joughin. New York: Columbia University Press, 1995.

———. *Spinoza: Practical Philosophy*. Trans. Robert Hurley. San Francisco: City Lights, 1988.

Deleuze, Gilles, and Michel Foucault. "Intellectuals and Power." In Foucault, *Language, Counter-Memory, Practice*. Ed. Donald Bouchard. Ithaca: Cornell University Press, 1977.

Deleuze, Gilles, and Félix Guattari. *Anti-Oedipus: Capitalism and Schizophrenia*. Trans. Robert Hurley, Mark Seem, and Helen R. Lane. Minneapolis: University of Minnesota Press, 1983.

———. *A Thousand Plateaus: Capitalism and Schizophrenia*. Trans. Brian Massumi. Minneapolis: University of Minnesota Press, 1987.

———. *What Is Philosophy?* Trans. Hugh Tomlinson and Graham Burchill. New York: Columbia University Press, 1994.

Diacu, Florin, and Philip Holmes. *Celestial Encounters: The Origins of Chaos and Stability*. Princeton: Princeton University Press, 1996.

Epstein, Russell, and Nancy Kanwisher. "A Cortical Representation of the Local Visual Environment." *Nature* 392 (9 April 1998): 598–601.

Etienne, Ariane S., Joëlle Berlie, Joséphine Georgakopoulos, and Roland Maurer. "Role of Dead Reckoning in Navigation" *Spatial Representation in Animals*, ed. Sue Healy. Oxford: Oxford University Press, 1998).

Evans, Ralph M. *The Perception of Color*. New York: John Wiley and Sons, 1974.

Foucault, Michel. *The Archaeology of Knowledge.* Trans. A. M. Sheridan. New York: Pantheon, 1972.

——. *Language, Counter-Memory, Practice.* Ed. Donald Bouchard. Trans. Donald Bouchard and Sherry Simon. Ithaca: Cornell University Press, 1977.

——. *L'Ordre du discours.* Paris: Gallimard, 1977.

Fried, Itzhak, Katherine A. MacDonald, and Charles L. Wilson. "Single Neuron Activity in Human Hippocampus and Amygdala during Recognition of Faces and Objects." *Neuron* 18 (May 1997): 753–65.

Gasquet, Joachim. *Joachim Gasquet's Cézanne.* London: Thames and Hudson, 1991.

Gershon, Michael D. "The Enteric Nervous System." *Encyclopedia of Neuroscience.* Vol. 1. Ed. George Adelman. Boston: Birhauser, 1987.

——. *The Second Brain: A Groundbreaking New Understanding of Nervous Disorders of the Stomach and Intestines.* New York: Harper, 1999.

Gibson, Eleanor J. *Principles of Perceptual Learning and Development.* New York: Appleton-Century-Crofts, 1969.

Gibson, James J., and Dickens Waddell. "Homogeneous Retinal Stimulation and Visual Perception." *American Journal of Psychology* 65, no. 2 (April 1952): 263–70.

Gil, José. *Metamorphoses of the Body.* Trans. Stephen Muecke. Minneapolis: University of Minnesota Press, 1998.

Gladstone, W. E. "Homer's Perceptions and Use of Colour." *Studies on Homer and the Homeric Age.* Vol. 3. Oxford: Oxford University Press, 1858.

Goethe, Johann Wolfgang von. *Theory of Colors.* Trans. Charles Lock Eastlake. Cambridge: MIT Press, 1970.

Grossberg, Lawrence. *We Gotta Get Out of This Place: Popular Conservatism and Postmodern Culture.* New York: Routledge, 1992.

Guattari, Félix. *Chaosmosis: An Ethico-Aesthetic Paradigm.* Trans. Paul Bains and Julian Pefanis. Bloomington: University of Indiana Press, 1995.

——. *The Three Ecologies.* Trans. Ian Pindar and Paul Sutton. London: Athlone, 2000.

Gurfinkel, V. S. and Yu S. Levick. "Perceptual and Automatic Aspects of the Postural Body Scheme." In Jacques Paillard, *Brain and Space.* New York: Oxford University Press, 1991.

Hacking, Ian. *The Social Construction of What?* Cambridge, Mass.: Harvard University Press, 1999.

Hardin, C. L. *Color for Philosophers: Unweaving the Rainbow.* Indianapolis: Hackett, 1986.

Harrison, John. *Synaesthesia: The Strangest Thing.* Oxford: Oxford University Press, 2001.

Hawking, Stephen. *A Brief History of Time.* New York: Bantam, 1988.

Heilbroner, Robert, and Lester Thurow. *Economics Explained: Everything You Need to Know about How the Economy Works and Where It Is Going.* New York: Simon & Schuster, 1994.

Held, Richard, and Alan Hein. "Movement-Produced Stimulation in the Development of Visually Guided Behavior." *Journal of Comparative and Physiological Psychology* 56, no. 5 (1963): 872–76.

Henle, Mary, ed. *Documents of Gestalt Psychology.* Berkeley: University of California Press, 1961.

Horgan, John. "Can Science Explain Consciousness?" *Scientific American,* July 1994, 76–77.

Hume, David. *A Treatise of Human Nature.* Intro. and ed. Ernest C. Mossner. London: Penguin, 1969.

Huyghe, René, ed. *Impressionism.* New York: Chartwell, 1973.

James, William. "The Feeling of Effort." *Collected Essays and Reviews.* New York: Russell and Russell, 1969.

———. *Essays in Radical Empiricism.* Lincoln: University of Nebraska Press, 1996.

———. *Principles of Psychology.* 2 vol. 1890. Reprint, New York: Dover, 1950.

Jameson, Fredric. *Postmodernism; or, The Cultural Logic of Late Capitalism.* Durham, N.C.: Duke University Press, 1991.

Katz, David. *The World of Colour.* Trans. R. B. MacLeod and C. W. Fox. London: Kegan, Paul, Trench, Trubner and Co., 1935.

Kinsbourne, Marcel. "Awareness of One's Body: An Attentional Theory of Its Nature, Development, and Brain Basis." In José Luis Bermúdez, Anthony Marcel, and Naomi Eilan, eds. *The Body and the Self.* Cambridge: MIT Press, 1995.

Klee, Paul. *Notebooks,* vol. 1. *The Thinking Eye.* Trans. Ralph Manheim. London: Lund Humphries, 1961.

Koffka, Kurt. *Principles of Gestalt Psychology.* New York: Harcourt, Brace, 1935.

Lamb, Trevor, and Janine Bourriau, eds. *Colour: Art and Science.* Cambridge: Cambridge University Press, 1995.

Latour, Bruno. *Petite réflexion sur le culte moderne des dieux faitiches.* Le Plessis-Robinson: Synthélabo, 1996.

———. *Science in Action: How to Follow Scientists and Engineers through Society.* Cambridge, Mass.: Harvard University Press, 1987.

———. *We Have Never Been Modern.* Trans. Catherine Porter. Cambridge, Mass.: Harvard University Press, 1993.

Leibniz, Gottfried Wilhelm. *G. W. Leibniz's* Monadology: *An Edition for Students.* Ed. Nicholas Rescher. Pittsburgh: University of Pittsburgh Press, 1991.

———. *Philosophical Writings.* Ed. G. H. R. Parkinson. Trans. Mary Morris and G. H. R. Parkinson. London: Everyman, 1995.

Lévy, Pierre. *Becoming Virtual: Reality in the Digital Age.* Trans. Robert Bononno. New York: Plenum, 1998.

Lewkowicz, David J., and Robert Lickliter, eds. *The Development of Intersensory Perception: Comparative Perspectives*. Hillsdale, N.J.: Lawrence Erlbaum, 1994.

Libet, Benjamin. "Unconscious Cerebral Initiative and the Role of Conscious Will in Voluntary Action." *Behavioral and Brain Sciences* 8 (1985): 529–66.

Lozano-Hemmer, Rafael. *Alzado Vectorial. Arquitectura Relacional No. 4/Vectorial Elevation. Relational Architecture No. 4*. Mexico City: National Council for Culture and the Arts, 2000.

Lucy, John A. "The Linguistics of Color." In *Color Categories in Thought and Language*, eds. C. L. Hardin and Luisa Maffi. Cambridge: Cambridge University Press, 1997.

Luminet, Jean-Pierre, Glenn D. Starkman, and Jeffrey R. Weeks. "Is Space Finite?" *Scientific American* (April 1999), 94.

Luria, A. R. *The Mind of the Mnemonist: A Little Book About a Vast Memory*. Cambridge, Mass.: Harvard University Press, 1968.

Lynn, Greg. *Animate Form*. New York: Princeton Architectural Press, 1999.

———. *Folds, Bodies, and Blobs: Collected Essays*. Brussels: La Lettre Volée, 1998.

Lyons, John. "Colour and Language." In Trevor Lamb and Janine Bourriau, *Colour: Art and Science*. Cambridge: Cambridge University Press, 1995.

Margulis, Lynn, and Dorion Sagan. *What Is Life?* London: Weidenfeld and Nicholson, 1995.

Marsh, Anne. *Body and Self: Performance Art in Australia, 1969–1992*. Melbourne: Oxford University Press, 1993.

Massumi, Brian. "The Diagram as Technique of Existence." *ANY (Architecture New York)* 23 (1998): 42–47.

———. "Requiem for Our Prospective Dead: Towards a Participatory Critique of Capitalist Power." In *Deleuze and Guattari: New Mappings in Politics, Philosophy, and Culture*. Ed. Eleanor Kauffman and Kevin John Heller. Minneapolis: University of Minnesota Press, 1998.

———, ed. *A Shock to Thought: Expression After Deleuze and Guattari*. London: Routledge, forthcoming.

Maturana, Humberto, and Franscisco Varela. *Autopoiesis and Cognition: The Realization of the Living*. Dordrecht: D. Reidel, 1980.

———. *The Tree of Knowledge: The Biological Roots of Human Understanding*. Boston: Shambhala, 1992.

Maurer, Daphne. "Neonatal Synaesthesia: Implications for the Processing of Speech and Faces." In *Synaesthesia: Classic and Contemporary Readings*, eds. Simon Baron-Cohen and John E. Harrison. London: Routledge, 1997.

Maxwell-Stuart, P. G. *Studies in Greek Colour Terminology*. Vol. 1. Leiden: E. J. Brill, 1981.

Milton, Julie, and Richard Wiseman. "Does Psi Exist? Lack of Replication of an

Anomalous Process of Information Transfer." *Psychological Bulletin* 125 (1999): 387–91.

Mollon, John. "Seeing Color." In *Colour: Art and Science,* eds. Trevor Lamb and Janine Bourriau. Cambridge: Cambridge University Press, 1995. 127–151.

Morris, Meaghan. *Too Soon, Too Late: History in Popular Culture.* Bloomington: Indiana University Press, 1998.

Moss, Frank, David Pearson, and David O'Gorman. "Stochastic Resonance: Tutorial and Update," *International Journal of Bifurcation and Chaos* 4, no. 6 (1994): 1383–97.

Mullarkey, John. *The New Bergson.* Manchester: University of Manchester Press, 1999.

Nathan, Tobie. *Fier de n'avoir ni pays, ni amis, quelle sottise c'était.* Paris: La pensée sauvage, 1999.

Nathan, Tobie, and Isabelle Stengers. *Médecins et sorciers.* Le Plessis-Robinson: Synthélabo, 1995.

Negroponte, Nicholas. *Being Digital.* New York: Alfred A. Knopf, 1995.

Nietzsche, Friedrich. *On the Genealogy of Morals.* Trans. Walter Kaufmann. New York: Vintage, 1967.

Norretranders, Tor. *The User Illusion: Cutting Consciousness Down to Size.* Trans. Jonathan Sydenham. New York: Viking, 1998.

O'Shaughnessy, Brian. "Proprioception and Body Image." In José Luis Bermúdez, Anthony Marcel, and Naomi Eilan, eds. *The Body and the Self.* Cambridge: MIT Press, 1995.

Paillard, Jacques, ed. *Brain and Space.* New York: Oxford University Press, 1991.

Pallasmaa, Juhani. *The Eyes of the Skin: Architecture and the Senses.* London: Academy Editions, 1996.

Peirce, C. S. *The Essential Peirce: Selected Philosophical Writings.* Vol. 1. Ed. Nathan Houser and Christian Kloesel. Bloomington: University of Indiana Press, 1992.

——. *Reasoning and the Logic of Things.* Ed. Kenneth Laine Ketner. Cambridge, Mass.: Harvard University Press, 1992.

Penrose, Roger. *The Large, the Small, and the Human Mind.* Cambridge: Cambridge University Press, 1997.

Pickering, Andrew. *The Mangle of Practice: Time, Agency, and Science.* Chicago: University of Chicago Press, 1995.

Platnauer, Maurice. "Greek Colour-Perception." *The Classical Quarterly* 15, nos. 3/4 (1921): 162.

Prigogine, Ilya. *Les lois du chaos.* Paris: Flammarion, 1994.

Prigogine, Ilya, and Isabelle Stengers. *The End of Certainty: Time, Chaos, and the Laws of Nature.* New York: Free Press, 1997.

——. *Entre le temps et l'éternité.* Paris: Fayard, 1988.

———. *La nouvelle alliance: Métamorphose de la science.* Paris: Gallimard, 1986.

———. *Order Out of Chaos: Man's Dialogue with Nature.* New York: Bantam, 1984.

Rajchman, John. *Constructions.* Cambridge: MIT Press, 1998.

Reagan, Ronald, and Richard B. Hubler. *Where Is the Rest of Me?* New York: Elsevier-Dutton, 1965; reprint, Karz Publishers, 1981.

Rogin, Michael. *Ronald Reagan, the Movie and Other Episodes in Political Demonology.* Berkeley: University of California Press, 1987.

Roll, Jean-Pierre, Régine Roll, and Jean-Luc Velay. "Proprioception as a Link between Body Space and Extra-personal Space." In *Brain and Space,* ed. Jacques Paillard. New York: Oxford University Press, 1991.

Ruyer, Raymond. *La conscience et le corps.* Paris: PUF, 1950.

———. *Néo-finalisme.* Paris: PUF, 1952.

Sacks, Oliver. *The Man Who Mistook His Wife for a Hat.* London: Picador, 1985.

Schatz, B., S. Chameron, G. Beugnon, and T. S. Collett. "The Use of Path Integration to Guide Route Learning in Ants." *Nature* 399 (24 June 1999): 769–72.

Schilder, Paul. *The Image and Appearance of the Human Body: Studies in the Constructive Energies of the Psyche.* New York: International Universities Press, 1950.

Serres, Michel. *The Parasite.* Trans. Lawrence R. Schehr. Baltimore: Johns Hopkins University Press, 1982.

Shaviro, Steven. *The Cinematic Body.* Minneapolis: University of Minnesota Press, 1993.

———. *Passion and Excess: Blanchot, Bataille, and Literary Theory.* Tallahassee: Florida State University, 1990.

Sherrington, Charles S. *The Integrative Action of the Nervous System.* New Haven: Yale University Press, 1906.

Simondon, Gilbert. *L'individuation psychique et collective.* Paris: Aubier, 1989.

———. *L'individu et sa genèse physico-biologique.* Grenoble: Millon, 1995.

Spinoza, Baruch. *The Ethics. The Collected Works of Spinoza.* Vol. 1. Ed. and trans. Edwin Curley. Princeton: Princeton University Press, 1985.

Spuybroek, Lars. *Deep Surface.* Rotterdam: NOX, 1999.

Stelarc. Stelarc Official Website. Http://www.stelarc.va.com.au/.

———. "The Body Obsolete: Paul McCarthy Interviews Stelarc." *High Performance* 24 (1983): 14–19.

———. Artist's Statement. In "The Function in Art and Culture Today." *High Performance* 11 (Spring/Summer 1988): 70.

———. "Portrait robot de l'homme-machine." Interview with Jean-Yves Katelan. *L'Autre journal* 27 (September 1992): 24–41.

———. Interview with Martin Thomas. In Nicholas Zurbrugg, ed. *Electronic Arts in Australia,* special issue, *Continuum* 8, no. 1 (1994): 376–93.

———. "Extended-Body: Interview with Stelarc." With Paolo Atzore and Kirk Woolford. *C-Theory* (1995). Http://www.ctheory.com.

——. Interview with Rosanne Bersten. *Internet.au* (1995): 34–35.

——. "From Psycho to Cyber Strategies: Prosthetics, Robotics and Remote Existence." *Canadian Theatre Review* 86 (Spring 1996): 19–23.

Stelarc and James D. Paffrath. *Obsolete Body/Suspensions/Stelarc*. Davis, California: JP Publications, 1984.

Stengers, Isabelle. *Cosmopolitiques*. 7 vol. Paris/Le Plessis-Robinson: La Découverte/Synthélabo, 1996.

Stengers, Isabelle, and Léon Chertok. *A Critique of Psychoanalytic Reason: Hypnosis as a Scientific Problem from Lavoisier to Lacan*. Trans. Martha Noel Evans. Stanford: Stanford University Press, 1992.

——. *L'Hypnose, blessure narcissique*. Paris: Editions des Laboratoires Delagrange, 1990.

Stern, Daniel. *The Interpersonal World of the Infant: A View from Psychoanalysis and Developmental Psychology*. New York: Basic Books, 1985.

Sturm, Hertha. *Emotional Effects of Media: The Work of Hertha Sturm*. Ed. Gertrude Joch Robinson. Working Papers in Communications. Montreal: McGill University Graduate Program in Communications, 1987.

Taussig, Michael. *The Nervous System*. New York: Routledge, 1992.

Thinès, Georges, Alan Costall, and George Butterworth, eds. *Michotte's Experimental Phenomenology of Perception*. Hillsdale, N.J.: Lawrence Erlbaum, 1991.

Thom, René. Interview. *Le Monde*, no. 15549 (January 22–23, 1995).

van Berkel, Ben, and Caroline Bos, eds. *ANY (Architecture New York)* 23 (1998), special "Diagram Work" issue.

Virilio, Paul. *The Art of the Motor*. Trans. Julie Rose. Minneapolis: University of Minnesota Press, 1995.

——. "Rat de laboratoire." *L'Autre journal* 27 (September 1992): 31–33.

von Senden, M. *Space and Sight: The Perception of Space and Shape in the Congenitally Blind before and after Operation*. Trans. Peter Heath. London: Methuen, 1960.

Walk, Richard D., and Herbert L. Pick, eds. *Intersensory Perception and Sensory Integration*. New York: Plenum Press, 1981.

Wallach, Hans. "Brightness Constancy and the Nature of Achromatic Colors." In *Documents of Gestalt Psychology*, ed. Mary Henle. Berkeley: University of California Press, 1961.

Weiskrantz, L. *Blindsight: A Case Study and Implications*. Oxford: Oxford University Press, 1986.

West, Geoffrey B., James H. Brown, and Brian J. Enquist. "A General Model for the Origin of Allometric Scaling Laws in Biology." *Science* 276 (4 April 1997): 12–126.

Westphal, Jonathan. *Colour: Some Philosophical Problems from Wittgenstein*. Aristotelian Society Series, vol. 7. Oxford: Basil Blackwell, 1987.

Whitehead, Alfred North. *Concept of Nature*. Cambridge: Cambridge University Press, 1964.

———. *Modes of Thought*. New York: Macmillan, 1938.

———. *Nature and Life*. Cambridge: Cambridge University Press, 1934.

———. *Process and Reality*. Eds. David Ray Griffin and Donald W. Sherburne. New York: Free Press, 1978.

Wiesenfeld, Kurt, and Frank Moss. "Stochastic Resonance and the Benefits of Noise: From Ice Ages to Crayfish and SQUIDS." *Nature* 373 (5 January 1995): 33–36.

Wilson, Edward O. *Consilience: The Unity of Knowledge*. New York: Alfred A. Knopf, 1998.

Wittgenstein, Ludwig. *Remarks on Colour*. Ed. G. E. M. Anscombe. Trans. Lindal L. McAlister and Margarate Schättle. Oxford: Basil Blackwell, 1978.

INDEX

Affect: (*cont.*)
32; structure and, 260 n.3; suspense and, 26–28, 31, 40–42; as synesthetic, 35; transition and, 15–16, 197; as trans-situational, 217–18; virtual and, 35, 197, 239; vision and, 56, 208–28, 238–39, 249–50; vitality and, 35, 41, 220

Affirmation, 12–13, 17, 18, 28, 132, 240

Agamben, Giorgio, 17, 242

Agency, 128–31

Agnosia, 39

Alchemy, 112

Amodality, 169–71, 282 n.25

Analog process, 84–85; digital vs., 133–43; power as, 43; reading as, 138–40; virtual and, 137–43

Anecdote, 214, 236

Animals: language and, 38; orientation abilities of, 180, 286 n.3

Anomaly, 29, 145, 162, 166, 226; conditions of, 222–23, 238

Ansell-Pearson, Keith, 297–98 n.33

Anthropomorphism, 39

Anticipation, 54, 91–92; and objectivity, 94, 233

Aphasia, 39

Arakawa, 192, 288 n.15

Architecture, 81, 87, 104, 218; deconstructive, 199; digital design in, 177, 191–92, 207–8; "lightness" in, 290 n.29; phenomenological, 191, 206, 287–88 n.14; relational, 192, 288 n.15; topology and, 177–78, 183, 191, 205–7

Art, 84, 95; construction and, 174; as cosmogenesis, 173; digital, 175; empirical and, 230; as minor science, 112; and philosophy, 175–76, 249, 252–53; popular vs. "high," 251–52; relation and, 173–74, 252; singularity and, 174–76, 249–52

Atomism, 280 n.13

Attention, 139, 155. *See also* Distraction

Attractor, 34, 72, 84, 159, 225; fractal vs. whole, 64; as limit, 159–60; visual, 147, 158

Autonomic process, 24–25, 28, 29, 32, 54–55, 129; art as, 173–74

Autonomy: of affect, 35–36, 43, 217; connective, 35, 235; of experience, 212–13, 221, 228; of relation, 35, 36–37, 165, 280 n.13; of sensation, 295 n.23

Autopoiesis, 206, 280 n.13. *See also* Self-organization

Bakhtin, Mikhail, 263–64 n.28, 277 n.13

Baudrillard, Jean, 137

Becoming, 5, 7, 21, 58, 63, 71, 80, 152, 200, 206, 217; active, 32; belonging and, 71, 76, 79, 81, 88, 128, 224; of the body, 104, 135, 205; cognition and, 231–32, 236; collective, 76–78, 86; "completion" of, 63–64, 66–67; of culture, 9–11; double, 12; of the event, 81–84, 86; history vs., 10, 80, 177, 207; immanence and, 83–84, 87; memory as, 210; other, 55, 63, 235, 254; virtual and, 237; of vision, 280 n.13. *See also* Emergence; Event; Evolution

Belief, 27, 40, 82, 258 n.8; lived, 220–21, 232, 237

Belonging: becoming and, 71, 76, 79, 81, 128, 224; capitalism and, 88; ethics as, 255–56; example and, 17; primacy of, 231. *See also* Relation

Bénard instability, 111, 223, 229, 241, 295 n.22

Benjamin, Walter, 43, 261–2 n.14, 289–90 n.25

Bennett, Jane, 258 n.8

Bergson, Henri, 5–7, 17, 31, 32, 136, 139, 167, 200, 239, 259 n.13, 267–8 n.23, 271 nn.13, 14, 283 n.34, 295 n.22, 298 n.33

Bifurcation point. *See* Critical point

Binarism (duality), 8, 33, 217, 293 n.17

Biogram: cognitive map vs., 187–94, 206, 207

Body: abstractness of, 5–6, 31–32, 41, 59, 61, 177–78, 190, 205, 207, 264 n.4; discursive, 2; as event, 14; expression and, 74–78, 104–6, 115–16, 126, 127–28; as fractal, 127, 131, 169, 202–3, 290 n.32; image and, 40, 46–67, 267 n.16; incorporeal and, 5, 14, 21, 31, 32, 44, 76, 205, 298 n.40; indeterminacy and, 5, 97, 103, 107; language and, 79; mind (cognition, consciousness) and, 29–32, 89, 190–91, 201, 206–7, 231; movement and, 1–5, 66, 149–51, 155, 178–84, 200–201, 249–50, 258 n.8; networked, 121–32, 142; objects and, 97, 99–100, 102, 103–5, 106, 150–51; "obsolescence" of, 89–132; openness of, 5, 29, 76, 104, 118–19, 126; organs and, 96; as part-object, 74–75, 78; as perception, 95; as potential, 30, 32, 58, 60, 63, 200–201; relation and, 4–5, 100, 116; sensation and, 1–5, 13–16, 74–76, 103–9, 114, 119, 120, 135, 139; as sensible concept, 89, 90, 100, 107, 118; space of, 57–61, 104, 127, 151, 177–78, 202–3, 205; in Spinoza, 15–16; thought and, 97, 106, 114; topology and, 177–20; transduction and, 74–78, 104–5, 115, 118, 131, 135; virtual and, 21, 30–31, 58, 66, 190, 205; without an image, 57–62, 63–64, 265 n.10, 277 n.13; without organs, 106, 109, 265

n.10. *See also* Affect; Habit; Incorporeality; Perception; Quasicorporeality; Sensation; Senses

Body image, 267 n.16

Bohm, David, 37, 263 n.24, 264 n.29

Brain, 28–31, 36–37, 190, 195, 198–99, 229, 286 n.2, 296 n.26; as computational, 281 n.16; as network, 296 n.25

Bruno, Giordano, 257–58 n.8

Buckley, Sandra, 285 n.1

Bush, George W., 268 n.24

Cache, Bernard, 279–80 n.13, 286 n.5

Capitalism: affect and, 27, 44–45, 219; art and, 251–52; becoming and, 88; power and, 43, 88; science and, 210, 219, 233, 234, 237; virtual and, 37, 42

Catalysis, 65, 71, 73–74, 80–81, 84, 87. *See also* Induction

Cause: nonlinear (recursive), 29–30, 33, 34, 37, 109–10, 203, 225, 295 n.25; quasi, 225–28, 234, 238–39, 250. *See also* Accompaniment; Effect; Nonlinearity; Requisites

Caygill, Howard, 289 n.25

Cézanne, Paul, 173

Chaos: laws of, 295 n.22; of vision, 146–51, 155–56, 168, 281 n.16

Chaos theory, 8, 19, 32, 37, 109–10, 147, 223–27, 229, 237, 244–45, 261 n.8, 276 n.6, 294–95 n.20, 295 n.22. *See also* Attractor; Bénard instability; Critical point; Emergence; Phase space; Self-organization

Change, 1–3, 6–8, 43, 48, 56, 64, 66, 69–71, 77, 199–201, 218, 225, 227, 243–44, 246, 253. *See also* Emergence; Incipience; Ingression; Invention; New; Ontogenesis; Qualitative transformation

n.30; on the virtual, 4–5, 190, 283 n.34, 286 n.6, 290 n.26, 292 n.10, 297–98 n.33, 298 n.38

Dephasing, 120

Derrida, Jacques, 37, 241

Desire, 108, 113, 120, 123, 132, 249

Determinable, 185, 232, 236

Determination, 161, 165, 190, 214–15, 219, 227, 241; movement and, 149, 184; pre-, 3–4, 69, 236; retrospective, 8–10, 78, 83, 102. *See also* Possibility

Determinism, 37, 152, 225, 246, 295 n.22

Deterritorialization, 88

Diagram, 33, 57, 134, 186–87, 191, 206

Difference: distinctive, 25; ontological (ontogenetic), 5, 8–9, 151–52, 159, 257–58 n.8, 284 n.35; reciprocal, 48–51; relational, 196–97, 224; repetition and, 63, 232, 267 n.22. *See also* Change; New; Qualitative transformation

Digital: vs. analog, 133–43; architectural design, 177, 191–92, 207–8; art, 175; virtual and, 137–43, 277 n.13

Distraction, 42, 84–85, 139. *See also* Attention

Doubling: of the actual by the virtual, 60, 64, 73, 76, 83–84, 98, 109, 110–11, 136, 153, 193–94, 196–97; of conceptual vocabulary, 266 n.15, 295 n.23; intensity as, 13, 16, 26, 31–32, 41–42

Duality (binarism), 8, 33, 217, 293 n.17

Ecology, 39; of knowledge practices, 215, 299 n.49; political, 255; relation and, 296 n.25

Effect: affect and, 28; vs. content, 24–25; dimensional, 185–86, 203–4; excess (supplemental), 119, 186, 196–97, 222, 224–25, 228, 234, 241, 245–46, 296 nn. 25, 26; field, 76–77, 79, 239, 245–46; force and, 160–61; infolding of, 31–32; operative reason and, 112; really-next-, 213–14; relational, 204, 228, 239, 243; virtual and 133, 136, 159

Einstein, Albert, 7

Electromagnetism, 117, 123

Emergence, 8–10, 12, 13, 16, 27, 31–35, 43, 71, 112, 121, 137, 164, 168, 172, 173–76, 206, 224, 241, 257 n.8, 266 n.15, 292 n.9; conditions of, 10, 33, 42, 72, 77, 140, 151–52, 154, 159–60, 284 n.35. *See also* Becoming; Form: germinal; Incipience; Ontogenesis

Emotion, 56–57, 64; affect vs., 27–28, 35, 41, 61, 217, 219, 294 n.17

Empirical, 57, 75, 77, 135, 159, 234, 245; art and, 230; conditions, 145–46, 148, 152, 280 n.13; infra-, 16, 56, 57, 156, 160, 266 n.15; pain and, 160–61; self-abstraction of, 147; super-, 16, 58, 76, 77, 152, 156, 160, 296 n.27

Empiricism, 11, 21; expanded, 230–21, 235–36, 238, 254–56; political, 243–44; radical, 16, 17, 230, 241, 296 n.27, 297 n.31; rationalist, 247–48; reductive, 1, 164–66, 175, 234, 236, 246; transcendental, 257–58 n.8

Energy, 5, 21; perceptual, 168–69; potential, 34, 37, 74, 92; transduction and, 104, 120, 130

Ethics, 28, 32, 34, 38, 210; of belonging, 255–56

Event, 11, 14, 16, 73, 212; acting and,

Function: possibility and, 241; potential, 34–35; suspension of, 101–9
Future-past, 31, 58, 64, 131, 194, 198, 200–201
Futurity: felt, 104, 107, 109, 116, 187; pure, 15, 30, 102, 122, 226. *See also* Anticipation; Possibility; Tendency

Ganzfeld, 147–61, 278–79 nn. 1, 2
Geometry. *See* Measure; Topology
Gender, 2, 8; domestic violence and, 80–82, 269 n.5; as interactive kind, 12
Generality, 98, 136; body and, 99–100, 109; event and, 79–80, 84–85, 222–26; example and, 79; language and, 169–70, 208–11, 236; movement and, 50; objectivity and, 93–94, 164–67, 174–75, 247, 253
Gestalt psychology, 209, 215, 278–79 n.1
Gibson, Eleanor, 287 n.12
Gibson, James J., 146, 266 n.16
Gil, José, 265 n.10
Gins, Madeleine, 192, 288 n.15
Gödel, Kurt, 37
Goethe, Johann Wolfgang von, 172, 173
Gore, Al, 268 n.24
Gossip, 214–15, 236
Gravity, 101, 104–7, 111–12, 114, 224, 290 n.29
Grossberg, Lawrence, 260 nn. 2, 3, 262 n.15
Guattari, Félix, 17, 42, 106, 108, 137, 172, 173, 206, 239, 242, 258 n.10, 261 n.8, 264 n.4, 265 n.10, 286 n.6, 290 n.26, 298 n.38

Habit, 82, 200, 205; matter and, 11, 236–37, 247, 299 n.44; perception and, 59, 150–51, 179–81, 188, 221; science and, 242. *See also* Reflex
Hacking, Ian, 12

Hallucination, 146, 151, 155–56, 178, 182–83, 190, 195, 206–7
Haptic, 158; tactile vs., 283 n.33
Hawking, Stephen, 248
Hearing, 145, 156, 186
Heidegger, Martin, 288 n.14
History, 194, 218, 220; becoming vs., 10, 77, 80, 207; philosophy and, 240; of science, 215; transhistorical, 77
Human: machine and, 118, 130; nonhuman and, 38–39, 92–97, 227, 237; posthuman evolution of, 112, 116, 121–32
Humanities, 1, 12, 240; science and, 8, 19–21, 248; writing in, 17–19
Hume, David, 11, 211, 247
Hybridity, 69–70, 76, 236, 277 n.13
Hypertext, 138–41, 175

Ideal, 44, 36, 63–64, 66–67, 165–67, 170, 174. *See also* Abstraction; Incorporeality; Incorporeal materialism
Identification, 40
Identity, 63, 151, 210, 231; nominal, 215–18, 234; reflective, 48–51; repetition and, 79, 218; virtual, 231–32
Ideology, 1–3, 5, 7, 40, 42, 263 n.24
Image: affect and, 24–26; body and, 40, 46–67, 267 n.16; "dialectical," 261–62 n.14; language and, 26, 47, 263–64 n.28; mass media and, 81, 84; power and, 42–46, 87–88; of thought, 137; virtual and, 133–34. *See also* Body: without an image; Form: visual
Imagination, 134, 136, 207
Immanence, 9, 33, 43, 71, 97–98, 100, 233; becoming and, 83–84, 87; capitalism and, 88; field of, 76–79, 85–86; transcendence and, 38, 78–79, 82–85, 262–63 n.22; virtual and,

Nervous system, 36–37; enteric, 265–66 n.13

Network, 85–88, 120–31, 142, 202

New, 12, 27, 33, 43, 97, 111, 160, 175–76, 214–15, 221, 224–25, 227, 239–40. *See also* Change; Emergence; Incipience; Ingression; Invention; Ontogenesis; Qualitative transformation

New media, 132, 192

Newton, Isaac, 7, 160, 163, 165, 172, 222, 247

Nietzsche, Friedrich, 283–84 n.35

Noise, 296 n.26

Nonconscious, 16, 25, 29, 31, 36, 60, 74, 100, 188, 195–96, 198–99, 230, 267 n.16, 284 n.9

Nonlinearity, 26, 33, 58, 113, 197, 229, 261–62 n.14, 264 n.3. *See also* Cause: nonlinear; Critical point; Feedback; Intensity; Interference; Linearity: super-; Resonance; Suspense

Nonlocality, 34, 159, 175

Nystagmus, 281 n.16

Object: body and, 97, 99–100, 102, 103–5, 106, 150–51; constancy, 149–50, 154; as differential, 216; eternal, 291–92 n.7; organ and, 106–7; part-, 74–75, 78; as prosthesis, 116, 127; quasi-, 71; scientific, 214, 218, 228, 236, 292 n.9; subject and, 50–51, 57–61, 73, 99, 127, 173, 201, 212, 217–19, 221, 231–32, 237–38; synesthetic, 193; technical, 214–15; thing vs., 94–96; vision and, 146, 149–51, 155, 156–57, 160–61, 168

Objectile, 279–80 n.13

Objectivity, 25, 94, 100, 145–47, 165–66, 174, 212, 214, 216–17, 221–27, 229

Observer: virtual, 51

Ontogenesis, 8–9, 12, 191, 206. *See also* New

Openness, 80, 85, 137, 138, 174, 243; of affect, 35, 43; of the body, 5, 29, 76, 104, 118–19, 126; qualitative, 219–20; and relation, 224–25, 227–28; systemic, 18–19

Order: implicate, 37, 263 n.24, 264 n.29

Order-word, 62, 63

Orientation: in space, 178–84

Organ: body and, 96; matter and, 271 n.14; object and, 106–7. *See also* Body: without organs

Pallasmaa, Juhani, 288 n.14, 290 n.29

Paradox, 13, 21, 24, 27, 38; lived, 30; Zeno's, 6–7

Parody, 69

Particular, 17, 35, 79–80, 93, 102–3, 109, 170, 208, 222–23, 226, 229, 235, 253

Passage: precedes position, 5–6, 8, 46, 66; regime of, 85, 203

Passion, 28, 32, 61, 63, 64

Past, 30, 58, 101–2, 155–56, 262 n.14; pure, 15, 103. *See also* Future-past; Memory

Peirce, C. S., 4, 247, 299 n.44

Perception: action and, 90–93, 103–4, 122, 137, 139; affect and, 35; amodal 169–71, 262 n.15, 282 n.25; body as, 95; constancy of, 150–51, 281 n.16; direct, 199; as event, 145, 156, 160, 172, 186–88, 190, 193, 206, 221–22; field of, 106, 120, 140, 144–61, 163, 167–68, 239, 278 n.1; force and, 95, 160–61; habit and, 59, 150–51, 179–81, 188, 221; hallucination and, 155–56, 182–83, 190, 207; indeterminacy and, 146, 153, 174, 232; intensity

Perception (*cont.*)
and, 31; memory and, 197, 209–11;
meso-, 62, 266 n.16; micro-, 16,
196–97; movement and, 108, 168,
199, 281 n.16; nature and, 221; nonconscious, 16, 198–99; of perception, 14–15, 258 n.11; potential and,
16, 92–99, 141, 186, 196, 232; "raw,"
66, 199; representational model of,
281 n.16; self-, 36, 220; sensation vs.,
1–2, 14–16, 21, 62, 97, 258–59 n.11,
271 n.13, 295 n.23; side-, 36, 170;
singularity and, 162–76, 210–21;
subthreshold, 296 n.26; thought and,
37, 91–92, 94–96, 98–99, 110–11,
141, 271 n.13; undecidability of, 37;
virtual and, 63, 98, 133, 140, 144–
76, 186–204, 241–42; of vitality, 35–
36, 41. *See also* Feedback: of higher
forms; Kinesthesia; Sensation;
Senses; Synesthesia; Vision
Performance, 2–3, 47–48, 56–57, 69–
70, 89, 97, 100, 190, 249
Period: phase vs., 113, 125
Perspective: event and, 79–80, 84–85;
relative, 48–49, 53–54, 56, 80, 84;
virtual (absolute), 35, 43, 50–51,
58–62
Phantasm, 63–64
Phase, 34, 77, 120, 159; dephasing,
120; period vs., 113, 125
Phase space, 33, 147, 153, 158–60
Phenomenology: architecture and, 191,
206, 287–88 n.14
Philosophy: actualization and, 241–42;
amodal perception and, 169, 171–
72, 282 n.25; art and, 175–76, 249,
252–53; concepts in, 16–21, 239–
44; cultural studies and, 252–56;
politics and, 242–44; science and,
214, 229–38, 244–48, 252; singularity and, 166, 213, 239–42; relation-

ality and, 210, 239–44; as useless,
241, 243; virtual and, 239–43, 252.
See also Concept; Thought
Pickering, Andrew, 292 n.9
Position, 2–10, 11–12, 15, 46, 66, 68–
70, 153, 180–83, 201
Possession, 63
Possibility: action and, 91–99, 101–6,
108–9, 137; conditions of, 33, 223–
25, 235, 238; digital and, 137–38;
law and, 247; position and, 3, 6–7,
70; potential vs., 9–10, 63, 92–99,
109–11, 113, 116, 119, 122–23, 131,
134–37, 141, 226, 240–43; probability and, 135–36; prosthesis and,
126; as retrospective, 272 n.24; virtual vs., 136–37, 141, 226, 229
Postmodern, 69, 173, 219; politics, 40–
42, 86
Poststructuralism, 4, 27, 70
Potential: abstraction and, 33, 34, 98,
204; affect and, 15, 76, 80, 228; body
and, 30, 32, 58, 60, 63, 200–201; energy, 34, 37, 74, 92; field of, 34–35,
38, 42, 72–86; for function, 34–35;
mass media and, 43–44, 86–88;
movement and, 4–5, 7, 15, 41, 72–
75, 77, 124, 250; nature and, 237–
40; perception and, 16, 92–99, 141,
186, 196, 232; possible vs., 9–10, 63,
92–99, 109–11, 113, 116, 119, 122–
23, 131, 134–37, 141, 226, 240–43;
probability and, 135–36, 226, 229;
sensation and, 33, 74–75, 97–99,
103, 136, 142, 153, 192, 197; space
and, 75; virtual and, 21, 30–31, 38,
43, 58, 60, 66, 98, 108, 113, 136–38,
141, 190, 197, 226
Power: affect and, 15, 42–44, 228; as
analog, 43; bio-, 82; capitalism and,
43, 88; as control, 88, 129, 226; disciplinary, 78, 82; ideology and, 5, 42;

mass media and, 43–44, 85–88; mediation and, 2; science and, 211–12; truth as, 246; as usurpation, 72, 88. *See also* Coding; Regulation

Pragmatic, 13, 33, 43, 113, 199, 206, 210, 243–44, 268–69 n.4

Pragmatism, 230–31, 246–47

Preindividual, 34

Prigogine, Ilya, 223–24, 229, 244, 294 n.18, 295 n.22

Probability, 135–36, 225–26, 229, 244–45, 295 n.22

Process, 7–9, 12, 113, 134–35, 139, 142, 165, 175, 177, 212–56, 258 n.10, 271 n.13

Process lines, 212–13, 234, 246–47. *See also* Seriality

Proprioception, 35, 58–61, 145, 154, 157, 168–69, 179–84, 186, 191–93, 197, 205, 265 n.11, 266 n.16, 284 n.9, 290 n.26

Prosthesis, 95–96, 107–8, 111, 116, 119, 120, 126–27

Psychology: evolutionary, 19; experimental, 144–45, 208; Gestalt, 209, 215, 278–79 n.1; para-, 279 n.2

Qualitative transformation, 1, 4, 8, 12, 66, 77, 84, 112, 120, 128–29, 136, 224–25, 243. *See also* Change; New

Quality, 42, 59, 135–36, 180–81, 183–84, 185–86, 197, 203, 266 n.15; affect and, 216–25, 232; expression and, 220, 235, 248–53; intensity and, 24–26, 60–61, 156, 261 n.9; as limit, 229, 234; quasi-, 61, 261 n.9, 266 n.15; secondary, 173

Quantification, 135–37, 181, 183–84, 225–26, 230, 235, 244, 259 n.11. *See also* Measure

Quantum, 37–39, 201, 203, 229, 259 n.11, 260 n.3, 264 n.3, 280 n.13

Quasicause, 225–28, 234, 238–39, 250, 257 n.5

Quasicorporeality, 57–62, 265 n.10

Queer theory, 69

Race, 8, 12

Reading, 2, 180, 277 n.13; as analog process, 138–40; as unmediated, 198–200

Reagan, Ronald, 39–42, 46–67, 268 nn. 4, 24

Realism, 1, 206–7, 230

Reason: contingent, 136, 240–41; instrumental, 94–96, 99, 102, 108, 110, 122, 128, 136; operative, 109–12, 122, 128, 136. *See also* Cognition; Common sense; Intelligence; Thought

Receptivity, 32, 55, 57, 61, 104, 207

Recognition, 47–51, 53–55, 60–61, 63, 64, 83–84, 91, 151, 161, 199, 204, 218, 220–21, 231, 233–34, 236–37, 240–41, 242, 252

Reflection, 31–32, 37–38, 50, 74–76, 110, 112, 127, 128, 132, 138, 140–41, 194–95, 205–6, 246; as retrospective, 123, 191; self-, 36–37. *See also* Reason; Self-referentiality; Vision: mirror-

Reflex, 74–75, 79, 81. *See also* Habit

Regularity, 20, 81–88, 93–94, 135, 218–19

Regulation: vs. regularization, 82–88

Relation: art and, 173–74, 252; autonomy of, 35, 36–37, 165, 280 n.13; body and, 4–5, 100, 116; as coded, 81–82; color and, 163–65; conservation of, 166–67; ecology and, 296 n.25; as exterior to its terms, 51, 58, 70–71, 76–79, 165, 168–69, 183, 231–32, 239, 242, 297 n.30; vs. interaction, 9, 164, 222–25, 238–42,

Relation (*cont.*)

245; language and, 297 n.30; as limit, 88, 229–30, 234–35, 238–40, 244–45; mass media and, 88–89, 262 n.20; matter (nature) as, 203–4, 238, 276 n.8; molar, 203; of movement and rest, 15, 20, 32, 59, 74; nature (matter) as, 203–4, 238; nonlocal, 34, 159, 175; openness and, 224–25, 227–28; perception and (as felt), 16–17, 163–65, 168, 170, 196–97, 221, 231–32, 234, 239, 241–42, 296 n.27; philosophy and, 210, 239–44; power and, 88; proprioception and, 183; radical empiricism and, 16, 230–31, 241–42; of relation, 203–4, 207; self-, 7–8, 14–16, 18, 180–81; virtual and, 35, 175, 197, 204, 229, 231–32, 245, 248, 252. *See also* Belonging; Quasicause; Resonance; Sensation

Relational architecture, 192

Relativity, 7, 90, 164, 229, 246

Religion, 247–48, 258 n.8, 299 n.46

Remainder, 25, 135–36, 151–52, 240, 242, 248–49; affective, 35–36, 219, 252, 255; virtual as, 226. *See also* Excess

Repetition, 10–11, 32, 54–57, 66, 77, 79, 83, 133, 150–51, 194, 213, 218, 222–23, 232, 292 n.10

Reproduction, 83, 96, 166, 210, 222–23, 225, 229–30, 233, 238

Requisites, 238, 245

Resistance, 2–3, 37, 43, 86–87

Resonance, 14, 25–26, 29–30, 33–34, 36, 37, 41, 62, 106–7, 110–11, 124, 136, 138–40, 142, 200, 273 n.48; stochastic, 229, 296 n.26

Retroduction, 10

Rhythm, 10, 20, 104, 115, 118, 139–40, 152, 160, 179–80, 190, 217–18

Ruyer, Raymond, 264 n.4, 278 n.1, 287 n.11, 297 n.33, 298 n.39

Sacks, Oliver, 39

Saussure, Fernand de, 4

Shilder, Paul, 267 n.16, 282–83 n.31

Schizophrenia, 155–56, 194

Science: capitalism and, 210, 219, 233, 234, 237; force in, 160; funding of, 215, 235, habit and, 242; history of, 215; humanities and, 8, 19–21, 248; limit of, 229–30, 234–35, 238–40; minor, 112; nature and, 236, 247–48; object of, 214, 218, 228, 236, 292 n.9; philosophy and, 214, 229–38, 244–48, 252; power and, 211–12; psychology and, 144–45, 208–9; techno-, 297 n.31; theology and, 247–48; virtual and, 229, 234, 245. *See also* Chaos theory; Cosmology; Empirical; Fact; Objectivity; Thermodynamics

Science "wars," 248

Selection, 33, 41, 92–94, 101, 134, 148–49; natural, 123, 125

Self, 48–50, 63, 74, 127; technologizing of, 55–56

Self-abstraction, 147, 161, 280 n.13

Self-organization (self-activity, self-variation), 32–34, 111, 128, 131, 164, 173–74, 181, 211–13, 219–20, 224–29, 234, 235, 237, 243–44, 295 n.22. *See also* Autopoiesis

Self-perception, 36, 220

Self-referentiality, 83–85, 109–10, 125–28, 133, 135, 139–40, 142, 156, 179–82, 194, 196, 295 n.23; vs. self-reflexivity, 13–14. *See also* Reflection

Self-relation, 7–8, 14–16, 18, 180–81

Self-survey, 264 n.4, 283 n.34

Sensation: action and, 75, 97–98, 103–4; affect and, 75, 97–98, 103–4, 109;

137; matter and, 37, 97, 107–8, 110, 114, 121, 131, 135, 173–74, 190, 195, 199, 206–7, 226–27, 271 nn. 13, 14; movement and, 6, 10, 98–99, 134, 137, 195; perception and, 37, 91–92, 94–98, 110–11, 141, 271 n.13; sensation and (as felt), 100–101, 109, 114, 121, 125, 134–35, 138–40, 242, 272 n.24; virtual and, 136, 241–43. *See also* Cognition; Concept: sensible; Conscious; Mind; Philosophy; Reason; Sensation: thought (intelligence) and; Reflection

Three-body problem, 37, 229, 281 n.16, 295–96 n.24

Threshold, 34, 38, 43, 86–88, 213, 229, 296 n.26

Time: architecture and, 194, 286 n.5; backward referral in, 28–29, 195; intensity and, 26, 54, 57, 61; linear, 15, 26, 28–31, 35, 60, 63, 80, 101–3, 167, 173, 197, 201; subject and, 174–75; virtual and, 58; vision and, 187, 190. *See also* Feedback; Future-past; Futurity; Nonlinearity; Past; Space-time continuum

Topology, 19; in architecture, 177–78, 183, 191, 205–7; body and, 177–207; virtual and, 134–35, 137, 194

Touch (tactility): field of, 152–53; haptic and, 283 n.33; proprioception and, 58–60, 157, 186; vision and, 35, 43, 91, 139, 145, 154, 156–58, 186, 189

Trace, 30, 32, 36, 54–56, 63, 155

Transcendence: becoming-immanent of, 38, 78–79, 82–85

Transcendental, 33

Transduction, 42–43, 74–76, 80–81, 86–87, 104, 106–7, 115–19, 121, 124, 130–31, 135, 141, 263 n.27

Transition: affect and, 15–16, 197;

form of, 213, 215, 291 n.5; immanence of, 86; topology and, 185, 201

Transversality, 42, 45, 215

Tropism, 34, 91, 180, 204, 205

Turrell, James, 279 n.2

Unconscious, 16, 130, 222–23, 230. *See also* Nonconscious

Undecidability, 37. *See also* Indeterminacy

Utility, 38, 95–97, 101–2, 108

Vacuum, 114, 146

Vague, 13, 74, 92, 97, 146, 156, 163–64, 173, 183, 214–16, 232, 242, 259 n.11; virtual as, 134, 140, 191

Varela, Francisco, 280 n.13

Vector, 59, 61, 76, 180, 183, 185, 192

Ventriloquism, 63

Vietnam War, 65

Virtual: abstraction and, 31–34, 58, 159–60, 175, 190, 197; actual and, 30–31, 37–38, 41, 43, 60, 63, 98, 136–38, 153–54, 159, 175, 241–42, 277 n.13; affect and, 35, 197, 239; analog/digital and, 137–43; attractors and, 159; becoming and, 237; body and, 21, 30–31, 58, 66, 190, 205; capitalism and, 37, 42; Deleuze on, 4–5, 190, 283 n.34; as doubling the actual, 60, 64, 73, 76, 83–84, 98, 109, 110–11, 136, 153, 193–94, 196–97; effect and, 133, 136, 159; event and, 58, 60, 105, 133, 136, 175, 204; everydayness of, 277–78 n.13, excess and, 98, 114, 190, 248; force and, 160–61; image and, 133–34; immanence and, 136, 141, 143; language and, 62–63, 277 n.13; as limited but unbounded, 289; mass media and, 41; memory and, 197; mime and, 41; movement and, 41, 51, 136–37, 159; nature and, 237–

Brian Massumi is
Associate Professor of Communications
at the Université de Montréal.